Regulating Unhealthy Lifestyles in the European Union

This book examines how European Union (EU) law regulates unhealthy lifestyles, focusing on the consumption of tobacco, alcoholic beverages and foods of poor nutritional quality. The first part of the book clarifies the EU's competences in this field and the content of its policy. It also outlines the main regulatory tools adopted in relation to each of the risk factors covered, such as product bans, labelling requirements or advertising restrictions. The second part of the book explores the fundamental tension between the commodification of these lifestyles and the pursuit of health policy objectives. It addresses two central questions: How does EU law reconcile the goal of creating a market for unhealthy products with that of reducing or eliminating their consumption? And how does EU law balance market uniformity with the diversity and scientific uncertainty inherent in lifestyle practices?

Vincent Delhomme is Assistant Professor of EU Law at Leiden University. He was previously a visiting professor at UCLouvain and the College of Europe. He specialises in EU internal market law, health law and food law. He offers expert advice to public institutions, including the Dutch Parliament and the European Commission.

Cambridge Studies in European Law and Policy

The focus of this series is European law broadly understood. It aims to publish original monographs in all fields of European law, from work focusing on the institutions of the EU and the Council of Europe to books examining substantive fields of European law as well as examining the relationship between European law and domestic, regional and international legal orders. The series publishes works adopting a wide variety of methods: comparative, doctrinal, theoretical and interdisciplinary approaches to European law are equally welcome, as are works looking at the historical and political facets of the development of European law and policy. The main criterion is excellence, i.e. the publication of innovative work, which will help to shape the legal, political and scholarly debate on the future of European law.

Books in the Series

Regulating Unhealthy Lifestyles in the European Union: The Dilemmas of an Internal Market for Tobacco, Alcohol and Foods
Vincent Delhomme

Market Regulation and Private Law: The Quest for Reconciliation in European Private Law
Olha O. Cherednychenko

Governance by Emulation: The Oversight Board, the Digital Services Act, and the Struggle for Platform Accountability
Moritz A. Schramm

Sustainability and EU Migration Law: Tracing the History of a Contemporary Concept
Alezini Loxa

Reimagining Prosperity: Toward a New Imaginary of Law and Political Economy in the EU
Marija Bartl

Open Strategic Autonomy in EU Trade Policy: Assessing the Turn to Stronger Enforcement and More Robust Interest Representation
Wolfgang Weiß and Cornelia Furculiţă

Trilogues: The Democratic Secret of European Legislation
Giacomo Rugge

The European Union, Emerging Global Business and Human Rights
Aleydis Nissen

The European Central Bank and the European Macroeconomic Constitution
Klaus Tuori

The Procedural and Organisational Law of the European Court of Justice: An Incomplete Transformation
Christoph Krenn

The New Economic Governance of the Eurozone: A Rule of Law Analysis
Paul Dermine

Digital Constitutionalism in Europe: Reframing Rights and Powers in the Algorithmic Society
Giovanni De Gregorio

Can the European Court of Human Rights Shape European Public Order?
Kanstantsin Dzehtsiarou

The Constitutional Boundaries of European Fiscal Federalism
Brady Gordon

Private Selves: Legal Personhood in European Privacy Protection
Susanna Lindroos-Hovinheimo

Fissures in EU Citizenship: The Deconstruction and Reconstruction of the Legal Evolution of EU Citizenship
Martin Steinfeld

The Boundaries of the EU Internal Market: Participation without Membership
Marja-Liisa Öberg

The Currency of Solidarity: Constitutional Transformation during the Euro Crisis
Vestert Borger

Empire of Law: Nazi Germany, Exile Scholars and the Battle for the Future of Europe
Kaius Tuori

In the Court We Trust: Cooperation, Coordination and Collaboration between the ECJ and Supreme Administrative Courts
Rob van Gestel and Jurgen de Poorter

Beyond Minimum Harmonisation: Gold-Plating and Green-Plating of European Environmental Law
Lorenzo Squintani

The Court of Justice of the European Union as an Institutional Actor: Judicial Lawmaking and its Limits
Thomas Horsley

The Politics of Justice in European Private Law: Social Justice, Access Justice, Societal Justice
Hans-W Micklitz

The Transformation of EU Treaty Making: The Rise of Parliaments, Referendums and Courts Since 1950
Dermot Hodson and Imelda Maher

Redefining European Economic Integration
Dariusz Adamski

Human Rights in the Council of Europe and the European Union: Achievements, Trends and Challenges
Steven Greer, Janneke Gerards and Rosie Slowe

Core Socio-Economic Rights and the European Court of Human Rights
Ingrid Leijten

Green Trade and Fair Trade in and with the EU: Process-based Measures within the EU Legal Order
Laurens Ankersmit

New Labour Laws in Old Member States: Trade Union Responses to European Enlargement
Rebecca Zahn

The Governance of EU Fundamental Rights
Mark Dawson

The International Responsibility of the European Union: From Competence to Normative Control
Andrés Delgado Casteleiro

Frontex and Non-Refoulement: The International Responsibility of the EU
Roberta Mungianu

Gendering European Working Time Regimes: The Working Time Directive and the Case of Poland
Ania Zbyszewska

EU Renewable Electricity Law and Policy: From National Targets to a Common Market
Tim Maxian Rusche

European Constitutionalism
Kaarlo Tuori

Brokering Europe: Euro-Lawyers and the Making of a Transnational Polity
Antoine Vauchez

Services Liberalization in the EU and the WTO: Concepts, Standards and Regulatory Approaches
Marcus Klamert

Referendums and the European Union: A Comparative Enquiry
Fernando Mendez, Mario Mendez and Vasiliki Triga

The Allocation of Regulatory Competence in the EU Emissions Trading Scheme
Josephine van Zeben

The Eurozone Crisis: A Constitutional Analysis
Kaarlo Tuori and Klaus Tuori

International Trade Disputes and EU Liability
Anne Thies

The Limits of Legal Reasoning and the European Court of Justice
Gerard Conway

New Governance and the Transformation of European Law: Coordinating EU Social Law and Policy
Mark Dawson

The Lisbon Treaty: A Legal and Political Analysis
Jean-Claude Piris

The European Union's Fight Against Corruption: The Evolving Policy Towards Member States and Candidate Countries
Patrycja Szarek-Mason

The Ethos of Europe: Values, Law and Justice in the EU
Andrew Williams

State and Market in European Union Law: The Public and Private Spheres of the Internal Market before the EU Courts
Wolf Sauter and Harm Schepel

The European Civil Code: The Way Forward
Hugh Collins

Ethical Dimensions of the Foreign Policy of the European Union: A Legal Appraisal
Urfan Khaliq

Implementing EU Pollution Control: Law and Integration
Bettina Lange

European Broadcasting Law and Policy
Jackie Harrison and Lorna Woods

The Transformation of Citizenship in the European Union: Electoral Rights and the Restructuring of Political Space
Jo Shaw

The Constitution for Europe: A Legal Analysis
Jean-Claude Piris

The European Convention on Human Rights: Achievements, Problems and Prospects
Steven Greer

Social Rights and Market Freedom in the European Constitution: A Labour Law Perspective
Stefano Giubboni

EU Enlargement and the Constitutions of Central and Eastern Europe
Anneli Albi

Regulating Unhealthy Lifestyles in the European Union

The Dilemmas of an Internal Market for Tobacco, Alcohol and Foods

Vincent Delhomme
Leiden University

CAMBRIDGE
UNIVERSITY PRESS

CAMBRIDGE
UNIVERSITY PRESS

Shaftesbury Road, Cambridge CB2 8EA, United Kingdom

One Liberty Plaza, 20th Floor, New York, NY 10006, USA

477 Williamstown Road, Port Melbourne, VIC 3207, Australia

314–321, 3rd Floor, Plot 3, Splendor Forum, Jasola District Centre, New Delhi – 110025, India

Cambridge University Press is part of Cambridge University Press & Assessment, a department of the University of Cambridge.

We share the University's mission to contribute to society through the pursuit of education, learning and research at the highest international levels of excellence.

www.cambridge.org
Information on this title: www.cambridge.org/9781009746991

DOI: 10.1017/9781009746946

When citing this work, please include a reference to the DOI 10.1017/9781009746946

First published 2026

Cover image: Wine and Smoking Stock Illustration / Collection: CSA Images / Getty Images

A catalogue record for this publication is available from the British Library

Library of Congress Cataloging-in-Publication Data
Names: Delhomme, Vincent author
Title: Regulating unhealthy lifestyles in the European Union : the dilemmas of an internal market for tobacco, alcohol, and foods / Vincent Delhomme.
Description: Cambridge, United Kingdom ; New York, NY : Cambridge University Press, 2026. | Series: Cambridge studies in European law and policy | Includes bibliographical references and index.
Identifiers: LCCN 2026011005 (print) | LCCN 2026011006 (ebook) | ISBN 9781009746991 hardback | ISBN 9781009746953 paperback | ISBN 9781009746946 ebook
Subjects: LCSH: Tobacco–Law and legislation–European Union countries | Tobacco use–Health aspects–European Union countries | Alcoholic beverage industry–Law and legislation–European Union countries | Alcoholic beverages–Labeling–Law and legislation–European Union countries | Alcoholic beverages–Health aspects–European Union countries | Drinking of alcoholic beverages–European Union countries | Food law and legislation–European Union countries | Food–Labeling–Law and legislation–European Union countries | Marketing–Law and legislation–European Union countries
Classification: LCC KJE6249 .D45 2026 (print) | LCC KJE6249 (ebook)
LC record available at https://lccn.loc.gov/2026011005
LC ebook record available at https://lccn.loc.gov/2026011006

ISBN 978-1-009-74699-1 Hardback
ISBN 978-1-009-74695-3 Paperback

Contents

Series Editors' Preface

Three themes lie at the heart of this very stimulating and dynamic work: the powers of the European Union (EU) to regulate unhealthy lifestyles and how those powers have been used so far; balancing the building of a market for unhealthy products with reducing or eliminating their consumption; and balancing the uniformity of the market with the diversity and scientific uncertainty associated with lifestyle practices. Delhomme examines and compares the EU's action relating to three types of products: tobacco, alcohol and foods, highlighting the various dilemmas in the regulation of each of them. The focus is on rules targeting the processing and marketing of products and their impact on consumer behaviour.

While the internal market was initially secured by putting the flesh of teleological case law on the skeleton of Treaty provisions, raising the hope that mutual recognition would reduce the need for regulation at EU level, in practice the internal market has seen a massive growth in EU-level regulation seeking to ensure a level playing field by substituting harmonisation for the plethora of divergent national rules, as it became clear that mutual recognition was not a panacea. The product areas examined here are clear illustrations of how legislative choices vary and show that positive integration measures by the EU in the internal market are targeted at the products and interests concerned, rather than driven by blind uniformity.

In Part I of this book, after setting the scene, Delhomme examines how unhealthy lifestyles are regulated in the EU, considering them first as a regulatory object, then dealing in turn with the question of EU competence to regulate trade in unhealthy products, to promote healthy lifestyles and to legislate in these domains. He then gives a fascinating account of the evolution of EU lifestyle regulation before examining the toolbox of measures at the EU's disposal to eliminate, guide, or enable choice of lifestyle. In Part II, Delhomme discusses the EU's internal market dilemmas regarding unhealthy lifestyles: striking the balance between health and free movement; between uncertainty and experimentation; and how to stimulate the change towards a (healthy) transnational lifestyle. Finally, he presents his conclusions. He notes that since the early 2000s, a genuine lifestyle policy has emerged at the EU level: identifying tobacco, alcohol use and unhealthy diets as major health risk factors, which are approached through a 'permit but discourage' policy. Having shown that this is fraught with contradictions and conceptual difficulties, Delhomme makes the case for considering Treaty change to avoid the need for judicial contortions. He also discusses taking account of differing cultural dimensions through creative solutions such as opt-outs and more systematic use of flexible modes of harmonisation, while being willing, if progress be elusive, to consider a return to national rather than European regulation to enable those Member States who wish to develop more far-reaching policies to do so. He argues that further EU intervention should be accompanied by reforms to the constitutional framework of competence and by greater engagement with the political, moral and cultural dimensions of unhealthy lifestyles.

Delhomme offers very rich perspectives on the development of positive integration in the fields it examines, and his recommendations provide considerable food for thought and stimuli for action. It is with great pleasure that we welcome this perceptive work to the Cambridge Studies in European Law and Policy series.

Laurence Gormley
Mark Dawson
Jo Shaw

Acknowledgements

This book reflects my enduring fascination with the role of risk in human existence and the way societies address it. Why do some embrace habits such as smoking, drinking, or drug use, while others abstain entirely? Should the State intervene and, if so, how should regulation be designed? These questions are examined here through the lens of EU law. Regulating lifestyles and promoting health in a federal, market-driven and diverse polity such as the EU presents both unique opportunities and distinct challenges. Unhealthy lifestyles ultimately touch on the very soul of the EU and its integration project. I hope the book not only illustrates this but also offers convincing answers and sparks further reflection and action.

As with any significant life journey, this research would not have been possible without the support of many individuals and institutions in Amsterdam, Bruges (College of Europe), Brussels, Louvain-la-Neuve (UCLouvain), Leiden (Universiteit Leiden) and Paris. To all of them, I extend my heartfelt thanks.

I am especially grateful to Anne-Lise Sibony, whose guidance and encouragement accompanied me throughout the doctorate that led to this book. Always respectful of my choices, she ensured they could withstand academic scrutiny. Her expertise and experience were instrumental in shaping the path of this research. I also owe sincere thanks to the members of my doctoral committee and jury – Alberto Alemanno, Loïc Azoulai, Henri Culot, Olivier De Schutter and Amandine Garde – for their generosity in sharing their time, insights and knowledge.

This book marks the culmination of a journey that began in 2017 at the College of Europe in Bruges, with a master's thesis on internal market harmonisation and tobacco legislation. That work convinced me that unhealthy lifestyles posed challenges for EU law worth exploring in depth. I remain deeply indebted to the College of Europe and to the inspiring people I met there. My passion for EU law was born in Bruges and nurtured during my years as both student and academic assistant. I wish to thank Sacha Garben for being a great teacher, colleague and mentor, always pushing me to treat legal authorities without too much deference and, most of all, to dream big. I am also grateful to Inge Govaere, whose trust allowed me to grow personally and professionally within the European Legal Studies Department. My thanks go as well to colleagues, students and friends from Bruges, with a special *merci* to Pierre and Celia, whose friendship has endured beyond those years.

The Netherlands has been both my academic and personal home for the past four years. I am especially thankful to Jorrit Rijpma and Armin Cuyvers for welcoming me to the Europa Instituut at Leiden University and providing a supportive environment in which to pursue this book project. Among my many colleagues there, I would like to mention Carina, Elena, Konstantinos, Martijn and Simona. Our conversations on law, the EU and much else have been a constant source of motivation and joy. Beyond Leiden, I am indebted to colleagues at other institutions who, through discussions, presentations and reviews, helped shape this work, whether knowingly or not. In particular, I would like to thank Floris De Witte and Hanna Schebesta. My gratitude also extends across the Channel to Tammy Hervey, who has been an outstanding mentor and role model, guiding me in the early stages of my career and opening important doors along the way.

I am grateful to the editors of the Cambridge Studies in European Law and Policy series for accepting this book, in particular Laurence Gormley, and to the manuscript reviewers and the Cambridge University Press editorial team for their assistance, Sharon McCann in particular.

Finally, I wish to thank those closest to me: family, old and new friends, lawyers and non-lawyers. Their belief in my abilities, whether expressed or unspoken, has been a constant source of motivation and comfort. I am especially grateful to Alex, Max and Morgane for their help in proofreading parts of the manuscript. To Stefan for being here, still. And to my parents and my brother, for their unconditional love and support.

1 Introduction

1.1 Setting the Scene: Unhealthy Lifestyles and the EU

This book examines how European Union (EU) law regulates unhealthy lifestyles: the consumption of tobacco, alcoholic beverages and foods of poor nutritional quality. What we eat, drink or smoke is an essential determinant of our health. Tobacco, alcohol and unhealthy diets are responsible for millions of deaths every year, in the EU and beyond, particularly in the form of non-communicable diseases (NCDs), such as cancer, diabetes or cardiovascular diseases.[1] Addressing lifestyle-related risk factors is therefore considered a top priority by public health authorities worldwide.[2] This is especially relevant to high-income countries, where sanitation policies and the development of public healthcare systems have led to a steady decrease in the burden of infectious diseases and other causes of ill-health, but where new lifestyle and environmental factors have led to an increase in the prevalence of NCDs.[3] The paradox is that, unlike many hazardous objects, tobacco, alcohol and unhealthy foods are ubiquitous in our societies. They are lawfully accessible to consumers and may be purchased with limited constraints. Regulators

[1] Regarding the EU, see OECD and European Commission, 'Health at a Glance: Europe 2024: State of Health in the EU Cycle' (2024) OECD Publishing.

[2] See United Nations General Assembly, 'Political Declaration of the High-level Meeting of the General Assembly on the Prevention and Control of Non-communicable Diseases' (2011), <https://digitallibrary.un.org/record/710899?ln=fr> accessed 8 September 2025; WHO, 'Global Noncommunicable Diseases (NCD) Compact 2020–2030', <https://cdn.who.int/media/docs/default-source/ncds/final_ncd-compact-(1).pdf?sfvrsn=d8895106_1> accessed 8 September 2025.

[3] Thomas Abel and David V McQueen, 'Current and Future Theoretical Foundations for NCDs and Health Promotion' in David V McQueen (ed), *Global Handbook on Noncommunicable Diseases and Health Promotion* (Springer 2013) 21–35.

tend to follow a 'permit but discourage' logic,[4] adopting taxes, labels and warnings to discourage consumption, but refraining from banning unhealthy practices altogether. Part of the explanation for such an approach is that unhealthy products represent a big segment of our economy, with billions in profits and millions of jobs dependent on them. Their consumption, while frowned upon by some, is also considered acceptable by many and experienced as pleasurable. Eating, drinking and smoking are entangled in a complex set of moral values, ethical norms and cultural practices. Alcohol is a good example. A toxic substance that does not meet any physiological needs in humans, and is hence best avoided, it remains widely consumed.[5] Many alcoholic beverages are seen as quality products, epitomising cultural traditions and know-how. On this basis, we can thus distinguish between (at least) three relevant dimensions of unhealthy lifestyles: a *health* dimension, a *market* dimension and an *ethical/cultural* dimension. These three dimensions are at the core of the regulatory process and at the core of this book.

The EU is increasingly aware of the need to tackle its growing lifestyle-related health burden. Over the last four decades, it has used its powers to promote healthier habits in its population, adopting various measures aimed at curbing the consumption of tobacco products, alcoholic beverages and unhealthy foods. The effort is particularly visible as regards tobacco, subject to a nearly complete advertising ban and to stringent labelling obligations.[6] Europeans, whether smokers or non-smokers, have grown accustomed to the graphic health warnings present on cigarette packs, one of the most visible aspects of the EU's lifestyle legal apparatus. Their food environment is also shaped by EU rules on labelling and nutritional information.[7] Lifestyles remain high on the

[4] William A Bogart, *Permit But Discourage* (Oxford University Press 2010).

[5] See Jürgen Rehm, Dirk W Lachenmeier and Robin Room, 'Why Does Society Accept a Higher Risk for Alcohol than for Other Voluntary or Involuntary Risks?' (2014) 12 BMC Medicine 189.

[6] Directive 2003/33/EC of the European Parliament and of the Council of 26 May 2003 on the approximation of the laws, regulations and administrative provisions of the Member States relating to the advertising and sponsorship of tobacco products, OJ L152/16; Directive 2014/40/EU of the European Parliament and of the Council of 3 April 2014 on the approximation of the laws, regulations and administrative provisions of the Member States concerning the manufacture, presentation and sale of tobacco and related products and repealing Directive 2001/37/EC, OJ L127/1.

[7] See, inter alia, Regulation (EC) No 1924/2006 of the European Parliament and of the Council of 20 December 2006 on nutrition and health claims made on foods (Claims Regulation), OJ L404/9; Regulation (EU) No 1169/2011 of the European Parliament and of

European Commission's public health agenda. The Europe's Beating Cancer Plan, released in 2021, puts preventive action on lifestyles at its core, with the ambitious objective to reach a 'tobacco-free generation' by 2040.[8] Nutrition is also a key component of the Farm to Fork Strategy, the Commission's road map to build a sustainable EU food system, by transitioning towards a more plant-based diet.[9] Up to 2025, however, the execution of these two strategies remained piecemeal, with little to none of the promised lifestyle-related legislation put forward as a formal proposal.[10] The difficulty to put these plans into motion is best illustrated by the controversy surrounding the 'Nutri-Score', a colour-coded nutrition label whose possible roll-out on all food packages in the EU has been vocally rejected by major food business operators and several Member States. Despite its wide support in the scientific community, this seemingly innocuous label, which ranks products according to their nutritional quality, is facing determined opposition.[11] What is disputed here is not only, or mostly, the scientific underpinning of the system, but the very legitimacy of the EU to adopt a label telling people which products are 'good' or 'bad'. This, according to some, would endanger traditional food productions and unduly interferes with people's dietary choices.[12] By offering a way for consumers to navigate their food choices more easily, the EU gets embroiled in political controversies that go well beyond health.

The Nutri-Score debate illustrates well the challenges of regulating unhealthy lifestyles at the EU level. These challenges are linked to the EU's characteristics as a supranational and functionally driven risk-

the Council of 25 October 2011 on the provision of food information to consumers (Food Information Regulation), OJ L304/18.

8 European Commission, Communication from the Commission to the European Parliament and the Council, 'Europe's Beating Cancer Plan', COM (2021) 44 final.

9 European Commission, Communication from the Commission to the Council, the European Parliament, the European Economic and Social Committee and the Committee of the Regions, 'A Farm to Fork Strategy for a fair, healthy and environmentally-friendly food system', COM (2020) 381 final.

10 See Hanna Schebesta, 'How to Save the Farm to Fork Strategy: A Two-Phased Approach' (2023) 18 European Food and Feed Law Review 231; Amandine Garde and others, 'Lobbying, Transparency and Trust: Power Imbalances and the Failure to Implement Europe's Beating Cancer Plan' (2025) 51 The Lancet Regional Health – Europe 101238.

11 Chantal Julia and others, 'Ten Years of Nutri-Score Front-of-Pack Nutrition Labelling in Europe' (2025) 6 Nature Food 239.

12 See Morgane Fialon, Lydiane Nabec and Chantal Julia, 'Legitimacy of Front-of-Pack Nutrition Labels: Controversy Over the Deployment of the Nutri-Score in Italy' (2022) 11 International Journal of Health Policy and Management 2574.

regulator,[13] a space where the health, market and cultural/ethical dimensions described above interact in a unique manner. This is due, first of all, to the importance of the market in EU law. As with other policy fields, the objective of establishing and ensuring the functioning of an internal market where goods, persons, services and capital circulate freely, as per Article 26 TFEU, has been central to the inception and development of EU lifestyle law and policy. National measures that seek to limit the consumption of unhealthy products are liable to constitute obstacles to trade between Member States, thus coming within the scope of the TFEU free movement provisions, Article 34 TFEU most notably. The clash between free movement and national rules on alcohol has given rise to some of EU law's most renowned judgments,[14] starting with the *Cassis de Dijon* case, where Germany unsuccessfully tried to prevent the sale on its territory of the French blackcurrant liqueur.[15] This ruling of the Court of Justice is thought to be the first expression of the principle of mutual recognition, later brought to the judicial and legislative pinnacle, as a foundation of the internal market and the broader EU legal order.[16] Creating and maintaining an internal market where unhealthy products can freely circulate across borders requires oversight of national control measures, to ensure that these do not unduly restrict the free flow of goods, services or persons. It also leads the EU to directly regulate these products by adopting common health standards, so as to offer a level-playing field to companies and other economic actors.

In the EU, the market logic often dominates for lack of other regulatory options. Article 114 TFEU, which allows the EU legislature to harmonise national laws with the view to facilitate the establishment and functioning of the internal market, compensates for the absence of direct legislative powers in the field of health.[17] The boundary between

[13] See Maria Weimer, *Risk Regulation in the Internal Market: Lessons from Agricultural Biotechnology* (Oxford University Press 2019).

[14] See e.g. Case 8/74 *Dassonville*, EU:C:1974:82; Case 178/84 *Commission v Germany (Beer purity)*, EU:C:1987:126; Case 170/78 *Commission v United Kingdom (beer and wine I)*, EU:C:1980:53; Case 170/78 *Commission v United Kingdom (beer and wine II)*, EU:C:1983:202; Case C-333/14, *The Scotch Whisky Association*, EU:C:2015:845.

[15] Case 120/78 *Rewe v Bundesmonopolverwaltung für Branntwein* (*Cassis de Dijon*), EU:C:1979:42.

[16] Albertina Albors-Llorens, Catherine Barnard and Brigitte Leucht (eds), *Cassis de Dijon: 40 Years On* (Hart Publishing 2021).

[17] As per Article 2(5) and 6(a) TFEU, the protection of human health predominantly falls within the field of supporting competences, for which no harmonisation of Member States' laws or regulations is possible.

the *health* and *market* dimensions of EU action was addressed by the Court of Justice in its landmark *Germany v European Parliament and Council* judgment,[18] better known as *Tobacco Advertising*. As rightly coined by Advocate General Kokott, '[h]ardly any EU legislation has led to such fierce legal disputes over the years as the various directives on [. . .] tobacco [. . .] in the European internal market'.[19] These judgments touch upon the EU's most fundamental constitutional questions, regarding the boundaries of its action and the respect for the principles of conferral, subsidiarity and proportionality. While much has already been written about it,[20] this book aims to take the reflection further, to explore the contradictions that exist in constructing a market for a category of products that one seeks, *at the same time*, to eliminate from that market. This is EU law's first dilemma. The study of unhealthy lifestyles leads us to rethink the meaning and content of the EU internal market, and re-evaluate the accounts made of a regulatory space where free movement and negative integration threaten the protection of non-market objectives.[21]

The second dilemma is related to the diversity inherent in lifestyle practices, which finds its expression not only in the ethical/cultural dimension described above, but also the health dimension, to the extent that the plurality of lifestyles leads to a different aetiology and prevalence of diseases and calls for different regulatory responses. Lifestyles

[18] Case C-376/98 *Germany v European Parliament and Council (Tobacco Advertising)*, EU:C:2000:544.

[19] Case C-477/14 *Pillbox 38*, Opinion of Advocate General Kokott, EU:C:2016:324, para 1. See in this regard Case C-380/03 *Germany v European Parliament and Council (Tobacco Advertising II)*, EU:C:2006:772; Case C-491/01 *British American Tobacco (Investments) and Imperial Tobacco*, EU:C:2002:741; Case C-547/14 *Philip Morris Brands*, EU:C:2016:325.

[20] In a vast literature, see in particular Derrick Wyatt, 'Community Competence to Regulate the Internal Market' in Michael Dougan and Samantha Currie (eds), *50 Years of the European Treaties: Looking Back and Thinking Forward* (Hart Publishing 2009); Stephen Weatherill, 'The Limits of Legislative Harmonization Ten Years after Tobacco Advertising: How the Court's Case-law Has Become a "Drafting Guide"' (2011) 12 German Law Journal 827; Vincent Delhomme, 'Emancipating Health from the Internal Market: For a Stronger EU (Legislative) Competence in Public Health' (2020) 11 European Journal of Risk Regulation 747.

[21] See, for recent accounts, Sacha Garben, 'The Constitutional (Im)Balance between "the Market" and "the Social" in the European Union' (2017) 13 European Constitutional Law Review 23; Sacha Garben, 'The "Fundamental Freedoms" and (Other) Fundamental Rights: Towards an Integrated Democratic Interpretation Framework' in Sacha Garben and Inge Govaere (eds), *The Internal Market 2.0* (Hart Publishing 2020). On the difference between positive and negative integration, see Robert Schütze, '"Integration-through-Law": Grand Theory, Revisionist History' (2025) 4 European Law Open 162.

are not 'the uncoordinated behaviours of disconnected individuals, but are personal routines that merge into an aggregate form representative of specific groups and classes'.[22] They are profoundly influenced by structural factors, such as age, wealth, gender and ethnicity.[23] These differences between groups highlight the power of social norms, that is, social attitudes of approval and disapproval towards certain behaviours.[24] This diversity is at odds with another fundamental feature of the EU's market dimension, the push towards harmonisation and uniformity, to iron out regulatory differences and install a level-playing field or economic actors. This dialectic creates two sets of challenges. The first is one of *effectiveness*, the ability of the EU as a functionally driven risk regulator to select the best health intervention, in terms of reduced mortality and morbidity. The prevention and control of NCDs is an area where scientific uncertainty persists regarding certain risks and where the effects of regulatory instruments are not always well-known. There is, for instance, still a considerable debate on the risks associated with electronic cigarettes and the role that this product may play in tobacco control.[25] The multifactorial nature of the underlying causes of NCDs renders the measurement of the effectiveness of different regulatory options difficult.[26] Uncertainty and diversity plead sometimes for a flexible use of EU powers, not always suited to the demands of market uniformity. The second is one of *acceptance*, the legitimacy of EU action in a culturally sensitive field, ripe with moral and ethical controversies. Opposition to governmental interference with lifestyle choices is reconfigured, and potentially amplified, when control measures are adopted at the EU level. That is because many foods or drinks are also 'heritage' products, that reflect 'what life "feels" like for local inhabitants',[27] and

[22] William C Cockerham, 'Health Lifestyle Theory and the Convergence of Agency and Structure' (2005) 46 Journal of Health and Social Behavior 51.

[23] ibid.

[24] Cass R Sunstein, 'Social Norms and Social Roles' (1996) 96 Columbia Law Review 903; Shaon Lahiri and others, 'Understanding the Mechanisms of Change in Social Norms around Tobacco Use: A Systematic Review and Meta-Analysis of Interventions' (2025) 120 Addiction 215.

[25] Susan Feeney, Victoria Rossetti and Jill Terrien, 'E-Cigarettes – a Review of the Evidence – Harm versus Harm Reduction' (2022) 15 Tobacco Use Insights 1179173X2210875.

[26] See Alberto Alemanno and Amandine Garde, 'The Emergence of EU Lifestyle Risk Regulation: New Trends in Evidence, Proportionality and Judicial Review' in Hans-W Micklitz and Takis Tridimas (eds), *Risk and EU law* (Edward Elgar Publishing 2015).

[27] Floris De Witte, 'You Are What You Ate: Food Heritage and the EU's Internal Market' (2022) 47 European Law Review 647.

which are particularly resistant to 'Europeanisation'. Lifestyle diversity might thus require us to accept a degree of market fragmentation, but, as the book will show, not necessarily at the expense of health.

1.2 Scope and Objectives of the Study

Against this background, the book addresses the three following questions:

What are the powers of the EU to regulate unhealthy lifestyles and how have these powers been used to date?

How does EU law balance the objective of building a market for unhealthy products and that of reducing and/or eliminating their consumption?

How does EU law balance market uniformity with the diversity and scientific uncertainty associated with lifestyle practices?

These questions have only been partially addressed. Some pioneer works by Alberto Alemanno and Amandine Garde have laid down the foundations of a study of 'lifestyle risks' in EU law, highlighting the specific questions arising from this regulatory field.[28] Some other works are dedicated to a single product or issue: food and nutrition,[29] tobacco,[30] alcohol,[31] or NCDs

[28] Simon Planzer and Alberto Alemanno, 'Lifestyle Risks: Conceptualising an Emerging Category of Research' (2010) 1 European Journal of Risk Regulation 335; Alberto Alemanno and Amandine Garde, 'The Emergence of an EU Lifestyle Policy: The Case of Alcohol, Tobacco and Unhealthy Diets' (2013) 50 Common Market Law Review 1745; Alberto Alemanno and Amandine Garde, *Regulating Lifestyle Risks: The EU, Alcohol, Tobacco and Unhealthy Diets* (Cambridge University Press 2015); Alberto Alemanno and Amandine Garde, 'The Emergence of EU Lifestyle Risk Regulation: New Trends in Evidence, Proportionality and Judicial Review' in Hans-W Micklitz and Takis Tridimas (eds), *Risk and EU Law* (Edward Elgar Publishing 2015).

[29] Caoimhín MacMaoláin, *EU Food Law: Protecting Consumers and Health in a Common Market* (Hart Publishing 2007); Amandine Garde, *EU Law and Obesity Prevention* (Kluwer Law International 2010); Caoimhín MacMaoláin, *Food Law: European, Domestic and International Frameworks* (Hart Publishing 2015); Hanna Schebesta and Kai Purnhagen, *EU Food Law* (Oxford University Press 2024).

[30] Scott Crosby, 'The New Tobacco Control Directive: An Illiberal and Illegal Disdain for the Law' (2002) 27 European Law Review 177; Alberto Alemanno, 'Out of Sight Out of Mind: Towards a New EU Tobacco Products Directive' (2012) 18 Columbia Journal of European Law 197.

[31] Ben Baumberg and Peter Anderson, 'Health, Alcohol and EU Law: Understanding the Impact of European Single Market Law on Alcohol Policies' (2008) 18 The European Journal of Public Health 392; Oliver Bartlett and Amandine Garde, 'Time to Seize the (Red) Bull by the Horns: The EU's Failure to Protect Children from Alcohol and

more generally.[32] Mostly, unhealthy lifestyles have been approached as a subset of EU health law and policy.[33] EU legal scholarship lacks a comprehensive study that allows an understanding of the basis on which the EU came to intervene in the field and offers a complete overview of its past and current action. Such comprehensive work is needed to characterise the EU's regulatory regime – that is, the measures adopted and the vision of the consumer that derives therefrom – and to draw useful comparisons between the three categories of products studied here. The book contributes to the expanding scholarship on risk regulation in the internal market and is thus closely connected to works such as that of Maria Weimer in the field of agricultural biotechnology.[34] It is motivated by the same desire to understand how 'EU regulators [can] secure the acceptability of risk regulation in the face of the legal-institutional, socio-economic and cultural diversity in the Member States, while acting on the basis of a narrow and functionally delineated mandate'.[35]

The book is thus written with two categories of readers in mind. The first are scholars and practitioners active in public health and NCDs prevention and control, who wish to know what the EU has done in the field and to understand better the specific challenges of conducting a lifestyle health promotion policy under the purview of EU law. The second are the readers interested in classic EU (internal market) law questions, regarding the division of competences between the EU and the Member States, the relationship between positive and negative integration and the tension between uniformity and diversity. They will feel

Unhealthy Food Marketing' (2013) 38 European Law Review 498; Oliver Bartlett and Angus Macculloch, 'Evidence and Proportionality in Free Movement Cases: The Impact of the Scotch Whisky Case' (2020) 11 European Journal of Risk Regulation 109.

32 Oliver Bartlett, 'The EU's Competence Gap in Public Health and Non-Communicable Disease Policy' (2016) 5 Cambridge International Law Journal 50; Oliver Bartlett, 'Power, Policy Ideas and Paternalism in Non-Communicable Disease Prevention' (2018) 24 European Law Journal 474; Nikhil Gokani, 'Regulation for Health Inequalities and Non-Communicable Diseases: In Want of (Effective) Behavioural Insights' (2018) 24 European Law Journal 490.

33 See, in particular, the relevant chapters in Elias Mossialos and others (eds), *Health Systems Governance in Europe: The Role of European Union Law and Policy* (Cambridge University Press 2010); Tamara K Hervey and Jean V McHale, *European Union Health Law: Themes and Implications* (Cambridge University Press 2015); Scott L Greer and Paulette Kurzer (eds), *European Union Public Health Policy: Regional and Global Trends* (Routledge 2016); Tamara K Hervey, Calum Alasdair Young and Louise E Bishop, *Research Handbook on EU Health Law and Policy* (Edward Elgar Publishing 2017).

34 Weimer, *Risk Regulation in the Internal Market*.

35 ibid 49.

familiar with the materials used in this work but may hopefully come to look at it in a different way.

As regards the scope of the study, further explanations will be given in Chapter 2. Some clarification is nonetheless necessary at this stage. Regulation is notoriously difficult to define as a concept and the book does not engage with the debates and controversies surrounding its use.[36] It follows a minimal definition, relevant to the field of health risks, according to which regulation is about 'which risks to accept and what measures need to be taken to minimise [these]'.[37] Regulation is typically exercised by public sector actors and interferes with market and social processes to minimise adverse consequences to protected interests such as health.[38] In the present EU law context, regulation is understood in a broad sense, as including not only the tools adopted by the EU to promote healthier lifestyles but also the effect of EU law, particularly free movement provisions, on national policies. This book is about the regulation of health risks associated with certain lifestyles, meaning that their environmental impact, while certainly an important aspect,[39] will only be addressed incidentally. It also focuses on internal EU action, that affecting the health of Europeans, citizens or residents of the EU. EU external action, which is also relevant to health and lifestyles, through trade policy for instance,[40] falls outside its scope.

[36] See Julia Black, 'Critical Reflections on Regulation' (2002) 27 Austrian Journal of Legal Philosophy 1; Robert Baldwin, Martin Cave and Martin Lodge, 'Introduction: Regulation – the Field and the Developing Agenda' in Robert Baldwin, Martin Cave and Martin Lodge (eds), *The Oxford Handbook of Regulation* (Oxford University Press 2010); Christel Koop and Martin Lodge, 'What Is Regulation? An Interdisciplinary Concept Analysis' (2017) 11 Regulation & Governance 95.

[37] Alberto Alemanno, 'Risk and Regulation' in Adam Burgess, Alberto Alemanno and Jens O Zinn (eds), *Routledge Handbook of Risk Studies* (Routledge 2016) 197. See also Weimer, *Risk Regulation in the Internal Market* 23.

[38] Weimer, *Risk Regulation in the Internal Market* 23. See also Christopher Hood, Henry Rothstein and Robert Baldwin, *The Government of Risk: Understanding Risk Regulation Regimes* (Oxford University Press 2001) 3.

[39] See as regards tobacco and food, Thomas E Novotny and Elli Slaughter, 'Tobacco Product Waste: An Environmental Approach to Reduce Tobacco Consumption' (2014) 1 Current Environmental Health Reports 208; Alessandro Banterle, Elena Claire Ricci and Alessia Cavaliere, 'Environmental Sustainability and the Food System' in Harry Bremmers and Kai Purnhagen (eds), *Regulating and Managing Food Safety in the EU: A Legal-Economic Perspective* (Springer International Publishing 2018); Anniek J Kortleve and others, 'Over 80% of the European Union's Common Agricultural Policy Supports Emissions-Intensive Animal Products' (2024) 5 Nature Food 288.

[40] On the role and place of health in EU external action, see Elisabet Ruiz Cairo, *The Promotion of Public Health in EU External Relations* (Schulthess LGDJ 2021).

The book is centred on three categories of products: tobacco, alcohol and unhealthy foodstuffs, that is, foods high in calories, fat, sugar or salt.[41] Other 'lifestyles' could have been included, such as gambling and the consumption of illicit drugs. Their exclusion is not only justified for practical reasons – the study could not possibly cover all unhealthy lifestyles – but because gambling and illicit drugs are subject to an entirely different regulatory regime under EU law. National gambling laws, on the one hand, are not harmonised and are solely governed by the TFEU freedoms of movement.[42] There is therefore no EU gambling policy. Illicit drugs, on the other hand, are subject to the full force of the law, with EU law prescribing the criminalisation of activities linked to drug trafficking.[43] EU policy on *illicit* drugs is therefore fundamentally different from its policy on *licit* drugs: the approach taken is not of 'permit but discourage', but prohibit to discourage. There are, for instance, no packaging and labelling rules or taxes on illicit drugs. In addition, while it is a policy relevant to unhealthy lifestyles, food and alcohol especially,[44] the choice was made to not cover the rules applicable to the common agricultural policy (CAP), which are legally distinct from those of the internal market.[45] Furthermore, while these rules govern primarily the production of agricultural products and raw materials, the book focuses on rules that target the processing and marketing of products and their impact on consumer behaviour.

41 The concept of healthiness as applied to foods is complex and goes beyond these aspects: see Chantal Julia and others, 'Are Foods "healthy" or "Healthier"? Front-of-Pack Labelling and the Concept of Healthiness Applied to Foods' (2022) 127 The British Journal of Nutrition 948. These issues are further explored in Section 2.5.

42 Stefaan Van den Bogaert and Armin Cuyvers, '"Money for Nothing": The Case Law of the EU Court of Justice on the Regulation of Gambling' (2011) 48 Common Market Law Review 1175; Simon Planzer, *Empirical Views on European Gambling Law and Addiction* (Springer 2014).

43 Article 83 TFEU. See Valsamis Mitsilegas, *EU Criminal Law* (Hart Publishing 2022).

44 Christopher Birt, 'A CAP on Health?' (Faculty of Public Health 2010); Nikolai Pushkarev, 'A CAP for Healthy Living Mainstreaming Health into the EU Common Agricultural Policy' (2015) 2 AIMS Public Health 844; F Recanati and others, 'Assessing the Role of CAP for More Sustainable and Healthier Food Systems in Europe: A Literature Review' (2019) 653 Science of The Total Environment 908; Kortleve and others, 'Over 80% of the European Union's Common Agricultural Policy Supports Emissions-Intensive Animal Products'.

45 The rules applicable to agriculture and fisheries are contained in Articles 38 to 44 TFEU.

1.3 Structure of the Book

The book is organised as follows. Part I addresses the first of the three research questions: determining what the EU's powers to regulate unhealthy lifestyles are and how these powers have been used thus far. Chapter 2 lays the foundations for the study and further clarifies its scope. Unhealthy lifestyles are defined here as collective patterns of unhealthy behaviour, based on choices from options available to people according to their life chances. This definition highlights four key dimensions central to the book: the health risks associated with those behaviours, their consumable nature, their voluntary character and, finally, the relevance of social norms and structural factors. The chapter explores the health dimension in greater detail for each of the three categories of products studied here, tobacco, alcohol and unhealthy foods, clarifying the health risks to which consumers are exposed and introducing the central regulatory questions raised by each category.

Chapter 3 investigates the EU's competence to regulate unhealthy lifestyles. Two main rationales for EU intervention in the field can be found in the TFEU. Both rationales carry a descriptive and normative value in the sense that, while allowing a better understanding of the shape and content of EU action, they also provide a defence for the EU's involvement in the field. The first, historically and conceptually predominant, is related to the market. EU regulation contributes to the establishment of the EU internal market, by addressing the externalities of Member State lifestyle policies and their restrictive effect on free movement, of goods in particular. This rationale corresponds to broad and functional powers to eliminate trade barriers between Member States, via the EU's fundamental free movement provisions, so-called negative integration, and the harmonisation of health standard at the EU level, positive integration. The second rationale concerns health as a standalone value, independent of the economic dimension of unhealthy lifestyles. For this rationale, the EU has been granted a much more limited competence. This explains why, in legal terms, EU law on unhealthy lifestyles remains a form of economic and market regulation, with a key role for Article 114 TFEU.

Chapter 4 provides an historical overview of the content and objectives of the EU's policy on unhealthy lifestyles. It distinguishes two periods. The first spans from the early days of European integration until the entry into force of the Treaty of Maastricht, in 1993. It is a period of negative integration: unhealthy products are regulated mostly through the prism of the TFEU internal market freedoms, with little role for harmonisation. One cannot yet speak of an EU 'policy' on the matter, in the sense of a deliberate and coordinated action made in response to the health burden associated with unhealthy lifestyles. This changes post-Maastricht, the second period, with the recognition of a formal competence for the EU in health matters. Unhealthy lifestyles are singled out as one of the key priorities of EU health action and a greater role is given to positive integration, with the adoption of various horizontal legislative instruments. Different approaches emerged for the three categories of products: while the declared goal is to bring tobacco consumption to a near end, alcohol consumption is considered to be a natural part of human life, not to be overly discouraged, with food and nutrition positioned somewhere in between.

Chapter 5 continues the overview through a different analytical lens. It investigates the EU's toolbox, describing and classifying the regulatory tools used by the EU legislature across the different lifestyles. It identifies four main types of interventions: ban and composition requirements, tax and price measures, rules on advertising and promotion and rules on mandatory and voluntary information. Beyond this systematic description and classification, the chapter serves three aims. First, it confronts the regulatory tools used with the stated objectives of EU lifestyle policy, assessing their adequacy and suggesting possible reforms. Second, it highlights the significant regulatory disparities existing between lifestyle risk factors, critically evaluating the justifications for such differential treatment. Third, it shows how health and internal market objectives are intertwined in EU lifestyle policy, generating legal frictions.

These frictions between health and the market are the focus of Part II, which aims to shed (a new) light on two perennial EU law questions: the balance between market and non-market objectives and the management of Member State diversity and autonomy in EU (internal market) law. Chapter 6 addresses the first of these questions. Its main contention is that the legal predominance of the internal market objective in this field of regulation has not been to the detriment of the protection of health. While the broad reach of the TFEU free movement provisions does mean that most Member State measures can be scrutinised by the Court of Justice for their restrictive effect on cross-border trade, the case law does not reveal a consistent hostility towards national control measures. The picture is rather one of unpredictability. In addition, the harmonisation practice of the EU legislature shows that the market functions mostly as an auxiliary to health, or, at times, fades away behind the objective of health protection. This invites a re-evaluation of the concept of the internal market in EU law.

Chapter 7 turns to the question of diversity from a health perspective, with a focus on scientific uncertainty and regulatory experimentation. This is about the *effectiveness* of EU intervention, the ability of the EU, as a functionally driven risk regulator, to select the best health intervention, in terms of reduced mortality and morbidity. It investigates how the principle of precaution is used by the Court to grant a certain leeway to the national and the EU legislature. Notably, the principle is applied not only to uncertainty about the existence of health risks, but also to uncertainty about the effects of policy interventions. The chapter then examines two legal devices designed to preserve the regulatory autonomy of Member States: subsidiarity and minimum harmonisation. Through three case studies – tobacco plain packaging, the ban on tobacco for oral use and front-of-pack nutrition labelling – the chapter highlights the contradiction between the need for regulatory diversity and the need for market uniformity, and the resultant tensions with the principles of conferral and subsidiarity.

Chapter 8 approaches diversity through cultural and moral lenses. It concerns the *acceptance* of EU intervention, the legitimacy of its action in a sensitive field, ripe with moral and ethical controversies. The EU's approach can broadly be divided into three strands, which are not mutually exclusive. The first is the Europeanisation of choice, most apparent in tobacco regulation, where the EU has adopted a quasi-prohibitionist stance with seemingly broad support from Member States. Strikingly, this occurs in the absence, both legally and politically, of arguments grounded in individual rights and autonomy. The second is an approach of insulation, relevant to alcohol and certain 'heritage' foods, where national regulatory choices remain shielded from European influence, either because of the EU's reluctance to act or because of political deadlock. The third concerns the application of proportionality in free movement cases, and the extent to which cultural and moral arguments are accommodated in the adjudication of national restrictive measures.

PART I

Regulating Unhealthy Lifestyles in the EU

2 Unhealthy Lifestyles as a Regulatory Object

2.1 Introduction

Government intervention in people's lifestyles is a relatively new phenomenon. Two factors may have accounted for this evolution. First, health has generally gained in importance as a value. Health may have been a long-standing preoccupation of most human groups, yet the extent and intensity of health-related concerns evident in contemporary societies are remarkable.[1] Whereas people used to take health for granted, this is no longer the case. Health is increasingly viewed as an achievement, something people are supposed to work on to enhance their quality of life and avoid premature death.[2] The concept of 'healthism' describes these concerns and the idea that individuals have a central role to play in maintaining their health.[3] Second, the nature of the health risks to which individuals are exposed has changed. Fuelled by the 'epidemiologic transition' described in Chapter 1,[4] a 'new' public health is coming of age. Contrary to the 'old' public health of the nineteenth century, preoccupied mostly with hygiene, filth and contagion, the new public health focuses on the root causes of diseases,

[1] Alan Petersen and Deborah Lupton, *The New Public Health: Health and Self in the Age of Risk* (SAGE Publications Ltd 2000) 1.

[2] Cockerham, 'Health Lifestyle Theory and the Convergence of Agency and Structure' 51.

[3] Nike Ayo, 'Understanding Health Promotion in a Neoliberal Climate and the Making of Health Conscious Citizens' (2012) 22 Critical Public Health 99, 100; Friedrich Schorb, 'Fat Politics in Europe: Theorizing on the Premises and Outcomes of European Anti-"Obesity-Epidemic" Policies' (2013) 2 Fat Studies 3, 6–7.

[4] Abdel R Omran, 'The Epidemiologic Transition: A Theory of the Epidemiology of Population Change' (2005) 83 The Milbank Quarterly 731; Robert E McKeown, 'The Epidemiologic Transition: Changing Patterns of Mortality and Population Dynamics' (2009) 3 American Journal of Lifestyle Medicine 19S.

non-communicable diseases (NCDs) mostly, where life habits play a key role.[5]

But not all hazardous lifestyles have attracted government attention. What do tobacco, alcohol and foods have in common? What justifies the focus on these three categories of products? This chapter seeks to answer these questions and to lay down the foundations for the entire book. Unhealthy lifestyles are defined here as collective patterns of unhealthy behaviour based on choices from options available to people according to their life chances. This definition highlights four key dimensions of the concept, central to the book: the health risks associated with those behaviours, their consumption nature, their voluntary character and, finally, the relevance of social norms and structural factors. The chapter then investigates, for each of the three relevant categories of products, the precise health risks associated with it and the main scientific debates that have arisen in the context of regulation.

2.2 Unhealthy Lifestyles: Content and Boundaries of the Concept

A person's health is determined by a number of factors. These 'determinants of health' are of behavioural, biological, socio-economic or environmental origin.[6] The European Union (EU), the World Health Organization (WHO) and other public health bodies recognise that lifestyles are an essential determinant of health.[7] Although there is neither a fixed list nor consensus as to which habits or activities constitute unhealthy lifestyles, this umbrella term usually includes the following: tobacco and alcohol consumption, unhealthy diets and the lack of physical activity.[8] These behaviours

[5] Petersen and Lupton, *The New Public Health* 2–4.

[6] Regulation (EU) 2021/522 of the European Parliament and of the Council of 24 March 2021 establishing a Programme for the Union's action in the field of health ('EU4Health Programme') for the period 2021–2027, OJ L107/1, art 2(11). See also WHO, 'Determinants of health' (2024), <www.who.int/news-room/questions-and-answers/item/determinants-of-health> accessed 12 September 2025.

[7] For the EU: see Regulation 2021/522, art 3(a); Council of the European Union, Council Conclusions on closing health gaps within the EU through concerted action to promote healthy lifestyle behaviours, OJ C359/5. For the WHO: see WHO, 'Healthy living: what is a healthy lifestyle?' (1999) WHO Regional Office for Europe, <https://apps.who.int/iris/handle/10665/108180> accessed 12 September 2025; WHO, 'Global Noncommunicable Diseases (NCD) Compact 2020–2030'.

[8] ibid; see also Alemanno and Garde, 'The Emergence of an EU Lifestyle Policy: The Case of Alcohol, Tobacco and Unhealthy Diets'; Alemanno and Garde, *Regulating Lifestyle Risks: The*

constitute risk factors for a range of harmful health outcomes, in particular NCDs,[9] a term that refers to 'any condition which is not transmissible between people'.[10] Countless NCDs exist, but four conditions exert a particularly high mortality and morbidity burden on the population globally: cardiovascular diseases, cancers, chronic respiratory diseases and diabetes.[11] It was estimated that these four NCDs claimed at least 25 per cent of health spending in the EU in 2020.[12] In 2021, approximately 1.1 million deaths, the equivalent of 21 per cent of all deaths, in the EU were attributable to the combined impact of smoking, excessive alcohol use and a high body mass index.[13]

Apart from their connection to a host of damaging health consequences, unhealthy lifestyles are rarely, if ever, defined in academic and policy contexts. According to the WHO a healthy lifestyle is 'a way of living that lowers the risk of being seriously ill or dying early',[14] implying that, on the contrary, an unhealthy lifestyle is a way of living that increases those risks. As such, most ways of living, most habits and behaviours influence our health, 'from brushing one's teeth and using automobile seat belts to relaxing at health spas',[15] or, conversely, from not wearing proper clothing during wintertime to cycling without a helmet. There is a need for a definition that is both *narrower in scope*, which allows us to focus on a set of specific lifestyles, and *wider in substance*, which unveils, beyond health, a number of key characteristics common to these various lifestyles.

EU, Alcohol, Tobacco and Unhealthy Diets; Dominic Upton and Kathryn Thirlaway, *Promoting Healthy Behaviour: A Practical Guide* (2nd edition, Routledge, Taylor & Francis Group 2014).

9 Mike Rayner and others, 'NCDs: Risk Factors and Determinants' in Mike Rayner and others (eds.), *An Introduction to Population-Level Prevention of Non-Communicable Diseases* (Oxford University Press 2017) 32; Christopher JL Murray and others, 'Global Burden of 87 Risk Factors in 204 Countries and Territories, 1990–2019: A Systematic Analysis for the Global Burden of Disease Study 2019' (2020) 396 The Lancet 1223.

10 Rayner and others, *An Introduction to Population-Level Prevention of Non-Communicable Diseases* 13.

11 Rayner and others, 'NCDs: Risk Factors and Determinants'.

12 Désirée Vandenberghe and Johan Albrecht, 'The Financial Burden of Non-Communicable Diseases in the European Union: A Systematic Review' (2020) 30 European Journal of Public Health 833.

13 OECD/European Commission, 'Health at a Glance: Europe 2024: State of Health in the EU Cycle'.

14 WHO, 'Healthy living: what is a healthy lifestyle?' 1.

15 William C Cockerham, Thomas Abel and Günther Lüschen, 'Max Weber, Formal Rationality, and Health Lifestyles' (1993) 34 The Sociological Quarterly 413, 419.

William Cockerham, one of the leading contemporary theorists of health lifestyles, offers such a definition. Drawing on elements from the sociology of Max Weber, Pierre Bourdieu and Anthony Giddens, Cockerham and his co-authors define health lifestyles as:

[C]ollective patterns of health-related behavior based on choices from options available to people according to their life chances.[16]

Unhealthy lifestyles may therefore be defined as *collective patterns of unhealthy behaviour based on choices from options available to people according to their life chances*. This definition underlines three central characteristics of the concept.[17] First, lifestyles are not only an individual but a collective phenomenon. Meals are often taken in common, as is the consumption of alcohol. Second – this is a central aspect of Max Weber's understanding of lifestyles in modern times – these status groups are defined by consumption rather than production. Consumption is regarded 'as a set of social and cultural practices that establish differences between social groups'.[18] Third, these lifestyles arise from the interplay between a person's 'life choices' – to smoke or not to smoke, to drink or not to drink – and 'life chances' – one's position in society which orients and limits the range of possible choices.[19] Life chances are affected by various structural variables, including social class, age, gender or race.[20] Lifestyle behaviours, while voluntary, do not appear in a vacuum. This definition is close to Thirlaway and Upton's conceptualisation of 'lifestyle behaviours':

[I]t is possible to put together a cohesive argument that *lifestyle behaviours share more than their ability to influence a range of chronic diseases*. First, lifestyle behaviours have multiple functions; *they are not simply or even primarily health focused*. Lifestyle behaviours can be mood enhancing; they can be used as a coping strategy; they are often *pleasurable*; and they play an important function in the development and maintenance of *social relationships*. Second, lifestyle behaviours are all *under some degree of volitional control*, although the amount of control individuals have

16 William C Cockerham, Alfred Rütten and Thomas Abel, 'Conceptualizing Contemporary Health Lifestyles: Moving beyond Weber' (1997) 38 The Sociological Quarterly 321, 338; Cockerham, 'Health Lifestyle Theory and the Convergence of Agency and Structure' 55.
17 ibid.
18 Cockerham, Rütten and Abel, 'Conceptualizing Contemporary Health Lifestyles' 324.
19 ibid 325; Cockerham, 'Health Lifestyle Theory and the Convergence of Agency and Structure' 55.
20 Cockerham, Rütten and Abel, 'Conceptualizing Contemporary Health Lifestyles' 338; Cockerham, 'Health Lifestyle Theory and the Convergence of Agency and Structure'.

over their lifestyle choices is *contentious and likely to vary widely from context to context.*[21]

To sum up, what unhealthy lifestyles have in common is that they are consumption behaviours, chosen by individuals within the constraints of their social position and expressing belonging to certain social groups, which expose individuals to certain health risks. Here appear the three dimensions highlighted in Chapter 1: health, market and ethical/cultural dimensions. Tobacco consumption, alcohol consumption and unhealthy diets undoubtedly fit that definition. These health-damaging behaviours are embedded in a set of cultural practices. It seems almost superfluous to stress the importance of food and alcohol for social groups, regardless of how these groups are defined, along ethnic lines or according to class, age or gender. These behaviours are also linked to an act of consumption, the purchase of a product which constitutes the entry point for regulation.

Unhealthy lifestyles are for the most part voluntary, activities for which individuals use their value system and experience to determine if the risk incurred is acceptable.[22] This is one of the main differences between lifestyle and systemic risks, for example, nuclear or environmental, where choice plays a far more minor role. This does not mean that lifestyle choices are fully desired or proceed from a perfectly reasoned and unfettered deliberation. As stressed by Cockerham, lifestyles are situated at the convergence of agency and structure,[23] meaning that individuals 'have the freedom to choose within the social constraints that apply to their situation in life'.[24] It is commonly accepted that NCDs are caused by a complex causal web of underlying socioeconomic, cultural, political and environmental determinants; personal factors like genetics; and common modifiable behavioural risk factors, such as tobacco, alcohol and unhealthy eating.[25]

The choice element in unhealthy lifestyles matters for regulation, for two main raisons. First, understanding why people act in a certain way is

[21] Kathryn Thirlaway and Dominic Upton, *The Psychology of Lifestyle: Promoting Healthy Behaviour* (Routledge, Taylor & Francis Group 2009) 6–7, emphasis added.

[22] Rehm, Lachenmeier and Room, 'Why Does Society Accept a Higher Risk for Alcohol than for Other Voluntary or Involuntary Risks?' 189.

[23] Cockerham, 'Health Lifestyle Theory and the Convergence of Agency and Structure'.

[24] Cockerham, Rütten and Abel, 'Conceptualizing Contemporary Health Lifestyles' 325. See also Cockerham, 'Health Lifestyle Theory and the Convergence of Agency and Structure' 55.

[25] Rayner and others, 'NCDs: Risk Factors and Determinants'.

crucial if one is to enact policies which can effectively achieve behavioural change. Simply informing people of the risks incurred with unhealthy drinking or eating, via labelling or educational campaigns, is unlikely to yield significant results if one considers the reality of human behaviour and the limits to standard rationality. For instance, lifestyle behaviours have most of their positive consequences in the present and the majority of their negative outcomes in the future. A large body of research shows that when the costs and benefits arising from a course of action materialise at different times, people display 'myopic' tendencies and tend to discount future costs and benefits compared with immediate ones.[26] This phenomenon is referred to as 'hyperbolic discounting' or 'present bias'.[27] This conflict of preferences partly explains failures of self-control.[28] As will be further explained in Section 5.5.1.2, pictorial health warnings on tobacco products function at least partly by bringing the long-term consequences of smoking more visibly to the consumer, to provoke a cognitive reaction. This is an example of behaviourally informed public policy.[29] Second, the centrality of choice in lifestyles matters from an ethical perspective. Save for cases of involuntary exposure to risk, like second-hand smoking or acts of violence provoked by alcohol, the harm arising from unhealthy lifestyles is largely self-inflicted. This raises specific questions as to the appropriate boundaries for State intervention, the legitimacy of paternalistic measures and the space given to individual autonomy.[30] These questions are central to the field of public health more generally, which is particularly likely to result in unsought interventions into people's lives.[31] They have a lot

[26] Eyal Zamir and Doron Teichman, *Behavioral Law and Economics* (Oxford University Press 2018) 88. See also Oleg Urminsky and Gal Zauberman, 'The Health Consequences of Intertemporal Preferences' in Denise de Ridder, Marieke Adriaanse and Kentaro Fujita (eds), *The Routledge International Handbook of Self-Control in Health and Well-Being: Concepts, Theories, and Central Issues* (Routledge 2018) 89.

[27] Urminksy and Zauberman, 'The Health Consequences of Intertemporal Preferences' (n 71) 89.

[28] Zamir and Teichman, *Behavioral Law and Economics* (n 71) 92.

[29] Marianna Baggio and others, 'The Evolution of Behaviourally Informed Policy-Making in the EU' (2021) 28 Journal of European Public Policy 658.

[30] Bartlett, 'Power, Policy Ideas and Paternalism in Non-Communicable Disease Prevention'.

[31] See Lindsay F Wiley, Micah L Berman and Doug Blanke, 'Who's Your Nanny? Choice, Paternalism and Public Health in the Age of Personal Responsibility' (2013) 41 The Journal of Law, Medicine & Ethics 88; Kalle Grill and Angus Dawson, 'Ethical Frameworks in Public Health Decision-Making: Defending a Value-Based and Pluralist Approach' (2017) 25 Health Care Analysis 291.

less relevance for involuntary risks. Few people would object to the State taking action to reduce the risk of a nuclear catastrophe. Intervening to protect people from their own choices is likely to raise more opposition. These debates influence law and policy, and the type of regulatory measures that may be enacted in the field, as will be further explored in Section 8.2.

As already mentioned in Chapter 1, the choice was made to exclude from the scope of the book two other unhealthy lifestyles that fit the definition retained here and are also regulated under EU law: gambling and the consumption of illicit drugs.[32] That is because, from the perspective of EU law and policy, significant differences exist between these behaviours and the consumption of tobacco, food and alcohol. The control of illicit drugs is not, contrary to a widely held belief, a retained competence of the Member States. The EU has used its criminal law competence under Article 83 TFEU to lay down minimum prescriptions regarding the repression of illicit drug trafficking.[33] Yet, precisely because of their illegal character, illicit drugs are a matter of criminal law and not of economic regulation. The tools used to discourage the consumption of legal products (taxation, labelling, restrictions on advertising, etc.) are, by definition, not available for illegal products. There are thus limited comparisons to make between drugs and the other lifestyles studied in this book. As regards gambling, leaving aside the specificities of the harm caused by that activity – gambling does not directly affect physical health – the main difference with tobacco, alcohol and food, is that there is little to no EU policy on the matter. Gambling is not considered a health issue by the EU,[34] and it is only weakly regulated at the EU level, even as an economic activity.[35] Not only has no sectoral legislation been adopted in the field, but gambling is also excluded from the main horizontal instruments governing the internal market, such as the Services

[32] See Bogart, *Permit But Discourage* (n 4); Planzer and Alemanno, 'Lifestyle Risks'.

[33] Council Framework Decision 2004/757/JHA of 25 October 2004 laying down minimum provisions on the constituent elements of criminal acts and penalties in the field of illicit drug trafficking, OJ L335/8.

[34] See Regulation (EU) 282/2014 of the European Parliament and of the Council on the establishment of a third Programme for the Union's action in the field of health (2014–2020), OJ L86/1, art 3(1); Regulation 2021/522, art 3(a).

[35] The adoption of sectoral legislation seems had been contemplated by the Commission. That option was abandoned in the 1990s: see European Council, Edinburgh 11–12 December 1992, Conclusions of the Presidency, 456/1/92, 28.

Directive[36] and the E-commerce Directive.[37] Member States may set independent policy objectives on gambling, organise the market in the way they see fit and decide on the level of protection to adopt regarding consumer safety and public health. The only limit to this autonomy is to be found in the TFEU free movement provisions, which are applied in a particularly lenient manner by the Court in that field (see Section 8.4). Finally, the book also leaves aside physical (in)activity, which differs from tobacco, food and alcohol consumption in at least two fundamental ways. First, the health risks or benefits involved with physical activity are not necessarily embedded in a consumer relationship, as is almost always the case for these other lifestyles. Second, the goal of public authorities as regards physical activity is not to prevent a certain behaviour from happening but is entirely aimed at promoting a healthy one. Hence, as for illicit drugs, albeit for different reasons, the usual lifestyle regulatory tools find little or no application here. In addition, there is very little EU law and policy applicable to physical activity.[38]

Some other activities, while being part of a person's lifestyle, understood broadly, fall outside the scope of unhealthy lifestyles as conceptualised here. Two of them deserve some more attention: sex and the consumption of unsafe food.[39] Sex is undoubtedly a lifestyle practice with strong moral, ethical and cultural dimensions. It is also hazardous, as it exposes people to sexually transmitted diseases. Yet, a crucial difference between sex and, say, tobacco or alcohol consumption, is the absence, in most cases, of an underlying economic or consumer relationship. Choice is also an important distinction. Sex-induced risks are not truly voluntary risks in the sense that few people would willingly engage in an unprotected sexual intercourse with someone that they know for

[36] Directive 2006/123/EC of the European Parliament and of the Council of 12 December 2006 on services in the internal market, OJ L376/36, art 2(2)(h) and recital 25.

[37] Directive 2000/31/EC of the European Parliament and of the Council of 8 June 2000 on certain legal aspects of information society services, in particular electronic commerce, in the Internal Market, OJ L178/1, art 1(5)(d) and recital 16.

[38] See Council of the European Union, Conclusions of the Council and of the Representatives of the Governments of the Member States, meeting within the Council, of 27 November 2012 on promoting health-enhancing physical activity (HEPA), OJ C393/22; Council of the European Union, Council conclusions on the promotion of motor skills, physical and sport activities for children, OJ C417/46.

[39] Regarding sex, see contra Upton and Thirlaway, *Promoting Healthy Behaviour*; Thirlaway and Upton, *The Psychology of Lifestyle*.

sure carries a disease. Sex can be risk-free, smoking and drinking are never risk-free.

The case of food safety is more complex, starting with the fact that food safety is the founding paradigm of EU food law.[40] As they both arise from food consumption, food safety risks are inevitably closely linked to the nutritional risks referred to under the term 'unhealthy diets'. Yet, it seems to be commonly accepted that a difference exists between food *safety* and food *quality*,[41] the latter being the focus of nutrition policy. Intuitively, most would agree that food safety and nutrition are not the same thing. Food safety usually refers to issues of contamination by an agent which leads to injurious consequences to health, or to food that is unfit for consumption. Similarly to sex-related health risks, the voluntary aspect seems to be lacking for food safety risks in the sense that, arguably, no one willingly consumes food infected with, say, salmonella or the *E. coli* bacteria.[42] From a legal perspective, food safety and food quality issues should also be distinguished.[43] Under EU law, a food is deemed unsafe within the meaning of Regulation 178/2002 (the 'General Food Law Regulation' or 'GFL Regulation') 'if it is considered to be *injurious to health* [or] *unfit for human consumption*'.[44] Unfit for human

40 Regulation (EC) No 178/2002 of the European Parliament and of the Council of 28 January 2002 laying down the general principles and requirements of food law, establishing the European Food Safety Authority and laying down procedures in matters of food safety, OJ L31/1 (General Food Law Regulation). More generally, see Schebesta and Purnhagen, *EU Food Law*.

41 MacMaoláin, *EU Food Law* 224; Garde, *EU Law and Obesity Prevention* 23; Wieke Willemijn Huizing Edinger, 'Food Health Law: A Legal Perspective on EU Competence to Regulate the "Healthiness" of Food' (2014) 9 European Food and Feed Law Review 11–12; Iris Goldner Lang, 'Public Health in European Union Food Law' in Tamara K Hervey, Calum Alasdair Young and Louise E Bishop (eds), *Research Handbook on EU Health Law and Policy* (Edward Elgar Publishing 2017) 405.

42 See Rehm, Lachenmeier and Room, 'Why Does Society Accept a Higher Risk for Alcohol than for Other Voluntary or Involuntary Risks?' 190.

43 A similar question arises regarding product safety more generally. Would cigarette qualify as a 'safe product' within the meaning of the EU General Product Safety Directive? See Directive 2001/95/EC of the European Parliament and of the Council of 3 December 2001 on general product safety, OJ L11/4, art 2(b). This question remains theoretical since the directive does not apply to tobacco and related products, because these are already subject to specific safety requirements under specific legislative instruments: see ibid art 1(2).

44 General Food Law Regulation, art 14(2), emphasis added. The alternative rather than cumulative character of these two conditions was confirmed in Case C-636/11 *Berger*, EU:C:2013:227, paras 36–37. See also Commission Standing Committee on the Food Chain and Animal Health, 'Guidance on the Implementation of Articles 11, 12, 14, 17, 18, 19 and 20 of Regulation (EC) 178/2002 on General Food Law' (2010) 8, <https://ec.europa

consumption refers to instances where there is something 'wrong' with a foodstuff,[45] 'for reasons of contamination, whether by extraneous matter or otherwise, or through putrefaction, deterioration or decay'.[46] A foodstuff of poor nutritional quality is not, for this reason alone, unfit for human consumption. It could, however, be considered as injurious to health within the meaning of that Regulation and hence be deemed unsafe.[47] Yet, the health risks that are considered under the GFL Regulation are those arising from exposure to a hazard, defined as 'a biological, chemical or physical agent in, or condition of, food or feed with the potential to cause an adverse health effect',[48] leaving aside the nutritional composition of food.[49] Hence, foodstuffs that are unhealthy due to their nutritional composition do not qualify as 'unsafe' under EU law. This finding is corroborated by the fact that, under the GFL Regulation, unsafe food must not be placed on the market, or must be withdrawn from the market if it is found to be unsafe,[50] a requirement which has obviously not been applied to fatty and salty food or alcoholic beverages. Similarly, under WTO law, a distinction can be drawn between measures coming under the Agreement on the Application of Sanitary and Phytosanitary Measures (SPS Agreement), 'measures regarding the spread of pests and diseases, food safety and "additives, contaminants [and] toxins" that are in some way unnatural or out of place (such as food colouring)', and 'measures relating to the provision of information about normal food nutrients that are not typically considered additives, contaminants or toxins, even if over-consumption may be detrimental for one's health'.[51] The difference between food safety and food quality is nonetheless not always clear-cut.[52] Could the 'hidden' sugars or the trans-fats added in processed food, insofar as they

.eu/food/system/files/2016-12/gfl_req_implementation-guidance_en.pdf> accessed 12 September 2025; Wieke Willemijn Huizing Edinger, 'Food, Safety and the Behavioural Factor of Risk' (2014) 5 European Journal of Risk Regulation 491, 497.

45 Edinger, 'Food, Safety and the Behavioural Factor of Risk' 498.

46 General Food Law Regulation, art 14(5). See also Garde, *EU Law and Obesity Prevention* 24.

47 See General Food Law Regulation, art 14(3).

48 ibid, art 3(14); see also art 3(9).

49 Edinger, 'Food, Safety and the Behavioural Factor of Risk' 500; Goldner Lang,'Public Health in European Union Food Law' 405.

50 General Food Law Regulation, arts 14(1) and 19.

51 Jessica C Lai and Shmuel I Becher, 'Front-of-Pack Labelling and International Trade Law: Revisiting the Health Star Rating System' (2020) 21 Melbourne Journal of International Law 24.

52 Garde, *EU Law and Obesity Prevention* 24–25; Edinger, 'Food, Safety and the Behavioural Factor of Risk'.

are not naturally present in our foods and are often consumed unbeknownst to consumers, be considered as hazardous agents within the meaning of the GLF Regulation? It is true, after all, that 'few gain enjoyment from consuming trans-fats in and of themselves; they just happen to be placed in some of the foods we eat'.[53] A similar interrogation arises with fortified foods, products reinforced with certain vitamins and minerals that are otherwise naturally present in food and also involve health risks. Furthermore, the safety and the quality of food can go hand in hand, as illustrated by the growing role played by the European Food Safety Authority in EU nutrition policy.[54] Hence, although food safety remains conceptually different from food quality and is therefore excluded from the ambit of this work, the EU food safety legal framework will nonetheless be used where pertinent.

2.3 Tobacco: Between Endgame and Harm Reduction

Tobacco is the common name used for a range of products prepared from the dried leaves of the tobacco plant. Originating from the Americas, tobacco grew in popularity in the nineteenth century and spread to the world through the industrial manufacturing of cigarettes. The tobacco plant contains nicotine, a highly addictive stimulant considered to be the major substance responsible for tobacco dependence.[55] While nicotine is harmful, it is not responsible for most of the diseases due to tobacco use, which are caused by the inhalation of smoke arising from the combustion of tobacco.[56] The smoke from cigarettes contains over 4,000 chemicals and at least seventy known carcinogens.[57] In 2011, it was estimated that, at current consumption patterns, one billion people would die from

53 Adam Oliver, 'Nudging, Shoving, and Budging: Behavioural Economic-Informed Policy' (2015) 93 Public Administration 700, 710. See also Edinger, 'Food, Safety and the Behavioural Factor of Risk' 492.

54 Marine Friant-Perrot and Amandine Garde, 'From BSE to Obesity: EFSA's Growing Role in the EU's Nutrition Policy' in Alberto Alemanno and Simone Gabbi (eds), *Foundations of EU Food Law and Policy: Ten Years of the European Food Safety Authority* (Ashgate 2013).

55 Jacques Le Houezec, Ann Mcneill and John Britton, 'Tobacco, Nicotine and Harm Reduction' (2011) 30 Drug and Alcohol Review 119.

56 ibid.

57 Shannon Gravely and others, 'European Adult Smokers' Perceptions of the Harmfulness of E-cigarettes Relative to Combustible Cigarettes: Cohort Findings from the 2016 and 2018 EUREST-PLUS ITC Europe Surveys' (2020) 30 European Journal of Public Health iii38.

smoking in the twenty-first century.[58] Tobacco consumption remains the leading cause of preventable mortality in the EU, resulting in approximately 500,000 deaths yearly.[59] These are mainly attributable to three types of NCDs: cancers, cardiovascular diseases and chronic respiratory diseases.[60] It should be stressed, regarding smoking, that *no safe level* of exposure exists. 'Light' or 'intermittent' smoking, regardless of how these terms are defined, poses significant health risks.[61]

Tobacco is not limited to cigarettes, it also includes a range of other products containing nicotine, including electronic cigarettes, smokeless tobacco products (STPs) – these are tobacco products that do not involve any inhalation – and heated tobacco products (HTPs). HTPs are a form of tobacco that is heated in a device at a high enough temperature to release an aerosol, without however burning it or producing smoke. Electronic cigarettes or e-cigarettes are electronic devices used to inhale an aerosol, or vapour – hence the use of the term 'vaping' – created from heating up a liquid that usually contains nicotine and different flavours. While not being made of tobacco, e-cigarettes are assimilated to a tobacco product due to the resemblance with traditional cigarettes and the presence of nicotine. Cigarettes are by far the most commonly used form of tobacco product in the European Union. The consumption of other tobacco products is marginal or confined to dual use.[62] In 2022, an average of 18.4 per cent of adults smoked daily across the EU, with significant variations between countries, from 25 per cent or more in Bulgaria, Greece, Hungary and France to below 12 per cent in Denmark, Finland and Sweden.[63]

In over half a century, tobacco has moved from an ubiquitous, fashionable practice to a habit viewed as filthy by many. In high-income

58 Prabhat Jha, 'Avoidable Deaths from Smoking: A Global Perspective' (2011) 33 Public Health Reviews 569–570.

59 OECD/European Commission, 'Health at a Glance: Europe 2024: State of Health in the EU Cycle' 118.

60 ibid.

61 K Bjartveit and A Tverdal, 'Health Consequences of Smoking 1–4 Cigarettes per Day' (2005) 14 Tobacco Control 315; Rebecca E Schane, Pamela M Ling and Stanton A Glantz, 'Health Effects of Light and Intermittent Smoking: A Review' (2010) 121 Circulation 1518.

62 European Commission, 'Attitudes of Europeans towards tobacco and electronic cigarettes' (2021) Special Eurobarometer 506, <https://europa.eu/eurobarometer/surveys/detail/2240> accessed 12 September 2025.

63 OECD/European Commission, 'Health at a Glance: Europe 2024: State of Health in the EU Cycle' 118.

countries, curbing tobacco consumption has become a top public health priority, with the adoption of ever tighter regulation on tobacco packaging and labelling, smoke-free environments and higher taxes. The policy debate has further shifted in recent years, with a growing part of the public health community calling for the adoption of an 'endgame' strategy. The term 'endgame' suggests moving beyond tobacco control, which assumes the continued presence of tobacco as a widely available consumer product, towards a future where tobacco products would be phased out and their use and availability significantly restricted.[64] Proponents of the endgame solution, however, advocate measures that go far beyond those currently in place in the EU and across the world: decreasing or removing nicotine from cigarettes, setting up licences for smokers, selling cigarettes as prescription drugs in pharmacies, restrict sales by year of birth, etc.[65]

A heated debate exists in the scientific community regarding the role that alternatives to tobacco should play in the context of an endgame strategy, more specifically about the 'harm reduction' potential of these alternatives, a term that refers 'to strategies designed to reduce the health risks associated with tobacco smoking but which may involve the continued use of nicotine'.[66] The starting point, overall uncontested, is that the harm resulting from smoking cigarettes outweighs the harm resulting from other tobacco products.[67] As previously explained, it is the smoke emitted during the combustion of cigarettes, cigarillos or cigars which is highly toxic, rather than the nicotine.[68] The supporters of harm reduction point at the difficulty that smokers have to quit to favour an approach based on the transition from cigarettes to other lower-risk products, such as e-cigarettes, tobacco for oral use or, less

64 Patricia A McDaniel, Elizabeth A Smith and Ruth E Malone, 'The Tobacco Endgame: A Qualitative Review and Synthesis' (2016) 25 Tobacco Control 594; Ruth E Malone, 'The Race to a Tobacco Endgame' (2016) 25 Tobacco Control 607.

65 For more strategies and measures, see Yvette van der Eijk, 'Development of an Integrated Tobacco Endgame Strategy' (2015) 24 Tobacco Control 336; Patricia A McDaniel, Elizabeth A Smith and Ruth E Malone, 'The Tobacco Endgame: A Qualitative Review and Synthesis' (2016) 25 Tobacco Control 594.

66 Sharon Cox and Lynne Dawkins, 'Global and Local Perspectives on Tobacco Harm Reduction: What Are the Issues and Where Do We Go from Here?' (2018) 15 Harm Reduction Journal 32.

67 David J Nutt and others, 'Estimating the Harms of Nicotine-Containing Products Using the MCDA Approach' (2014) 20 European Addiction Research 218.

68 Cox and Dawkins, 'Global and Local Perspectives on Tobacco Harm Reduction'; Renée O'Leary and Riccardo Polosa, 'Tobacco Harm Reduction in the 21st Century' (2020) 20 Drugs and Alcohol Today 219, 226.

so, HTPs.[69] Following this approach, these alternative products should not be assimilated to cigarettes and should be regulated in a less stringent way, so that they constitute a suitable alternative to smokers while remaining as little attractive as possible to non-users of tobacco. Other actors in the scientific community, while acknowledging that these alternatives may be adapted to some individuals wishing to reduce their risks, oppose recommending their use at a population level. They defend a regulatory model that treats tobacco for oral use, e-cigarettes or HTPs similarly to tobacco products for smoking.[70] They consider that the effectiveness of these alternatives as cessation tools has not been established and that a risk exists that these products act as a gateway towards cigarette consumption, as well as contribute to the renormalisation of smoking.[71]

STPs are an interesting case in this regard. Their use is negligible in the EU as a whole, to the notable exception of Sweden, where 16 per cent of the population declare using *snus* daily.[72] Snus is a 'moist oral tobacco product which is placed behind the upper lip, either loose or in portioned sachets, which resemble miniature tea bags'.[73] While the sale of any form of tobacco for oral use is prohibited in the EU since 1992, such sales remain legal in Sweden. As will be discussed further in Section 7.4.2, the EU-wide prohibition of tobacco for oral use is contested by some experts who defend its harm reduction potential. While not devoid of health risks, that of oral cancer especially, consuming snus is substantially less hazardous than smoking and brings health benefits if used as a substitute.[74] The wide consumption of snus in Sweden explains why

[69] ibid.

[70] See Charlotta Pisinger and others, 'ERS and Tobacco Harm Reduction' (2019) 54 European Respiratory Journal 1902009; Mohammed Al-Hamdani and Eden Manly, 'Harm Reduction in Tobacco Control: Where Do We Draw the Line?' (2022) 43 Journal of Public Health Policy 149.

[71] ibid. See also Kristin Voigt, 'Smoking Norms and the Regulation of E-Cigarettes' (2015) 105 American Journal of Public Health 1967.

[72] European Commission, 'Attitudes of Europeans towards tobacco and electronic cigarettes' 48.

[73] Elizabeth Clarke and others, 'Snus: A Compelling Harm Reduction Alternative to Cigarettes' (2019) 16 Harm Reduction Journal 62, 1.

[74] ibid; Konstantinos Farsalinos, 'Snus: Swedish Snus Is Different' (2019) 226 British Dental Journal 85; LM Ramström, 'Much Safer with Snus' (2019) 226 British Dental Journal 85; Ellen Meier and others, 'A Randomized Clinical Trial of Snus Examining the Effect of Complete Versus Partial Cigarette Substitution on Smoking-Related Behaviors, and Biomarkers of Exposure' (2020) 22 Nicotine & Tobacco Research 473.

tobacco-related mortality is much lower in Sweden than in the rest of the EU.[75]

E-cigarettes, because they resemble traditional cigarettes, are often considered as offering the most potential for harm reduction purposes. Although the debate is rife within the scientific community – the WHO does not acknowledge, for instance, that e-cigarettes pose a smaller risk to health than conventional cigarettes –[76] ample evidence seems to show that users of e-cigarettes are only exposed to a small fraction of the risks posed by conventional cigarettes.[77] Apart from the risks arising from contact with the liquid contained in e-cigarettes, most of the harmful effects from e-cigarettes come from the chemicals present in the aerosol that is released when vaping, with acute and local effects on the respiratory systems.[78] The question of passive vaping is debated, with weak to moderate evidence establishing the existence of a risk for bystanders,[79] although that risk is significantly lower than that resulting from exposure to second-hand tobacco smoke. Uncertainty remains as to the role played by e-cigarettes in smoking initiation or cessation, that is, whether these products help smokers to quit and hence reduce their exposure to risk, or whether, on the contrary, e-cigarettes act as a gateway towards smoking, especially for young people.[80] As to their use for cessation purposes, e-cigarettes do offer

[75] Lars Ramström and Tom Wikmans, 'Mortality Attributable to Tobacco among Men in Sweden and Other European Countries: An Analysis of Data in a WHO Report' (2014) 12 Tobacco Induced Diseases 14; Lars Ramström, Ron Borland and Tom Wikmans, 'Patterns of Smoking and Snus Use in Sweden: Implications for Public Health' (2016) 13 International Journal of Environmental Research and Public Health 1110; Lars M Ramstrom, 'If There Had Been No Snus in Sweden: The Impact of Snus on Mortality Attributable to Smoking' (2024) 21 Harm Reduction Journal 176.

[76] WHO, 'Tobacco: E-cigarettes' (2020), <www.who.int/news-room/questions-and-answers/item/tobacco-e-cigarettes> accessed 12 September 2025.

[77] Ann McNeill and others, 'Evidence review of e-cigarettes and heated tobacco products 2018: A report commissioned by Public Health England' (2018) Public Health England 20, <www.gov.uk/government/publications/e-cigarettes-and-heated-tobacco-products-evidence-review> accessed 12 September 2025; Scientific Committee on Health, Environmental and Emerging Risks (SCHEER), 'Opinion on electronic cigarettes' (2021) 7, <https://ec.europa.eu/health/document/download/50b3adac-5451-47c1–8427-ea67e874c970_en> accessed 12 February 2025.

[78] SCHEER, 'Opinion on electronic cigarettes' (n 123) 7.

[79] McNeill and others, 'Evidence review of e-cigarettes and heated tobacco products 2018: A report commissioned by Public Health England' 19.

[80] Regarding the gateway hypothesis, see Simon Chapman, David Bareham and Wasim Maziak, 'The Gateway Effect of E-Cigarettes: Reflections on Main Criticisms' (2018) 21 Nicotine & Tobacco Research 695; Peter N Lee, Katharine J Coombs and Esther

an interesting potential since they release nicotine and involve a gesture very similar to that of smoking.[81] Although they are increasingly popular as a cessation tool among smokers in the EU,[82] their effectiveness remains unclear. They may help to reduce smoking but not to quit altogether, leading to dual use and hence potentially increased harm.[83] The use of e-cigarettes is more common than that of STPs but remains nonetheless limited. In the EU and the United Kingdom, more than eight in ten (85 per cent) respondents of the 2021 Eurobarometer had never used e-cigarettes and only a small proportion (2 per cent) declared to currently use them.[84]

As regards HTPs, still relatively new products, evidence remains scant as to the health risks associated with their consumption and the relationship between HTPs consumption and that of cigarettes. It seems that such products expose users and bystanders to fewer risks than conventional cigarettes and to probably more risks than e-cigarettes.[85] They are currently a niche market in the EU, with more than nine in ten respondents (93 per cent) from the 2021 Eurobarometer declaring that they have never used these products and only 1 per cent declaring to currently use them.[86]

F Afolalu, 'Considerations Related to Vaping as a Possible Gateway into Cigarette Smoking: An Analytical Review' (2019) 7 F1000Research 1915.

81 Caitlin Notley and others, 'The Unique Contribution of E-Cigarettes for Tobacco Harm Reduction in Supporting Smoking Relapse Prevention' (2018) 15 Harm Reduction Journal 31.

82 Filippos T Filippidis and others, 'Changes in Smoking Cessation Assistance in the European Union between 2012 and 2017: Pharmacotherapy versus Counselling versus e-Cigarettes' (2019) 28 Tobacco Control 95.

83 Sara Kalkhoran and Stanton A Glantz, 'E-Cigarettes and Smoking Cessation in Real-World and Clinical Settings: A Systematic Review and Meta-Analysis' (2016) 4 The Lancet: Respiratory Medicine 116; McNeill and others, 'Evidence review of e-cigarettes and heated tobacco products 2018' 16; Peter Hajek and others, 'A Randomized Trial of E-Cigarettes versus Nicotine-Replacement Therapy' (2019) 380 New England Journal of Medicine 629.

84 European Commission, 'Attitudes of Europeans towards tobacco and electronic cigarettes' 63.

85 Małgorzata Znyk, Joanna Jurewicz and Dorota Kaleta, 'Exposure to Heated Tobacco Products and Adverse Health Effects, a Systematic Review' (2021) 18 International Journal of Environmental Research and Public Health 6651. See also European Commission, 'Support study to the report on the application of Directive 2014/40/EU' (2021) 392–394, <https://op.europa.eu/en/publication-detail/-/publication/9ce15083-b931–11eb-8aca-01aa75ed71a1> accessed 12 September 2025.

86 European Commission, 'Attitudes of Europeans towards tobacco and electronic cigarettes' 64.

2.4 Alcohol: The Fallacies of Responsible Drinking

Alcohol is the term commonly used to refer to ethanol, an organic compound naturally produced by the fermentation process of sugars, present in drinks such as beer, wine and distilled spirits. Ethanol is a psychoactive substance with a variety of short-term and long-term adverse effects. Alcohol is a leading factor of mortality and morbidity globally, responsible for 255,000 to 290,000 deaths per year across EU countries.[87] Its impact on health is complex but well-established. Alcohol is linked to sixty acute and chronic diseases,[88] NCDs in particular, such as cancer, diabetes, neuropsychiatric diseases (including alcohol use disorders), cardiovascular diseases and liver and pancreas diseases.[89] Alcohol consumption affects health in various ways, through cumulative consumption affecting organs and tissues and by acute intoxication.[90] The harm incurred depends on one's volume of consumption and frequency of drinking. A moderate but frequent consumption of alcohol may result in the development of NCDs, while heavy episodic drinking, defined as the consumption of sixty or more grams of pure alcohol on at least one single occasion at least once a month,[91] might also result in poisoning, injuries and violence. Alcohol is not only detrimental to the one that consumes it but also to third parties: to the foetus, in case of prenatal alcohol exposure, or to bystanders, victims of intentional or unintentional injuries and homicides. The link between alcohol and violence clearly sets that lifestyle risk factor apart from tobacco and nutritional risks.

As for tobacco, and contrary to a widely held opinion, no level of alcohol consumption can be considered risk-free. The prevailing view in the scientific community is that the safest level of drinking is none.[92] Another belief that has existed in the general population is that health

[87] OECD/European Commission, 'Health at a Glance: Europe 2024: State of Health in the EU Cycle' 15.

[88] Max G Griswold and others, 'Alcohol Use and Burden for 195 Countries and Territories, 1990–2016: A Systematic Analysis for the Global Burden of Disease Study 2016' (2018) 392 The Lancet 1015.

[89] Jürgen Rehm, 'The Risks Associated with Alcohol Use and Alcoholism' (2011) 34 Alcohol Research & Health 135.

[90] Griswold and others, 'Alcohol Use and Burden for 195 Countries and Territories, 1990–2016' 1015.

[91] WHO, 'Global Status Report on Alcohol and Health 2018' (2018) 47, <www.who.int/publications/i/item/9789241565639> accessed 12 September 2025.

[92] Griswold and others, 'Alcohol Use and Burden for 195 Countries and Territories, 1990–2016'.

benefits could arise from moderate alcohol use,[93] the so-called French paradox,[94] an expression coined after some studies had found a protective effect of a moderate consumption of alcohol, wine especially, on cardiovascular diseases. The most recent evidence has fully discredited this idea, not only because the protective effect of wine has been found to be non-existent or non-significative, but because any such effect would in any case be offset by the overall risk of harm associated with alcohol.[95] Scientific experts consider that the hypothesis of health benefits from moderate drinking should no longer play a role at the policy level.[96]

Because complete abstinence is unattractive to most people, public health authorities have devised 'low-risk' drinking guidelines. These are based on 'units of alcohol' or 'standard drinks', a single unit of measurement that takes into account the strength and volume of a beverage and allows for comparisons across alcohol products.[97] A unit of alcohol contains a fixed amount of alcohol, set in most countries at 8, 10 or 12 g.[98] For instance, if taking the 8 g unit used in the United Kingdom, there is twice as much alcohol in a pint of regular strength beer (50 cl, 5.2 per cent vol, 3 units) than there is in a small glass of wine (12.5 cl, 12 per cent vol, 1.5 units).[99] The guidelines for low-risk alcohol consumption are usually expressed as a maximum of unit consumed per day and per week. These guidelines vary significantly across the EU but tend for the most part to be set at an excessive level. While it is estimated that the threshold for the lowest risk of all-cause mortality is situated at

[93] Tanya Chikritzhs and others, 'Has the Leaning Tower of Presumed Health Benefits from "moderate" Alcohol Use Finally Collapsed?' (2015) 110 Addiction 726.

[94] Jules Constant, 'Alcohol, Ischemic Heart Disease, and the French Paradox' (1997) 20 Clinical Cardiology 420; Serge Renaud and René Gueguen, 'The French Paradox and Wine Drinking' (1998) 216 Novartis Foundation Symposia 208.

[95] Griswold and others, 'Alcohol Use and Burden for 195 Countries and Territories, 1990–2016'; World Heart Federation, 'The Impact of Alcohol Consumption on Cardiovascular Health: Myths and Measures' (2022), <https://world-heart-federation.org/wp-content/uploads/WHF-Policy-Brief-Alcohol.pdf> accessed 12 September 2025.

[96] Chikritzhs, 'Has the Leaning Tower of Presumed Health Benefits from "moderate" Alcohol Use Finally Collapsed?'.

[97] Ashley Wettlaufer, 'Can a Label Help Me Drink in Moderation? A Review of the Evidence on Standard Drink Labelling' (2018) 53 Substance Use & Misuse 585.

[98] Agnieszka Kalinowski and Keith Humphreys, 'Governmental Standard Drink Definitions and Low-Risk Alcohol Consumption Guidelines in 37 Countries' (2016) 111 Addiction 1293.

[99] See NHS, 'Alcohol units', <www.nhs.uk/live-well/alcohol-support/calculating-alcohol-units/> accessed 12 September 2025.

about 100 g of alcohol per week[100] – equivalent to ten regular glasses (25 cl) of light beer (5% vol) – many guidelines advise to limit consumption for men to a level that is twice as high (200 g).[101] The promotion of 'responsible' drinking, a term left purportedly vague by those using it, is the approach championed by the industry, whose usual response to alcohol control measures has been to frame the issue as concerning a minority of heavy alcohol users, shifting the focus away from the majority of drinkers.[102] As it happens, the alcohol industry is heavily reliant on episodes of intense drinking for its sales. A policy that would effectively eliminate heavy drinking while leaving moderate patterns of consumption untouched would be detrimental to these companies.[103]

While alcoholic beverages bear much resemblance to food – both are agricultural products, they contain calories and similar nutrients, they are often consumed simultaneously, etc. – they are, in terms of harm, more comparable to tobacco products. Alcoholic beverages make no positive contribution to health and should, from that perspective, be entirely avoided. The picture is quite different for food, which may bring benefits to health and is overall indispensable to human life. The positive image of alcoholic beverages, which are central to many food and drink cultures, yields a direct influence on the perception of these products as less risky than they really are. Alcohol, in spite of its harmfulness, is generally more lightly regulated than comparable risk factors such as tobacco or cannabis.[104] As we shall see, this is also true of the EU.

2.5 (Un)healthy Diets: A Complex Reality

Unhealthy diets have been singled out as the largest cause of health loss globally, posing a greater risk of morbidity and mortality than unsafe

[100] Angela M Wood and others, 'Risk Thresholds for Alcohol Consumption: Combined Analysis of Individual-Participant Data for 599 912 Current Drinkers in 83 Prospective Studies' (2018) 391 The Lancet 1513.

[101] Kalinowski and Humphreys, 'Governmental Standard Drink Definitions and Low-Risk Alcohol Consumption Guidelines in 37 Countries'.

[102] Pham Viet Cuong and others, 'Cross-country Comparison of Proportion of Alcohol Consumed in Harmful Drinking Occasions Using the International Alcohol Control Study' (2018) 37 Drug and Alcohol Review 45–46.

[103] ibid.

[104] Rehm, Lachenmeier and Room, 'Why Does Society Accept a Higher Risk for Alcohol than for Other Voluntary or Involuntary Risks?'. See also Robin Room, 'Global Intergovernmental Initiatives to Minimise Alcohol Problems: Some Good Intentions, but Little Action' (2021) 12 European Journal of Risk Regulation 419.

sex, alcohol, drug and tobacco use combined.[105] Defining what constitutes an (un)healthy diet is a difficult endeavour. The link between nutrition and health is not only extremely complex – countless nutrients and compounds are involved, whose effects are not all yet well-known – but people also have different dietary needs according to their age, sex, physical activity or health status.[106] Unlike for alcohol and tobacco products, where abstinence is the healthiest choice, some nutrients associated with health risks when consumed in excess, such as salt or fat, are actually necessary to healthy bodily functions. Regulatory approaches must therefore be more nuanced with foods than they are with tobacco and alcohol.

The use of the term 'unhealthy diets', rather than 'unhealthy foods', reflects that complexity: that is, the fact that a given food may contain both 'positive' and 'negative' nutrients and that healthiness is best assessed in the context of a person's overall diet. To improve nutritional knowledge in the population about healthy diets, the most common approach has been to develop and disseminate food-based dietary guidelines, which recommend the consumption of certain foods and, conversely, advise to limit the consumption of others.[107] The latter may be referred to as 'unhealthy' foods, with all the necessary precaution. The consumption of processed, high-calorie foods rich in fat, salt and sugar (HFSS foods) and the disbalance in energy/calorie intake are among the best-established dietary risk factors.[108] They have been to date a central focus of nutrition policy,[109] with the use of a mix of tools – labels, taxes,

[105] Walter Willett and others, 'Food in the Anthropocene: The EAT–Lancet Commission on Healthy Diets from Sustainable Food Systems' (2019) 393 The Lancet 447; Ashkan Afshin and others, 'Health Effects of Dietary Risks in 195 Countries, 1990–2017: A Systematic Analysis for the Global Burden of Disease Study 2017' (2019) 393 The Lancet 1958, 1967; Boyd A Swinburn and others, 'The Global Syndemic of Obesity, Undernutrition, and Climate Change: The Lancet Commission Report' (2019) 393 The Lancet 791, 795.

[106] Willet and others, 'Food in the Anthropocene' 453.

[107] Chantal Julia and others, 'Are Foods "healthy" or "Healthier"? Front-of-Pack Labelling and the Concept of Healthiness Applied to Foods' (2022) 127 The British Journal of Nutrition 948.

[108] Anna Herforth and others, 'A Global Review of Food-Based Dietary Guidelines' (2019) 10 Advances in Nutrition 590; WHO, 'Healthy Diet' (2020), <www.who.int/news-room/fact-sheets/detail/healthy-diet> accessed 12 September 2025.

[109] Regarding the EU, see European Commission, White Paper: 'A Strategy for Europe on Nutrition, Overweight and Obesity Related Health Issues' (EU Nutrition Strategy) COM (2007) 279 final. See also Council of the European Union, Council conclusions on obesity, nutrition and physical activity (2005) 9803/5; Council of the European Union, Council conclusions on nutrition and physical activity (2014) OJ C213/1; Council of the

advertising rules – to discourage their consumption. Evidence is mounting on the association between red and processed meat and certain types of cancer.[110] On the other hand, nutrition policy should not only focus on discouraging the consumption of unhealthy foods, but encourage the consumption of the healthy sort, such as fruits, vegetables, legumes, whole grains and nuts. This is sometimes overlooked, even though increasing such consumption might have a greater positive effect on health than reducing sugar and fat.[111]

While salt excess is primarily targeted for its association with cardiovascular risks, over-consumption of sugar and fat is closely associated with excessive calorie intake and weight gain. The global rise in overweight and obesity, the so-called obesity epidemic,[112] is one of today's main public health challenges. Obesity and overweight are major risk factors for NCDs such as cardiovascular diseases – heart disease and stroke – diabetes and cancer.[113] Whether obesity should be considered as a disease in itself or simply a risk factor for other diseases is debated.[114] Based on self-reported data, in 2022, over half of the EU population was either overweight or obese, a sharp increase over the last twenty years, but a rate that has stabilised and even slightly decreased since 2017.[115] In 2021, an estimated 420,000 deaths in the EU were associated with an excessive body mass index (BMI), highlighting the large impact of overweight and obesity on population

European Union, Council conclusions - Healthy Nutrition for Children: The Healthy Future of Europe (2018) OJ C23/1.

110 Luis D Boada, LA Henríquez-Hernández and OP Luzardo, 'The Impact of Red and Processed Meat Consumption on Cancer and Other Health Outcomes: Epidemiological Evidences' (2016) 92 Food and Chemical Toxicology 236; Maryam S Farvid and others, 'Consumption of Red Meat and Processed Meat and Cancer Incidence: A Systematic Review and Meta-Analysis of Prospective Studies' (2021) 36 European Journal of Epidemiology 937.

111 Afshin and others, 'Health Effects of Dietary Risks in 195 Countries, 1990–2017: A Systematic Analysis for the Global Burden of Disease Study 2017' 1967.

112 WHO, 'Controlling the global obesity epidemic', <www.who.int/activities/controlling-the-global-obesity-epidemic> accessed 12 September 2025. See also Schorb, 'Fat Politics in Europe: Theorizing on the Premises and Outcomes of European Anti-"Obesity-Epidemic" Policies' 6.

113 WHO, 'Obesity and overweight' (2021), <www.who.int/news-room/fact-sheets/detail/obesity-and-overweight> accessed 12 September 2025.

114 See Howard Rosen, 'Is Obesity A Disease or A Behavior Abnormality? Did the AMA Get It Right?' (2014) 111 Missouri Medicine 104; John PH Wilding, Vicki Mooney and Richard Pile, 'Should Obesity Be Recognised as a Disease?' (2019) 366 BMJ l4258.

115 OECD/European Commission, 'Health at a Glance: Europe 2024: State of Health in the EU Cycle' 136.

health.[116] Simply put, obesity can be defined as an excess of body fat.[117] Qualifying an individual as obese is usually done by relying on a specific metric, the BMI, which is calculated by dividing a person's weight in kilograms by the square of that person's height in metres (kg/m^2).[118] A BMI situated between 18.5 and 24.9 is considered to reflect a normal weight and one between 25 and 29.9 to signal overweight. Above 30, one is considered obese. The BMI is however a contested tool. Many consider that it is a poor proxy for body fat mass and criticise the fact that it does not account for how fat is distributed in the body, which greatly matters as far as health risks are concerned.[119] Some consider, however, that evidence for the health risks associated with being overweight, with a BMI below 30, is unclear and that it is not proven that 'pre-obesity' on its own leads to higher morbidity and mortality.[120] Furthermore, the causes of obesity are complex.[121] At the individual level, obesity and overweight are primarily caused by an energy imbalance, thus directly linked to poor dietary habits and physical inactivity, but are also largely influenced by genetic factors.[122] The global rise in obesity can only be explained by structural population-level factors, which pertain to changes in, among other things, food supply, eating, life habits and working environments.

2.6 Conclusion

Under the definition adopted in this chapter and throughout the book, unhealthy lifestyles are consumption behaviours chosen by individuals

[116] ibid. [117] Frank Q Nuttall, 'Body Mass Index' (2015) 50 Nutrition Today 117–118.

[118] WHO, 'A healthy lifestyle - WHO recommendations' (2010), <www.euro.who.int/en/health-topics/disease-prevention/nutrition/a-healthy-lifestyle/body-mass-index-bmi> accessed 12 September 2025.

[119] Julie Guthman, 'Fatuous Measures: The Artifactual Construction of the Obesity Epidemic' (2013) 23 Critical Public Health 263; Lee F Monaghan, Rachel Colls and Bethan Evans, 'Obesity Discourse and Fat Politics: Research, Critique and Interventions' (2013) 23 Critical Public Health 249; Nuttall, 'Body Mass Index' 120–121.

[120] Katherine M Flegal and others, 'Association of All-Cause Mortality With Overweight and Obesity Using Standard Body Mass Index Categories: A Systematic Review and Meta-Analysis' (2013) 309 Journal of the American Medical Association 71; Guthman, 'Fatuous Measures: The Artifactual Construction of the Obesity Epidemic' 268; Nuttall, 'Body Mass Index' 123–124.

[121] See Christopher JL Murray and others, 'Global Burden of 87 Risk Factors in 204 Countries and Territories, 1990–2019: A Systematic Analysis for the Global Burden of Disease Study 2019' (2020) 396 The Lancet 1223.

[122] ibid.

within the constraints of their social position, reflecting belonging to certain social groups, and exposing individuals to specific health risks. Both the voluntary nature of these behaviours and their collective dimension are significant. Lifestyle-related risks raise particular questions compared with other publicly regulated risks, largely because of the strong behavioural component of risk-control measures and their ethical implications.

Tobacco, alcohol and unhealthy diets are the leading causes of avoidable mortality and morbidity in the EU, exposing individuals to a range of health risks, most notably NCDs such as diabetes, cardiovascular diseases and cancer. Public policy approaches to these risks have differed, reflecting variations in both the degree of risk and its perception among the population. In the case of tobacco, there is broad consensus on the need to eliminate products for smoking, such as cigarettes, though debate continues over the best means to achieve this and the role of alternative products such as e-cigarettes. With alcohol, despite established scientific consensus that no level of consumption is entirely safe, abstinence is generally not considered a realistic or desirable policy goal. Nutrition presents a further complexity, as very few nutrients are inherently unhealthy, with risk depending on dosage and individual characteristics.

Against this backdrop, the next chapter examines the mandate conferred upon the EU to regulate lifestyles and the powers assigned to it in this domain. It introduces the reader to the two principal objectives of EU regulation of lifestyle risks: protecting public health and ensuring the establishment and functioning of an internal market in which goods, persons and services circulate freely. The interaction between these two objectives provides the central thread running throughout this book.

3 EU Competence to Regulate Unhealthy Lifestyles

3.1 Introduction

The European Union is best understood as a federation which, as it is common for such systems, acts within the limits of a delineated mandate.[1] Federalism operates from the assumption that action at the local level is preferable, for reasons of effectiveness or legitimacy, and is transferred upwards only where necessary to achieve a certain objective.[2] Member States have granted competences to the EU to pursue objectives they have in common, which they consider can be best achieved at the EU rather than the national or sub-national levels.[3] Under the principle of conferral, the EU shall act only within the limits of the competences conferred upon it and competences not conferred upon it remain with the Member States.[4]

This chapter investigates the reasons that might justify the existence of an EU policy on unhealthy lifestyles, and a corresponding body of law. Two main rationales provide a solid basis for EU intervention, to which correspond a different set of competences under the EU Treaties. The first one, historically and conceptually predominant, as will appear

[1] In an abundant literature on federalism and the EU, readers may refer to Robert Schütze, *From Dual to Cooperative Federalism: The Changing Structure of European Law* (Oxford University Press 2009); Signe Rehling Larsen and Signe Rehling Larsen, *The Constitutional Theory of the Federation and the European Union* (Oxford University Press 2021).

[2] Daniel Halberstam, 'Federalism: Theory, Policy, Law' in Michel Rosenfeld and Andras Sajo (eds), *The Oxford Handbook of Comparative Constitutional Law* (Oxford University Press 2012). See also Roger Van den Bergh, 'Farewell Utopia? Why the European Union Should Take the Economics of Federalism Seriously' (2016) 23 Maastricht Journal of European and Comparative Law 937; Michael Faure, 'The Economics of Harmonization of Food Law in the EU' in Harry Bremmers and Kai Purnhagen (eds), *Regulating and Managing Food Safety in the EU* (Springer International Publishing 2018).

[3] Art 1 TEU. [4] Art 5(4) TEU.

throughout the book, relates to the internal market. EU regulation contributes to the establishment of the EU internal market, by addressing the externalities of Member State lifestyle policies and their restrictive effect on free movement, that of goods in particular. The second one concerns health as a stand-alone value. Promoting good health and evening out health inequalities across the EU justifies for Member States to lose part of their autonomy on the matter of lifestyles. Both rationales carry a descriptive and normative value. While allowing to better understand the shape and content of EU action, they also provide a defence of the EU's involvement with healthy lifestyles, and possible future developments.

3.2 Regulating Trade in Unhealthy Products

3.2.1 *Transboundary Effects: The Spillover of Free Movement*

One of the arguments most frequently advanced to justify the exercise of power at the federal/central level rather than at the national/local level is the existence of transboundary effects, externalities resulting from government action or inaction which may render local regulation ineffective.[5] A good example is climate change. The rejection of greenhouse gases in the atmosphere affects the entire planet, even though most of these emissions originate from a limited number of industrialised countries. In this case, action at the national level alone is insufficient and countries may be tempted to free ride on the efforts of others so as to reap the benefits of lower emissions without affecting the functioning of their economies. From this perspective, climate action at the EU level appears thus relatively uncontroversial. Many other contemporary risks are global in nature and require transnational cooperation to be addressed. This is the case, for public health, of *communicable* diseases. As pathogenic agents spread across borders, unilateral action is unlikely to be sufficient to control the diffusion of a disease. Decisions taken in one jurisdiction may have significant consequences in others, especially in an area such as the EU where, in principle, internal borders have been eliminated. The Covid-19 pandemic has shown the necessity to

[5] Faure, 'The Economics of Harmonization of Food Law in the EU' 267–268; Van den Bergh, 'Farewell Utopia? Why the European Union Should Take the Economics of Federalism Seriously' 941.

coordinate non-pharmaceuticals interventions between countries, such as stay-at-home orders, closures of businesses and international travel bans.[6]

The situation is different for *non-communicable* diseases, which cannot be transmitted from one individual to the other and cannot 'travel' across borders. In the case of NCDs, what connects States is trade. Trade in hazardous products disseminates the associated risk. For a State, on the one hand, accepting that an alcoholic beverage or an unhealthy foodstuff is placed on its market means exposing its population to the associated risk and, as regulatory standards may differ, in a potentially more dangerous form. On the other hand, diverging national health standards constitute impediments to cross-border trade, usually in the form of non-tariff barriers. Eliminating these barriers to trade requires supranational action, in a gradual way. As a first step, in the absence of common rules, national rules restricting trade may be scrutinised and set aside if they do not prove to be useful for the protection of human health or if the standards applicable in different jurisdictions are given recognition beyond national borders. This is the role of the free movement provisions contained in TFEU. Forcing States to recognise laxer foreign standards, however, affects the level of public health protection and may lead to a 'race to the bottom'.[7] To enable cross-border trade without undermining the control of the risks associated with unhealthy goods, States may decide, as a second step, to adopt common rules at the supranational level, ensuring a level-playing field for economic operators and retaining a degree of regulatory control. The competence to regulate is thus progressively transferred to the supranational level. These two modes of economic regulation, the elimination of barriers to trade via the disapplication of national rules on the one hand and the harmonisation of national standards on the other, are central to the regulation of unhealthy lifestyles in the EU. They are the focus of this book.

[6] Vincent Delhomme and Tamara Hervey, 'The European Union's Response to the Covid-19 Crisis and (the Legitimacy of) the Union's Legal Order' (2022) 41 Yearbook of European Law 48. On Covid-19 and border closures, see Case C-128/22, *Nordic Info*, EU:C:2023:951 and Vincent N Delhomme, 'The Legality of Covid-19 Travel Restrictions in an "Area without Internal Frontiers": Court of Justice (Grand Chamber) 5 December 2023, Case C-128/22, Nordic Info' (2024) 20 European Constitutional Law Review 307.

[7] Faure, 'The Economics of Harmonization of Food Law in the EU' 270–273; Halberstam, 'Federalism: Theory, Policy, Law' 590–591.

Supranational action may also be necessary to safeguard the free movement of people. People suffering from cancer or diabetes cannot infect others but cross-border movements affect national policies in other ways. Individuals may, for instance, take advantage of open borders to acquire products in countries where less stringent public health measures apply. The incentive is particularly strong if a given product cannot be sold in one's home country but is available abroad, or if there is a significant price difference between two legally accessible products. Lifestyle control measures can thus be circumvented, deterring a country from adopting a stricter health policy or undermining its effectiveness. European border regions are all too familiar with this problem. Shortly after its accession to the EU in 1995, Sweden experienced a drastic increase in cross-border shopping for alcohol, its population taking advantage of the laxer rules and lower prices in place in neighbouring countries. The liberalisation of cross-border movements risked undermining the Swedish effort to limit the consumption of alcoholic beverages.[8] Another example is the Danish fat tax of 2011. It was repealed a bit more than a year after its adoption, among other reasons because of an increase in the cross-border purchases of butter and other high-saturated fat products from Germany to Denmark.[9]

3.2.2 *The EU's Broad Internal Market Competence*

Eliminating barriers to free movement is the core purpose of the EU's internal market, defined in Article 26(2) TFEU as 'an area without internal frontiers in which the free movement of goods, persons, services and capital is ensured'. The EU's competence reflects the two modes of regulation previously mentioned: preventing Member States from adopting unjustified barriers to trade and adopting common regulatory standards at the EU level.

Regarding the first mode, one has to turn to the free movement provisions contained in the TFEU, often referred to as the 'fundamental'

[8] Paulette Kurzer, *Markets and Moral Regulation: Cultural Change in the European Union* (Cambridge University Press 2001) 74, 81. A similar phenomenon took place in Finland, see Case C-394/97 *Heinonen*, EU:C:1999:308, para 18.

[9] Sinne Smed and others, 'The Effects of the Danish Saturated Fat Tax on Food and Nutrient Intake and Modelled Health Outcomes: An Econometric and Comparative Risk Assessment Evaluation' (2016) 70 European Journal of Clinical Nutrition 681, 685; Signild Vallgårda, Lotte Holm and Jorgen D Jensen, 'The Danish Tax on Saturated Fat: Why It Did Not Survive' (2015) 69 European Journal of Clinical Nutrition 223, 225.

freedoms.[10] They are found primarily in Title II and IV of the TFEU, dealing respectively with the free movement of goods and the free movement of persons, services and capital. The provisions on goods are applicable here, as tobacco, alcohol and food constitute goods under EU law.[11] The most relevant provision is Article 34 TFEU, which prohibits quantitative restrictions on imports and all measures having equivalent effect. As will be discussed in Chapter 4 (Section 4.2) and Chapter 6 (Section 6.2.1, the broad scope of Article 34 TFEU, which include 'any measure of the Member States that is capable of hindering, directly or indirectly, actually or potentially, intra-Union trade',[12] allows the capture of a wide range of non-tariff measures, such as import bans,[13] licencing and authorisation requirements,[14] rules on the composition of products,[15] packaging and labelling requirements,[16] advertising restrictions[17] or price measures.[18] These measures are in principle prohibited, unless they are justified under Article 36 TFEU, which mentions health as a protected interest, or by other 'overriding reason[s] in the public interest'.[19]

Article 37 TFEU, a somewhat overlooked provision dealing with the free movement of goods, is also relevant to the regulation of unhealthy lifestyles. The article applies to the operation of State monopolies of a commercial character. According to Article 37(1) TFEU, 'Member States shall adjust any State monopolies of a commercial character so as to ensure that no discrimination regarding the conditions under which

10 Case 240/83, *ADBHU*, EU:C:1985:59, para 9.

11 Under the definition provided by the Court, 'goods' are 'products which can be valued in money and which are capable, as such, of forming the subject of commercial transactions': Case 7/68, *Commission v Italy*, EU:C:1968:51. The same can be said of Article 110 which applies to 'products'.

12 Case C-591/17, *Austria v Germany*, EU:C:2019:504, para 120. See *Dassonville*.

13 Case C-170/04, *Rosengren*, EU:C:2007:313.

14 Case C-198/14, *Visnapuu*, EU:C:2015:751; Case C-434/04, *Ahokainen and Leppik*, EU:C:2006:609; Case C-394/97, *Heinonen*, EU:C:1999:308.

15 Case C-17/93, *Van der Veldt*, EU:C:1994:299; Case C-123/00, *Bellamy and English Shop Wholesale*, EU:C:2001:214; Case 274/87, *Commission v Germany (Meat products)*, EU:C:1989:51.

16 *Cassis de Dijon*, Case 59/82, *Weinvertriebs-GmbH*, EU:C:1983:101.

17 Joined cases C-1/90 and C-176/90, *Aragonesa*, EU:C:1991:327; Case C-405/98, *Gourmet International Products*, EU:C:2001:135.

18 Case 88/77, *Van Tiggele*, EU:C:1978:10 Case 3/77 *INNO v ATAB*, EU:C:1977:185, paras 53-54. See also Joined Cases 177 and 178/82 *Van de Haar*, EU:C:1984:144, paras 20-21. See *Scotch Whisky*.

19 Case C-649/18, *A (Advertising and sale of medicinal products online)*, EU:C:2020:764, para 66.

goods are procured and marketed exists between nationals of Member States'.[20] Generally speaking, Article 37 TFEU applies in circumstances where the State grants exclusive purchase or sales rights to a public undertaking or institution or, by means of delegation, to a private organisation, thus enabling the control of imports or exports.[21] Alcohol and tobacco monopolies were originally in place in most Member States, leading to a number of cases before the Court of Justice, dealing especially with the tax treatment of foreign products,[22] and the rules governing retail sales.[23] As commercial monopolies were progressively abolished throughout the EU, to the notable exception of the Swedish and Finnish retail monopolies on alcohol, that provision has lost in importance.

Article 110 TFEU, which prohibits discriminatory or protectionist internal taxation, while not part of Title II TFEU on the free movement of goods, is also relevant to lifestyle regulation, where tax measures play a key role. According to Article 110 TFEU,

> No Member State shall impose, directly or indirectly, on the products of other Member States any internal taxation of any kind *in excess* of that imposed directly or indirectly on *similar* domestic products.
>
> Furthermore, no Member State shall impose on the products of other Member States any internal taxation of such a nature as to afford *indirect protection* to other products.[24]

As the Court recalled on multiple occasions, 'the aim of Article [110 TFEU] as a whole is to ensure free movement of goods between the Member States in normal conditions of competition by the *elimination of all forms of protection* which result from the application of internal taxation which discriminates against products from other Member States and to guarantee the *complete neutrality* of internal taxation as regards competition between domestic products and imported products'.[25] This

[20] Under Art 37(2), 'Member States shall refrain from introducing any new measure which is contrary to the principles laid down in paragraph 1 or which restricts the scope of the articles dealing with the prohibition of customs duties and quantitative restrictions between Member States'. The Court does not usually differentiate between the two paragraphs and makes a general application of Article 37 TFEU.

[21] European Commission, Commission Notice: Guide on Articles 34-36 of the Treaty on the Functioning of the European Union (TFEU), OJ C100/38, 80.

[22] Case 91/75, *Miritz*, EU:C:1976:23; Case 90/82, *Commission v France*, EU:C:1983:169.

[23] Case C-189/95 *Franzen*, EU:C:1997:504.

[24] Emphasis added.

[25] Case 106/84 *Commission v Denmark*, EU:C:1986:99, para 10, emphasis added.

brought the Court to examine national rules on the taxation of spirits,[26] wine and/or beer,[27] to ensure that these measures were not designed in a way that would benefit domestic production.

Finally, to the extent that Member States rules also regulate the provision of a service linked to a lifestyle product, advertising services for instance, Article 56 TFEU is also applicable. That provision prohibits restrictions on freedom to provide services within the EU, unless, as is the case for Article 34 TFEU, they can be justified.[28] The variety of ways in which advertising rules can restrict the freedom to provide services appears clearly from the judgments in *Commission v France* and *Bacardi France*,[29] where the Court analysed the compatibility of the French Loi Evin, which prohibits all television advertising for alcoholic beverages.

Harmonisation, the adoption of common standards at the EU level, is the second mode of regulation in the internal market. It has also become the main tool used by the EU to regulate unhealthy lifestyles. Article 114 TFEU is here the central provision. It empowers the EU to adopt measures for the approximation of Member States rules 'which have as their object the establishment and functioning of the internal market'.[30] Article 114 TFEU serves to remove barriers to trade that cannot be eliminated by free movement provisions alone, usually because the national rules giving rise to such barriers pursue a legitimate public interest. To take a concrete example, if the market is fragmented by divergent labelling rules for alcohol or tobacco products, adopting a single EU rule on labelling facilitates the free movement of such products while retaining regulatory control over them. The use of Article 114 TFEU is subject to two conditions. First, there needs to be actual divergences between the laws of the Member States which create obstacles to free movement or appreciable distortions of competition[31] or

[26] *Commission v Denmark* (106/84); Case 243/84, *John Walker*, EU:C:1986:100; Joined Cases C-367/93 to C-377/93, *Roders*, EU:C:1995:261.

[27] *Commission v United Kingdom (beer and wine I)*; *Commission v United Kingdom (beer and wine II)*; See also Case 356/85, *Commission v Belgium*, EU:C:1987:353.

[28] See Articles 52 and 62 TFEU. The Court has also recognised the existence of overriding reasons in the public interest in the case of services: see e.g. Case C-463/13, *Stanley International Betting and Stanleybet Malta*, EU:C:2015:25, para 47.

[29] Case C-492/02 *Bacardi France*, EU:C:2004:432; Case C-262/02 *Commission v France*, EU: C:2004:431.

[30] Art 114(1) TFEU.

[31] Case C-58/08 *Vodafone e.a.*, EU:C:2010:321, para 32. More recent cases do not explicitly refer to these two concepts of 'obstacles to free movement' and 'distortions of competition' but tend to refer to those under the common term of 'obstacles to trade':

future divergences likely to give rise to such obstacles or distortions.[32] Second, the adopted measure must remove these obstacles or distortions.[33] The case law offers little guidance as to what constitutes an appreciable distortion of competition. In the *Tobacco Advertising* judgment, the Court considered that a general ban on tobacco advertising adopted at the national level did not constitute such distortion.[34] In some judgments, the Court did identify appreciable distortions. In *Titanium Dioxide*, this was the case of differences in legislation affecting the production costs in the titanium dioxide industry,[35] and, in *Vodafone*, of divergent national laws regarding roaming charges which could significantly affect the production costs of the service provider.[36] The presence of an appreciable distortion of competition, it seems, cannot be established without 'showing that a national rule puts an industry in at least some Member States in a particular disadvantage'.[37] It is a concept 'founded in the presence of inequality'.[38] Determining what constitutes an obstacle to free movement is easier, because there is a symmetry between the concept of 'obstacle' and that of a 'restriction' under free movement provisions, Articles 34 and 56 TFEU for our purpose.[39] This symmetry is justified by the fact that harmonisation seeks to eliminate the barriers that cannot be overcome by negative integration alone.[40] Through the prism of trade restrictions and the internal market,

see *Philip Morris*, paras 58–59; Case C-358/14 *Poland v European Parliament and Council*, EU:C:2016:323, paras 32–33. See also Case C-482/17 *Czech Republic v Parliament and Council*, EU:C:2019:321, Opinion of Advocate General Sharpston, para 44.

32 *Philip Morris*, para 59; *Poland v Parliament and Council*, para 33.

33 *Tobacco Advertising*, paras 84, 95; *Tobacco Advertising II*, para 69. The measure may alternatively remove obstacles or distortions: *Tobacco Advertising II*, para 67.

34 *Tobacco Advertising*, para 113.

35 Case C-300/89, *Commission v Council*, EU:C:1991:244, para 12. See also *Tobacco Advertising*, para 109.

36 *Vodafone*, para 47.

37 Gareth Davies, 'Can Selling Arrangements Be Harmonized?' (2005) 30 European Law Review 373.

38 ibid.

39 See *British American Tobacco*, para 64; *Tobacco Advertising II*, para 57. See also Case C-154/04 *Alliance for Natural Health and Others*, EU:C:2005:199, Opinion of Advocate General Geelhoed, para 35.

40 This 'symmetry thesis' is, for instance, defended by Alexander Somek: Alexander Somek, *Individualism: An Essay on the Authority of the European Union* (Oxford University Press 2008) 103–105. Somek opposes the 'asymmetry thesis' defended by Gareth Davies: Davies, 'Can Selling Arrangements Be Harmonized?' 105–107. See, however, the recent evolution in Davies' argument: Gareth Davies, 'The Competence to Create an Internal Market: Conceptual Poverty and Unbalanced Interests' in Sacha Garben and Inge Govaere (eds),

Article 114 TFEU has allowed the EU to act in various fields relevant to the regulation of unhealthy lifestyles.[41]

In addition to Article 114 TFEU, the Treaty contains other provisions that allow for harmonisation in specific fields of the internal market. Pursuant to Article 53(1) TFEU, the Union may adopt directives 'for the coordination of the provisions laid down by law, regulation or administrative action in Member States concerning the taking-up and pursuit of activities as self-employed persons', a power which, by virtue of Article 62 TFEU, also extends to the free movement of services.[42] The conditions for recourse to these two provisions are similar to that of Article 114 TFEU.[43] Article 113 TFEU concerns indirect taxation. It allows the EU to 'adopt provisions for the harmonisation of legislation concerning turnover taxes, excise duties and other forms of indirect taxation to the extent that such harmonisation is necessary to ensure the establishment and the functioning of the internal market and to avoid distortion of competition'. Article 113 TFEU is the legal basis underpinning EU legislation on tobacco and alcohol excise duties.[44] Differences in tax rates between Member States create distortions of competition and diverging rules as regards chargeability may create obstacles to the free movement of goods or people. Reasoning by analogy with Articles 53(1), 62 and 114 TFEU, one can consider that, to be lawfully used, Article 113 TFEU should help removing such obstacles and restrictions.

The Division of Competences Between the EU and the Member States: Reflections on the Past, the Present and the Future (Hart Publishing 2017) 76.

41 Among others, the following pieces of lifestyle legislation are based on Article 114 TFEU: Directive 2003/33/EC of the European Parliament and of the Council of 26 May 2003 on the approximation of the laws, regulations and administrative provisions of the Member States relating to the advertising and sponsorship of tobacco products (Tobacco Advertising Directive), OJ L152/16; Claims Regulation; Regulation (EU) No 1169/2011 of the European Parliament and of the Council of 25 October 2011 on the provision of food information to consumers (Food Information Regulation) OJ L304/18; Tobacco Products Directive.

42 The AVMS Directive is based on Articles 53(1) and 62 TFEU: Directive 2010/13/EU of the European Parliament and of the Council of 10 March 2010 on the coordination of certain provisions laid down by law, regulation or administrative action in Member States concerning the provision of audiovisual media services (Audiovisual Media Services (AVMS) Directive), OJ L95/1. The Tobacco Products Directive is also based on both provisions, together with Article 114 TFEU.

43 *Tobacco Advertising*, para 87.

44 Council Directive 2011/64/EU of 21 June 2011 on the structure and rates of excise duty applied to manufactured tobacco (Tobacco Excise Duties Directive) OJ L176/24.

3.3 Promoting Healthier Lifestyles

3.3.1 Healthy Lifestyles Beyond the Market

The focus so far has been on the economic and trade-related aspects of the regulation of unhealthy products. Under certain circumstances, however, national measures do not affect cross-border trade. Where none of transboundary effects previously described are present, it is possible to regulate unhealthy lifestyles at the local level in a manner both effective and responsive to local circumstances and preferences. Enacting a smoking ban in cafés and restaurants or prohibiting the consumption of alcohol in outdoor public spaces, for instance, does not affect the free movement of goods or persons and the capacity of another jurisdiction to conduct an independent policy on such matters. There is thus a certain logic in leaving the regulatory choice to the local level. Yet, even in this context, various reasons may be identified that would warrant action at the supranational level. As regards the EU, three appear particularly pertinent.

Good health may be considered so important as a value that it justifies trumping regulatory diversity, because a low standard of protection contradicts 'widely held perceptions of human rights' or simply for reason of 'equity, justice or [. . .] paternalism'.[45] In that regard, the right to health fulfils an important function for the EU, not only as a source of legal obligations, but as an overarching norm justifying the enaction of protective measures at the Union level.[46] A raison d'être for EU supranational integration may be found in the protection of fundamental rights,[47] considering especially that the burden of NCDs and other damaging health consequences arising from lifestyles is unevenly distributed both within and between Member States.[48] In a country where no rules

45 Faure, 'The Economics of Harmonization of Food Law in the EU' 277.

46 See Anniek de Ruijter, *EU Health Law & Policy: The Expansion of EU Power in Public Health and Health Care* (Oxford University Press 2019). On the right to health in general, see Jean McHale, 'Fundamental Rights and Health Care' in Elias Mossialos and others (eds), *Health Systems Governance in Europe: The Role of EU Law and Policy* (Cambridge University Press 2010) 282–314; Hervey and McHale, *European Union Health Law: Themes and Implications* 156–183; Calum Alasdair Young, 'Fundamental Rights and EU Health Law and Policy' in Tamara K Hervey, Calum Alasdair Young and Louise E Bishop (eds), *Research Handbook on EU Health Law and Policy* (Edward Elgar Publishing 2017) 82–108. As regards lifestyle risks and NCDs, see Alemanno and Garde, 'The Emergence of an EU Lifestyle Policy: The Case of Alcohol, Tobacco and Unhealthy Diets' 1783–1784; Marie Elske Gispen and Brigit Toebes (eds), *Human Rights and Tobacco Control* (Edward Elgar Publishing 2020).

47 de Ruijter, *EU Health Law & Policy*' 18.

48 Alemanno and Garde, 'The Emergence of an EU Lifestyle Policy' 1783.

regulating indoor smoking are in place, hence exposing the population to second-hand smoke, one could argue that this constitutes an infringement on the rights of non-smokers to live in a clean, non-harmful environment. Granting supranational bodies an oversight on fundamental rights may appear necessary so that the population of States which fail to adequately protect these rights are not left without remedies.

In budgetary terms, promoting good health is also a sound investment. Preventive action on NCDs constitutes an efficient way to reduce the significant financial burden that these diseases impose on national healthcare systems and the broader costs to society incurred. Under this 'health is wealth' approach, the positive contribution that a healthy population makes to the economy is underlined. Health promotion is not only a way to save government revenue but also to increase it, by allowing people to live longer and more productive lives. This framing of health is increasingly present in the EU's discourse.[49] In the aftermath of the 2008 financial and subsequent sovereign debts crisis, the EU considerably strengthened its fiscal and economic governance instruments, to the extent that some considered that 'austerity' had become a new facet of EU health policy.[50]

Finally, for the EU, acting in health matters also has a strategic appeal, contributing to improving its image and increasing its legitimacy in the eyes of the public.[51] This is especially pertinent for the EU, which is often criticised for being too 'economic' and too remote from citizens' concerns. As said by former EU Commissioner for Health David Byrne:

> Health is a preoccupation of Europeans. We need to get it right on health, if we are to get it right on a new Europe that means something to our citizens. [...] Indeed our citizens are telling us that the European Union should not only be preoccupied with better markets, predictable rules, stable international

[49] See European Commission, 'Investing in Health' (Staff Working Document) SWD (2013) 43 final.

[50] See Scott L Greer, 'The Three Faces of European Union Health Policy: Policy, Markets, and Austerity' (2014) 33 Policy and Society 13. See also Scott L Greer, 'Health, Federalism and the European Union: Lessons from Comparative Federalism about the European Union' (2021) 16 Health Economics, Policy and Law 94–96.

[51] Sébastien Guigner, 'De « La Santé dans Toutes les Politiques » à « Toutes les Politiques dans la Santé » : le Régime de Visibilité de la Prise en Compte de la Santé dans les Politiques de l'Union Européenne' (2016) 34 Sciences Sociales et santé 71. See also Somek, *Individualism* 12: 'For an organization such as the European Union that notoriously lacks appeal to ordinary people, posturing as being concerned about the well-being of citizens plays part of a strategy to look "nice"'.

relations, sustainable jobs and public finances. They are telling us that there can be no Europe without a Europe of Health.[52]

This concern for EU's image and appeal was instrumental in the launch of the European programme against cancer,[53] one of the first public health policies devised at the Union level. Amidst the budgetary crisis of the mid-1980s, at a time when the European integration process had come to a stalemate, this programme was considered a way to bridge the gap existing between the EU and its citizens and to improve the EU's image. The French President at the time, François Mitterrand, was especially vocal in pushing for a 'People's Europe', a plan to reinforce the legitimacy of European integration by responding 'to the expectations of the people of Europe by adopting measures to strengthen and promote its identity and its image both for its citizens and for the rest of the world'.[54] This resulted in the adoption of the first EU measures in the field of tobacco, which represented a significant improvement for some of the Member States that had no such rule in place at the time.

3.3.2 *The EU's Limited Competence in Health*

The protection of human health is one of the EU's core objectives. According to Article 3 TEU, '[t]he Union's aim is to promote peace, its values and the *well-being* of its peoples'. Further, pursuant to Article 9 TFEU, '[i]n defining and implementing its policies and activities, the Union shall take into account requirements linked to the promotion of a high level of [...] human health', an obligation reiterated in Article 168(1) TFEU and Article 35 of the Charter of Fundamental Rights of the European Union (CFR). These various horizontal clauses reflect a 'health in all policies' approach to policymaking, that is, 'the recognition that a

52 David Byrne, 'Future priorities in EU health policies' (2002) Speech at the European Health Forum Gastein, <https://ec.europa.eu/commission/presscorner/api/files/document/print/en/speech_02_426/SPEECH_02_426_EN.pdf> accessed 17 September 2025.

53 Council of the European Union, Resolution of the Council and the Representatives of the Governments of the Member States, meeting within the Council of 7 July 1986, on a programme of action of the European Communities against cancer, OJ C184/19.

54 European Council, Fontainebleau 25–26 June 1984, Conclusions of the Presidency, 8. See Sébastien Guigner, 'La Dynamique d'Intégration par Sédimentation: Retour sur l'Inscription de la Santé dans les Compétences de l'Union' in Estelle Brosset (ed), *Droit Européen et Protection de la Santé – Bilan et Perspectives* (Bruylant 2015) 38–43; de Ruijter, *EU Health Law & Policy* 72.

broader range of factors, other than those traditionally addressed within the "health" field, affect population health'.[55]

Health has a 'mixed competence structure' under the TFEU.[56] Article 6 (a) TFEU grants a competence to the Union to carry out actions to support, coordinate or supplement the actions of the Member States as regards the 'protection and improvement of human health'. Under Article 4(2) (k), the Union also shares competence with the Member States in the area of 'common safety concerns in public health matters'.[57] No authoritative legal text defines 'health' under EU law. According to Anniek de Ruijter, the concept of health in EU law and policy 'refers to the normal functioning of the (human) species and also to a more subjective expression of a (social) state of physical and mental well-being, depending on individual and social (national) backgrounds'.[58] Article 168 TFEU is the specific health legal basis contained in the TFEU. It lays down the objectives of EU health policy and the specific powers granted to the Union to achieve these objectives. According to Article 168(1),

> Union action, which shall complement national policies, shall be directed towards improving public health, *preventing physical and mental illness and diseases*, and *obviating sources of danger to physical and mental health*. Such action shall cover the fight against the major health scourges, by promoting research into their causes, their transmission and their *prevention*, as well *as health information and education*, and monitoring, early warning of and combating serious cross-border threats to health.
>
> The Union shall complement the Member States' action in *reducing drugs-related health damage*, including information and prevention.[59]

Union action is centred on 'public health' issues, understood as the management of health risks and the prevention of disease,[60] as opposed

[55] Oliver Bartlett and Anja Naumann, 'Reinterpreting the Health in All Policies Obligation in Article 168 TFEU: The First Step towards Making Enforcement a Realistic Prospect' (2021) 16 Health Economics, Policy and Law 8. The precise meaning of these horizontal clauses remains somewhat unclear and open to different interpretations: ibid 12–16.

[56] Sacha Garben, 'Article 168 TFEU' in Manuel Kellerbauer, Marcus Klamert and Jonathan Tomkin (eds), *The EU Treaties and the Charter of Fundamental Rights: A Commentary* (Oxford University Press 2019) 1448.

[57] It should be borne in mind that 'public health' and 'human health' have the same meaning under EU law and can be used interchangeably: de Ruijter, *EU Health Law & Policy* 55.

[58] ibid, 57–58. [59] Emphasis added.

[60] Greer, 'The Three Faces of European Union Health Policy: Policy, Markets, and Austerity' (n 217) 13; Hervey and McHale, *European Union Health Law* 69.

to 'healthcare', the provision of health services and medical care,[61] an area which remains more firmly within the ambit of Member State competence.[62] Aside from the general reference to 'physical and mental illness and diseases' and to 'sources of danger to physical and mental health', which are wide enough to cover all kinds of health hazards, lifestyle risks are directly referred to in Article 168(1) via the mention of 'drugs-related health damage'. A clearer reference to unhealthy lifestyles is contained in Article 168(5), which grants the power to the Union to adopt 'measures which have as their *direct objective* the protection of public health regarding *tobacco and the abuse of alcohol*'.[63]

It is thus clear from Article 168 TFEU that the prevention of health damages associated with hazardous lifestyles is one of the EU's main health priorities. Yet, as health falls predominantly within the category of complementary competences, Union action in that field is limited to measures that 'support, coordinate or supplement' those adopted by the Member States.[64] Most importantly, this excludes harmonisation measures.[65] This prohibition should be understood as prohibiting *de jure* harmonisation, the harmonisation of existing national provisions and could even be interpreted as denying all pre-emptive effect to EU acts adopted under Article 168.[66] One can consider with Bartlett that 'the prohibition on harmonisation means that Article 168(5) TFEU confers no authority upon the EU to engage in any type of [...] prevention that would prevent the Member States from enacting their own policy on the same topic'.[67] A derogation exists for the 'common safety concerns in

[61] For the difference between 'public health' and 'health-care', see de Ruijter, *EU Health Law & Policy* 62–63.

[62] Under Article 168(7) TFEU: 'Union action shall respect the responsibilities of the Member States for the definition of their health policy and for the organisation and delivery of health services and medical care. The responsibilities of the Member States shall include the management of health services and medical care and the allocation of the resources assigned to them'.

[63] Art 168(5) TFEU, emphasis added. On the meaning of 'direct objective', see Bartlett, 'The EU's Competence Gap in Public Health and Non-Communicable Disease Policy' 62–63.

[64] Art 2(5) TFEU. [65] ibid. See also Art 168(5) TFEU.

[66] See Robert Schütze, 'Co-operative Federalism Constitutionalized: The Emergence of Complementary Competences in the EC Legal Order' (2006) 31 European Law Review 167; Bartlett, 'The EU's Competence Gap in Public Health and Non-Communicable Disease Policy' 63–64; Robert Schütze, 'Classifying EU Competences: German Constitutional Lessons?' in Garben and Govaere, *The Division of Competences Between the EU and the Member States: Reflections on the Past, the Present and the Future* 50–51.

[67] Bartlett, 'The EU's Competence Gap in Public Health and Non-Communicable Disease Policy' 64.

public health matters' referred to in Article 4(2)(k) TFEU, in relation to which the Union may adopt harmonisation measures.[68] These common safety concerns include food safety but do not extend, as explained in Section 2.2, to the aspects studied in this book.[69] Under Article 168 TFEU, the EU may only adopt incentive measures[70] or recommendations.[71] Through incentive measure, which may have binding force, the EU can spend 'small sums of money to promote European networks that connect people and organizations, put items on the agenda for the future, and [...] produce research'.[72] It can engage in benchmarking exercises and facilitate the sharing of information and best practices. The EU health programmes are examples of incentive measures.[73] This form of intervention is not devoid of any influence and may contribute positively to lifestyle health promotion,[74] but is nonetheless limited in nature. Recommendations, for their part, are legal acts devoid of any binding effect[75] and can therefore not form the basis of a genuine policy.

As discussed at the beginning of this section, as public health is affected by almost every policy, 'almost every policy in government could potentially be seen as more or less successful public health policy'.[76] Other legal bases belonging to other fields and categories of competence could also be used for the purpose of regulating lifestyles, allowing the Union to enact more forceful measures. One should mention Article 121 TFEU, which relates to the coordination of Member States' economic policies and empowers the Council to adopt economic

[68] Art 168(4).

[69] Art 168(4)(b) refers to 'measures in the veterinary and phytosanitary fields which have as their direct objective the protection of public health'. This provision serves, for instance, as a legal basis for the General Food Law Regulation.

[70] Article 168(5) refers both to 'incentive measures' and 'measures'. Following Bartlett's contextual and historical interpretation of this provision, one may conclude that these two terms refer to the same type of act, which excludes harmonisation, and that the use of both results from poor drafting: Bartlett, 'The EU's Competence Gap in Public Health and Non-Communicable Disease Policy' 60.

[71] Art 168(6) TFEU.

[72] Greer, 'The Three Faces of European Union Health Policy: Policy, Markets, and Austerity' (n 217) 15. See also Greer, 'Health, Federalism and the European Union: Lessons from Comparative Federalism about the European Union' 93.

[73] See most recently Regulation (EU) 2021/522.

[74] Bartlett, 'The EU's Competence Gap in Public Health and Non-Communicable Disease Policy' 61–62.

[75] Art 288 TFEU.

[76] Scott L Greer, 'Introduction - What is Public Health Policy?' in Scott L Greer and Paulette Kurzer (eds), *European Union Public Health Policy: Regional and Global Trends* (Routledge 2016) 1. See also de Ruijter, *EU Health Law & Policy* 52.

policy guidelines in the form of country specific recommendations (CSRs) to Member States. These CSRs address the question of the sustainability of national healthcare systems and include recommendations related to people's lifestyles.[77] Another field of EU policy related to health and lifestyles is the Common Agricultural Policy (CAP). What Article 39 TFEU shows, however, is that health promotion and protection are not part of the CAP's objectives.

If one focuses on legal bases that specifically refer to health as an objective, other than Article 168 TFEU, the conclusion still holds that the EU is deprived of direct and general harmonisation powers applicable to health and lifestyles.[78] Under Article 153 TFEU on social policy, the Union may adopt harmonisation measures aimed at improving 'the working environment to protect workers' health and safety'.[79] This legal basis has been used to legislate in the field of lifestyles, but limited to aspects related to the health of workers. Directive 89/654/EEC requires, for instance, employers to introduce appropriate measures for the 'protection of non-smokers against discomfort caused by tobacco smoke'.[80] Article 153 TFEU could also be employed to adopt measures encouraging physical activity at work, a useful objective if considering that the tertiarization of work is one of the structural explanations for the general decline in physical activity in society.[81] Article 191 TFEU on the environment mentions the protection of human health as one of the main objectives of Union policy in that field.[82] This makes sense, as many activities are equally detrimental to the environment and to

[77] See Natasha Azzopardi-Muscat and others, 'EU Country Specific Recommendations for Health Systems in the European Semester Process: Trends, Discourse and Predictors' (2015) 119 Health Policy 375.

[78] Article 352 TFEU, the 'flexibility clause', which was used to adopt harmonisation measures in the early days of EU health policy, is no longer an available option. Since the Lisbon Treaty revision, 'measures based on this Article shall not entail harmonisation of Member States' laws or regulations in cases where the Treaties exclude such harmonisation', which is the case of health.

[79] Art 153(1)(a) TFEU, harmonisation powers are granted pursuant to Article 153(2)(b).

[80] See Council Directive 89/654/EEC of 30 November 1989 concerning the minimum safety and health requirements for the workplace (first individual directive within the meaning of Article 16 (1) of Directive 89/391/EEC), OJ L393/1, annex I, para 16.3, and annex II, para 11.3.

[81] Garde, *EU Law and Obesity Prevention* 321–326.

[82] Under Art 191 TFUE, 'Union policy on the environment shall contribute to pursuit of the following objectives: preserving, protecting and improving the quality of the environment, protecting human health [. . .]'. 'Environment' is in itself a contested concept, 'ripe for discussion': see Nicolas de Sadeleer, *EU Environmental Law and the Internal Market* (Oxford University Press 2014) 5–7.

human health.[83] To the knowledge of the author, there is no case law that would shed light on the relationship between health and environmental concerns in the choice of legal basis. To the extent that a lifestyle measure with a predominantly environmental objective also benefits human health, Article 192 TFEU would constitute a suitable legal basis. Such could be the case of a rule addressing the pollution resulting from cigarette use. The potential of that provision remains yet limited to the environmental aspects of lifestyle consumptions. Consumer protection, finally, is also relevant. Under this policy, 'the Union shall contribute to protecting the *health*, safety and economic interests of consumers'.[84] Article 169 TFEU, however, does not offer more powers than those existing under other legal bases. Article 169(2)(a) refers to measures adopted pursuant to Article 114 TFEU and Article 169(2)(b) allows the EU to adopt measures 'which support, supplement and monitor the policy pursued by the Member States', hence excluding harmonisation.

3.4 The Scope of the EU's Legislative Competence

The EU's limited mandate in health matters stands in contrast with its broad internal market competence. Harmonisation under Article 114 TFEU and the related legal bases seems, prima facie, to contradict the exclusion contained in Article 168 TFEU. How can these provisions be reconciled? What are, ultimately, the powers of the EU legislature to regulate unhealthy lifestyles? These questions were at the core of the *Germany v European Parliament and Council* judgment, better known as *Tobacco Advertising*, a landmark ruling familiar to students and scholars of EU law alike. That case concerned the validity of Directive 98/43/EC on the advertising and sponsorship of tobacco products.[85] Germany claimed that the Directive was a public health measure which could not have been lawfully adopted under Article 114 TFEU. According to Germany, 'recourse to Article [114 TFEU] is not possible where the centre of gravity of a measure is focused not on promoting the internal market but on protecting public health'.[86] Germany considered that the Directive,

[83] ibid, 36–37; David Langlet and Said Mahmoudi, *EU Environmental Law and Policy* (Oxford University Press 2016) 35.

[84] Art 169 TFEU, emphasis added.

[85] Directive 98/43/EC of the European Parliament and of the Council of 6 July 1998 on the approximation of the laws, regulations and administrative provisions of the Member States relating to the advertising and sponsorship of tobacco products, OJ L213/9.

[86] *Tobacco Advertising*, para 32.

because it introduced a general ban on tobacco advertising and sponsorship in the EU, was predominantly a public health measure, unlawfully adopted under Article 114 TFEU. The Court rejected that argument and ruled that:

> [P]rovided that the conditions for recourse to Articles [114, 53(1) and 62 TFEU] as a legal basis are fulfilled, the [Union] legislature cannot be prevented from relying on that legal basis *on the ground that public health protection is a decisive factor in the choices to be made.*[87]

For the Court, Article 168(5) TFEU cannot be interpreted as preventing the EU legislator from adopting harmonisation measures having health as an objective under other provisions. The only limit to the use of Article 114 TFEU, and related legal bases, is to be found in the conditions for recourse to these provisions, the removal of obstacles to trade. As long as this is the case, the importance of the public health objective is irrelevant to the legality of the act. The importance of the Court's pronouncement for the development of EU lifestyle policy, and EU health policy in general, cannot be overstated. Thus doing, the Court allowed the EU legislature to make up for its lack of harmonisation powers in public health through the use of its internal market competence.

Does this interpretation constitute an undue extension of the EU's powers? It is not in itself objectionable that measures adopted pursuant to Article 114 TFEU have a bearing on health. Article 114 TFEU is purposive in nature: it seeks the achievement of an objective but does not regulate any particular area.[88] As observed by Advocate General Fennelly, this competence 'is not limited in advance by reference to a particular subject-matter defined *ratione materiae*'.[89] To exclude from the scope of Article 114 TFEU the areas where the EU is not granted harmonisation powers would considerably weaken its function. This is even more true in relation to health, the protection of which creates restrictions to free movement that cannot, and should not, be solved by TFEU free movement provisions alone. Moreover, in requiring that the European Commission take as a base a high level of protection in its legislative proposals 'concerning health, safety, environmental

[87] ibid, para 88, emphasis added.

[88] For a critical approach towards purposive legal bases, see Gareth Davies, 'Democracy and Legitimacy in the Shadow of Purposive Competence' (2015) 21 European Law Journal 2.

[89] Case C-376/98 *Germany v European Parliament and Council (Tobacco Advertising)*, EU:C:2000:324, Opinion of Advocate General Fennelly, para 62. See also Davies, 'Democracy and Legitimacy in the Shadow of Purposive Competence' 3.

protection and consumer protection [. . .]', Article 114(3) TFEU itself foresees the integration of health concerns within internal market measures. Yet, the Court, while recognising the fact that health and market concerns are often intertwined, could have decided to limit the weight of the health objective that a measure adopted under Article 114 TFEU can lawfully pursue. It could have applied the centre of gravity doctrine, according to which 'if examination of [an EU] act shows that it has a twofold purpose or twofold component and if one of these is identifiable as main or predominant, whereas the other is merely incidental, the act must be founded on a sole legal basis, that is, the one required by the main or predominant purpose or component'.[90] Following this approach, a purpose other than a strictly internal market one, such as health, could be validly pursued by a measure adopted via Article 114 TFEU, under the condition that this purpose remains of a lesser weight than the internal market component of the measure. This was essentially the point that Germany was making in *Tobacco Advertising*, when arguing that 'the legislative history of the Directive and its content and purpose show that the centre of gravity of the measure is public health protection'.[91] In the judgment, however, the Court refrained from discussing the respective importance of the internal market and public health objectives pursued by the Directive.[92] Had it done so, it would have probably concluded that health was prevailing, for it is clear that a piece of legislation setting up a wide ban on tobacco advertising and sponsorship is more concerned with the protection of health than the free movement of tobacco products. The Court had nonetheless good reasons to abstain from such reasoning, for the very idea of applying a centre of gravity test to a piece of legislation adopted under Article 114 TFEU seems ill-suited. It is indeed 'of the essence of any internal-market measure that it pursues, quite legitimately, two objectives - one the removal of obstacles to trade or distortions of competition; the other (the means of achieving the first) the adoption of harmonised EU measures to replace national measures in the field in question'.[93] Every time an EU measure harmonises national health standards, an obstacle to trade is lifted while *at the same time* a new standard of protection is set.

[90] *British American Tobacco* para 94. [91] *Tobacco Advertising* para 34.
[92] Bruno de Witte, 'Exclusive Member State Competences - Is There Such a Thing?' in Garben and Govaere, *The Division of Competences Between the EU and the Member States: Reflections on the Past, the Present and the Future* 63.
[93] *Tobacco Advertising*, Opinion of Advocate General Fennelly para 75.

These two objectives cannot legally be severed. Setting the level of protection, one could argue, is a political matter that should escape the Court's review.[94] To conclude with Bruno de Witte: '[i]nternal market legislation is always also "about something else", and that something else may in fact be the main reason why the internal market measure was adopted'.[95] Implicitly or explicitly, all EU lifestyle risk harmonisation measures follow a double objective: internal market and health.[96]

That being said, even if the solution adopted by the Court appears the most adapted to the logic of Article 114 TFEU, it is not without raising questions. The extensive use of EU internal market powers to harmonise matters which, according to the legal bases relevant to these specific fields, should remain free from EU harmonisation, creates problems of clarity, effectiveness and legitimacy, which will be further explored in Chapters 6 and 7. Suffice to say, at this stage, that the extensive use of Article 114 TFEU sits uneasily with the principle of conferral, according to which 'the Union shall act only within the limits of the competences conferred upon it by the Member States in the Treaties to attain the objectives set out therein'.[97] EU action in the field of unhealthy lifestyles may be regarded as a form of competence creep, understood as 'a process whereby the powers of the EU [are] perceived as expanding in covert or somehow unclear ways, including into areas where Member States were supposed to remain fully in charge'.[98] The contradiction between the legislative practice in the area of lifestyles and the content of Article 168 (5) TFEU illustrates an incoherence that goes deeper in the EU Treaty system. The idea of categorising competences in different policy areas attached to specific legal bases goes against the purposive nature of Article 114 TFEU. In fact that provision 'makes a mockery of the

[94] René Barents, 'The Internal Market Unlimited: Some Observations on the Legal Basis of Community Legislation' (1993) 30 Common Market Law Review 85, 101. This argument was further unpacked by Advocate General Poiares Maduro in Case C-58/08 *Vodafone Ltd*, EU:C:2009:596, para 9.

[95] De Witte, 'Exclusive Member State Competences - Is There Such a Thing?' 63.

[96] See e.g. Claims Regulation, art 1(1); AVMS Directive, recital 104; Tobacco Excise Duties Directive, recital 2; Food Information Regulation, art 3; Tobacco Products Directive, art 1.

[97] Article 5(2) TEU.

[98] Sacha Garben and Inge Govaere, 'The Division of Competences Between the EU and the Member States: Reflections on the Past, the Present and the Future' in Garben and Govaere, *The Division of Competences Between the EU and the Member States: Reflections on the Past, the Present and the Future* 7.

carefully drawn restrictions in provisions such as Article 168 TFEU'.[99] The drafting of the latter provision could thus be qualified as 'cynical',[100] insofar as it leads the EU legislature to justify politically desired health measures with the vocabulary of the internal market.[101] Ultimately though, this deficiency results from the Treaty's drafting and it is arguably not for the Court to correct.

3.5 Conclusion

The EU, as other 'post-national risk governance regimes', is 'at one and the same time, a modern normative commitment to the establishment of a global economy, with all the risks that that entails, as well as a manifestation of an unprecedented ambition to control or govern that same risk'.[102] This is true for lifestyle-related health risks, as well as other risks emerging from market activities.[103] Free movement has played a key role in the emergence of the EU governance regime on lifestyles and it represents a powerful justification for its existence. The establishment of the internal market requires to eliminate the barriers to trade resulting from national risk control measures. The EU has been granted with sweeping legislative and judicial powers to do so. The adoption of common European standards facilitates free movement while at the same time allowing the EU to set the content of a genuine policy on lifestyle risks, compensating for the EU's lack of general harmonisation powers in the field of public health.

Legally speaking then, the regulation of unhealthy lifestyles in the EU remains a form of internal market regulation, with a key role for Article 114 TFEU. Politically, however, it is increasingly framed as a public health policy, both in terms of the objectives pursued and the regulatory tools used. This will hopefully clearly appear to the reader in Chapters 4 and 5. This evolution is in line with the Treaty-sanctioned objectives of promoting the health of Europeans, and, as it has been argued, does not

[99] Stephen Weatherill, *The Internal Market as a Legal Concept* (Oxford University Press 2017) 171.

[100] Schütze, *From Dual to Cooperative Federalism: The Changing Structure of European Law* 282.

[101] ibid 283.

[102] Michelle Everson, 'Three Intimate Tales of Law and Science: Hope, Despair and Transcendence' in Ellen Vos and Michelle Everson (eds), *Uncertain Risks Regulated* (Routledge-Cavendish 2009).

[103] See Micklitz and Tridimas (eds), *Risk and EU Law*; Weimer, *Risk Regulation in the Internal Market: Lessons from Agricultural Biotechnology*.

raise any principled issue of competence. Yet, as one can imagine, a tension exists between the objective of building a market for unhealthy products and that of reducing their consumption, or eliminating their use altogether. This is one of the fundamental questions explored in this study, which will be further analysed in Part II of the book, Chapter 6 especially.

4 The Evolution of EU Lifestyle Regulation

4.1 Introduction

From a mere by-product of the internal market, governed by the TFEU free movement provisions and the related case law, the regulation of unhealthy lifestyles has turned into a genuine policy field, with the EU legislature setting goals and deciding on the measures to adopt. Negative and positive integration have always coexisted, but the latter has now gained in prominence. This chapter describes this transition, taking the entry into force of the Treaty of Maastricht in 1993, which introduced a formal health competence in the EU treaty system, as a milestone. This evolution corresponds to the changing perception and status of tobacco, alcohol and unhealthy foods in public policy. No longer seen as ordinary goods, they are increasingly treated as hazardous and unsafe products whose place on the market should be restricted. The EU has followed this evolution, by making the fight against NCDs one of its main public health priorities. The level of ambition varies greatly, however, whether one considers tobacco, alcohol or food. While the EU openly advocates for a 'smoke-free' future, alcoholic beverages and unhealthy foods are considered to be an unescapable feature of life, to be consumed with moderation.

Section 4.1 covers the application of free movement provisions to national lifestyle measures, with a focus on the fields where EU law has had the most impact: product requirements, monopolies and price measures. This section provides only an overview of the issue, which will further be taken up in Chapter 6. Section 4.2 describes the main orientations of the EU's policy on lifestyle and NCDs, generally first, and then for tobacco, diets and alcohol specifically. It provides the background to Chapter 5, where EU regulatory interventions are systematically analysed and classified.

4.2 From Rome to Maastricht: Building a Market for Unhealthy Products

After the creation of the European Economic Community in 1957, the first decades of European integration corresponded to the establishment of a common market, later to become the internal market. The common market was to be built during the first transitional period of twelve years (1958–1969), during which, on the one hand, existing trade restrictions were to be eliminated by way of legislation and, on the other hand, Member States were to refrain from enacting new ones.[1] While early food legislation did incorporate health concerns,[2] linked to additives and food safety, the question of healthy lifestyles remained largely ignored. After the expiry of the transition period, the TFEU free movement provisions played a key role, bolstered by the twin doctrines of primacy and direct effect.[3] A large body of cases on food and alcoholic beverages emerged, sparked by disgruntled traders challenging national rules preventing their access to foreign markets.[4] Most of these cases involved product requirements, price measures and monopoly rules and were decided under Articles 34, 37 and 110 TFEU. The TFEU provisions on services and establishment played a negligible role.[5] Through its case law, the Court of Justice participated in building a market for unhealthy lifestyles and, with judgments such as *Dassonville*, *Cassis de Dijon* and *Beer Purity*,[6] laid down the foundation for the internal market at large.

In the wake of the *Cassis de Dijon* ruling, many of the cases adjudicated under Article 34 TFEU involved 'product requirements', that is, 'rules that lay down requirements to be met by [. . .] goods (such as those relating to designation, form, size, weight, composition, presentation,

[1] For an overview of the transitional period, see Schütze, '"Integration-through-Law": Grand Theory, Revisionist History' 167–173.

[2] See Council Directive on the approximation of the rules of the Member States concerning the colouring matters authorized for use in foodstuffs intended for human consumption, OJ 115/2645; Council Directive 64/54/EEC of 5 November 1963 on the approximation of the laws of the Member States concerning the preservatives authorized for use in foodstuffs intended for human consumption, OJ 12/161.

[3] On this foundational period for the EU legal order, see Joseph HH Weiler, 'The Transformation of Europe' (1990) 100 Yale Law Journal 2403; Schütze, '"Integration-through-Law": Grand Theory, Revisionist History' 11–13.

[4] For an overview of the food and alcohol case law, see Schebesta and Purnhagen, *EU Food Law* 79–110.

[5] Articles 49 and 56 are especially relevant to the regulation of gambling, starting from *Schindler* in 1994: Case C-275/92, *H.M. Customs and Excise v Schindler*, EU:C:1994:119.

[6] *Dassonville*; *Cassis de Dijon*; *Beer purity*.

labelling, packaging)'.[7] Many of these rules were not primarily, if at all, meant to protect the health of consumers. Rather, by ensuring that foods sold under a given name complied with certain composition or production standards, their aim was to protect consumers' expectation, together with their domestic market.[8] Notable cases involved Italian rules reserving the name 'pasta' to products made of durum wheat,[9] or Dutch and German rules protecting the traditional methods of brewing beer.[10] Some food cases did involve rules with a stronger link to nutrition. In *Sandoz*, the national measure at stake prohibited the marketing of food to which vitamins had been added without prior administrative authorisation.[11] The Court found that a rule of this kind was likely to impede trade between Member States and therefore constituted a measure having equivalent effect to a quantitative restriction. Many 'vitamins' cases followed.[12] In *Commission v Germany (Meat products)*, a rule prohibiting the marketing of meat products containing other ingredients than meat, which aimed to preserve protein intake in the population, was found to be a restrictive measure.[13] Similarly, in *Commission v France (Milk substitutes)*,[14] the Court declared that the French rule prohibiting the import and sale of substitutes for milk powder and concentrated milk was in breach of Article 34 TFEU. The case most illustrative of a 'lifestyle' measure, though, is *Van der Veldt*, which involved a Belgian rule prohibiting the sale of bread and other bakery products with a salt content higher than 2 per cent,[15] ultimately struck down by the Court.

Regarding alcoholic beverages, two early cases on advertising had a clear public health bearing. In *Aragonesa*, the rule adopted by the Autonomous Community of Catalonia prohibited the advertising of beverages having an alcoholic strength of more than 23 per cent vol. in the media, on streets and highways, in cinemas and on public transport. The Court ruled that a measure 'which restricts or prohibits certain forms of

[7] Case C-267/91, *Keck and Mithouard*, EU:C:1993:905, para 15.

[8] For an overview of various types of 'quality requirements', see Onno Brouwer, 'Free Movement of Foodstuffs and Quality Requirements: Has the Commission Got It Wrong?' (1988) 25 Common Market Law Review 26; Schebesta and Purnhagen, *EU Food Law*.

[9] Case 90/86, *Zoni*, EU:C:1988:403; Case 407/85, *3 Glocken*, EU:C:1988:401.

[10] Case 94/82, *Kikvorsch*, EU:C:1983:85; *Beer purity*.

[11] Case 174/82, *Sandoz*, EU:C:1983:213.

[12] Case C-24/00, *Commission v France*, EU:C:2004:70; Case C-192/01, *Commission v Denmark*, EU:C:2003:492; Case C-41/02 *Commission v Netherlands*, EU:C:2004:762.

[13] *Commission v Germany (Meat products)*.

[14] Case 216/84 *Commission v France (Milk substitutes)*, EU:C:1988 :81.

[15] *Van der Veldt* (n 182). See also *Bellamy*.

advertising and certain means of sales promotion may, although it does not directly affect trade, [is] such as to restrict the volume of trade because it affects marketing opportunities' and must therefore be regarded as a measure having equivalent effect within the meaning of Article 34 TFEU.[16] The Court ultimately found the restriction to be justified on grounds of public health. In *Gourmet*, the quasi-total Swedish ban on alcohol advertising and promotion was challenged.[17] The Court ruled that it was a restriction under Article 34 TFEU but deferred the assessment on proportionality to the national court.

A number of judgments rendered by the Court of Justice concerned the operation of State monopolies for tobacco and alcohol. These monopolies, many of which have now been dismantled, apply to the import, export, wholesale or retail sale of goods. They pursue an economic/fiscal objective, ensuring that the revenues accrued from the sale of monopolised goods benefit the public purse, and may also be adopted for health purposes, controlling the import and sale of hazardous goods to the population.[18] This is, for instance, the case of the Swedish and Finnish alcohol retail monopolies, still in place today. The most relevant provision here is Article 37 TFEU, which applies in circumstances where the State grants exclusive purchase or sales rights to a public undertaking or institution or, by means of delegation, to a private organisation, thus enabling the control of imports or exports.[19] Article 37(1) precludes discrimination regarding the conditions under which monopolised goods are procured and marketed.

Two streams of cases may be identified. A first stream involved the tax treatment of imported goods coming under the monopoly. In *Cinzano*, the Court considered that a duty levied on imports did not amount to an infringement of Article 37 TFEU if such a charge was imposed similarly to imported and domestic products.[20] Logically, it is also permitted to impose internal taxation on domestic products superior to similar products imported from other Member States.[21] On the contrary, in *Miritz*, the Court ruled that Article 37 TFEU prevented a Member State from

[16] *Aragonesa* paras 10–11. [17] *Gourmet*.

[18] See Graham Butler, 'State Monopolies and the Free Movement of Goods in EU Law: Getting Beyond Obscure Clarity' (2021) 48 Legal Issues of Economic Integration 285.

[19] See European Commission, Commission Notice: Guide on Articles 34-36 of the Treaty on the Functioning of the European Union (TFEU), OJ C100/38, 80.

[20] Case 13/70 *Cinzano*, EU:C:1970:110, para 12. See also Case 45/75 *Rewe*-Zentrale, EU: C:1976:22, para 27.

[21] Case 86/78 *Peureux*, EU:C:1979:64, para 38.

levying a charge imposed only on imported products, for the purpose of compensating for the difference between the selling price of such products and the higher price paid by the state monopoly to domestic producers of the same products.[22] In *Commission v France*, the Court considered that the setting of a uniform retail price for tobacco products was contrary to Article 37 TFEU, as it was 'of such a nature as adversely to affect the marketing of imported tobacco under normal conditions of competition'.[23] Questions quickly arose regarding the boundary between Article 37 TFEU and Article 110 TFEU, which prohibits discriminatory or protective taxation. In earlier cases, the Court applied both provisions, favouring a broad reading of Article 37 TFEU.[24] It changed its approach in later cases, applying Article 110 TFEU only.[25]

Another stream of cases touched upon the core of the monopolies, the exclusive rights on import or retail granted to one or several operators. Article 37 precludes the existence of import monopolies,[26] whose elimination was one of the Commission's main priorities in the early years of the internal market.[27] The Court considers that the prohibition of exclusive rights for import is required so as 'to eliminate even the possibility of any discrimination being practised against [...] exporters'.[28] Retail monopolies, on the other hand, are permitted if they are devoid of any discriminatory feature. In *Franzen*, the Court analysed the product selection system, the monopoly's sale network and the promotion policy operated by Systembolaget, the Swedish monopoly on alcohol. It concluded that no difference in treatment existed between foreign and imported products. The product selection system is the aspect of a retail monopoly that appears most problematic, due to the possibility of favouring domestic goods. In *Franzen*, the Court concluded that products were selected by Systembolaget on the basis of criteria independent of the origin of the products, 'their quality, lack of adverse effects on human health, consumer demand and business or ethical considerations'.[29] It also welcomed the existence of procedural guarantees

[22] *Miritz*, para 12.

[23] *Commission v France* (90/82), para 27. For another price measure on tobacco, see also Case 78/82 *Commission v Italy*, EU:C:1983:159.

[24] See *Rewe-Zentrale*.

[25] See *Peureux*.

[26] Case 59-75 *Manghera e.a.*, EU:C:1976:14, para 13.

[27] See the various Commission recommendations of 22 December 1969, OJ L31; Council Resolution of 21 April 1970 on national monopolies of commercial character in manufactured tobacco, OJ C50/2.

[28] *Manghera*, para 3.

[29] *Franzen*, para 44.

allowing traders whose products are not selected to challenge the decision of the monopoly.[30]

In *Franzen*, the Court also clarified another judicial debate, regarding the boundaries between Articles 34 and 37 TFEU. While Article 37 TFEU is 'specifically applicable to the exercise, by a domestic commercial monopoly, of its exclusive rights', provisions which 'are separable from the operation of the monopoly although they have a bearing upon it' are not covered by Article 37 TFEU but must be examined under Article 34 TFEU.[31] This represented a significant change from earlier cases,[32] where both provisions had been applied simultaneously. The judgment in *Rosengren*, dealing with another aspect of the Swedish monopoly on alcohol, confirmed the test devised in *Franzen*.[33]

Beyond monopolies, a number of cases that reached the Court of Justice involved internal taxation and Article 110 TFEU. Article 110 TFEU aims to ensure that taxation is neutral vis-à-vis imported goods.[34] Where Member States enact taxation measures to discourage the consumption of certain products, they must do so in a manner that does not favour their domestic production, directly or indirectly. The two paragraphs of Article 110 TFEU address different situations. Article 110 (1) TFEU is essentially concerned with discrimination. Member States may not enact measures that would result in foreign products being more heavily taxed than similar domestic products. Article 110(2) TFEU, however, is broader in scope, as it prevents Member States from using their taxation as a protectionist tool. Article 110(1) TFEU applies to situations where domestic and foreign products are similar while Article 110(2) TFEU applies to situations where those are in competition. The two paragraphs of Article 110 TFEU should therefore, in principle, be applied separately. This has not always been the Court's practice, which, in certain judgments, applied the article in its entirety, without distinguishing between the two paragraphs.[35] This approach was later abandoned.

[30] ibid, paras 50–51. [31] ibid, paras 35–36.

[32] Case 119/78 *Grandes distilleries Peureux*, EU:C:1979:66, para 28; *Commission v France* (90/82), para 27. Advocate General Elmer himself followed this approach in Franzen: Case C-189/95 *Franzen*, EU:C:1997:101, Opinion of Advocate General Elmer, paras 97 and 106.

[33] *Rosengren*. [34] *Commission v Denmark* '(106/84)' para 10.

[35] This appears particularly clearly in a series of three judgments rendered in the 1980s dealing with Danish, French, and Italian taxes on spirits: Case 169/78 *Commission v Italy*, EU:C:1980:52; Case 168/78 *Commission v France*, EU:C:1980:51; Case 171/78 *Commission v Denmark*, EU:C:1980:54.

Many Article 110 TFEU cases concerned the taxation of alcohol and the different rates applicable to different categories of beverages: between different spirits,[36] between wines,[37] wine and spirits[38] or beer and wine.[39] Regarding tobacco, the Court found dark-tobacco and light-tobacco cigarettes to be similar products. This can be seen in *Commission v France* where a different tax rate applied to dark-tobacco and light-tobacco cigarettes. The Court noted that 'cigarettes falling within the most favourable tax category come almost exclusively from domestic production whereas almost all imported products come within the least advantageous category', resulting therefore in discriminatory taxation.[40] Regarding Article 110(2), the cases involving beer and wine show an evolution. In *Commission v United Kingdom (beer and wine II)* the Court established that wine bore a tax burden which, by reference to alcoholic strength, was more than twice as heavy as that borne by beer.[41] The information provided to the Court did not allow to establish precisely the influence of this tax difference on the respective prices of the two products,[42] so the Court decided that the difference in tax burden was enough to identify a protective effect.[43] The Court fortunately changed its approach in *Commission v Belgium.*[44] It held that 'any assessment of the compatibility of a given tax with the second paragraph of Article [110 TFEU] must take account of the impact of that tax on the competitive relationship between the products concerned', looking essentially at whether this tax can reduce the potential consumption of imported products to the advantage of competing domestic products.[45] In this regard, the price difference between the products at stake is an element that cannot be disregarded.[46] The Court acknowledged that a deceleration of the rise in wine consumption had been observed after the introduction of the tax increase but considered that no causal connection had been

[36] ibid. [37] *Commission v Denmark* (106/84). [38] *(John Walker)*; *Roders*.

[39] *Commission v United Kingdom (beer and wine I)*; Case 170/78 *Commission v United Kingdom (beer and wine II)*; see also *Commission v Belgium* (356/85).

[40] Case C-302/00 *Commission v France*, EU:C:2002:123, paras 22–29.

[41] *Commission v United Kingdom (beer and wine II)* para 21. [42] ibid.

[43] ibid, paras 26–27.

[44] *Commission v Belgium* (356/85). The formal approach was, however, still used in the latter Case C-230/89, *Commission v Greece*, EU:C:1991:156, para 10.

[45] *Commission v Belgium*356/85 para 15. See also *Roders* para 39; Case C-167/05 *Commission v Sweden*, EU:C:2008:202, para 52.

[46] *Commission v Belgium*356/85 para 16.

established between the two.[47] No protective effect was found in this case.[48]

In order to deter the consumption of certain products, altogether or in excess, Member States might adopt measures that regulate the price at which these products are sold. These measures usually seek to eliminate products that are too cheap from the market. They can take various forms: rules that directly set a minimum or maximum retail price, rules on minimum or maximum profit margins and rules on resale price maintenance, whereby the retailer is prevented from selling a product at a different price from the one set by the manufacturer.[49] This latter type of measure is used to prevent retailers from offering discounts on products. The circumstances in which various price measures can constitute a measure having equivalent effect within the meaning of Article 34 TFEU have given rise to a steady stream of, sometimes contradictory, case law. Under Article 34 TFEU, the picture that emerges from these early cases is that price measures are not held to have restrictive effects on trade, provided they apply equally to foreign and domestic products,[50] unless the level at which the price or profit margin is set puts imported products at a disadvantage, in which case the measure constitutes a measure having equivalent effect prohibited by Article 34 TFEU.[51] Any restrictive effect is especially unlikely where the retail price is freely set by the manufacturer or importer. This line of case law essentially subjects price measures to a discrimination test,[52] an approach which has been further challenged and refined in subsequent case law (see Section 6.2.1).

Free movement of goods provisions have lost in importance today. Since 2010, the Court adjudicates a very low number of cases under Article 34 TFEU every year, comparable to the pre-*Dassonville* era.[53]

47 ibid, para 20. 48 See also *Commission v Sweden*(C-167/05).

49 See European Commission, Commission Notice: Guide on Articles 34-36 of the Treaty on the Functioning of the European Union 53–55.

50 *INNO v ATAB*; *Van de Haar*.

51 See *Van Tiggele*; Case 116/84, *Roelstraete*, EU:C:1985:237, Case 188/86 *Ministère public v Lefèvre*, EU:C:1987:327.

52 See Case C-333/14, *Scotch Whisky*, Opinion of Advocate General Bot, EU:C:2015:527, para 65. See also the analysis of the arguments put forward by the European Commission in this case in Angus MacCulloch, 'State Intervention in Pricing: An Intersection of EU Free Movement and Competition Law' (2017) 42 European Law Review 190, 202–203.

53 Jan Zglinski, 'The End of Negative Market Integration: 60 Years of Free Movement of Goods Litigation in the EU (1961–2020)' (2024) 31 Journal of European Public Policy 633.

While there might be many reasons for such a decline,[54] the rise of legislation, as will appear from this chapter and Chapter 5, is one of the main explanatory factors, since harmonising measures remove (parts of) a product from the scope of the free movement provisions.[55] Articles 37 and 110 TFEU cases, for their part, have virtually disappeared from the Court's docket, probably because the body of rules concerned at the national level was much narrower in the first place. Crucially, this does not mean that free movement provisions are no longer relevant. First of all, the decline in cases that can be observed is specific to the free movement of goods and does not apply to the free movement of services or establishment.[56] Further, there are still large holes in EU legislation, which allow Member States to act, triggering the application of free movement provisions. Important judgments in the field of alcohol have been rendered more recently, such as *Visnapuu*,[57] where the Court examined the restrictive effects of the Finnish alcohol monopoly on imports, or *Scotch Whisky*,[58] where the Court scrutinised the Scottish minimum unit pricing (MUP) rule for alcoholic beverages. This is also the case in the field of tobacco.[59] Finally, depending on policy developments at the national level, regarding food taxation or reformulation, for instance, free movement provisions could also come back to the forefront.[60]

4.3 After Maastricht: The Emergence of an EU Lifestyle Policy

4.3.1 A Growing Public Health Priority

While health only formally became an EU competence with the Maastricht revision of the EC Treaty,[61] which entered into force on

On food and alcohol more specifically, see Schebesta and Purnhagen, *EU Food Law* 79–110.

54 Zglinski, 'The End of Negative Market Integration: 60 Years of Free Movement of Goods Litigation in the EU (1961–2020)' 639–649.

55 This may be referred to as the legislative priority rule, see Eadaoin Ní Chaoimh, *The Legislative Priority Rule and the EU Internal Market for Goods: A Constitutional Approach* (Oxford University Press 2022).

56 Barend van Leeuwen, 'Repositioning Free Movement of Services: A Substantive Perspective on the Structure and Dynamics of the Internal Market' (2025) 62 Common Market Law Review 705.

57 *Visnapuu*. 58 *Scotch Whisky*. 59 Case C-96/22, *CDIL*, EU:C:2023:1025.

60 Schebesta and Purnhagen, *EU Food Law* 102. See in that regard European Commission, 'Health taxes from an EU perspective' (2025) Final report.

61 The first health legal basis was Article 129 EC, now Article 168 TFEU.

1 November 1993, health concerns were not absent from the early days of European integration. The creation of a 'European Health Community' had been contemplated before the European Economic Community was even born in 1957, although that project would ultimately not come to life.[62] Yet, action on health in the pre-Maastricht period was conducted in an uncoordinated and patchy way, with most initiatives relating to the free movement of goods, services and economically active citizens: social security coordination, recognition of medical qualifications, safety of medicinal products.[63] Some measures potentially had an impact on lifestyles but did not represent a systematic and coherent attempt to promote healthier behaviours.[64]

Cancer was a notable exception to this state of affairs. Starting from the mid-1980s, the fight against the disease became a focal point of the EU's nascent public health policy. In 1986, the Council adopted the first resolution laying down a programme of action against cancer.[65] Despite its embryonic character, the Resolution already identified tobacco, alcohol and poor nutrition as key lifestyle risk factors to be addressed, with different degrees of priority. The focus is on tobacco, for which 'rules on advertising, rules on labelling, tax legislation, sponsorship, enforcement of no-smoking rules, extension of no-smoking areas' could be adopted, 'if appropriate', at the European level.[66] Nutrition and alcohol are only briefly mentioned, the Resolution stressing the necessity, as regards alcoholic beverages, to 'tak[e] account of differing circumstances and habits in the Member States'.[67] This would become, as we shall see, one of the EU's leitmotivs on alcohol. Three action plans on cancer were subsequently adopted, for the periods 1987 to 1989, 1990 to 1994 and

[62] See Alban Davesne and Sébastien Guigner, 'La Communauté Européenne de la Santé (1952-1954): Une Redécouverte Intergouvernementaliste du Projet Fonctionnaliste de « Pool Blanc »' (2013) 41 Politique Européenne 40.

[63] See Mary Guy and Wolf Sauter, 'The History and Scope of EU Health Law and Policy' in Tamara K Hervey, Calum Alasdair Young and Louise E Bishop (eds), *Research Handbook on EU Health Law and Policy* (Edward Elgar Publishing 2017) 23–29; Hervey and McHale, *European Union Health Law* 31–40. See also Tamara Hervey and Anniek De Ruijter, 'The Dynamic Potential of European Union Health Law' (2020) 11 European Journal of Risk Regulation 726, 723–724.

[64] Alemanno and Garde, 'The Emergence of an EU Lifestyle Policy' 1747.

[65] Council of the European Union, Resolution of the Council and the Representatives of the Governments of the Member States, meeting within the Council of 7 July 1986, on a programme of action of the European Communities against cancer (Resolution on a programme of action against cancer), OJ C184/19.

[66] ibid 20. [67] ibid.

1996 to 2000.[68] The first cancer plan resulted with the adoption of three instruments, on the labelling of tobacco products, the tar yield of cigarettes[69] and on tobacco advertising.[70]

It is only after Maastricht that a genuine EU health policy came of age, starting with the release in 1993 of the Commission Communication on the framework for action in the field of public health.[71] The Communication mentions the 'risks to health from one's chosen lifestyle' and observes the growing emphasis in the public health community on 'the responsibility of the individual for his/her own health and the modifications he can make to his/her own behaviour to prevent the onset of disease'.[72] Action on health determinants was also at the core of the EC Health Strategy of 2000, which addressed key lifestyle factors, 'such as smoking, alcohol, nutrition, physical activity, stress and drug abuse', with a focus on young people, 'since key decisions on lifestyle and health-related behaviour are taken in youth and adolescence'.[73] These priorities are reflected in the four consecutive programmes for Community and Union action in the field of public health adopted since 2003.[74] The fourth and current programme for Union action in the field

[68] European Commission, 'Europe against cancer' programme: Proposal for a plan of action 1987 to 1989, OJ C50/1; Decision 90/238/Euratom, ECSC, EEC of the Council and the Representatives of the Governments of the Member States meeting within the Council, on 17 May 1990 adopting a 1990 to 1994 action plan in the context of the "Europe against Cancer" programme, OJ L137/31; Decision No 646/96/EC of the European Parliament and of the Council of 29 March 1996 adopting an action plan to combat cancer within the framework for action in the field of public health (1996 to 2000), OJ L95/9.

[69] Council Directive 89/622/EEC of 13 November 1989 on the approximation of the laws, regulations and administrative provisions of the Member States concerning the labelling of tobacco products, OJ L359/1; Council Directive 90/239/EEC of 17 May 1990 on the approximation of the laws, regulations and administrative provisions of the Member States concerning the maximum tar yield of cigarettes, OJ L137/36.

[70] Council Directive 89/552/EEC of 3 October 1989 on the coordination of certain provisions laid down by Law, Regulation or Administrative Action in Member States concerning the pursuit of television broadcasting activities, OJ L298/23 (Television without Frontiers (TWF) Directive), art 13.

[71] European Commission, 'Commission Communication on the framework for action in the field of public health', COM (93) 559 final.

[72] ibid 6.

[73] European Commission, Communication from the Commission to the Council, the European Parliament, the Economic and Social Committee and the Committee of the Regions on the health strategy of the European Community, COM (2000) 285 final, 3.1.

[74] See Decision No 1786/2002/EC of the European Parliament and of the Council of 23 September 2002 adopting a programme of Community action in the field of public health (2003-2008), OJ L271/1, art 2(2)(c); Decision No 1350/2007/EC of the European

of health, or 'EU4Health Programme', spanning from 2021 to 2027, while being heavily influenced by the Covid-19 pandemic and its consequences, also shows the enduring importance of action on lifestyles.[75] The programme's first general objective remains to 'improv[e] and foster [. . .] health in the Union to reduce the burden of communicable and non-communicable diseases, by supporting health promotion and disease prevention, by reducing health inequalities, by fostering healthy lifestyles and by promoting access to healthcare'.[76] During this period, the Council also adopted two sets of conclusions on lifestyles, the 2003 Conclusions on 'healthy lifestyles: education, information and communication'[77] and the 2011 Conclusions on 'closing health gaps within the EU through concerted action to promote healthy lifestyle behaviours'.[78] In 2017, the three Commissioners for Health, Agriculture and Sports[79] signed the 'Tartu Call for a Healthy Lifestyle', a pledge of fifteen commitments aimed at boosting the adoption of healthy lifestyles by Europeans, with focus mostly on physical activity and dietary choices.[80] To support Member States in reaching their policy objectives, the Commission created a Steering Group on Health Promotion, Disease Prevention and Management of Non-Communicable Diseases in 2018.[81] The enduring importance of lifestyles in EU public health policy was symbolically reflected with the inclusion in Article 168 TFEU, after Lisbon, of a reference to tobacco and alcohol, the only explicit mention of these two risk factors appearing in the EU Treaties.

Parliament and of the Council of 23 October 2007 establishing a second programme of Community action in the field of health (2008-13), OJ L301/13, art 2(2); Regulation 282/2014, art 3(1).

[75] Regulation 2021/522. [76] ibid, art 3(a).

[77] Council of the European Union, Council Conclusions of 2 December 2003 on healthy lifestyles: education, information and communication, OJ C22/1.

[78] Council of the European Union, Council Conclusions on closing health gaps within the EU through concerted action to promote healthy lifestyle behaviours, OJ C359/5.

[79] Tibor Navracsics, Commissioner for Education, Culture, Youth and Sport; Vytenis Andriukaitis, Commissioner for Health and Food Safety; Phil Hogan, Commissioner for Agriculture and Rural Development.

[80] Available at <https://ec.europa.eu/sport/sites/sport/files/ewos-tartu-call_en.pdf> accessed 17 September 2025. The commitments consisted of incentive measures and not of concrete legislative action. For the evaluation of the action taken two years later, see <https://ec.europa.eu/commission/presscorner/detail/en/IP_19_3028> accessed 17 September 2025.

[81] Commission Decision of 17 July 2018 setting up a Commission expert group 'Steering Group on Health Promotion, Disease Prevention and Management of Non-Communicable Diseases', OJ C251/9.

For cancer, after a loss of momentum of over two decades, during which no specific programmes or action plans were adopted,[82] the release of the 2021 'Europe's Beating Cancer Plan' provided a new impetus for EU action in the field.[83] It is by far the EU's most ambitious cancer plan to date, reaffirming the importance of preventive action in view of the disease's growing burden in Europe. In relation to lifestyles, the plan sets the three following objectives: 'achieving a tobacco-free Europe', 'reducing harmful alcohol consumption' and 'improving health promotion through access to healthy diets and physical activity',[84] and puts forward a number of initiatives for each of these risk factors, which will be referred to in the following sections.[85] The importance of lifestyles in EU cancer prevention efforts is particularly apparent in the European Code Against Cancer, the '10 European commandments for cancer prevention',[86] a rule book containing simple and actionable recommendations for Europeans to limit their cancer risk. Twelve rules feature in the current fourth edition of the Code,[87] adopted in 2015, out of which the first six are lifestyle-related:

1. Do not smoke. Do not use any form of tobacco.
2. Make your home smoke free. Support smoke-free policies in your workplace.
3. Take action to be a healthy body weight.
4. Be physically active in everyday life. Limit the time you spend sitting.
5. Have a healthy diet:
    - Eat plenty of whole grains, pulses, vegetables and fruits.
    - Limit high-calorie foods (foods high in sugar or fat) and avoid sugary drinks.
    - Avoid processed meat; limit red meat and foods high in salt.

[82] See Louise Trubek, Mark Nance and Tamara Hervey, 'The Construction of Healthier Europe: Lessons from the Fight against Cancer' (2008) 26 Wisconsin International Law Journal 804. See, however: European Commission, Communication from the Commission to the European Parliament, the Council, the European Economic and Social Committee and the Committee of the Regions, 'Action Against Cancer: European Partnership', COM (2009) 291 final.

[83] European Commission, 'Europe's Beating Cancer Plan'.

[84] ibid 8–11.

[85] On the limited regulatory impact of the Plan to date, see Amandine Garde and others, 'Lobbying, Transparency and Trust: Power Imbalances and the Failure to Implement Europe's Beating Cancer Plan' (2025) 51 The Lancet Regional Health – Europe 101238.

[86] European Commission, 'Europe against cancer' programme: Proposal for a plan of action 1987 to 1989 32.

[87] The first three editions of the Code were published in 1987, 1994 and 2003.

6. If you drink alcohol of any type, limit your intake. Not drinking alcohol is better for cancer prevention.[88]

This Code is particularly interesting, on several grounds. An emphasis on individual choice and responsibility is apparent,[89] although the Code has evolved in this regard. It no longer invites Europeans to 'avoid becoming overweight',[90] seemingly suggesting that being overweight is simply a matter of choice. The different amendments made to the Code reveal the evolution of scientific knowledge since it was first published in 1987. While the first version only advised Europeans to 'moderate [their] consumption of alcoholic drinks',[91] the current version now clearly acknowledges that 'not drinking alcohol is better for cancer prevention'. The first version did not mention processed or red meat,[92] the consumption of which is now linked by a growing body of evidence to several types of cancer.[93] Most interestingly perhaps, the Cancer Code lays down some of the main orientations of EU lifestyle policy as regards specific risk factors, as will appear in the next sections and throughout the book. Tobacco should be avoided without any qualification, including in smokeless form. The alcohol statement is written in more careful terms, so as to raise 'awareness of the increased risk of cancer resulting from consumption of any amount of alcohol, consistent with current evidence, [while] not recommending total abstinence'.[94] Regarding nutrition, the words have also been carefully chosen. The terms 'avoid' and 'limit' were selected to reflect the fact that the authors of the Code did not expect the public to entirely cut out unhealthy foods, a suggestion

[88] Available at <https://cancer-code-europe.iarc.fr/index.php/en/> accessed 17 September 2025. For the methodology and evidence underpinning the current version of the code, see Joachim Schüz and others, 'European Code against Cancer 4th Edition: 12 Ways to Reduce Your Cancer Risk' (2015) 39 Cancer Epidemiology 1.

[89] A footnote to the Code does mention the following: 'The European Code Against Cancer focuses on actions that individual citizens can take to help prevent cancer. Successful cancer prevention requires these individual actions to be supported by governmental policies and actions'.

[90] European Commission, 'Europe against cancer' programme: Proposal for a plan of action 1987 to 1989 32.

[91] ibid. [92] ibid 32–33.

[93] Boada, Henríquez-Hernández and Luzardo, 'The Impact of Red and Processed Meat Consumption on Cancer and Other Health Outcomes: Epidemiological Evidences'; Abou Diallo and others, 'Red and Processed Meat Intake and Cancer Risk: Results from the Prospective NutriNet-Santé Cohort Study' (2018) 142 International Journal of Cancer 230.

[94] Schüz and others, 'European Code against Cancer 4th Edition: 12 Ways to Reduce Your Cancer Risk' 6.

that was seen as unrealistic.[95] Hence, although it is based on robust scientific evidence regarding cancer risk, the Code incorporates other aspects that reflect the relative value held by some unhealthy habits if compared to one another. Whereas cutting drastically alcohol consumption would bring far more benefits to Europeans and their societies than avoiding smokeless tobacco, it is probably more realistic to expect a total abstinence from niche tobacco products than it is for alcohol.

4.3.2 *Towards a Smoke-Free Europe*

Since the 1980s, the EU has taken resolute action to reduce smoking prevalence in its population and positioned itself as a leader in global tobacco control. Reflecting the evolution of tobacco's perception in the second half of the twentieth century, early EU action was actually 'almost completely concerned with promotion rather than control'.[96] Tobacco was included in the Common Agricultural Policy (CAP) and became among the most heavily EU-subsidised crop, this financial support greatly surpassed tobacco reduction efforts.[97] It is only with the first cancer programme that the EU's dealings with tobacco gained a distinctive public health turn. As we have seen tobacco was from the onset the main priority of EU cancer policy.[98] The first cancer action plan identified a wide range of policy options for EU level action: upward alignment of tobacco taxation, harmonisation of health warnings and product composition, rules restricting smoking in public places, etc.[99] In 1989 and 1990, the EU adopted its first tobacco legislations: a directive on tobacco labelling, which included provisions on health warnings, a directive limiting the tar yield of cigarettes[100] and, as part of the Television Without Frontiers (TWF) Directive,[101] the prohibition of television advertising for tobacco products. These texts helped improve tobacco

95 ibid.

96 Donley T Studlar, 'Tobacco Control: The End of Europe's Love Affair with Smoking?' in Scott L Greer and Paulette Kurzer (eds), *European Union Public Health Policy: Regional and Global Trends* (Routledge 2016) 186. See also Martin McKee, Tamara Hervey and Anna Gilmore, 'Public Health Policies' in Elias Mossialos and others (eds), *Health Systems Governance in Europe: The Role of EU Law and Policy* (Cambridge University Press 2010) 57.

97 Studlar, 'Tobacco Control: The End of Europe's Love Affair with Smoking?' 186. See also Hervey and McHale, *European Union Health Law* 390.

98 Council of the European Union, Resolution on a programme of action against cancer 20.

99 European Commission, 'Europe against cancer' programme: Proposal for a plan of action 1987 to 1989.

100 Council Directive 89/622 and Council Directive 90/239.

101 Television Without Frontiers Directive, art 13.

prevention in Europe, as some countries had not yet adopted any relevant legislation.[102] In 1996 and 1999, respectively, the Council adopted a resolution on the reduction of smoking and a set of conclusions urging the European Commission to adopt an overall strategy aimed at diminishing the prevalence of tobacco use in the European population.[103] Although no comprehensive EU strategy on tobacco would ever be devised by the Commission, contrary to what would be the case for nutrition and alcohol, the early 2000s saw the adoption of two important milestones for EU tobacco control: Directive 2001/37 on tobacco products (the 2001 TPD),[104] later revised and repealed, and the Tobacco Advertising Directive (TAD),[105] still in force today, which introduced a comprehensive advertising ban in cross-border audiovisual and printed media.

Over the same period, the EU negotiated and concluded the Framework Convention on Tobacco Control (FCTC).[106] The first and ever convention negotiated under the auspices of the WHO,[107] the FCTC reflects the international community's recognition of the harm resulting from tobacco and its commitment to curb its consumption. Due to the globalised nature of the tobacco epidemic, fuelled by a handful of powerful market players, the need was felt to have a common instrument in place that would help governments better coordinate their action and scale up their policies. An early actor in global tobacco control, the EU was a driving force in the negotiation and adoption of the FCTC.[108] Along with the EU, the twenty-seven Member States are also parties to it. The

102 McKee, Hervey and Gilmore, 'Public Health Policies' 257–258.

103 Council of the European Union, Council Resolution of 26 November 1996 on the reduction of smoking in the European Community, OJ C374/4; Council of the European Union, Council conclusions of 18 November 1999 on combating tobacco consumption, OJ C86/4.

104 Directive 2001/37/EC of the European Parliament and of the Council of 5 June 2001 on the approximation of the laws, regulations and administrative provisions of the Member States concerning the manufacture, presentation and sale of tobacco products, OJ L194/26.

105 Directive 2003/33.

106 Council Decision of 2 June 2004 concerning the conclusion of the WHO Framework Convention on Tobacco Control, OJ L213/8.

107 The World Health Assembly, the decision-making body of the WHO, can adopt three kinds of normative instruments: conventions, regulations, and recommendations. See Constitution of the World Health Organisation, Basic Documents: arts 19, 21 and 23.

108 Hadii M Mamudu and Donley T Studlar, 'Multilevel Governance and Shared Sovereignty: European Union, Member States, and the FCTC' (2009) 22 Governance: An International Journal of Policy, Administration, and Institutions 73; Miriam Faid and David Gleicher, 'Dancing the Tango: The Experience and Roles of the European

FCTC is governed by the Conference of the Parties, whose main tasks are to regularly review the implementation of the FCTC and to take the necessary decisions to facilitate such implementation.[109] The Conference can adopt protocols and guidelines on specific FCTC articles. One protocol, the Protocol to Eliminate Illicit Trade in Tobacco Products, and eight guidelines have so far been adopted. The FCTC's core obligations are organised between demand reduction measures and supply reduction measures. Demand reduction measures (Articles 6 to 14) cover price and fiscal measures, rules on the protection from exposure to tobacco smoke, regulation of the contents of tobacco products and their disclosures, rules on packaging and labelling, measures aiming at informing and educating the public and, finally, measures restricting tobacco advertising, promotion and sponsorship. Supply reduction measures (Articles 15 to 17) cover measures to fight illicit trade in tobacco products and to prevent sales to and by minors.[110] The FCTC is widely seen as a success and a model for international cooperation in other fields of health.[111]

The Tobacco Products Directive, adopted in 2014 as a revision of the former 2001 instrument, is the EU's main effort to implement the key demand and supply reduction measures contained in the FCTC.[112] Wide

Union in Relation to the Framework Convention on Tobacco Control' (2011) Global Health Europe.

[109] For further details on the development and functioning of the FCTC, see Suzanne Zhou and Jonathan Liberman, 'The Global Tobacco Epidemic and the WHO Framework Convention on Tobacco Control – the Contributions of the WHO's First Convention to Global Health Law and Governance' in Gian Luca Burci and Brigit CA Toebes (eds), *Research Handbook on Global Health Law* (Edward Elgar Publishing 2018).

[110] In Case C-452/20 *Agenzia delle dogane e dei monopoli and Ministero dell'Economia e delle Finanze*, EU:C:2022:111, the Court of Justice ruled that, in implementing Article 16 of the FCTC on the prohibition of sales to minors, Italy complied with the principle of proportionality. The Italian rule provided, in the case of a first infringement of the prohibition on selling tobacco products to minors, in addition to the imposition of an administrative fine, for the suspension, for a period of fifteen days, of the trading licence authorising the economic operator who has infringed that prohibition to sell such products.

[111] Zhou and Liberman, 'The Global Tobacco Epidemic and the WHO Framework Convention on Tobacco Control – the Contributions of the WHO's First Convention to Global Health Law and Governance'; Janet Chung-Hall and others, 'Impact of the WHO FCTC over the First Decade: A Global Evidence Review Prepared for the Impact Assessment Expert Group' (2019) 28 Tobacco Control 119; Gian Luca Burci, 'A Global Legal Instrument for Alcohol Control: Options, Prospects and Challenges' (2021) 12 European Journal of Risk Regulation 499, 503–504.

[112] Tobacco Products Directive, art 1. See also recitals 7, 15, 24 and 29.

in coverage – it includes tobacco products for smoking,[113] smokeless tobacco products[114] and non-tobacco related products,[115] such as e-cigarettes – the TPD introduced some of the key elements of the EU's current tobacco control framework: large and mandatory textual and pictorial health warnings, ban on characterising flavours in tobacco products, rules on e-cigarettes and traceability system to fight illicit trade.[116] It is the main piece of EU tobacco legislation currently in force.

Although ambitious on substance, the TPD legislative process illustrated the difficulty for the EU to prevent policy interference from the tobacco industry. The TPD is considered to have been 'the most lobbied dossier in the history of the EU institutions'.[117] The industry deployed a massive lobbying effort, securing access to the highest echelon of EU decision-making. This culminated with the resignation of the Health Commissioner John Dalli in 2012 following allegations of bribe solicitation from the tobacco manufacturer Swedish Match.[118] It is considered that tobacco industry tactics managed to delay the TPD adoption process by several years and led to have some measures removed from the final legislative proposal.[119] The EU's permeability to tobacco corporate interests has been an enduring problem, putting the Union in breach of its obligations under Article 5(3) of the FCTC. This provision requires that tobacco control policies are protected from 'commercial and other vested interests of the tobacco industry', on grounds of a 'fundamental and irreconcilable conflict between the tobacco industry's interests and

113 Tobacco products are defined under the TPD as 'products that can be consumed and consist, even partly, of tobacco, whether genetically modified or not': art 2(4). Tobacco is further defined as 'leaves and other natural processed or unprocessed parts of tobacco plants, including expanded and reconstituted tobacco': art 2(1).

114 Under the TPD, STPs are tobacco products that do not involve a combustion process: art 2(5).

115 These are herbal products for smoking and electronic cigarettes and their refill containers. Other products related to tobacco but that do not contain tobacco, such as nicotine pouches, are not currently regulated under the TPD.

116 See European Commission, '10 key changes for tobacco products sold in the EU' (2016), <https://ec.europa.eu/commission/presscorner/detail/en/IP_16_1762> accessed 17 September 2025.

117 Silvy Peeters and others, 'The Revision of the 2014 European Tobacco Products Directive: An Analysis of the Tobacco Industry's Attempts to "Break the Health Silo"' (2016) 25 Tobacco Control 108. See also Florence Berteletti and others, 'Campaign for a Revised Tobacco Products Directive in the European Union: Lessons Learnt' (2017) 26 Tobacco Control 464.

118 ibid.

119 Peeters and others, 'The Revision of the 2014 European Tobacco Products Directive' 109.

public health policy interests'.[120] In a decision rendered in 2016, the European Ombudsman concluded that the Commission's refusal to publish online details of all the meetings held with the tobacco industry constituted maladministration.[121] These findings were repeated in 2023, after the Ombudsman conducted another probe into the European Commission's interactions with tobacco interest representatives.[122] The Ombudsman observed in particular that the lack of proper record keeping made it difficult to assess whether the European Commission only interacted with the tobacco industry to the extent strictly necessary to regulatory endeavours, as per the FCTC guidelines on Article 5(3).[123] More generally, a 2018 study showed a relative lack of awareness on the part of Commission officials and Members of the European Parliament (MEPs) as to the importance of keeping the political process free from tobacco industry interference and as to the various techniques used by the industry in this regard, due in part to the lack of a specific code of conduct.[124]

Improvement on that front will prove all the more important as the EU is set to strengthen its tobacco control effort in the coming years.[125] In the 2021 Beating Cancer Plan, the Commission spelled out for the first time its ultimate policy objective of creating a 'tobacco-free generation', with less than 5 per cent of the European population using tobacco by 2040.[126] In that context, the Commission will make new proposals in all areas currently regulated under EU law: product regulation, taxation, commercial communications and smoke-free environments. The

120 Conference of the Parties to the FCTC, 'Guidelines for implementation of Article 5.3 of the WHO Framework Convention on Tobacco Control on the protection of public health policies with respect to tobacco control from commercial and other vested interests of the tobacco industry' (2008) Decision FCTC/COP3(7), Principle 1.

121 European Ombudsman, 'Decision concerning the European Commission's compliance with the Tobacco Control Convention' (2016) Case 852/2014/LP. Regarding the European Ombudsman and its role, see Article 228 TFEU.

122 European Ombudsman, 'Preliminary findings in the OI/6/2021/KR on the European Commission's interactions with tobacco interest representatives' (2023).

123 ibid, p 3.

124 Benjamin Hawkins and Chris Holden, 'European Union Implementation of Article 5.3 of the Framework Convention on Tobacco Control' (2018) 14 Globalization and Health 79.

125 As regards current developments in EU tobacco policy and Article 5(3) of the FCTC, see the recent speech by the European Ombudsman: European Ombudsman, 'Importance of FCTC Article 5.3 in the EU context' (2021), <www.ombudsman.europa.eu/en/speech/en/139671> accessed 19 July 2025.

126 European Commission, 'Europe's Beating Cancer Plan' 8.

'tobacco-free' objective of 5 per cent prevalence is the one usually retained for a tobacco endgame.[127] Whether that objective is realistic under current circumstances is an open question. Tobacco prevalence remains high in the EU, at about 20 per cent, and no EU country is considered today as 'endgame ready', meaning a prevalence situated below 15 per cent.[128] Further, none of the measures usually put forward in the context of the endgame seem to be considered by the European Commission, whether it is a regulation of the nicotine contained in cigarettes or treating tobacco like an illicit drug by adopting a lifetime ban on the sales of tobacco products for people born after a certain date.[129] In that regard, on 24 August 2022, the Commission officially registered a European citizen's initiative titled 'Call to achieve a tobacco-free environment and the first European tobacco-free generation by 2030', whose first objective was to 'promote the first tobacco-free European generation by 2028, ending the sale of tobacco and nicotine products to citizens born since 2010'.[130] That initiative was withdrawn at the end of 2023. The Beating Cancer Plan also confirms the EU's strict approach towards alternatives to tobacco products, such as e-cigarettes, STPs and HTPs, and its rejection of any harm reduction strategy at the level of the general population.[131] Whether a drastic reduction of smoking prevalence can be achieved without recourse to these tobacco alternatives, or even a form of promotion thereof, remains an open question which will undoubtedly be central in the coming years.[132]

4.3.3 *Promoting Healthier Diets and Preventing Obesity*

Food was an early focus of EU integration. While the primary objective was and remains to give Europeans access to a diversified and stable food

[127] Hanna Ollila and others, 'Tobacco Endgame Goals and Measures in Europe: Current Status and Future Directions' (2024) 34 Tobacco Control e1.

[128] Sahaana Tamil Selvan, Xue Xin Yeo and Yvette van der Eijk, 'Which Countries Are Ready for a Tobacco Endgame? A Scoping Review and Cluster Analysis' (2024) 12 The Lancet Global Health e1049.

[129] ibid.

[130] Commission Implementing Decision (EU) 2022/1430 of 24 August 2022 on the request for registration of the European citizens' initiative titled 'Call to achieve a tobacco-free environment and the first European tobacco-free generation by 2030', pursuant to Regulation (EU) 2019/788 of the European Parliament and of the Council, OJ L221/103, recital 2.

[131] European Commission, 'Europe's Beating Cancer Plan' 9.

[132] See Amy L Fairchild, Ronald Bayer and James Colgrove, 'The Renormalization of Smoking? E-Cigarettes and the Tobacco "Endgame"' (2014) 370 The New England Journal of Medicine 293; Malone, 'The Race to a Tobacco Endgame'.

supply, through CAP and the establishment of the internal market, health and nutrition concerns have been progressively integrated to EU action in the field. The CAP, launched in 1962, pursued a nutrition objective from the onset, although framed in terms of food security rather than food quality, in a post-war context where shortages had not been completely eliminated. As explained above, early legislation from the 1970s and 1980s was primarily concerned with the free movement of foodstuffs. In the 1990s, health and safety concern raised to the top of the agenda with the Bovine spongiform encephalopathy (BSE), or 'mad cow disease', crisis,[133] which resulted in the slaughter of millions of cattle and the deaths of dozens of people. The crisis ultimately led to the creation of the European Food Safety Authority (EFSA).[134] The nutritional quality of diets and the related chronic diseases were for a long time no more than a secondary priority for the EU, often mixed with food safety issues.[135] It is not before the 2000s that nutrition started to be dealt with in its own right, with obesity as the main focus.[136]

The first push for a stronger EU engagement in such matters originated from the Member States, under the influence of international NGOs and organisations such as the WHO.[137] In a first resolution adopted in 1990, the Council acknowledged that 'the Community ha[d] dealt on various occasions with nutritional problems and related measures in sectoral contexts, [...] *but ha[d] not given overall consideration to aspects of nutritional education and consumer information taken as a whole* with the aim of promoting eating habits in keeping with individual needs'.[138] It invited the Commission to submit a proposal for an action programme on nutrition and health and proposed to declare the year 1994 the

[133] The BSE is a neurodegenerative disorder affecting cattle that can be transmitted to humans, leading to death on average after one year. For an overview of the crisis, see MacMaoláin, *Food Law* 124–132.

[134] See the General Food Law Regulation.

[135] MacMaoláin, *EU Food Law* 221–222.

[136] Tim Lang and Geof Rayner, 'Obesity: A Growing Issue for European Policy?' (2005) 15 Journal of European Social Policy 301; Paulette Kurzer and Alice Cooper, 'Hold the Croissant! The European Union Declares War on Obesity' (2011) 21 Journal of European Social Policy 107; Paulette Kurzer, 'Non-communicable diseases: The EU declares war on "fat"', in Scott L Greer and Paulette Kurzer (eds), *European Union Public Health Policy: Regional and Global Trends* (Routledge 2016) 155–167.

[137] Kurzer and Cooper, 'Hold the Croissant! The European Union Declares War on Obesity'; Kurzer, 'Non-communicable diseases 157.

[138] Council of the European Union, Resolution of the Council and of the Representatives of the Governments of the Member States, meeting within the Council of 3 December 1990 concerning an action programme on nutrition and health, OJ C329/1, 1, emphasis added.

'European Nutrition Year'.[139] This call for action was repeated by the Council on multiple occasions, singling out obesity as the main cause for concern.[140] In 2003, the Commission put forward its proposal for a Regulation on nutrition and health claims made on foods (Claims Regulation),[141] adopted in 2006, arguably the first piece of EU legislation putting food quality at its core. It also established a number of forums aimed at facilitating exchange and cooperation between stakeholders: the Network on Nutrition and Physical Activity in 2003,[142] the European Platform for Action on Diet, Physical Activity and Health in 2005 (see Section 5.4.2) and the High Level Group on Nutrition and Physical Activity in 2007.[143]

The first building brick of a coherent nutrition policy came with the publication in 2005 of the Commission Green Paper on healthy diets and physical activity,[144] followed two years later by the adoption of the White Paper 'A Strategy for Europe on Nutrition, Overweight and Obesity related health issues' (the EU Nutrition Strategy).[145] This White Paper remains the only comprehensive strategy document on nutrition and health adopted by the EU. Although the focus is mostly on obesity,

[139] Council of the European Union, Resolution concerning an action programme on nutrition and health, 2–3.

[140] Council of the European Union, Council Resolution of 14 December 2000 on health and nutrition, OJ C20/1; Council of the European Union, Council Conclusions of 2 December 2002 on obesity, OJ C11/3; Council of the European Union, Council Conclusions on obesity, nutrition and physical activity (2005).

[141] European Commission, Proposal for a Regulation of the European Parliament and of the Council on nutrition and health claims made on foods (Claims Regulation Proposal) COM (2003) 424.

[142] The Network on Nutrition and Physical Activity gathered representatives of the Commission, the WHO, Member States and civil society organisation. See the mandate adopted on 15 September 2003, <http://ec.europa.eu/health/ph_determinants/life_style/nutrition/documents/ev_20030630_rd02_en.pdf> accessed 17 September 2025.

[143] Led by the Commission and gathering representative from EU Member States and EFTA States, this group is a network devoted to the sharing of evidence, data and best practice, working in cooperation with the EU Platform.

[144] European Commission, 'Promoting healthy diets and physical activity: a European dimension for the prevention of overweight, obesity and chronic diseases' Green Paper COM (2005) 637 final.

[145] European Commission, EU Nutrition Strategy. See the reaction of the Council and the European Parliament to this strategy: Council of the European Union, Council Conclusions on Putting an EU strategy on Nutrition, Overweight and Obesity related Health Issues into operation, 15612/07; European Parliament, European Parliament Resolution of 25 September 2008 on the White Paper on nutrition, overweight and obesity-related health issues, OJ C8/97.

the Strategy targets all risks associated with poor diet and limited physical activity.[146] According to the Commission,

> Any public action, including those possibly undertaken at [Union] level, in this field should take into account three factors. Firstly, *the individual is ultimately responsible for his lifestyle*, and that of his children, *while recognising the importance and the influence of the environment on his behaviour*. Secondly, *only a well-informed consumer is able to make rational decisions*. Finally, an optimal response in this field will be achieved by promoting both the complementarity and integration of the different relevant policy areas (horizontal approach), and of the different levels of action (vertical approach).[147]

The perspective adopted here is heavily influenced by the Court of Justice's early free movement of goods case law, where the consumer is depicted as a rational and diligent agent able to make the right food choices on the basis of the information received (see Section 6.2.3). Food information and labelling are therefore given a key role in the Strategy. Among the options put forward by the Commission were the introduction of a mandatory nutrition declaration on foodstuffs, which would be effective with the adoption of Regulation 1169/2011 (Food Information Regulation), and the adoption of rules on harmful food advertising and other promotional practices.[148] The EU Nutrition Strategy makes children a priority target, in reaction to the steep rise in obesity witnessed in this segment of the population and because 'childhood is an important period to instil a preference for healthy behaviours'.[149] This orientation was deepened with the adoption in 2014 of the EU Action Plan on Childhood Obesity,[150] and in 2021 of the EU Strategy on the Rights of the Child.[151]

Nutrition remains a public health priority for the Commission, which increasingly tries to address the issue in conjunction with the environmental impacts of food consumption. The Commission's Farm to Fork Strategy 'for a fair, healthy and environmentally-friendly food system', published in 2020, observes in that regard that 'current food

[146] European Commission, EU Nutrition Strategy 3. [147] ibid. [148] ibid 5–6.
[149] ibid 8.
[150] European Commission, 'EU Action Plan on Childhood Obesity 2014-2020' (2014). See also Council of the European Union, Council Conclusions to contribute towards halting the rise in Childhood Overweight and Obesity, OJ C205/46; Council of the European Union, Council Conclusions on the promotion of motor skills, physical and sport activities for children, OJ C417/51; Council of the European Union, Council Conclusions - Healthy Nutrition for Children: The Healthy Future of Europe, OJ C232/1.
[151] European Commission, Communication from the Commission to the Council, the European Parliament, the European Economic and Social Committee and the Committee of the Regions, 'EU strategy on the rights of the child' COM (2021) 142 final.

consumption patterns are *unsustainable from both health and environmental points of view*', due in particular to excessive 'average intakes of energy, red meat, sugars, salt and fats' and insufficient 'consumption of wholegrain cereals, fruit and vegetables, legumes and nuts'.[152] According to the Commission, 'moving to a more plant-based diet with less red and processed meat and with more fruits and vegetables will reduce not only risks of life-threatening diseases, but also the environmental impact of the food system'.[153] Neither the Farm to Fork Strategy, however, nor the Beating Cancer Plan, deviates from the approach taken until now to favour information-based interventions or interventions that limit, weakly, as we shall see, the possibility for companies to promote unhealthy foodstuffs.[154] Save for minor exceptions, food business operators face few constraints as to the kind of food that can be placed on the market and advertised for. The conclusions drawn in the EU Nutrition Strategy evaluation report, conducted in 2013, still hold true today:

> [I]t is worth highlighting that most of the action taken in Europe to date (both at the EU and at the national levels) has been of a relatively *soft nature*, and has relied primarily (although the extent varies by country) *on information provision and education*, limited interventions in specific environments (such as schools), and voluntary actions by the food industry and other private actors, so as to generate an impact via a series of relatively subtle changes.[155]

As argued by the Group of Chief Scientific Advisors to the European Commission, a transformational policy mix should combine softer measures aimed at influencing and reshaping social norms – interventions that aim to improve consumers' knowledge, skills and awareness – with stronger measures impacting directly the food environment – including taxes, bans, mandatory product reformulations and other measures that do not require high agency at consumer level.[156]

[152] European Commission, 'A Farm to Fork Strategy for a fair, healthy and environmentally-friendly food system' 13, emphasis added.

[153] ibid. [154] ibid. See also European Commission, 'Europe's Beating Cancer Plan' 10.

[155] European Commission, 'Evaluation of the implementation of the Strategy for Europe on Nutrition, Overweight and Obesity related health issues' (2013) Final Report, 162, emphasis added. See also European Commission, 'Supporting the mid-term evaluation of the EU Action Plan on Childhood Obesity 2014-2020: The Childhood Obesity Study' (2018) 7–9, <https://op.europa.eu/en/publication-detail/-/publication/7e0320dc-ee18-11e8-b690–01aa75ed71a1> accessed 17 September 2025.

[156] European Commission, Group of Chief Scientific Advisors, 'Towards Sustainable Food Consumption: Promoting Healthy, Affordable and Sustainable Food Consumption Choices' (2023) 7, emphasis added.

4.3.4 *Reducing the Harmful Consumption of Alcohol*

It is important to clarify that alcoholic beverages fall within the definition of 'food' under EU law. Under the General Food Law Regulation, a 'food' is 'any substance or product, whether processed, partially processed or unprocessed, intended to be, or reasonably expected to be ingested by humans',[157] regardless of its liquid form or its alcohol content. In the common language, however, alcoholic beverages are usually not referred to as foods, which can be a source of confusion. The book follows both approaches. Depending on the context, it uses the term 'food' to refer to all foods or to refer to non-alcoholic products specifically. The terms 'alcohol' or 'alcoholic' apply to beverages that contain alcohol.

From being treated as any other commodity, subject to free movement rules and food legislation, and, for agricultural products like wine, to the CAP framework, alcoholic beverages have slowly emerged as an area of concern for EU health policy.[158] In the mid-1980s, the EU took first steps to address the health aspects of alcohol consumption, in the framework of its newly developed cancer policy. The Resolution of the Council and Member States on alcohol abuse,[159] adopted shortly before the 1986 Action programme against cancer, recognised that 'in many countries the increase in alcohol abuse [...] is causing serious concern for public health and social welfare'.[160] Yet, while acknowledging the problem, it invited the Commission 'to *weigh carefully* the interests involved in the production, distribution and promotion of alcoholic beverages, and public health interests and to conduct a *balanced* policy to this end'.[161] As we shall see, this cautious approach set the tone for the development of EU alcohol policy in the following decades. Although the first action plan against cancer recognised that alcohol consumption was the second most important cancer risk factor in Europe after tobacco, it contained virtually no proposal on the matter.[162] Throughout the 1990s, alcohol

[157] General Food Law Regulation, art 2

[158] For a more detailed account of the early period, see Jenny Cisneros Örnberg, 'Alcohol Policy in the European Union' in Scott L Greer and Paulette Kurzer (eds), *European Union Public Health Policy: Regional and Global Trends* (Routledge 2016) 168–180.

[159] Council of the European Union, Resolution on a programme of action against cancer.

[160] Council of the European Union, Resolution of the Council and of the Representatives of the Governments of the Member States, meeting within the Council, of 29 May 1986, on alcohol abuse, OJ C184/3.

[161] ibid, emphasis added.

[162] European Commission, 'Europe against cancer' programme: Proposal for a plan of action 1987 to 1989 15–18.

remained absent from the EU's early public health efforts. The accession of Finland and Sweden to the EU in 1995 brought changes to this state of play. The two countries, acting as 'policy entrepreneurs' through their Council presidencies, in 1999 and 2000 respectively, sought to put alcohol back on the agenda.[163] This resulted in the adoption in 2001 of the Council Recommendation on the drinking of alcohol by young people,[164] adopted by unanimity and subsequently endorsed by the European Parliament,[165] and, the same year, of the Council Conclusions on a Community strategy to reduce alcohol-related harm.[166] The latter invited the Commission to adopt a comprehensive strategy on alcohol.

This was taken up by the Commission in 2006 with the publication of the EU Alcohol Strategy. The overall approach, which is worth reproducing in full, is laid down as follows:

> [The Strategy] focuses on preventing and cutting back *heavy and extreme* drinking patterns, as well as under-age drinking, and some of their *most harmful* consequences such as alcohol-related road accidents and Foetal Alcohol Syndrome. *The Communication therefore is not a reflection on alcohol use as such, but on misuse and its harmful consequences*. The Communication recognises that there are *different cultural habits* related to alcohol consumption in the various Member States. *There is no intention to substitute Community action to national policies*, which have already been put in place in most of the Member States and relate to national competences in accordance with the *principle of subsidiarity* and Article 152 of the EC Treaty. In particular, the Commission *does not intend as a consequence of this Communication to propose the development of harmonised legislation* in the field of the prevention of alcohol-related harm.[167]

With this Strategy, it is not alcohol consumption per se which is targeted but only 'heavy' and 'extreme' patterns. The objectives of EU alcohol

[163] Trygve Ugland, 'Promoting Policy Consistency and Continuity in the EU through the Trio: Alcohol-Related Harm on the Council Presidency Agenda' (2019) 29 Journal of European Social Policy 515, 520–522. See also Jenny Cisneros Örnberg, 'The Europeanization of Swedish Alcohol Policy: The Case of ECAS' (2008) 18 Journal of European Social Policy 380.

[164] Council Recommendation of 5 June 2001 on the drinking of alcohol by young people, in particular children and adolescents, OJ L161/38.

[165] Jenny Cisneros Örnberg, 'Escaping Deadlock – Alcohol Policy-Making in the EU' (2009) 16 Journal of European Public Policy 755, 760.

[166] Council of the European Union, Council Conclusions of 5 June 2001 on a Community strategy to reduce alcohol-related harm, OJ C175/1.

[167] European Commission, Communication from the Commission to the Council, the European Parliament, the European Economic and Social Committee and the Committee of the Regions, 'An EU strategy to support Member States in reducing alcohol related harm' (EU Alcohol Strategy), COM (2006) 625 final, 1, emphasis added.

policy thus appear plainly different from that followed for tobacco, although, as previously explained (see Section 2.4), 'moderate' alcohol consumption is no less hazardous than 'moderate' tobacco consumption. The 'different cultural habits' existing between Member States are mentioned several times through the text, the Commission insisting on the variations in 'drinking patterns and cultures [existing] across the EU',[168] as well as the particular context on which 'measures adopted by Member States to reduce alcohol-related harm with a view to protecting public health are based'.[169] Although the reference made to subsidiarity in this context lacks clarity, we will come back to this in Chapter 8, it is undeniable that types and patterns of alcohol consumption differ widely between Member States, which could warrant a supporting role for the EU. The same thing could however be said of dietary habits and, to a lesser extent, of tobacco consumption. Yet, no references to cultural diversity and subsidiarity are made in the EU Nutrition Strategy or any tobacco-related document. The EU Alcohol Strategy is essentially a mapping of good practices implemented at national level in a number of priority areas.[170] EU harmonisation is only mentioned with regards to consumer information.[171]

The Strategy was received with disappointment within the public health community.[172] The predominant feeling was that 'the European Commission ha[d] correctly diagnosed the alcoholic disease ravaging Europe and announced its determination to keep the patient under close observation from now on, but perversely insist[ed] that no treatment [was] called for at this time'.[173] According to some, the EU's lack of ambition resulted in part from the heavy opposition of the alcohol industry towards stronger regulatory action.[174] The Strategy expired in 2012, prompting the European Parliament and the Council to call for the

[168] ibid 4. [169] ibid 13.

[170] There are five of them: (i) protecting young people, children and the unborn child; (ii) reducing injuries and deaths from alcohol-related road traffic accidents; (iii) preventing alcohol-related harm among adults and reducing the negative impact on the workplace; (iv) informing, educating and raising awareness on the impact of harmful and hazardous alcohol consumption and on appropriate consumption patterns; and (v) developing, supporting and maintaining a common evidence base.

[171] European Commission, EU Alcohol Strategy 13.

[172] See Jonathan Gornall, 'Europe under the Influence' (2014) 348 British Medical Journal 1166.

[173] Ben Baumberg and Peter Anderson, 'The European Strategy on Alcohol: A Landmark and a Lesson' (2007) 42 Alcohol and Alcoholism 1.

[174] ibid; Gornall, 'Europe under the Influence'.

adoption of a new strategy covering the years 2016–2022.[175] Both institutions did not intend to depart from the general orientation of EU alcohol policy, continuing to stress the need to respect national policy and the important cultural aspect of alcohol, and focusing on excessive drinking rather than drinking in general.[176] The European Parliament stressed in particular that 'a clear distinction between responsible and harmful alcohol consumption [was] needed [because] *responsible alcohol consumption is compatible with a healthy way of living*',[177] oblivious to the fact that alcohol can never be 'healthy'. Intensive lobbying efforts have been reported, to ensure that no new strategy entailing a stronger response on alcohol-related harm would be put on the table.[178] Since then, EU alcohol policy has come 'close to deadlock'.[179] The Beating Cancer Plan may represent a new impetus, although the objective laid down as regards alcohol is modest if compared to the 'smoke-free' approach adopted for tobacco, with a goal of a relative reduction of at least 10 per cent in the harmful use of alcohol by 2025, compared to 2021.[180] For that purpose, the Commission announced that it would work on new proposals in the area of taxation, commercial communications and labelling.[181] Regarding labelling, the policy priority should be to bring the regime applicable to alcoholic beverages closer to the one applicable to food in general, with the inclusion of information on ingredients, energy and nutrients (see Section 5.5).

The near absence of binding alcohol control legislation adopted at the EU level, as will appear more clearly from Chapter 5, may be regretted. The contrast is particularly strong with tobacco and related products, which are not only subject to far more restrictive rules but also governed by two specific legislative instruments, the Tobacco Products Directive

[175] European Parliament, European Parliament Resolution of 29 April 2015 on Alcohol Strategy, OJ C346/32; Council of the European Union, Council Conclusions on an EU strategy on the reduction of alcohol-related harm, OJ C418/6; Council of the European Union, Council Conclusions on cross-border aspects in alcohol policy – tackling the harmful use of alcohol, OJ C441/3. See also Council of the European Union, Council Conclusions of 1 December 2009 on alcohol and health, OJ C302/15.

[176] See European Parliament Resolution of 29 April 2015 on Alcohol Strategy. See also European Parliament, European Parliament Resolution of 5 September 2007 on a European Union strategy to support Member States in reducing alcohol-related harm, OJ C187/160.

[177] European Parliament Resolution of 29 April 2015 on Alcohol Strategy 34.

[178] Gornall, 'Europe under the Influence'.

[179] Pieter de Coninck and Ian Gilmore, 'Long Overdue: A Fresh Start for EU Policy on Alcohol and Health' (2020) 395 The Lancet 10.

[180] European Commission, 'Europe's Beating Cancer Plan' 9.

[181] ibid 9–10.

and the Tobacco Advertising Directive. No such piece of legislation exists for alcoholic beverages, for which rules are scattered across different instruments. This lack of ambition leaves regulatory space for those of the Member States that wish to act, as illustrated by the recent Irish decision to introduce new health warning labels on alcoholic beverages in 2022, after the European Commission raised no objection to its draft regulation.[182] Yet, what appears most questionable with the EU approach is not this regulatory restraint – these are, after all, political choices for which the Member States are also responsible – but the reliance on fallacies to justify this restraint. A first serious problem is the use of vague terms such as 'appropriate', 'reasonable' and 'responsible' consumption, on the one hand, and 'harmful', 'excessive' or 'heavy' drinking, on the other. These terms lack any proper scientific basis. The entire EU alcohol policy is based on concepts which are never defined and perpetuate the idea that alcohol is safe under a certain threshold of consumption and that only a minority of users will be exposed to harm during their lifetime. A second problem is the heavy emphasis laid on the diversity of habits and preferences as a justification for the lack of action. No one denies that alcohol presents an important cultural aspect, but the same can be said of other lifestyle risk factors too. This lack of engagement with alcohol-related harm is not specific to the EU.[183] Global action in this field remains limited.[184] Unlike for tobacco and illicit drugs, no international convention on alcohol has been adopted, although the burden of alcohol worldwide, in terms of deaths and disabilities, far exceeds the one attributable to illicit drugs and is comparable to the one of tobacco. Conceptualising alcohol as a global challenge is not only warranted because countries experience similar alcohol-related problems and harm, but because of the global nature of the alcohol industry and its products, in terms of market concentration, trade and cross-border marketing.[185] A number of voices

[182] The text of the notification can be retrieved at <https://ec.europa.eu/growth/tools-databases/tris/en/search/?trisaction=search.detail&year=2022&num=441>. The notification was made pursuant to Directive (EU) 2015/1535 and the Food Information Regulation.

[183] See Jan van Amsterdam and Wim van den Brink, 'The High Harm Score of Alcohol. Time for Drug Policy to Be Revisited?' (2013) 27 Journal of Psychopharmacology 248.

[184] See Sally Casswell, 'Will Alcohol Harm Get the Global Response It Deserves?' (2019) 394 The Lancet 1396; Paula O'Brien, 'Public Health and the Global Governance of Alcohol' (2021) 12 European Journal of Risk Regulation 415; Room, 'Global Intergovernmental Initiatives to Minimise Alcohol Problems'.

[185] O'Brien, 'Public Health and the Global Governance of Alcohol' 416.

have therefore called for the adoption of a comprehensive international legal instrument similar to the FCTC, a Framework Convention on Alcohol Control.[186]

4.4 Conclusion

Since the middle of the 1980s, altering peoples' lifestyles to reduce the associated health risks has remained a cornerstone of EU health policy, both to combat the harmful consequences falling on individuals and society and to help reducing the financial burden on health systems. Consistent reference is made to tobacco, diets and alcohol in the various programmes, strategies or action plans on health that have been devised in the last forty years. A large body of rules has been adopted that prescribe the conditions under which unhealthy products may be marketed in the EU. Why do lifestyles feature so prominently in EU public health policy? The reason may be twofold. From a political perspective, there are reasons to tackle the burden of chronic non-communicable diseases and their causes, which now constitute the main cause of mortality and morbidity in the EU. From a legal perspective, the exercise of EU *regulatory* power, 'influencing people by establishing rules on how they should live', compensates for the lack of EU *spending* power, 'influencing people through resources and the distribution of money', which is so crucial as regards health and the welfare state.[187] This is an area where the EU can easily act, thanks to its broad internal market harmonisation powers, and where action may appear, precisely because of this internal market aspect, less objectionable.

The EU lays emphasis on individual choices and one's responsibility to adopt a healthier lifestyle, an approach which must be questioned, considering the complexity of the root causes of unhealthy behaviours

[186] The Lancet, 'A Framework Convention on Alcohol Control' (2007) 370 The Lancet 1102. For recent discussions on what an international convention would bring and how it would go about in reality, see Robin Room and Jenny Cisneros Örnberg, 'A Framework Convention on Alcohol Control: Getting Concrete about Its Contents' (2021) 12 European Journal of Risk Regulation 433; Burci, 'A Global Legal Instrument for Alcohol Control'; Suzanne Zhou, 'What Difference Would a Binding International Legal Instrument on Alcohol Control Make? Lessons from the World Health Organization Framework Convention on Tobacco Control's Impact on Domestic Litigation' (2021) 12 European Journal of Risk Regulation 514.

[187] Mark Dawson and Floris de Witte, *EU Law and Governance* (Cambridge University Press 2022) 73. See also Greer, 'Health, Federalism and the European Union: Lessons from Comparative Federalism about the European Union'.

and their largely collective aspect. This approach corresponded, for a time, with the adoption of measures aiming primarily at informing consumers of the characteristic of products and the risks incurred with their consumption. This has nonetheless not prevented the EU from enacting rules which go beyond the simple dissemination of information, as will be shown in Chapter 5. Although the different lifestyle risk factors are considered jointly at the policy level, this does not result in them being subject to the same regulatory regime. On the one hand, the EU embraces the 'endgame' approach, under which tobacco products, for smoking especially, need to be phased out entirely. This ideal of a 'smoke-free' world reflects the view that the risks entailed by the consumption of those products outweigh possible benefits, bringing an overall negative contribution to human lives and society. For alcohol, on the other hand, in spite of harm levels comparable to that of tobacco, the EU has taken a much more hands-off approach. For foods and alcohol, the idea is to promote 'responsible' consumption, that is, limited intake in the framework of a balanced diet. This difference in treatment, as should be clear by now, cannot be explained by purely 'risk' concerns. It has to do with economic considerations, as well as cultural and ethical factors, further explored in Chapter 8.

5 The EU's Lifestyle Toolbox

5.1 Introduction

Considering the variety of factors influencing unhealthy lifestyles, effective prevention strategies require a multisectoral approach, involving not only public health *stricto sensu* but sectors such as education, agriculture, sports, transport, urban planning or trade.[1] This section, and the book more generally, focuses on interventions that directly regulate the product or activity in question: its characteristics, its availability, its price or its use. These operate at the level of the general population. Unlike individual-level interventions performed by a health professional, involving counselling or treatment and taking the physical and psychological characteristics of the individual into account,[2] population-level interventions target the environment, that is, the general context in which individual choices are made. The EU, as reflected in its competence framework,[3] is not directly involved in the delivery of healthcare services.

Because there is no 'silver bullet', population-level interventions are typically used in combination rather than separately, as part of a regulatory mix.[4] They tend to operate according to a 'permit but discourage' logic,[5] under which the activity in question remains lawful but consumers are, through various means, discouraged from partaking in it. The 'Nuffield intervention ladder', a classification developed by the

[1] United Nations General Assembly 36.
[2] For a presentation of individual-level interventions in healthy lifestyles promotion, see Upton and Thirlaway.
[3] Article 168(7) TFEU.
[4] Alemanno and Garde, 'The Emergence of an EU Lifestyle Policy' 1773–1774.
[5] Bogart.

Table 5.1 A 'Nuffield inspired' ladder of lifestyle interventions.

Level	Description	Example
Eliminate choice	Entirely eliminating choice	Ban on illicit drugs
Restrict choice	Restricting available options	Regulate ingredients used in food or tobacco products
Guide choice through disincentives	Price or other disincentives	Taxes on tobacco Minimum unit pricing for alcoholic beverages Smoke-free environments
Guide choice through incentives	Price or other incentives	Tax-break on healthy food options
Guide choice through changing the default policy	Changing the default option	Change the default option in restaurant menus or cafeteria
Enable choice	Helping individuals change their behaviour	Advertising restrictions[6]
Provide information	Inform and educate the public	Health warnings, nutrition labelling, information campaigns
Do nothing		

Nuffield Council on Bioethics,[7] is a useful method to rank public health interventions, in function of how severely individual choice is restricted.[8] Table 5.1 classifies some typical lifestyle risks measures

[6] Advertising rules does not appear in the original ladder developed by the Nuffield Council on Bioethics 42 and that developed by Upton and Thirlaway 358. We consider that restrictions on advertising, by limiting 'unhealthy' influences on choice, participate to enabling the healthy choice. In that, we follow Willet and others who consider that a role for the industry under the 'enable choice' level is to 'focus [. . .] marketing on only healthy and sustainably produced foods': Willett and others, 'Food in the Anthropocene' 478.

[7] The Nuffield Council on Bioethics is a UK-based independent charitable body that examines and reports on ethical issues in biology and medicine: <www.nuffieldbioethics.org/about-us> accessed 19 September 2025.

[8] Nuffield Council on Bioethics 'Public Health: Ethical Issues' (2007) 42, <www.nuffieldbioethics.org/assets/pdfs/Public-health-ethical-issues.pdf> accessed 19 September 2025. See also Upton and Thirlaway 358; Willet and others 478. See the Criticism by PE Griffiths and C West, 'A Balanced Intervention Ladder: Promoting Autonomy through Public Health Action' (2015) 129 Public Health 1092.

according to this ladder. [9] Where possible, interventions that are part of the EU regulator's toolbox are included.

This chapter presents the EU's lifestyle toolbox, the measures adopted by the EU to limit the consumption of tobacco products, alcoholic beverages and unhealthy foodstuffs. Based on the intervention ladder, these may be regrouped into four main categories: measures that restrict choice by prohibiting the placing on the market of certain products or setting the composition thereof; tax measures which disincentivise the unhealthy choice; rules that enable choice by restricting or prohibiting the use of commercial communications and; finally, rules on the provision of information to the consumer. The choice was made to focus on binding EU measures, regulations and directives, leaving aside the recommendations addressed to the Member States, which do not have binding effect. Beyond the systematic description and classification of EU lifestyle interventions, the chapter serves two other purposes. The first is to confront the regulatory tools used by the EU with the stated objectives of its lifestyle policy, to assess the adequacy of these tools and suggest, where pertinent, avenues for reform. The second is to highlight the vast regulatory differences that exist across lifestyle risk factors and to critically evaluate the justifications for such a differential treatment.

5.2 Restricting and Eliminating Choice: Bans and Composition Requirements

For consumers, the most prescriptive form of intervention is to simply prohibit a product or to restrict the use of certain ingredients or components therein. Overall, the EU has made a limited use of these policy options, granting consumers access to a wide range of hazardous products. Only two categories of products are banned at the EU level, tobacco for oral use and tobacco containing characterising flavours. On composition, most of the relevant rules also concern tobacco products. Few of the composition requirements that apply to alcoholic beverages and foods pursue a distinctive health purpose. They rather serve to ensure the quality of products: protecting consumers' expectations and, ultimately, protecting the internal market.

[9] Adapted from Upton and Thirlaway 358.

5.2.1 *The Prohibition of Tobacco for Oral Use and Flavoured Tobacco*

Since 1992, the EU prohibits the placing on the market of tobacco for oral use,[10] on grounds of the specific health risks associated with it, oral cancer in particular, and its potential role as a gateway to the consumption of other and more dangerous forms of tobacco products, such as cigarettes.[11] The ban does not apply in Sweden, which secured an opt-out upon its accession to the EU in 1995.[12] Tobacco for oral use is still widely consumed in Sweden, in a specific form known as *snus* (see Section 2.3). Under the Tobacco Products Directive, tobacco for oral use belongs to the broader category of smokeless tobacco products, which also includes chewing tobacco and nasal tobacco.[13] Although the consumption of chewing and nasal tobacco also involves health risks, the EU legislator has decided not to ban these products, which are deemed to be less appealing to consumers than tobacco for oral use. Hence, for the former, 'strict provisions on labelling and certain provisions relating to their ingredients are considered sufficient to contain their expansion in the market beyond their traditional use'.[14] The Court of Justice upheld this reasoning, ruling that, as regards tobacco for oral use and other STPs, no breach of the principle of equal treatment could be established.[15]

With the adoption of the TPD in 2014, another ban was enacted on tobacco containing a characterising flavour.[16] The measure was adopted due to the appeal of such products, among young people especially, as

[10] Tobacco Products Directive, arts 1(c) and 17. The ban was first introduced by Council Directive 92/41/EEC of 15 May 1992 amending Directive 89/622/EEC on the approximation of the laws, regulations and administrative provisions of the Member States concerning the labelling of tobacco products, OJ L158/30, art 1. The definition of tobacco for oral use is contained in art 2(8) TPD.

[11] Council Directive 92/41/EEC, recitals.

[12] Act concerning the conditions of accession of the Kingdom of Norway, the Republic of Austria, the Republic of Finland and the Kingdom of Sweden and the adjustments to the Treaties on which the European Union is founded, OJ C241/9, art 151. See also Article 17 TPD.

[13] TPD, art 2(5). The definition of chewing and nasal tobacco may be found in arts 2(6) and (7), respectively. In *Günter Hartmann*, the Court of Justice provided some guidance as to how to differentiate between these two categories of products: see Case C-425/17 *Günter Hartmann Tabakvertrieb*, EU:C:2018:830, paras 30–35.

[14] TPD, recital 32.

[15] Case C-434/02 *Arnold André*, EU:C:2004:800, para 69; Case C-210/03 *Swedish Match*, EU: C:2004:802, para 71; Case C-151/17 *Swedish Match AB v Secretary of State for Health (Swedish Match II)*, EU:C:2018:938, para 28.

[16] TPD, arts 7(1) and (7). The prohibition currently applies to cigarettes and roll-your-own (RYO) tobacco only, see art 7(12).

flavours mask the taste and smell of tobacco and function as a gateway to the consumption of traditional tobacco products.[17] Prohibited flavours include, for instance, fruit, candy, menthol or vanilla.[18] For menthol cigarettes and other products whose EU sales volumes represented 3 per cent or more in a particular category in 2014, the application of the measure was delayed to 20 May 2020.[19] Since October 2023, the ban on characterising flavours also applies to heated tobacco products.[20] The ban was unsuccessfully challenged before the Court of Justice on three occasions,[21] the Court considering, among other arguments, that tobacco products containing a characterising flavour have similar characteristics and effects as regards tobacco uptake and use which justify to treat them differently from unflavoured products.[22]

5.2.2 *The Galaxy of Composition Requirements*

5.2.2.1 Tobacco Products: Health as the Main Objective

The Tobacco Products Directive contains a number of rules on ingredients and emissions, contained in Articles 3 to 7 for tobacco products and Article 20 for e-cigarettes. These requirements pursue two different but complementary objectives: preventing, on the one hand, the intake of substances which are intrinsically harmful to health and preventing, on the other hand, the use of substances which, even if per se innocuous, are susceptible to mislead consumers and alter their perception of risks, thereby contributing to a greater consumption of the products in question. It is the case, for instance, of vitamins.

Article 3 lays down maximum emission levels for tar, nicotine, carbon monoxide and other substances contained in cigarettes (TNCO

[17] TPD, recital 16. For evidence of this, see James C Hersey and others, 'Are Menthol Cigarettes a Starter Product for Youth?' (2006) 8 Nicotine & Tobacco Research 403; Kim Klausner, 'Menthol Cigarettes and Smoking Initiation: A Tobacco Industry Perspective' (2011) 20 Tobacco Control 12; James Nonnemaker and others, 'Initiation with Menthol Cigarettes and Youth Smoking Uptake' (2013) 108 Addiction 171; Cristine D Delnevo and others, 'The Influence of Menthol, e-Cigarettes and Other Tobacco Products on Young Adults: Self-Reported Changes in Past Year Smoking' (2016) 25 Tobacco Control 571.

[18] TPD, art 2(25).

[19] ibid, art 7(14), as interpreted by the Court in Case C-220/17 *Planta Tabak*, EU:C:2019:76, paras 60–67.

[20] Commission Delegated Directive (EU) 2022/2100 of 29 June 2022 amending Directive 2014/40/EU of the European Parliament and of the Council as regards the withdrawal of certain exemptions in respect of heated tobacco products, OJ L283/4, art 1.

[21] *Poland v European Parliament and Council*; *Philip Morris*; *Planta Tabak*.

[22] *Poland v European Parliament and Council*, para 48; Philip Morris, para 114; Planta Tabak, para 40.

emissions). Article 4 sets methods for the measurement of emissions, which must be verified by approved laboratories that are not directly or indirectly controlled by the tobacco industry.[23] The Commission may, by means of delegated acts, decrease these maximum emission levels or adopt supplementary maximum levels, applicable to other products or other types of emissions.[24] Article 7 prohibits the use of a number of additives in tobacco products, including (i) vitamins and other substances which may create a false impression of a health benefit, (ii) additives that are associated with energy and vitality, such as caffeine or taurine and (iii) additives that have carcinogenic, mutagenic or reprotoxic (CMR) properties.[25] To facilitate the regulation of ingredients and emissions, Articles 5 and 6 lay down a number of reporting obligations applicable to importers and manufacturers.[26] In order to monitor market developments, Article 19 lays down specific obligations regarding novel tobacco products. Manufacturers and importers are required to submit a notification to the competent authorities of the Member State where they intend to place such product on the market, at least six months before the date of introduction.[27]

E-cigarettes and their refill containers are subject to an entirely distinct set of provisions in the TPD, contained in Article 20.[28] It must be borne in mind that the TPD does not apply to e-cigarettes and refill containers regulated as medicinal products or medical devices, which fall within the scope of Directive 2001/83 and Regulation 2017/745 (former Directive 93/42).[29] Article 20 sets prescriptions on the volume of refill containers and single use cartridges that contain the nicotine-containing liquid used for e-cigarettes.[30] The liquid must not exceed the threshold of 20 mg of nicotine per millilitre and must not contain the

[23] Regarding the interpretation and validity of Article 4 TPD, see Case C-160/20 *Stichting Rookpreventie Jeugd and Others*, EU:C:2022:101.

[24] TPD, arts 3(2) and (4). [25] ibid, art 7(6). [26] See art 20(2) for e-cigarettes.

[27] ibid, art 19(1).

[28] Electronic cigarette and refill container are defined at Articles 2(16) and (17) of the TPD. In Case C-477/14 *Pillbox 38 (UK) Ltd v Secretary of State for Health*, EU:C:2016:324, the Court ruled that Article 20 was valid, in light, among other things, of the principle of proportionality, subsidiarity and equal treatment.

[29] TPD, art 20(1). See Directive 2001/83/EC of the European Parliament and of the Council of 6 November 2001 on the Community code relating to medicinal products for human use, OJ L311/67; Regulation (EU) 2017/745 of the European Parliament and of the Council of 5 April 2017 on medical devices, amending Directive 2001/83/EC, Regulation (EC) No 178/2002 and Regulation (EC) No 1223/2009 and repealing Council Directives 90/385/EEC and 93/42/EEC, OJ L117/1.

[30] Tobacco Products Directive, art 20(3)(a).

aforementioned additives prohibited for tobacco products.[31] E-cigarettes and their containers must also be child- and tamper-proof, and prevent any breakage and leakage.[32] The TPD does not regulate the use of flavours in e-cigarettes, which Member States are free to prohibit or not.[33] As for tobacco products, flavours may constitute a gateway to the consumption of e-cigarettes and tobacco in general, especially for youngsters.[34] To ensure consistency across the range of products regulated by the TPD, the Commission is currently considering introducing a full ban on flavours in the next revision of the TPD.[35]

Although it is not per se a composition requirement, it is worth mentioning the rule contained at Article 14, which sets a minimum content for unit packets of cigarettes and roll-your-own (RYO) tobacco. These must contain, respectively, at least twenty cigarettes and no less than 30 g of tobacco.[36] This rule seeks to increase the upfront cost of tobacco so as to deter its purchase, for young people especially.[37] As explained by the Court in *Philip Morris*, 'smaller sales units are more of an inducement to start smoking because the consumer is inclined to think that they are cheaper, less of a constraint and psychologically more acceptable'.[38] On the other hand, the EU does not set a maximum number of cigarettes per unit packet. The respective merits of such minimum and maximum thresholds are debated. Some authors think that a cap on the number of cigarettes in one pack, set for instance at twenty, could be beneficial, because greater cigarette pack size is associated with higher cigarette consumption.[39] Others think that a cap is unlikely to bring benefits, rather favouring a dramatic scale-up of the

[31] ibid, arts 20(3)(b) to (e). The Court clarified in *Pillbox 38*, paras 94–95, that electronic cigarettes whose liquid contains more than 20 mg/ml of nicotine are not prohibited under EU law. Pursuant to Article 20(1), read in the light of Recital 36 the TPD, such products may be placed on the market under the conditions laid down by Directive 2001/83/EC and Regulation 2017/745. This is meant to take account of the need for some consumers, based on their state of dependence or their habits, to use electronic cigarettes with a higher nicotine strength as an aid to quit smoking.

[32] TPD, art 20(3)(g).

[33] See ibid, recital 47.

[34] European Commission, 'Support study to the report on the application of Directive 2014/40/EU' 117–118.

[35] European Commission, 'Europe's Beating Cancer Plan' 9.

[36] TPD, art 14(1).

[37] See European Commission, '10 key changes for tobacco products sold in the EU'; Anna KM Blackwell and others, 'Should Cigarette Pack Sizes Be Capped?' (2020) 115 Addiction 802.

[38] *Philip Morris*, para 197.

[39] Blackwell and others, 'Should Cigarette Pack Sizes Be Capped?'. See also European Commission, 'Support study to the report on the application of Directive 2014/40/EU' 66.

minimum content of packets, set for instance at 100 units, so as to increase price and further deter consumption.[40]

5.2.2.2 Foods and Alcoholic Beverages: Health as an Ancillary Objective

Overall, there are (very) few rules in place in the EU mandating or steering the reformulation of HFSS foods.[41] Most EU rules on food composition, that is, regulating the type and quantity of nutrients present in a given product, are concerned with the protection of the 'quality' of products rather than their healthiness. Their aim is to ensure that foods are in conformity with consumers' expectations or with a protected name, thus promoting free movement and a well-functioning internal market. This is, for instance, the case of the marketing standards contained in the CAP CMO Regulation,[42] the rules on geographical indications[43] or the so-called breakfast directives on cocoa, chocolate and fruit juices.[44] Nutrition and health concerns are mostly absent from these instruments, although some provisions, taken in isolation, may contribute to improve the nutritional quality of certain products.[45] It is, for instance, telling that health is nowhere mentioned in the directive on cocoa and chocolate or the regulation on spirit drinks.[46] The EU's powers to set the composition of foods and alcoholic beverages remain vastly underused. Rather than adopting binding rules, the EU has consistently favoured an approach based on the adoption of voluntary commitments by the industry through self-regulatory schemes (see Section 5.4.2.). The

[40] See Kenneth M Cummings, 'What's in a Number?' (2020) 115 Addiction 814.

[41] Food reformulation can be defined as the process of altering the processing or composition of a food or beverage product, to improve its nutritional profile or to reduce its content of ingredients or nutrients of concern.

[42] Regulation (EU) No 1308/2013 of the European Parliament and of the Council of 17 December 2013 establishing a common organisation of the markets in agricultural products (CMO Regulation), OJ L 347/671.

[43] Regulation (EU) 2024/1143 of the European Parliament and of the Council of 11 April 2024 on geographical indications for wine, spirit drinks and agricultural products, as well as traditional specialities guaranteed and optional quality terms for agricultural products, amending Regulations (EU) No 1308/2013, (EU) 2019/787 and (EU) 2019/1753 and repealing Regulation (EU) No 1151/2012, OJ L1143.

[44] Directive 2000/36/EC of the European Parliament and of the Council of 23 June 2000 relating to cocoa and chocolate products intended for human consumption, OJ L197/19, Council Directive 2001/112/EC of 20 December 2001 relating to fruit juices and certain similar products intended for human consumption, OJ L10/58.

[45] Such would be the case, for instance, of the prohibition of added sugars in fruit juices contained in Directive 2001/112, annex I.

[46] Directive 2000/36/EC and Regulation (EU) 2024/1143.

first of those was the EU Platform for Action on Diet, Physical Activity and Health, created in 2004.[47] After twenty years of existence, the EU Platform has led to the adoption of few commitments regarding food composition, with no visible effect on the quality of the food supplied.

A notable exception to this state of inaction is the regulation of trans fatty acids or trans fats (TFAs). While limited in scope, it is the EU's clearest legislative effort to date to improve the nutritional composition of food products sold on its market. TFAs are a particular type of unsaturated fatty acids naturally present in some foods and which can also be artificially added.[48] TFAs bring no nutritional benefits and are a risk factor for coronary heart disease. It is therefore recommended to keep TFAs intake as low as possible within the context of a nutritionally adequate diet.[49] On this basis, the Commission adopted a regulation in 2019, placing a limit on the content of TFAs in food.[50] Save for TFAs naturally present in fat of animal origin, the Regulation sets an upper limit of 2 g of TFAs per 100 g of fat, for food intended for the final consumer and food intended for supply to retail.[51] This threshold corresponds to the limit set by the WHO of maximum 1 per cent of TFAs in the daily energy intake.[52] Interestingly enough, the Commission decided to regulate the content of TFAs in food after a report had discarded a labelling option. The report established that consumer knowledge of TFAs and their effects on health was low and that information about TFAs had little impact on consumers' ability to identify the healthier product in a real-life situation.[53]

[47] See <https://health.ec.europa.eu/other-pages/basic-page/eu-platform-diet-physical-activity-and-health-database_en#the-platform-visualised> accessed 19 September 2025.

[48] The legal definition of TFAs is contained in the Food Information Regulation, annex 1 art 4.

[49] European Commission, 'Report from the Commission to the European Parliament and the Council regarding trans fats in foods and in the overall diet of the Union population', COM (2015) 619 final, see also EFSA, 'Scientific and technical assistance on trans fatty acids' (2018) Technical report.

[50] Commission Regulation (EU) 2019/649 of 24 April 2019 amending Annex III to Regulation (EC) No 1925/2006 of the European Parliament and of the Council as regards trans fat, other than trans fat naturally occurring in fat of animal origin, OJ L 110/17.

[51] ibid, art 1.

[52] European Commission, Factsheet, 'Trans fats in foods a new regulation for EU consumers' (2019).

[53] European Commission, Report from the Commission to the European Parliament and the Council regarding trans fats in foods and in the overall diet of the Union population 9.

Some nutrition-related composition requirements may also be found in food-specific instruments, such as the Regulation on Foods for Specific Groups,[54] the Regulation on Food Fortification[55] and the Food Supplements Directive.[56] The Regulation on Foods for Specific Groups regulates foods that are vital for the management of certain conditions or essential to vulnerable population groups, such as infants and young children, as well as foods that are used as diet replacement for weight control. It applies to the following categories of food: (i) infant formula and follow-on formula, (ii) processed cereal-based food and baby food, (iii) food for special medical purposes and (iv) total diet replacement for weight control.[57] The basic requirement is that only foods compliant with the Regulation may be placed on the market.[58] The Regulation on Food Fortification and the Food Supplements Directive have drawn up a list of vitamins and minerals that may be added to foods or sold as supplements and regulate the quantities thereof.[59] The Regulation prohibits the addition of vitamins and minerals to beverages containing more than 1.2 per cent vol of alcohol,[60] on the ground that such fortified foods are perceived by consumers as having a health advantage over products that do not contain such nutrients.[61] Alcoholic beverages should therefore not benefit from such a promotional effect.

5.3 Guide Choice through Disincentives: The EU's Misused Taxation Powers

Measures affecting price and disincentivising the purchase of unhealthy goods are widely seen as the most effective type of lifestyle

[54] Regulation (EU) No 609/2013 of the European Parliament and of the Council of 12 June 2013 on food intended for infants and young children, food for special medical purposes and total diet replacement for weight control and repealing Council Directive 92/52/EEC, Commission Directives 96/8/EC, 1999/21/EC, 2006/125/EC and 2006/141/EC, Directive 2009/39/EC of the European Parliament and of the Council and Commission Regulations (EC) No 41/2009 and (EC) No 953/2009, OJ L181/35.

[55] Regulation (EC) No 1925/2006 of the European Parliament and of the Council of 20 December 2006 on the addition of vitamins and minerals and of certain other substances to foods, OJ L404/26.

[56] Directive 2002/46/EC of the European Parliament and of the Council of 10 June 2002 on the approximation of the laws of the Member States relating to food supplements, OJ L183/51.

[57] Regulation 609/2013, arts 1 and 2. [58] ibid, art 4.

[59] Regulation 1925/2006, art 3 and annexes I and II; Directive 2002/46, art 4.

[60] Regulation 1925/2006, art 4(b). A very narrow exception exists, see points (i) to (iii).

[61] ibid, recital 12.

intervention.[62] Evidence is particularly robust as regards tobacco products and alcoholic beverages, two categories of products regulated at the EU level.[63] No rules have yet been adopted on the taxation of unhealthy foodstuffs, an area under review as part of the 2021 Beating Cancer Plan.[64]

Article 113 empowers the EU to adopt harmonisation measures in the field of indirect taxation, as regards turnover taxes and excise duties in particular. Excise duties, on the one hand, are taxes levied on the sale or use of specific products and are characterised by a selectivity in coverage and discrimination in intent. Turnover taxes, such as the VAT, tend to be of general application, that is, they apply to most of the sales of goods and provisions of services within a country, and are generally levied to raise revenue rather than to pursue other public policy objectives. This section focuses on three categories of rules of specific interest for public health: (i) fiscal provisions *stricto sensu*, dealing with the structure and the rates of excise duty for tobacco and alcohol; (ii) rules that govern the cross-border acquisitions of products by individuals within and towards the EU; (iii) rules that seek to prevent illicit trade in tobacco products, one of the main obstacles to the effective payment of excise duties and other dues.

As we shall see, rules on excise duties and other indirect forms of taxation are primarily concerned with the proper functioning of the EU internal market. Health is largely absent as a concern. Worse, due to their full harmonisation effect, some of the rules come to undermine the autonomy and effectiveness of Member State fiscal policies and negatively impact public health. The potential offered by that legal framework for the purpose of lifestyle health promotion is thus far from

62 WHO, 'Tackling NCDs: Best buys and other recommended interventions for the prevention and control of noncommunicable diseases' (2nd edition, 2024), <https://apps.who.int/iris/handle/10665/259232> accessed 19 September 2025.

63 Alexander C Wagenaar, Matthew J Salois and Kelli A Komro, 'Effects of Beverage Alcohol Price and Tax Levels on Drinking: A Meta-Analysis of 1003 Estimates from 112 Studies' (2009) 104 Addiction 179; Robyn Burton and others, 'A Rapid Evidence Review of the Effectiveness and Cost-Effectiveness of Alcohol Control Policies: An English Perspective' (2017) 389 The Lancet 1558; Shannon Gravely and others, 'Implementation of Key Demand-Reduction Measures of the WHO Framework Convention on Tobacco Control and Change in Smoking Prevalence in 126 Countries: An Association Study' (2017) 2 The Lancet Public Health e166; Ariadna Feliu and others, 'Impact of Tobacco Control Policies on Smoking Prevalence and Quit Ratios in 27 European Union Countries from 2006 to 2014' (2019) 28 Tobacco Control 101.

64 See European Commission, 'Europe's Beating Cancer Plan' 11.

exploited. This may change in the coming years. The European Commission, as part of its Beating Cancer Plan, expressed its intention to review existing rules on excise duty to take better account of the public health dimension, both regarding the rate and structure of duties and cross-border acquisitions.[65]

5.3.1 *Excise Duties: General Rules, Structure and Rate*

Excise duties for tobacco and alcohol are subject to a general legal framework and to product-specific instruments. Directive 2020/262 (the General Excise Duties Directive),[66] former Directive 2008/118,[67] contains the general arrangements for the payment of excise duties in the EU. The General Excise Duties Directive seeks to unify the concept of excise duty and the conditions for its chargeability, by making clear when excise goods are released for consumption and who is liable to pay the excise duty.[68] It applies to three categories of products: energy products and electricity; alcohol and alcoholic beverages; manufactured tobacco.[69] From a health point of view, a key provision is Article 1, which lays down the conditions under which Member States may continue to adopt autonomous tax measures. Article 1(2) of the Directive allows Member States to levy other indirect taxes on these three categories of products, 'for specific purposes' other than budgetary, including public health.[70] Article 1(3) makes clear that Member States are free to impose taxes on products other than excise goods and on the supply of services.[71] Articles 6 and 8 of the Directive, although bearing no obvious link to health, have been found to tamper with Member State health policies. These articles provide that excise duty becomes chargeable when a given product is released for consumption,[72] subject to the chargeability conditions and

[65] European Commission, 'Europe's Beating Cancer Plan' 9. See also European Commission, Communication from the Commission to the European Parliament and the Council, 'An action plan for fair and simple taxation supporting the recovery strategy', COM (2020) 312 final, 2–3.

[66] Council Directive (EU) 2020/262 of 19 December 2019 laying down the general arrangements for excise duty (recast) (General Excise Duties Directive), OJ L58/4.

[67] Council Directive 2008/118/EC of 16 December 2008 concerning the general arrangements for excise duty and repealing Directive 92/12/EEC, OJ L9/12.

[68] General Excise Duties Directive, recitals 2 and 7. [69] ibid, art 1(1).

[70] Case C-434/97 *Commission v France*, EU:C:2000:98, para 19. For an unsuccessful reliance on public health as the specific purpose of a tax on alcoholic beverages, see *EKW and Wein & Co.*, para 37.

[71] See Case C-491/03 *Hermann*, EU:C:2005:157.

[72] General Excise Duties Directive, art 6(2).

rate of excise duty applicable at that time in the Member State concerned.[73] These rules came to clash with a Portuguese measure preventing economic operators from releasing an excessive and artificial quantity of tobacco products on the market ahead of a future increase in excise duty, so as to benefit from the lower rate. In *Commission v Portugal*, the Court ruled that the Directive did not prevent Portugal from adopting such a rule as such but that proportionality had nonetheless been violated.[74] In *CDIL*, the Portuguese rule was considered to be directly in breach of the Directive, undermining the level of harmonisation reached by the instrument.[75]

Directive 2011/64 ('Tobacco Excise Duties Directive') contains the rules governing the structure and rate of excise duty for tobacco products.[76] The Directive applies to cigarettes, cigars, cigarillos and smoking tobacco.[77] It avowedly pursues both an internal market and public health objective,[78] recognising that 'the level of taxation is a major factor in the price of tobacco products, which in turn influences consumers' smoking habits'.[79] While this statement represents an improvement if compared to previous legislative versions – health was mentioned with the sole reference to the need of preserving a 'healthy competition' in the internal market[80] – in practice, the Directive does little to promote health. This is the case, first of all, because the minimum excise duty rate provided for under the Directive is set at a level too low to influence the rates adopted by Member States.[81] In addition, the Directive prevents Member States from adopting effective minimum pricing rules, that is, measures adopted to prevent products below a certain price to be placed

[73] ibid, art 8. [74] Case C-126/15, *Commission v Portugal*, EU:C:2017:504. [75] *CDIL*.

[76] See also the two previous directives: Council Directive 72/464/EEC of 19 December 1972 on taxes other than turnover taxes which affect the consumption of manufactured tobacco, OJ L303/1; Council Directive 95/59/EC of 27 November 1995 on taxes other than turnover taxes which affect the consumption of manufactured tobacco, OJ L291/40.

[77] Tobacco Excise Duties Directive, art 2(1). See the precise definitions contained in arts 3 to 5. See also Case C-638/15 *Eko-Tabak*, EU:C:2017:277; Case C-638/17 *Skonis ir kvapas*, EU:C:2019:316; Case C-674/19 *Skonis ir kvapas*, EU:C:2020:710.

[78] Tobacco Excise Duties Directive, recital 2. [79] ibid, recital 16.

[80] Directive 72/464/EEC, recital 1; Directive 95/59/EC, recital 2.

[81] The minimum rate of excise duty for cigarettes consists of a specific component and an *ad valorem* component. The overall excise rate should be of at least 90 euros per 1,000 cigarettes and represent 60 per cent of the weighted average retail selling price of cigarettes. See European Commission, 'Evaluation of Council Directive 2011/64/EU of 21 June 2011 on the structure and rates of excise duty applied to manufactured tobacco' (Staff Working Document) SWD (2020) 32 final, 51.

on the market. This is the case of Article 8(6), which permits Member States to levy a minimum excise duty.[82] The Court found in *Yesmoke* that the minimum duty had to be applied to all cigarettes, irrespective of their characteristics or price.[83] This prevented Italy from maintaining a minimum rate specific to the cheapest cigarettes, meant to ensure that the price of all cigarettes would reach a certain level. Furthermore, to protect 'the imperative needs of competition',[84] Article 15(1) prevents Member States from directly regulating the price of tobacco. In a series of cases, the Court confirmed that Member State rules imposing a minimum retail selling price for cigarettes contravened the Directive and could not be justified on ground of public health.[85] Such legislation is indeed 'capable of undermining competition by preventing some of those producers or importers from taking advantage of lower cost prices so as to offer more attractive retail selling prices'.[86] Here as well, the detrimental effect of the level of harmonisation reached under the Directive can be seen.

Finally, the rules governing the structure and rate of excise duty for alcoholic beverages are contained in Directive 92/83 (the 'Alcohol Excise Duties Structure Directive')[87] and Directive 92/84 (the 'Alcohol Excise Duties Rates Directive').[88] Five categories of products are subject to excise duties: (i) beer; (ii) wine; (iii) fermented beverages other than beer and wine; (iv) 'ethyl alcohol', including spirits and (v) other alcoholic beverages with an alcoholic volume comprised between 1.2 per cent vol and 22 per cent, called intermediate products. Health concerns are also

[82] Tobacco Excise Duties Directive, art 8(6). [83] Case C-428/13 *Yesmoke*, EU:C:2014:2263.

[84] Tobacco Excise Duties Directive, recital 10.

[85] Case C-216/98 *Commission v Greece*, EU:C:2000:571; *Commission v France*C-.02/00; Case C-197/08 *Commission v France*, EU:C:2010:111; Case C-198/08 *Commission v Austria*, EU:C:2010:112; Case C-221/08 *Commission v Ireland*, EU:C:2010:113; Case C-571/08 *Commission v Italy*, EU:C:2010:367.

[86] *Commission v France*C-197/08 , para 37; *Commission v Ireland*C-221/08 , para 40; *Commission v Italy*C-571/08, para 39. See also *Commission v Austria* C-198/08, para 33. Not all pricing measures are prohibited under the Directive, see Case C-221/15 *Etablissements Fr. Colruyt*, EU:C:2016:704; Case C-596/17 *Japan Tobacco International*, EU:C:2018:996, Opinion of Advocate General Saugmansgaard Øe.

[87] Council Directive 92/83/EEC of 19 October 1992 on the harmonisation of the structures of excise duties on alcohol and alcoholic beverages (Alcohol Excise Duties Structure Directive), OJ L316/21.

[88] Council Directive 92/84/EEC of 19 October 1992 on the approximation of the rates of excise duty on alcohol and alcoholic beverages (Alcohol Excise Duties Rates Directive), OJ L316/29.

largely absent from that legal framework.[89] The minimum rates are (very) low and have not been modified since 1992. These are set at 0.748 or 1.87 euros per hectolitre for beer, depending on how the quantity is calculated, at 0 euro per hectolitre for wine and other fermented beverages, at 45 euros per hectolitre for intermediate products and at 550 euros per hectolitre of pure alcohol for spirits.[90] Some positive steps have been taken with the adoption of Directive 2020/1151, amending the Alcohol Excise Duties Structure Directive.[91] In order to encourage the development of low-strength beer, the alcohol content under which a reduced rate may be applied to beer is increased from 2.8 to 3.5 per cent vol.[92] The Commission is also required to submit a report on the implementation of the Alcohol Excise Duties Structure Directive every five years, taking account, inter alia, of the impact of its provisions on public health.[93] Much remains nonetheless to be done in this area.

5.3.2 *Cross-Border Acquisition of Excised Goods*

While existing rules on the structure and rates of excise duties appear insufficient and even counterproductive from a public health perspective, they are not the most problematic aspect of the tobacco and alcohol taxation framework. In an internal market such as the EU, which guarantees the free movement of goods and people, consumers can take advantage of free movement to acquire excised goods in other Member States, where lower taxation rates are applicable. Divergent excise duties rates provide a powerful incentive for such cross-border movements,[94] potentially undermining Member States' public health policies. Two situations must be distinguished, depending on whether individuals make the journey themselves to acquire goods in another country or

[89] See European Commission, Report from the Commission to the Council on the evaluation of Council Directive 92/83/EEC on the structures of excise duties on alcohol and alcoholic beverages, COM (2016) 676 final, 8.

[90] Alcohol Excise Duties Rates Directive, arts 3 to 6.

[91] Council Directive (EU) 2020/1151 of 29 July 2020 amending Directive 92/83/EEC on the harmonisation of the structures of excise duties on alcohol and alcoholic beverages, OJ L256/1, art 2. The main change introduced is the extension of the possibility of applying a reduced rate to independent small producers other than breweries and distilleries: Alcohol Excise Duties Structure Directive, arts 9a, 13a and 18a.

[92] Alcohol Excise Duties Structure Directive, art 5(1). See also Directive 2020/1151, recital 4.

[93] Alcohol Excise Duties Structure Directive, art 28b.

[94] See Pete Driezen and others, 'Cross-Border Purchasing of Cigarettes among Smokers in Six Countries of the EUREST-PLUS ITC Europe Surveys' (2019) 16 Tobacco Induced Diseases 13.

purchase such goods at a distance. In the first case, current EU rules entirely fail to discourage cross-border acquisitions made to escape domestic taxes. As regards distance sales, the situation is much more satisfactory.

5.3.2.1 Cross-Border Movement of Individuals

As already mentioned, the general rule for excise duty is that it becomes chargeable at the time and in the Member State of release for consumption.[95] Where goods have been released for consumption in one Member State and are subsequently moved to another to be delivered there, the goods are subject to excise duty in the Member State of destination.[96] The idea is that products consumed in one Member State are subject to the rate that is applicable in that Member State. That system, however, does not apply to cross-border purchases made by private individuals, outside a commercial activity. Pursuant to Article 32(1) of the General Excise Duties Directive, 'excise duty on excise goods *acquired by a private individual for his or her own use*, and transported from the territory of one Member State to the territory of another Member State by this private individual, shall be charged only *in the Member State in which the excise goods are acquired*'.[97] This means that individuals may freely purchase excised goods while travelling without having to pay the excise duty applicable in the place where the goods are consumed. Such exception makes sense from the perspective of free movement. If individuals had to go through a lengthy and complicated procedure to correct the payment of the excise duty every time they exercised their rights to free movement, this would disincentivise cross-border movement and shopping. At the same time, such a rule creates a number of risks, linked to 'tax fraud, avoidance or abuse, threatening or undermining public policy or protection of health and life of humans'.[98] As the Court of Justice recognised itself, there is a financial incentive to purchase goods on which lower excise duties have been paid and import them into a Member State where excise duties are higher.[99] A risk also exists that commercial entities disguise their imports as private acquisitions, to circumvent the rule that goods moved to other Member States for

[95] General Excise Duties Directive, art 6(2). [96] ibid, art 33(1).
[97] ibid, art 32(1). Regarding the definition of 'own use', see Case C-5/05 *Joustra*, EU:C:2006:733.
[98] Recital 41 of the Directive, emphasis added.
[99] Case C-315/12 *Metro Cash and Carry Denmark*, EU:C:2013:503, para 12.

commercial purposes are subject to excise duties in the Member States of destination and not that of origin.

Article 32 of the General Excise Duties Directive acknowledges the problem. It lays down the criterion that Member States shall take into account for the purpose of assessing whether the movement of goods crossing a border is meant for an individual's personal use or for commercial purposes[100] – in the latter case, as explained above, the excise duty is the one of the country of destination. In particular, Member States shall take into account the quantity of the goods transported and, for that purpose, may adopt 'guide levels',[101] quantitative thresholds over which a shipment may be presumed to be of a commercial nature. Crucially, these guide levels may not be set at a level lower than that provided for in the Directive: as regards tobacco products, 800 cigarettes, 400 cigarillos, 200 cigars and 1 kg of smoking tobacco; as regards alcoholic beverages, 10 litres of spirit drinks, 20 litres of intermediate products,[102] 90 litres of wines, including a maximum of 60 litres of sparkling wines and 110 litres of beer. These lower limits were set in Directive 92/12/EEC,[103] which came into force on 1 January 1993, and have not been changed ever since.

These thresholds are set at an extremely high level if compared to the average consumption of tobacco and alcohol in the European population. After controlling for those that do not drink, the limits for alcoholic beverages represent 4 litres more of pure alcohol than the *annual* consumption of Lithuania, Czechia or Bulgaria, among the heaviest EU drinkers.[104] This is all the more problematic when considering that the guide levels apply per trip and not per year. The situation is slightly better for tobacco, the limits equating, for instance, to around one and a half months of average consumption in Greece and two and a half months in the Netherlands.[105] Yet, this still means that a smoker only needs to make a handful of trips abroad every year to source all its

[100] Directive 2020/262, art 32(2). [101] ibid, art 32(3).

[102] See the preceding section for the definition of intermediate products.

[103] Council Directive 92/12/EEC of 25 February 1992 on the general arrangements for products subject to excise duty and on the holding, movement and monitoring of such products, OJ L 76/1.

[104] European Commission, 'Study assessing articles 32 and 36 of Council Directive 2008/118/EC concerning the general arrangements for excise duty' (2020) Final Report 65, <https://op.europa.eu/en/publication-detail/-/publication/4dffa2d3-a92e-11ea-bb7a-01aa75ed71a1/language-en> accessed 19 September 2025.

[105] ibid 66.

consumption from a country where taxes are lower. Worse, the Court of Justice's interpretation of Article 32 reinforces the problem. In *Commission v France*, the Court made clear that Article 32 does not permit Member States 'to determine that products are held for commercial purposes *solely on the basis of a purely quantitative threshold* for products held'[106] and that the lower limits cannot be aggregated but apply for each distinct categories of products.[107] This means, for instance, that a private person travelling back to its Member State of origin with 11 litres of spirit drinks purchased abroad cannot automatically be considered as acting commercially, and be required to pay the excise duties in that Member State. Further, a private person transporting 9 litres of spirit drinks and 109 litres of beer must be considered as falling below the threshold. Relatedly, the Court also held in that judgment that lower limits should be applied per person and not per vehicle.[108]

A large study published in 2020 confirmed that Article 32 was deficient from a public health point of view,[109] and had been unable, if such was ever its purpose, to stem the development of cross-border acquisitions of tobacco and alcohol by individuals. The phenomenon is not marginal. In the previous twelve months before the study was made, around 14 per cent of the total EU adult population purchased alcohol products in another Member State and 12 per cent purchased tobacco products.[110] Unsurprisingly, Member States with particularly stringent tobacco or alcohol control policies, such as France, Sweden or Finland, have the highest per capita cross-border purchases of cigarettes and alcohol.[111] Border regions are particularly affected. Evidence of the negative impact of cross-border personal acquisition of alcohol and tobacco on public health is overall limited but exists for countries that are most severely hit by the phenomenon. In Finland, Sweden, Denmark and Estonia, there is proof that cross-border movements through the internal market have contributed to a higher total alcohol consumption than otherwise would be the case.[112] Finland and Denmark, in particular,

[106] Case C-216/11 *Commission v France*, EU:C:2013:162, para 17. [107] ibid, para 22.
[108] ibid, para 23.
[109] European Commission, 'Study assessing articles 32 and 36 of Council Directive 2008/118/EC'.
[110] ibid 57. [111] ibid 58.
[112] ibid 71. For Finland, see Thomas Karlsson, 'Nordic alcohol policy in Europe: The adaptation of Finland's, Sweden's and Norway's alcohol policies to a new policy framework 1994–2013' (Doctoral thesis Åbo Akademi University 2014) 47. See also *Heinonen*.

significantly lowered their taxes after joining the EU, due to the rules on travellers' allowances.[113] In Finland, domestic prices were further reduced after Estonia's accession to the EU, due to its inability to block imports of cheaper drinks from this country.[114] This resulted in a steep rise in alcohol-related deaths.[115] In France, one in five smokers report getting their supply often or almost always from purchases abroad.[116] The list could go on. The study suggests a number of changes to remedy this problem: reduce the minimum guide levels to better reflect the average consumption of private individuals, add a frequency to the guide levels or replace the guide levels with binding thresholds.[117] The most effective way would probably be to allow Member States to derogate from the provisions of Article 32, where justified on grounds of their specific situation and subject to the requirements of proportionality. While eliminating the practice of cross-border purchases seems illusory, more can be done to limit its magnitude.

This is clear if one is to compare the rules applicable to *intra-EU* purchases with that applicable to *extra-EU* cross-border purchases. Directive 2007/74 lays down a framework for the exemption from VAT and excise duty of non-commercial imports of goods transported in the personal luggage of travellers coming from third countries.[118] This is to avoid double-taxation. To prevent that such rules are circumvented for the purpose of buying tobacco or alcohol, the Directive also sets quantitative limits, but at levels significantly lower than those provided for in the General Excise Duties Directive.[119] Furthermore, these limits are not indicative but binding on Member States and travellers, and the quantities for different categories of products may not be combined.[120] The greater weight given to public health concerns also appears from Regulation 1186/2009, which establishes exemptions from the application of the EU's Common Customs Tariff, where 'the usual need to

[113] Jenny Cisneros Örnberg, 'Sweden, the EU and the Alcohol Traveller's Allowances' (2010) 37 Contemporary Drug Problems 3, 16; Karlsson, *Nordic Alcohol Policy in Europe* 45.

[114] McKee, Hervey and Gilmore, 'Public Health Policies' 235.

[115] Anna Koski and others, 'Alcohol Tax Cuts and Increase in Alcohol-Positive Sudden Deaths-a Time-Series Intervention Analysis' (2007) 102 Addiction 362.

[116] European Commission, 'Study assessing articles 32 and 36 of Council Directive 2008/118/EC' 72.

[117] ibid 106.

[118] Council Directive 2007/74/EC of 20 December 2007 on the exemption from value added tax and excise duty of goods imported by persons travelling from third countries, OJ L346/6. Formerly Council Directive 69/169/EEC.

[119] ibid, arts 8 and 9.

[120] ibid.

protect the economy is absent':[121] goods imported on the occasion of a marriage, property acquired by inheritance, consignments of negligible value, etc. This instrument is the most protective of public health when it comes to the cross-border movement of alcohol and tobacco. The exemption of customs duty is first of all almost never granted to such products.[122] Second, the relief is subject to low monetary and quantitative limits: for instance, a maximum of fifty cigarettes and one or two litres of alcohol.[123] Lessons can therefore be drawn from these two instruments to reform the rules applicable to intra-EU movements.

5.3.2.2 Distance Sales

The rules on distance sales, that is, sales where the goods are transported to the final consumer, are much stricter. The principle set out by Article 44(1) of the General Excise Duties Directive is that excise goods already released for consumption in the territory of one Member State and sold and delivered to a person in another Member State, where that person does not carry an independent economic activity, are subject to excise duties in the Member State of destination. There is hence no financial incentive for individuals to buy tobacco products or alcoholic beverages at a distance, as far as the level of excise duties is concerned. A possible problem with cross-border distance selling could be the circumvention of age checks for the purchase of tobacco and alcohol. The TPD seeks to address this for tobacco products. Article 18 allows Member States to prohibit cross-border distance sales altogether.[124] Where such sales are not prohibited, retail outlets must register with their Member State of establishment and the Member States where their consumers are located.[125] These outlets must operate an age verification system to ensure that buyers comply with the minimum age requirements in force in the Member State of destination.[126] In May 2021, nineteen Member States had prohibited tobacco distance sales.[127] Enforcing the ban has

[121] Council Regulation (EC) No 1186/2009 of 16 November 2009 setting up a Community system of reliefs from customs duty, OJ L324/23, see recital 3.

[122] ibid, arts 14, 18, 24, 62, 83 and 94. [123] ibid, arts 26–27.

[124] Tobacco Products Directive, art 18(1). Under the TPD, cross-border distance sales are defined as 'distance sales to consumers where, at the time the consumer orders the product from a retail outlet, the consumer is located in a Member State other than the Member State or the third country where that retail outlet is established': art 2(34). Pursuant to art 20(6), art 18 also applies to e-cigarettes.

[125] ibid. [126] ibid, art 18(4).

[127] European Commission, 'Support study to the report on the application of Directive 2014/40/EU' 99.

given rise to difficulties and most retailers across Member States seem to only rely on weak self-reporting age checks, which do not correctly prevent underaged shoppers to access tobacco products.[128] Regarding alcoholic beverages, most Member States have consumer age verification measures in place and do not report any significant impact of alcohol distance selling on public health.[129]

Where these are not prohibited, rules governing cross-border distance sales, which give a certain leeway to Member States, result in a high administrative burden for companies.[130] In the present configuration, tax differences are neutralised and the incentive for individuals to purchase goods abroad is limited. The balance found as regards distance sales is the opposite as that found for cross-border acquisitions: public health is better protected, but at the expense of free movement. The difference in treatment between the two situations may be justified by the fact that cross-border acquisitions require individuals to undertake a journey, providing a physical limit to the practice. Conversely, if the excise duties for cross-border distance sales were to be paid in the country of purchase, consumers in highly taxed country could, regardless of their location, easily source their entire consumption from abroad, with disastrous effect on Member State health policies. That being said, more should be done to limit the cross-border acquisitions of tobacco and alcohol.

5.3.3 *Traceability and Security: The Fight against Illicit Trade in Tobacco Products*

Illicit trade in tobacco products is recognised internationally as one of the main challenges to effective tobacco control, allowing for products to be purchased in violation of fiscal rules and other requirements.[131] It does not only lead to foregone revenues for governments – the loss

[128] ibid. For more details, see 99–105.

[129] European Commission, 'Study assessing articles 32 and 36 of Council Directive 2008/118/EC' 171.

[130] See ibid 174, 178.

[131] Illicit tobacco products 'is understood to include different types of (international) smuggling of both genuine and counterfeit tobacco products (mainly cigarettes), as well as illicit internal EU production and distribution': European Commission, Communication from the Commission to the Council and the European Parliament, 'Stepping up the fight against cigarette smuggling and other forms of illicit trade in tobacco products - A comprehensive EU Strategy', COM (2013) 324 final, 4.

was estimated in 2023 at 10.6 billion euros in the EU[132] – but fuels the shadow economy and organised crime, and undermines tobacco control policies.[133] To address and ultimately eliminate the phenomenon, the parties to the FCTC adopted a specific Protocol on illicit trade in tobacco products, which entered into force in 2018.[134] The European Commission adopted a dedicated strategy and a first action plan in 2013,[135] laying down a number of measures aimed at decreasing the incentives to fraud, securing the supply chain and strengthening enforcement and sanctions.[136] As regards securement of the supply chain, the FCTC Protocol obliges parties to adopt a tracking and tracing system of tobacco products, which was introduced at the EU level with the adoption of the TPD. Articles 15 and 16 TPD set up a system of traceability and security features for tobacco products.[137] All unit packets of tobacco products must be marked with a unique identifier allowing to determine the movement of the product through the supply chain.[138] To ensure traceability, operators involved in the trade of tobacco products must keep a record of all the movement of unit packets and transactions, information that must be stored in an independent data storage facility.[139] In addition to the unique identifier, all unit packets of tobacco products must carry a tamper proof security feature, which must be 'irremovably printed or affixed, indelible and not hidden or interrupted in any form'.[140] Obligations regarding traceability and

[132] KPMG, 'Illicit cigarette consumption in Europe: Results for the calendar year 2023' (2024), <www.pmi.com/resources/docs/default-source/itp/illicit-cigarette-consumption-in-europe_2023-results_final.pdf?sfvrsn=7a64b1c9_4>, accessed 19 September 2025.

[133] European Commission, 'Stepping up the fight against cigarette smuggling and other forms of illicit trade in tobacco products - A comprehensive EU Strategy' 4.

[134] WHO, 'Protocol to eliminate illicit trade in tobacco products, WHO Framework Convention on Tobacco Control' (2013), <https://apps.who.int/iris/bitstream/handle/10665/80873/9789241505246_eng.pdf> accessed 19 September 2025.

[135] European Commission, 'Stepping up the fight against cigarette smuggling and other forms of illicit trade in tobacco products - A comprehensive EU Strategy'; European Commission, 'Anti-smuggling Action Plan' (Staff Working Document) SWD (2013) 193 final. See also European Commission, Communication from the Commission to the Council, the European Parliament and the European Economic and Social Committee, '2nd Action Plan to fight the illicit tobacco trade 2018-2022', COM (2018) 846 final, 1.

[136] European Commission, 'Stepping up the fight against cigarette smuggling and other forms of illicit trade in tobacco products - A comprehensive EU Strategy' 14–21.

[137] See Tobacco Products Directive, recital 29.

[138] TPD, arts 15(1)–(4).

[139] TPD, arts 15(5)–(9) and recitals 30 and 31.

[140] Tobacco Products Directive, art 16(1), see Commission Implementing Decision (EU) 2018/576 of 15 December 2017 on technical standards for security features applied to tobacco products, OJ L 96/57.

security have been applicable to cigarettes and RYO tobacco since 20 May 2019 and will apply to tobacco products other than cigarettes and RYO tobacco from 20 May 2024.[141]

5.4 Enabling Choice: The EU's Contrasted Regulation of Commercial Communications

To promote their products and stimulate consumption, economic operators rely on various advertising techniques and other forms of commercial communications.[142] Restricting or prohibiting such communications is regarded as crucial to limit exposure to harmful products, change consumer perception and ultimately reduce consumption.[143] In this area of regulation, the contrast between risk factors appears particularly stark. The EU has adopted a general ban on cross-border commercial communications for tobacco products. Conversely, operators of the food and drink industry face minor constraints when advertising for their products, as far as EU law is concerned.

5.4.1 *The Wide Ban on Tobacco Advertising and Promotion*

EU law prohibits all forms of tobacco advertising and sponsorship with a cross-border dimension. This is one of the EU's oldest public health measures. The EU adopted a ban on television advertising for tobacco products in 1989, with the Television Without Frontiers (TWF) Directive, as part of its early efforts to combat cancer.[144] The TWF Directive was later repealed by the Audiovisual Media Services Directive (AVMSD), which currently prohibits all forms of audiovisual commercial communications for tobacco products, electronic cigarettes and refill containers.[145] Beyond advertising *stricto sensu*, this ban covers the sponsorship of audiovisual services or programmes by tobacco companies,[146] and the

[141] Tobacco Products Directive, arts 15(13) and 16(3).

[142] The term 'commercial communication' is used in this section as an umbrella term covering not only advertising but also a range of other promotional techniques, such as sponsorship and product placement, in an audiovisual form or not: see AVMS Directive, art 1(1)(h).

[143] WHO, 'Tackling NCDs: Best buys and other recommended interventions for the prevention and control of noncommunicable diseases'.

[144] TWF Directive, art 13. For the definition of 'television advertising', see art 1(1)(i) of the AVMS Directive.

[145] AVMS Directive, art 9(1)(d). For the definition of 'audiovisual commercial communications', see AVMS Directive, art 1(1)(h).

[146] ibid, art 10(2). For the definition of 'sponsorship', see art 1(1)(k).

product placement of such products as well as any other product from tobacco companies.[147]

For commercial communications outside the audiovisual sphere, the first directive was adopted in 1998, banning all forms of advertising and sponsorship in media such as radio, newspapers and magazines, through merchandising and on billboards.[148] The Directive was however annulled by the Court of Justice in its (in)famous *Tobacco Advertising* judgment, on the ground that the EU lacked competence to adopt such a comprehensive ban.[149] The implications of this judgment will be further analysed in Section 6.3. A new and narrower directive was adopted in 2003, upheld this time by the Court after Germany had mounted another challenge.[150] Directive 2003/33 (the Tobacco Advertising Directive or TAD) prohibits the advertising of tobacco products in the press and other printed publications, in information society services (i.e. electronic services) and on radio.[151] Sponsorship by tobacco companies is prohibited for radio programmes.[152] The sponsorship of events or activities involving or taking place in several Member States or having cross-border effects is also prohibited.[153] This includes sports events with a European wide audience, which may no longer be sponsored by tobacco companies, as it had often been the case in the past.[154] As strange as it may seem today, it is only after the Los Angeles 1984 edition that the Olympic Games ceased to have an official cigarette sponsor. The provisions of the TAD also apply to e-cigarettes and refill containers.[155]

5.4.2 *Limited Rules on Foods and Alcoholic Beverages*

The regulation of commercial communications for unhealthy foods and alcoholic beverages stands in stark contrast with that of tobacco

147 ibid, art 11(4). For the definition of 'product placement', see art 1(1)(m).

148 Directive 98/43, art 3(1). 149 *Tobacco Advertising.* 150 *Tobacco Advertising II.*

151 Tobacco Advertising Directive, arts 3 and 4(1). For the definition of 'information society service', see Directive (EU) 2015/1535 of the European Parliament and of the Council of 9 September 2015 laying down a procedure for the provision of information in the field of technical regulations and of rules on Information Society services, OJ L 241/1, art 1(1)(b).

152 Tobacco Advertising Directive, art 4(2). Sponsorship is defined as 'any form of public or private contribution to any event, activity or individual with the aim or direct or indirect effect of promoting a tobacco product': art 2(c).

153 ibid, art 5.

154 See John L Crompton, 'Sponsorship of Sport By Tobacco and Alcohol Companies: A Review of the Issues' (1993) 17 Journal of Sport and Social Issues 148; Alan Blum, 'Tobacco in Sport: An Endless Addiction?' (2005) 14 Tobacco Control 1.

155 Tobacco Products Directive, art 20(5).

products. Advertising and sponsorship is generally authorised on all media and the content of such communications is subject to limited rules. The EU's approach is characterised by a strong preference given to self-regulation through codes of conduct, rather than the adoption of binding rules, with limited effectiveness. This section focuses on the general rules applicable to all categories of foods and drinks, contained primarily in the AVMS Directive, leaving aside product-specific rules such as those applicable to fortified foods, food supplements and foods with a specific health purpose (see Section 5.2.2.2).

Most of the EU rules on commercial communications for food and alcohol concern minors and children. These indeed deserve greater protection. Children are less able to distinguish between neutral information and promotional messages. Exposure to advertising for unhealthy foods influences their dietary habits.[156] To reach them, companies advertise during children's TV viewing hours and, increasingly, on social media platforms.[157] Evidence also shows that young people who have been more exposed to alcohol promotion are more likely to initiate alcohol use and to engage in binge and hazardous drinking.[158]

Under Article 9 AVMSD, audiovisual commercial communications shall not 'encourage behaviour prejudicial to health or safety'[159] and shall not 'cause physical, mental or moral detriment to minors' – that is, 'directly exhort minors to buy or hire a product or service by exploiting their inexperience or credulity, directly encourage them to persuade their parents or others to purchase the goods or services being advertised [. . .]'.[160] There is, to the author's best knowledge, no indication that these vague provisions apply to food or alcohol advertising as such. The Directive also encourages Member States to develop codes of conduct that limit '*inappropriate*' audiovisual commercial communications for

156 Emma Boyland and Mimi Tatlow-Golden, 'Exposure, Power and Impact of Food Marketing on Children: Evidence Supports Strong Restrictions' (2017) 8 European Journal of Risk Regulation 224.

157 ibid 225–228.

158 David Jernigan and others, 'Alcohol Marketing and Youth Alcohol Consumption: A Systematic Review of Longitudinal Studies Published since 2008: Alcohol Marketing and Youth Drinking' (2017) 112 Addiction 7.

159 AVMSD, art 9(1)(c)(iii).

160 ibid, art 9(1)(g). A provision similar to Article 9(1)(g) can be found in the Unfair Commercial Practices Directive, which prohibits the inclusion 'in an advertisement [of] a direct exhortation to children to buy advertised products or persuade their parents or other adults to buy advertised products for them': Unfair Commercial Practices Directive, art 5(5) and annex I.

alcoholic beverages and for foods promoted in children's programmes.[161] Rules are slightly stricter for alcohol. Under Article 22 of the AVMS Directive, whose drafting has remained the same since the TWF Directive of 1989,[162] television advertising and teleshopping for alcoholic beverages shall not be aimed '*specifically*' at minors or depict minors consuming these beverages and shall not encourage the '*immoderate*' consumption of alcohol.[163]

The code of conducts referred to in Article 9 AVMSD apply to foods and beverages containing nutrients of which excessive intakes in the overall diet are not recommended, in particular fat, salt and sugar. These codes shall ensure that audiovisual commercial communications 'do not emphasise the positive quality of the nutritional aspects of such foods and beverages' and shall serve to 'effectively reduce' the exposure of children to harmful commercial communications.[164] Codes of conduct may be drawn up at the national or EU level.[165] Despite such codes being in place in most Member States, the number of self-regulatory initiatives adopted by operators remains limited.[166] The EU Pledge, a voluntary initiative from major food and beverage companies launched in 2007, is the industry's main effort in the field of unhealthy food advertising and promotion.[167] It consists of two main commitments. Members must, first, refrain from advertising their unhealthy products to children under the age of twelve on TV, print and Internet and, second, abstain from communicating in primary schools, save for specific exceptions.[168] These commitments, regardless of their actual implementation by the signatories, remain largely insufficient in terms of products, media and ages covered.[169]

[161] AVMSD, art 9(3)–(4). See also art 28(b)2 as regards video-sharing platforms. Product placement for unhealthy foods in children's programmes is prohibited under Article 11 (2) of the AVMSD. Article 10(4) also permits Member States to prohibit the sponsorship of such programmes.

[162] TWF Directive, art 15.

[163] AVMSD, art 22(a) and (e), emphasis added. See also art 9(1)(e).

[164] AVMSD, art 9(4). See also the further requirements contained in art 4a(1).

[165] AVMSD, art 4a(2).

[166] European Commission, 'Reporting on the application of Directive 2010/13/EU "Audiovisual Media Services Directive" for the period 2014-2019' (Staff Working Document) SWD (2020) 228 final.

[167] See <https://eu-pledge.eu/> accessed 19 September 2025.

[168] ibid.

[169] Amandine Garde, Bill Jeffery and Neville Rigby, 'Implementing the WHO Recommendations Whilst Avoiding Real, Perceived or Potential Conflicts of Interest' (2017) 8 European Journal of Risk Regulation 237, 245–248. See also Bartlett and Garde, 'Time to Seize the (Red) Bull by the Horns' 506–507.

The weakness of this soft law approach is reinforced by the limitations in the scope and wording of the AVMSD's provisions. The scope of 'audiovisual commercial communications' is too narrow, leaving out many social media platforms[170] and other promotional tools such as corporate websites.[171] It also fails to address marketing techniques that are particularly powerful at influencing children, such as engaging celebrities for endorsement or the offer of free toys.[172] These weaknesses must be compared to the recognition by the EU, in its Action Plan on Childhood Obesity, that efforts to reduce harmful advertising to children should include 'not only TV but *all marketing elements*, including in-store environments, promotional actions, internet presence and social media activities'.[173] Further, the terms used in the provisions of the AVMSD outlined above – inappropriate, immoderate – seem to be deliberately weak and vague. Article 9(1)(g) only refers to 'direct' exhortation or encouragement, while most advertising aimed at children or minors operates in an indirect manner.[174] Articles 9(3) and (4) mention 'inappropriate' commercial communications, an unclear term that leaves companies with a broad margin of discretion.[175] One could think that any communication promoting unhealthy foods or alcoholic beverages to children or minors is inappropriate. Article 9(4) also refers to 'children's programmes', a narrow reach which leaves out programmes that are not specifically aimed at children but are watched by many of them nonetheless. Finally, as regards alcohol, other vague and undefined expressions are used, such as programmes 'not specifically aimed at minors' or 'immoderate' consumption.[176] Moreover, contrary to tobacco, there are no provisions restricting the sponsorship of programmes or events by

[170] Directive (EU) 2018/1808 of the European Parliament and of the Council of 14 November 2018 amending Directive 2010/13/EU on the coordination of certain provisions laid down by law, regulation or administrative action in Member States concerning the provision of audiovisual media services (Audiovisual Media Services Directive) in view of changing market realities, OJ L303/69, recital 5.

[171] Oliver Bartlett and Amandine Garde, 'The EU's Failure to Support Member States in Their Implementation of the WHO Recommendations: How to Ignore the Elephant in the Room?' (2017) 8 European Journal of Risk Regulation 251, 254.

[172] ibid.

[173] European Commission, 'EU Action Plan on Childhood Obesity' 16, emphasis added.

[174] Garde, *EU Law and Obesity Prevention* 188.

[175] Bartlett and Garde, 'Time to Seize the (Red) Bull by the Horns' 506.

[176] See Oliver Bartlett and Amandine Garde, 'EU Public Health Law and Policy – on the Rocks? A Few Sobering Thoughts on the Growing EU Alcohol Problem' in Tamara K Hervey, Calum Alasdair Young and Louise E Bishop (eds), *Research Handbook on EU Health Law and Policy* (Edward Elgar Publishing 2017) 389–390.

alcohol of predominantly HFSS foods companies. The absence of such restrictions for events with a cross-border dimension is to be regretted, considering that such events, sports competitions in particular, are susceptible to attract a large young audience. Evidence shows that unhealthy food sports sponsorship achieves enormous population reach and exposure and contributes to increased brand awareness, preference and consumption of the sponsored products.[177]

The EU's approach towards commercial communications for food and alcohol remains thus largely insufficient, despite a growing international recognition of the need to better protect children from harmful commercial practices,[178] including from a children's right perspective,[179] and despite the growing evidence as to the effectiveness of mandatory restrictions.[180] The 2005 Green Paper on food and nutrition mentioned that 'other options [than self-regulation] would need to be considered should self-regulation fail to deliver satisfactory results'.[181] The moment has probably come to draw such conclusion. Yet, the EU stands firm on its preference for non-binding and non-effective schemes, as illustrated by the adoption in 2021 of an EU Code of Conduct on Responsible Food Business and Marketing Practices, within the framework of the Farm to Fork Strategy.[182] Under the Beating Cancer Plan, the Commission

[177] Helen Dixon, Angelyna Lee and Maree Scully, 'Sports Sponsorship as a Cause of Obesity' (2019) 8 Current Obesity Reports 480. See also Timothy Chambers and Franco Sassi, 'Unhealthy Sponsorship of Sport' (2019) 367 British Medical Journal 16718; Robin Ireland and others, 'Commercial Determinants of Health: Advertising of Alcohol and Unhealthy Foods during Sporting Events' (2019) 97 Bulletin of the World Health Organization 290.

[178] WHO, 'Set of recommendations on the marketing of foods and non-alcoholic beverages to children' (2010), <www.who.int/dietphysicalactivity/marketing-food-to-children/en/> accessed 19 September 2025. See Amandine Garde and Godfrey Xuereb, 'The WHO Recommendations on the Marketing of Food and Non-Alcoholic Beverages to Children' (2017) 8 European Journal of Risk Regulation 211.

[179] Amandine Garde and others, 'For a Children's Rights Approach to Obesity Prevention: The Key Role of an Effective Implementation of the WHO Recommendations' (2017) 8 European Journal of Risk Regulation 327; Amandine Garde, 'Harmful Commercial Marketing and Children's Rights: For a Better Use of EU Powers' (2020) 11 European Journal of Risk Regulation 841.

[180] Emma Boyland and others, 'Systematic Review of the Effect of Policies to Restrict the Marketing of Foods and Non-Alcoholic Beverages to Which Children Are Exposed' (2023) 8 Obesity Reviews e13447.

[181] European Commission, Green Paper 'Promoting healthy diets and physical activity: a European dimension for the prevention of overweight, obesity and chronic diseases' 8.

[182] See <https://ec.europa.eu/food/horizontal-topics/farm-fork-strategy/sustainable-food-processing/code-conduct_fr> accessed 19 September 2025.

committed to 'develop and implement guidance for codes of practice on reducing unhealthy food marketing to children, including online marketing through the provisions of AVMSD'[183] and to further monitor the implementation of the AVMSD.[184] No significant changes are therefore to be expected. The discrepancy between the treatment of commercial communications across lifestyle risk factors is likely to remain in the near future.

5.5 Informing Choice

The last category of rules analysed in this chapter are those regulating information to consumers, whether it is the information freely given by economic operators, or that mandated by law. EU (consumer) law has been described as subscribing to an 'information paradigm',[185] whereby the provision of information is seen as an ideal regulatory solution which allows consumers' interests to be protected while imposing little burden on economic operators. This vision is based on the vision of 'an average consumer who is reasonably well-informed and reasonably observant and circumspect',[186] and who reads labels when their purchasing decisions depend on the composition of the products in question.[187] As we shall see, while such paradigm is undoubtedly visible in the field of lifestyles, a more nuanced picture emerges. The limits to consumers' processing of information, as underlined by behavioural sciences, are acknowledged in EU legislation, and increasingly so.

The overall objective of EU information requirements on unhealthy food, tobacco and alcohol is to provide consumers with an accurate knowledge and perception of the risk, so that, as a result, consumers

183 European Commission, 'Europe's Beating Cancer Plan' annexes. 184 ibid 10–11.

185 Anne-Lise Sibony and Geneviève Helleringer, 'EU Consumer Protection and Behavioural Sciences: Revolution or Reform?' in Alberto Alemanno and Anne-Lise Sibony (eds), *Nudge and the Law: A European Perspective* (Hart Publishing 2015) 214; Geneviève Helleringer and Anne-Lise Sibony, 'European Consumer Protection Through The Behavioral Lens' (2017) 23 Columbia Journal of European Law 607, 623–624. As rightly pointed out by Helleringer and Sibony, the case *GB-INNO-BM* offers one of the clearest illustrations of this approach. In this case, the Court seems indeed to rule out the mere possibility that limiting information could ever be beneficial to consumers: see *GB-INNO-BM*, para 18. See also para 15.

186 Case C-210/96 *Gut Springenheide*, EU:C:1998:369, para 31; Case C-220/98 *Estée Lauder*, EU:C:2000:8, para 27.

187 See Case C-51/94 *Commission v Germany*, EU:C:1995:352, para 34; Case C-465/98 *Darbo*, EU:C:2000:184, para 22.

adopt healthier behaviours. This is done in two manners. First, a number of provisions require operators to disclose information considered relevant for consumer choice – mandatory disclosure of information. This mostly applies to food. Second, EU law regulates the information voluntarily given by operators, to ensure that it does not mislead consumers – voluntary disclosure of information. In this latter case, the law can either way set requirements as to the content of the information given or its form, to ensure its truthfulness and non-misleading character, or simply bar operators from providing that information altogether. The prohibition of information mostly applies to tobacco products. In that area of the law, a divergence between risk factors may also be seen, with tobacco being the most regulated risk, alcohol the least and food standing in the middle.

As regards tobacco, the relevant piece of legislation is the Tobacco Products Directive. The relevant rules on food and alcohol are contained in two main instruments: Regulation 1169/2011 on the provision of food information to consumers and Regulation 1924/2006 on nutrition and health claims made on food. The food-specific legislative instruments mentioned in Section 5.2.2.2 also contain provisions that combine elements related to mandatory and voluntary information, as well as advertising. These rules are stricter than those applicable to food in general. It is worth mentioning here the provisions on infant formulae, whose goal is to encourage breastfeeding and limit the use of these substitute products.[188]

5.5.1 *Mandatory Disclosure of Information*

A variety of rules apply to the mandatory disclosure of information for tobacco products, food and alcoholic beverages. Their aim is to inform consumers of the products' content and to make them aware of the risks incurred. As well summarised by Advocate General Saugmandsgaard Øe, the logic differs between tobacco products, on the one hand, and food and alcohol on the other:

> In certain fields, including that of *food*, consumers must indeed be given information about the ingredients in the products they consume, so that *they can identify and make appropriate use of a food and make choices that suit their individual needs*.

[188] Commission Delegated Regulation (EU) 2016/127. For further restrictions on the promotion and advertising of infant formula, see art 10 specifically. On the benefits of breastfeeding for children, see Willett and others, 'Food in the Anthropocene' 459.

However, *tobacco products are not ordinary commodities*. The aim is not to enable consumers to choose more easily between different products. Here, *giving consumers appropriate information amounts essentially to highlighting the particularly harmful effects of tobacco on their health*.[189]

This difference is reflected in the two main policy tools that the EU had adopted in the area: the food nutrition declaration and the tobacco health warnings. As we shall see, the difference is not only in the nature of the information that is given to consumers, but also its form. While health warnings have integrated behavioural insights so as to maximise their potential for behaviour change, nutrition information, and food information in general, continues to be given in a format that is largely ineffective.

5.5.1.1 Foods, Alcoholic Beverages and the Nutrition Declaration

The general requirements on food information, in particular nutrition information, are contained in Regulation 1169/2011 (Food Information Regulation).[190] Transparency as regards the composition and the nutritional content of foods is a cornerstone of EU food law. It aims at providing consumers with the necessary elements to make informed choices[191] and, as far as nutrition is concerned, is also seen as a public health tool.[192]

Articles 9 and 10 of the Regulation lay down a list of information items that must be communicated to consumers, called 'mandatory particulars'. A number of these items have a link with health and nutrition, such as the list and quantity of ingredients or the name and net quantity of the food.[193] The most important mandatory particular, for our

[189] Case C-220/17 *Planta Tabak*, EU:C:2018:530, Opinion of Advocate General Saugmansgaard Øe, paras 76–77, emphasis added.

[190] The Food Information Regulation applies to all foods intended for the final consumer, including mass catering, without prejudice to labelling requirements provided for in other Union instruments applicable to particular foods: arts 1(3) and (4). The final consumer is 'the ultimate consumer of a foodstuff who will not use the food as part of any food business operation or activity': General Food Law Regulation, art 3(18). Food that is not intended for the final consumer but is used as part of a food business operation or activity falls outside the scope of the Food Information Regulation.

[191] General Food Law Regulation, art 8(1).

[192] See in that regard Article 3(1) of the Food Information Regulation: '[t]he provision of food information shall pursue a *high level of protection of consumers' health and interests* by providing a basis for final consumers to *make informed choices and to make safe use of food, with particular regard to health*, economic, environmental, social and ethical considerations', emphasis added.

[193] ibid, art 9(1)(a) to (e). See art 20 for situations where constituents of food can be omitted from the list of ingredients.

purpose, is the nutrition declaration,[194] governed by Articles 29 to 35 of the Regulation. This declaration contains a number of mandatory elements – the energy value and the amounts of fat, saturates, carbohydrates, sugars, protein and salt – to which other optional elements, such as fatty acids or fibre, may be added.[195] The energy value and the content of nutrients must be given per 100 g or 100 ml and may also additionally be expressed per portion or consumption unit.[196] For cereals, a portion would, for instance, represent what is typically consumed in a regular size bowl. For beverages, it is usually equivalent to the amount of liquid contained in a single glass. Although expressing the nutrition declaration per portion or per unit can be useful to consumers, who might struggle to grasp what 100 g or ml of a product represent, it can also be misleading, as food business operators can set portion sizes freely. Operators may select sizes that are smaller than what is typically consumed in one serving, so as to make consumers believe that a serving contains less fat, salt or sugar than it actually does.[197] This practice, which appears to be widespread,[198] threatens the truthfulness of the information given and may lead to increased consumption of the products whose portion sizes have been manipulated.

As it stands, the mandatory nutrition declaration suffers from several defects, limiting consumer understanding. Because the declaration is expressed textually and numerically,[199] consumers need to have sufficient nutrition knowledge and computational skills to be able to determine whether a product contains too much of a given nutrient, taking into account their overall diet and the daily reference intake for that

[194] ibid, art 9(1)(l).

[195] Food Information Regulation, art 30. The energy value and the amounts of nutrients referred to in Article 30(1) to (5) shall be those of the food as sold: art 31(3). 'Where appropriate, the information may relate to the food after preparation, provided that sufficiently detailed preparation instructions are given and the information relates to the food as prepared for consumption': ibid. Article 31(3) must be interpreted as applying only to foods for which preparation is necessary and the method of preparation is predetermined, see Case C-388/20 *Dr. August Oetker* Nahrungsmittel, EU:C:2021:913. Some foods are exempted from the declaration, those in particular that comprise a single ingredient: ibid, art 16(3), see the complete list in annex V.

[196] ibid, arts 32 and 33.

[197] Ossama Elshiewy, Steffen Jahn and Yasemin Boztug, 'Seduced by the Label: How the Recommended Serving Size on Nutrition Labels Affects Food Sales' (2016) 1 Journal of the Association for Consumer Research 104; Nathalie Kliemann and others, 'Serving Size and Nutrition Labelling: Implications for Nutrition Information and Nutrition Claims on Packaged Foods' (2018) 10 Nutrients 891.

[198] ibid. [199] Food Information Regulation, art 9(2).

nutrient.[200] This information is also difficult to notice. Under the Regulation, it must be given in tabular format, if space permits, otherwise in linear format,[201] in characters using a font size with a minimum height of 1.2 mm.[202] Furthermore, the Regulation allows food business operators to choose whether to include the mandatory nutrition declaration on the front or the back of the packaging.[203] Operators usually choose to feature this information on the back, which means that it is not immediately accessible to consumers when looking at products in a retail environment.

As could be expected, there is ample evidence showing that nutrition information of the kind provided for in the Food Information Regulation does not have any significant impact on people's dietary choices and is unlikely to lead to any meaningful improvement from a public health perspective.[204] As it is currently expressed and presented, the nutrition declaration fails to 'appeal to the average consumer and to serve the informative purpose for which it is introduced'.[205] Given the current level of knowledge on the subject of nutrition, it cannot be considered as 'simple and easily understood', in contradiction with the very objectives of the Regulation.[206] To address this problem, Article 35 allows food business operators to use additional forms of expression and presentation, including graphical forms or symbols.[207] The implication of that provision and the relevance of these additional forms of expression and presentation for EU nutrition information are further discussed in Section 7.3.3.

The Food Information Regulation applies to all foods intended for the final consumer, including alcoholic beverages. As regards alcohol, however, there are two important caveats to the aforementioned rules. Beverages containing more than 1.2 per cent by volume of alcohol are exempted from the mandatory nutrition declaration as well as the

[200] See ibid, annex XIII. [201] ibid, art 34. See also annex XV.

[202] Food Information Regulation, art 13(2). The 'x-height' is defined at Annex IV.

[203] According to Article 34(1) of the Food Information Regulation, the particulars referred to in Article 30(1) and (2) shall be included in the 'same field of vision', without any reference to its location. See ibid, art 2(2)(k).

[204] Gill Cowburn and Lynn Stockley, 'Consumer Understanding and Use of Nutrition Labelling: A Systematic Review' (2005) 8 Public Health Nutrition 21; JM Bauer and LA Reisch, 'Behavioural Insights and (Un)Healthy Dietary Choices: A Review of Current Evidence' (2019) 42 Journal of Consumer Policy 3, 29; Shmuel I Becher and others, 'Hungry for Change: The Law and Policy of Food Health Labeling' (2019) 54 Wake Forest Law Review 1305, 1314, 1318.

[205] Food Information Regulation, recital 41. [206] ibid. [207] ibid, art 35 and recital 43.

obligation to provide the list of ingredients.[208] This exemption does not apply to wine.[209] Food business operators are encouraged to provide the energy value of their drinks on a voluntary basis,[210] and Member States are authorised to adopt binding measures requiring the provision of the list of ingredients for these beverages.[211] The only supplementary rule that alcoholic beverages must comply with is the indication of the actual alcoholic strength by volume ('% vol').[212]

These exemptions for alcoholic beverages are a long-standing feature of EU food labelling legislation.[213] The Food Information Regulation offers little by way of justifying this difference in treatment, simply referring to the 'specific nature' of the alcohol sector.[214] The original legislative proposal only excluded beer, wine and spirits from the mandatory nutrition declaration.[215] The European Parliament subsequently extended this exemption to all alcoholic beverages.[216] Nothing justifies the current lack of transparency as to the content of drinks and the difference in treatment between alcoholic beverages and other food products. Mentioning the energy content appears particularly important if one considers that alcohol contains seven calories per gram, meaning that it is more calorie dense than carbohydrates or proteins (both four calories per gram), and a little less calorie dense than fat (nine calories per gram).[217] In 2017, the Commission noted it 'ha[d] not identified objective grounds that would justify the absence of information on ingredients and nutrition information on alcoholic beverages' but decided nonetheless not to adopt binding legislation, relying instead on

[208] ibid, art 16(4). Specific labelling rules apply to wine, aromatised wines and spirits, supplementing those contained in the Food Information Regulation: CMO Regulation, art 118; Regulation 251/2014, art 1; Regulation 2019/787, art 9.

[209] CMO Regulation, art 119. [210] ibid, art 30(4) and recital 42. [211] ibid, art 41.

[212] ibid, art 9(1)(k). Pursuant to Article 28(1) of the Food Information Regulation, rules governing the indication of the alcoholic strength are contained in Annex XII. In particular, the alcoholic strength must be determined at 20°C and must be indicated by a figure followed by the symbol '% vol.'.

[213] See Directive 79/112, art 6(3). [214] Food Information Regulation, recital 40.

[215] European Commission, Proposal for a Regulation of the European Parliament and of the Council on the provision of food information to consumers, COM(2008) 40 final, art 20(e).

[216] European Commission, European Commission, 'Report from the Commission to the European Parliament and the Council regarding the mandatory labelling of the list of ingredients and the nutrition declaration of alcoholic beverages' COM (2017) 58 final, 4.

[217] Adam Sherk and others, 'Calorie Intake from Alcohol in Canada: Why New Labelling Requirements Are Necessary' (2019) 80 Canadian Journal of Dietetic Practice and Research 111.

voluntary action by the industry.[218] The Commission's commitment to propose, before the end of 2022, the extension of the mandatory indication of ingredients and the nutrition declaration to alcoholic beverages have so far not materialised.[219]

5.5.1.2 Tobacco Health Warnings

If compared to foods and alcoholic beverages, tobacco and related products have to comply with far fewer information disclosure requirements. The goal here is not to enable consumers to choose more easily between different products, but to discourage them to consume tobacco altogether. Tobacco health warnings are the EU's key instrument in this regard. They were first introduced in 1989 at the EU level,[220] then subsequently strengthened,[221] culminating with the adoption of provisions on large combined health warnings in the 2014 TPD.

The general provisions on health warnings are contained in Article 8 TPD, which sets requirements on language(s), presentation and on the visibility and integrity of the warnings.[222] Specific provisions apply to different categories of tobacco products, contained in Articles 9 to 12. Each unit packet or outside packaging of tobacco product for smoking must carry: (i) one the two general warnings 'Smoking kills – quit now' or 'Smoking kills', and (ii) the information message 'Tobacco smoke contains over 70 substances known to cause cancer'.[223] Both the general warning and the information message shall cover 50 per cent of the surfaces on which they are printed and must comply with a number of other presentation requirements.[224] Rules are most stringent for products for smoking, cigarettes especially,[225] as these are both the most harmful and most widespread form of tobacco. E-cigarettes and refill containers are subject to text-only warnings.[226] They are the only category of products to which 'classic' information disclosure requirements apply under the TPD, including the disclosure of the ingredients

[218] European Commission, 'Report from the Commission to the European Parliament and the Council regarding the mandatory labelling of the list of ingredients and the nutrition declaration of alcoholic beverages' 12.

[219] European Commission, 'Europe's Beating Cancer Plan' 10.

[220] Directive 89/622/EEC, art 4. [221] Directive 2001/37/EC, art 5.

[222] Regarding Article 8(8) TPD, see Case C-370/20 *Pro Rauchfrei*, EU:C:2021:988 and Case C-356/22 *Pro Rauchfrei e v V JS eK*, EU:C:2023:174.

[223] Tobacco Products Directive, arts 9(1) and (2). [224] ibid, arts 9(3) and (4).

[225] See ibid, arts 11, 12 and 20 for specific rules applying to certain tobacco products for smoking and tobacco products other than for smoking.

[226] ibid, art 20(4)(b)(iii).

used[227] and the presence of a leaflet containing health and safety information.[228]

The main change brought by the TPD was the introduction of large combined health warnings for tobacco products for smoking, consisting of a text message and a photograph, and covering 65 per cent of both the front and back surface of the packaging.[229] The required text warnings and photographs are contained, respectively, in Annex I and Annex II of the Directive.[230] Text warnings include for instance 'Smoking damages your lungs' or 'Your smoke harms your children, family and friends'. The photographs used are meant to shock, with the depiction of wounds, damaged teeth or hospital patients. The combined health warnings are grouped into three sets which must be used in a given year and rotated on an annual basis.[231] Each set contains fourteen combined health warnings which must be displayed to the extent possible in equal numbers on each brand of tobacco products.[232]

The Guidelines for implementation of Article 11 of the FCTC provide the rationale for the introduction of the TPD combined health warnings: 'in comparison with small, text only health warnings, larger warnings with pictures are more likely to be noticed, better communicate health risks, provoke a greater emotional response and increase the motivation of tobacco users to quit and to decrease their tobacco consumption'.[233] They are also 'more likely to retain their effectiveness over time and are particularly effective in communicating health effects to low-literacy populations, children and young people'.[234] The introduction of combined health warnings illustrates the 'behavioural turn' in EU tobacco control and EU lifestyle policy more generally.[235] The disgusting and troubling character of the images is used to induce fear and to negatively

[227] ibid, art 20(4)(b)(i). [228] ibid, art 20(4)(a). [229] ibid, art 10(1).

[230] See the Commission Delegated Directive 2014/109/EU of 10 October 2014 amending Annex II to Directive 2014/40/EU of the European Parliament and of the Council by establishing the library of picture warnings to be used on tobacco products, OJ L360/22.

[231] Tobacco Products Directive, art 10(2). [232] ibid and Annex II.

[233] WHO, 'Guidelines for implementation of Article 11 of the WHO Framework Convention on Tobacco Control (Packaging and labelling of tobacco products)', para 7, <www.fctc.org/wp-content/uploads/2007/06/fca-2007-cop-article11-cop2-recommendations-en.pdf> accessed 11 September 2025.

[234] ibid. For more evidence on the effectiveness of combined warnings on smoking reduction and deterrence, see Bo Pang and others, 'The Effectiveness of Graphic Health Warnings on Tobacco Products: A Systematic Review on Perceived Harm and Quit Intentions' (2021) 21 BMC Public Health 884.

[235] Alberto Alemanno, 'Nudging smokers: The Behavioural Turn of Tobacco Risk Regulation' (2012) 3 European Journal of Risk Regulation 32.

affect consumers' emotions and evaluation of the risk.[236] The rotation of the warnings is meant to ensure that consumers are not too often confronted to the same texts and images, thus avoiding a 'washing out' or 'wear out' effect from materialising, whereby exposure to similar messages leads to habituation and decreased attention.[237]

5.5.2 *Voluntary Disclosure of Information*

Information voluntarily given by business operators can be useful to consumers, in which case its provision may be encouraged. It is however reasonable to consider that operators will not disclose information that cannot benefit them in one way or another, also because such disclosure entails costs. Voluntary information has often a promotional intent and can mislead consumers, especially as regards hazardous products. Rules have therefore been adopted to ensure that voluntary information is accurate, that it does not distort risk perception and thus encourage the consumption of unhealthy products. The main instrument in that regard is the Food Claims Regulation. In certain circumstances, information is deemed to be misleading per se, regardless of its accurate character, in which case its provision is prohibited. This stricter approach is especially visible as regards tobacco products.

5.5.2.1 Claims on Foods and Alcoholic Beverages

Generally, food law 'shall aim at the prevention of fraudulent or deceptive practices [and] other practices which may mislead the consumer'.[238] The relevant provisions for health and nutrition are contained in the Food Claims Regulation and, to a lesser extent, in the Food Information Regulation. Pursuant to Article 7 of the Food Information Regulation, food information shall not be misleading and shall be accurate, clear and easy to understand for the consumer. In particular, Article 7(1)(a) prohibits the provision of misleading information relating to the characteristics of the food, including its ingredients. If the voluntary information

[236] Jennifer S Blumenthal-Barby and Hadley Burroughs, 'Seeking Better Health Care Outcomes: The Ethics of Using the "Nudge"' (2012) 12 The American Journal of Bioethics 5–6; Sophie Lacoste-Badie and others, 'How Do Smokers Respond to Pictorial and Threatening Tobacco Warnings? The Role of Threat Level, Repeated Exposure, Type of Packs and Warning Size' (2019) 36 Journal of Consumer Marketing 461–471.

[237] Eva Woelbert and Béatrice d'Hombres, 'Pictorial Health Warnings and Wear-out Effects: Evidence from a Web Experiment in 10 European Countries' (2019) 28 Tobacco Control e71, 71–76.

[238] General Food Law Regulation, art 8.

provided refers to one of the mandatory particulars mentioned in Articles 9 or 10 of the Regulation, it shall comply with the requirements applicable to these particulars.[239] Voluntary information shall also not be ambiguous or confusing, shall be based, where relevant, on scientific data,[240] and shall not be displayed to the detriment of the space available for mandatory food information.[241]

The Food Claims Regulation, adopted in 2006,[242] is, with the Food Information Regulation, the other main instrument applicable to nutrition information. It regulates the use of health-related claims on products, messages used by food operators to claim particular health benefits for their products: 'good for your heart', 'rich in fibre' or 'increases your well-being'.[243] Claims are generally perceived positively by consumers and evidence shows that they incite to the purchase and consumption of foods.[244] Claims are therefore useful to food operators, as promotional tools. When truthful and correctly understood, claims are also beneficial to consumers, enabling them to make dietary choices aligned with their needs or interests. Yet, a number of behavioural phenomena suggest that consumers can easily be misled by claims. The 'halo effect', for instance, is a widely known psychological phenomenon whereby the positive or negative impression one has of an aspect of a person or object is extended to other unrelated aspects.[245] In the context of claims, emphasising one aspect of the food as being healthy can lead to the creation of a 'health halo', which makes the food appear healthier than it is, leading to overconsumption.[246] Consumers could, for instance, wrongly infer from a

[239] Food Information Regulation, art 36(1) and (2)(a). [240] ibid, art 36(2)(b) and (c).

[241] ibid, art 37.

[242] For a brief overview of the developments leading to this adoption, see Wieke Huizing Edinger, 'Promoting Educated Consumer Choices. Has EU Food Information Legislation Finally Matured?' (2016) 39 Journal of Consumer Policy 9.

[243] Under the Regulation, a claim is 'any message or representation, which is not mandatory under [EU] or national legislation, including pictorial, graphic or symbolic representation, in any form, which states, suggests or implies that a food has particular characteristics': Claims Regulation, art 2(2)(1).

[244] Asha Kaur, Peter Scarborough and Mike Rayner, 'A Systematic Review, and Meta-Analyses, of the Impact of Health-Related Claims on Dietary Choices' (2017) 14 International Journal of Behavioral Nutrition and Physical Activity 93. See also Claims Regulation, recital 10.

[245] Kai Purnhagen, Erica van Herpen and Ellen van Kleef, 'The Potential Use of Visual Packaging Elements as Nudges' in Klaus Mathis and Avishalom Tor (eds), *Nudging - Possibilities, Limitations and Applications in European Law and Economics* (Springer International Publishing 2016) 204.

[246] Aparna Sundar and others, 'Is Unnatural Unhealthy? Think about It: Overcoming Negative Halo Effects from Food Labels' (2021) 38 Psychology & Marketing 1280;

low cholesterol claim on butter that this product also has less calories. Against that background, the Food Claims Regulation pursues two main functions: (i) ensuring that the claims used by food business operators are accurate, based on appropriate scientific evidence and are not misleading to consumers, and (ii) restricting the use of claims for products that are deemed too harmful to human health.

The Regulation covers two kind of claims: nutrition claims and health claims.[247] A nutrition claim is defined as 'any claim which states, suggests or implies that a food has particular beneficial nutritional properties', due to its content of energy, nutrients or other substances, or to its lack thereof.[248] Typical examples include 'low sugars' or 'sugars-free', for a nutrient whose intake must be limited, or 'source of fibre' or 'high fibre', for a nutrient whose intake is recommended.[249] Health claims form a broader category, and are defined as 'any claim that states, suggests or implies that a relationship exists between a food category, a food or one of its constituents and health'.[250] The Regulation sets a number of general principles applicable to all claims. Claims must not be false, ambiguous or misleading,[251] and must fulfil a number of general conditions as to their truthfulness.[252] They shall be based on and substantiated by generally accepted scientific evidence, which must be adduced by the food business operators using them.[253]

Beyond these general principles, the Regulation lays down specific requirements applicable to each of the two categories of claims, resulting in a significantly different regulatory framework. Authorised nutrition claims are limited to a list annexed to the Regulation, which may be

Zenobia Talati and others, 'Consumers' Responses to Health Claims in the Context of Other on-Pack Nutrition Information: A Systematic Review' (2017) 75 Nutrition Reviews 260.

247 For a critical discussion of the difference made between those two categories of claims in the Claims Regulation, see Ellen Van Nieuwenhuyze, 'Regulating nutrition and health claims: EU food law's poisoned chalice?' (2015) Thèse présentée en vue de l'obtention du grade de docteur en sciences juridiques, 269–271, <https://dial.uclouvain.be/pr/boreal/object/boreal:167583> accessed 19 September 2025.

248 Claims Regulation, art 2(2)(4).

249 See ibid, annex.

250 ibid, art 2(2)(5). See the interpretation of the Court in Case C-544/10 *Deutsches Weintor*, EU:C:2012:526, para 35. Distinguishing between a health and a nutrition claim is not always easy, as both refer, directly or indirectly, to health benefits, see Nikhil Gokani, 'Front-of-Pack Nutrition Labelling: A Tussle between EU Food Law and National Measures' (2022) 47 European Law Review 153, 163.

251 Claims Regulation, art 3.

252 ibid, art 5.

253 ibid, art 6(1).

amended by way of an implementing act.[254] The use of any other nutrition claim is prohibited. The list lays down the conditions governing the use of each claim. The message 'energy-reduced' may, for instance, only be used 'where the energy value is reduced by at least 30%, with an indication of the characteristic(s) which make(s) the food reduced in its total energy value'.[255] The use of claims based on percentages is not authorised, on grounds of their misleading effect on consumers.[256] Indeed, referring to a product as '90 per cent fat-free' may, for instance, give the impression that this product contains little fat, even though a 10 per cent fat content can be very high for certain categories of products. At play here is a behavioural phenomenon known as 'framing', which the prohibition of percentage-based claims seeks to neutralise.[257] Framing refers to a situation where people are influenced by the way information is presented and judge differently equivalent statements depending on the point of reference chosen.[258] In our example, people would believe that a product '90 per cent fat-free' is healthier than one containing '10 per cent fat', where these two statements are obviously equivalent.

To be lawfully used, health claims must comply with a number of requirements.[259] Health claims must clearly specify the benefits brought by the nutrient or food. References attributing general and non-specific health benefits to a product are prohibited, unless accompanied by a specific health claim complying with the Regulation.[260] This prohibition aims at preventing consumers from being misled by a potential halo effect.[261] The Regulation differentiates between two kinds of health claims, governed by specific sets of conditions. The first category

[254] ibid, art 8 and annex. An exception applies for trademarks, brand names or fancy names, see art 1(3). For additional requirements applicable to comparative claims, see art 9.

[255] ibid, annex.

[256] European Commission, Claims Regulation Proposal, Explanatory Memorandum, para 18.

[257] See Baggio and others, 'The Evolution of Behaviourally Informed Policy-Making in the EU' 4.

[258] Zamir and Teichman, *Behavioral Law and Economics* 46–48.

[259] Claims Regulation, art 10.

[260] ibid, art 10(3). The meaning of 'accompanied' was discussed by the Court in the *Willmar Schwabe* case: Case C-524/18 *Willmar Schwabe*, EU:C:2020:60.

[261] See point 3 of the Annex to Commission Implementing Decision 2013/63/EU of 24 January 2013 adopting guidelines for the implementation of specific conditions for health claims laid down in Article 10 of Regulation (EC) No 1924/2006 of the European Parliament and of the Council, OJ L22/25.

contains claims referring to a reduction of disease risk or to children's development. The second category contains so-called function claims, which refer to the role of a nutrient or other substance in bodily or psychological functions.[262] Claims referring to a reduction of disease risk or to children's development must undergo an authorisation procedure.[263] They are first reviewed by EFSA, to ensure proper scientific substantiation and compliance with the Regulation, before being authorised by the Commission.[264] Function claims escape this authorisation procedure if they are based on generally accepted scientific evidence, are well understood by the average consumer and feature on a pre-approved list adopted by the Commission on the basis of submissions Member States had to make before 31 January 2008.[265] The reason is that these claims are less controversial and were based, at the time of the adoption of the Regulation, on long-standing evidence.[266] The list was finally adopted in 2012, after some difficulties.[267]

Apart from these conditions dealing with the truthfulness and the clarity of claims, the Claims Regulation also sets requirements as to the composition of products carrying claims, contained in Article 4. The idea is that unhealthy products should not benefit from claims, however accurate, so as to limit their attractiveness.[268] This applies to two categories of products: alcoholic beverages and products that contain certain nutrients in excess. For alcoholic beverages, the rule is simple: Article 4(3) prohibits the use of health or nutrition claims for beverages containing more than 1.2 per cent vol of alcohol. As stated by the Court in *Deutsches Weintor*, claims made on alcoholic beverages are 'likely to encourage [the consumption of these products] and, ultimately, to increase the risks for consumers' health inherent in the immoderate

[262] Claims Regulation, art 13(1). For examples, see the Annex of Commission Regulation (EU) No 432/2012 of 16 May 2012 establishing a list of permitted health claims made on foods, other than those referring to the reduction of disease risk and to children's development and health, OJ L136/1.

[263] Claims Regulation, art 14.

[264] ibid, arts 15–19.

[265] ibid, art 13. Supplementary claims may be added to this list in light of newly developed scientific evidence after complying with a specific authorisation procedure: ibid, see also art 18.

[266] Patrick Coppens, 'Regulation (EU) No. 432/2012 Establishing a List of Permitted Health Claims' (2012) 2012 European Food and Feed Law Review 162–163.

[267] Commission Regulation (EU) No 432/2012. See Coppens, 'Regulation (EU) No. 432/2012 Establishing a List of Permitted Health Claims' 162–163.

[268] For a detailed description of the behavioural phenomena that can lead to these wrong inferences, see Van Nieuwenhuyze, 'Regulating nutrition and health claims: EU food law's poisoned chalice?' 285–289.

consumption of any alcoholic beverage'.[269] There is an exception to this rule for three types of nutrition claims: those referring to low alcohol levels, to the reduction of the alcohol content or to the reduction of the energy content.[270]

The situation is more complex as regards foodstuffs containing certain nutrients in excess. To prevent a situation where nutrition or health claims would mask the overall nutritional status of a food product,[271] Article 4(1) of the Regulation provides for the establishment of nutrient profiles for foods or categories of foods. Products that do not comply with such nutrient profiles would be prohibited from using claims. Nutrient profiling can be defined as 'the classification of foods for specific purposes based on their nutrient composition',[272] relying, for instance, on maximum thresholds of nutrients. To take a concrete example, a nutrient profile set at 5 g of fat per 100 g would mean that all products in the relevant category with a fat content above that threshold would be prevented from using any claim. The Commission had until 19 January 2009 to adopt the nutrient profiles provided for in Article 4(1).[273] No such profiles have been adopted to date. In 2009, the Commission presented a proposal in this regard,[274] which was rejected due to the opposition from the industry and some Member States. These wished to establish exemptions or apply more lenient conditions to certain categories of foods.[275] As part of its Farm to Fork Strategy and Beating Cancer Plan, the Commission announced that a new proposal

[269] *Deutsches Weintor* para 52.

[270] In the absence of Union legislation, relevant national rules apply to these three kinds of permitted alcohol claims, see Claims Regulation, art 4(4).

[271] Claims Regulation, recital 11. See also Pierre Chandon, 'How Package Design and Packaged-Based Marketing Claims Lead to Overeating' (2013) 35 Applied Economic Perspectives and Policy 7; Asha Kaur, Peter Scarborough and Mike Rayner, 'A Systematic Review, and Meta-Analyses, of the Impact of Health-Related Claims on Dietary Choices'; Talati and others, 'Consumers' Responses to Health Claims in the Context of Other on-Pack Nutrition Information'.

[272] Scientific Opinion of the Panel on Dietetic Products, Nutrition and Allergies, 'The setting of nutrient profiles for foods bearing nutrition and health claims pursuant to article 4 of the Regulation (EC) no 1924/2006' (2008) 644 EFSA Journal 1.

[273] Claims Regulation, art 4(1).

[274] European Commission, 'Evaluation of the Regulation (EC) No 1924/2006 on nutrition and health claims made on foods with regard to nutrient profiles and health claims made on plants and their preparations and of the general regulatory framework for their use in foods' SWD (2020) 95 final, 17. For the proposed thresholds, see ibid, appendix 2.

[275] ibid 17.

would be put forward, with no success until now.[276] Some of the reasons behind these difficulties are further analysed in Section 8.3. Suffice to say, at this stage, that renouncing the adoption of nutrient profiles restricting the use of claims for unhealthy foodstuffs would be a step back for consumer protection and public health.

5.5.2.2 Misleading Tobacco Information

Following a logic similar to that of Article 4 of the Food Claims Regulation, Article 13 TPD prohibits the use of a number of elements on the packaging and labelling of tobacco products, which, while factually true, may mislead consumers or reinforce the attractiveness of these products.[277] It is worth reproducing those provisions in full:

1. The labelling of unit packets and any outside packaging and the tobacco product itself shall not include any element or feature that:
   (a) promotes a tobacco product or encourages its consumption by creating an erroneous impression about its characteristics, health effects, risks or emissions; labels shall not include any information about the nicotine, tar or carbon monoxide content of the tobacco product;
   (b) suggests that a particular tobacco product is less harmful than others or aims to reduce the effect of some harmful components of smoke or has vitalising, energetic, healing, rejuvenating, natural, organic properties or has other health or lifestyle benefits;
   (c) refers to taste, smell, any flavourings or other additives or the absence thereof;
   (d) resembles a food or a cosmetic product;
   (e) suggests that a certain tobacco product has improved biodegradability or other environmental advantages.
2. The unit packets and any outside packaging shall not suggest economic advantages by including printed vouchers, offering discounts, free distribution, two-for-one or other similar offers.[278]

[276] European Commission, 'A Farm to Fork Strategy for a fair, healthy and environmentally-friendly food system' 12; European Commission, 'Europe's Beating Cancer Plan' 10.

[277] See TPD, recitals 24, 25, 27; *Philip Morris* paras 138–145. See also David Hammond and Carla Parkinson, 'The Impact of Cigarette Package Design on Perceptions of Risk' (2009) 31 Journal of Public Health 345.

[278] Article 13 is partially applicable to e-cigarettes and herbal products for smoking: TPD, arts 20(4)(b)(ii) and 21(4).

Concretely, under Article 13, tobacco products are prevented from using words such as 'low-tar', 'light', 'ultra-light', 'mild', 'natural', 'organic', 'without additives', 'without flavours' or 'slim'.[279] The prohibition of any reference to the TNCO content of products reflects the fact that this information has been used by manufacturers to present some of their products as light and less dangerous.[280] Article 13 TPD can be seen as complementary to the TPD provisions on health warnings, ensuring that information on tobacco products only highlights the harmful effects of tobacco on health, to the exclusion of any promotional feature.

5.6 Conclusion

Save for some exceptions, such as tobacco for oral use and tobacco with a characterising flavour, unhealthy products may be lawfully placed on the EU market, at a price freely set by the relevant economic operators. The conditions under which such products may be marketed, however – their composition, packaging, labelling, advertising, etc. – are subject to a variety of requirements under EU law. Significant differences exist between products, reflecting the different policy objectives discussed in Chapter 4. The rules on tobacco products form a dense regulatory net whose objective is to reduce their attractiveness and to communicate to consumers, in clear and vivid terms, that these are hazardous products that are best avoided. By contrast, the rules governing unhealthy foods and alcoholic beverages concern primarily information, seeking to ensure that consumers are aware of what these products contain – nutrients, additives, alcohol, etc. – without placing restrictions on their composition. The EU thus promotes the 'responsible' consumption of

[279] TPD, recital 27. As regards Article 13 in general, the Court declared the following in *Philip Morris* para 160: 'It cannot be accepted that those elements and features may be included for the purpose of giving consumers clear and precise information, inasmuch as they are intended more to exploit the vulnerability of consumers of tobacco products who, because of their nicotine dependence, are particularly receptive to any element suggesting there may be some kind of benefit linked to tobacco consumption, in order to vindicate or reduce the risks associated with their habits'.

[280] Nigel Gray and Peter Boyle, 'Publishing Tobacco Tar Measurements on Packets' (2004) 329 BMJ: British Medical Journal 813. The press release published upon expiration of the deadline for transposition of the Tobacco Products Directive stressed that 'research has shown that TNCO labelling is misleading to consumers as it makes them believe that some products are less risky to their health. The new information message will more accurately reflect the true health consequences of smoking': European Commission, '10 key changes for tobacco products sold in the EU'. See also Tobacco Products Directive, recital 25.

these products, laying emphasis on individual choice and personal responsibility for adopting a healthier lifestyle. Another notable feature of the EU's approach towards food and alcohol is the reliance on industry self-regulation, to be contrasted with the strict exclusion of tobacco companies from policymaking, as required under the FCTC (see Section 4.3.2). This contrast is equally apparent when EU law is compared with the WHO's 'best buys', namely the most cost-effective interventions to tackle NCDs. While the EU has adopted two of the tobacco-related best buys, together with a number of other recommended measures, it has adopted none in relation to alcohol.[281] As should be clear by now, this divergence in treatment is not justified on health grounds but rests on broader economic and societal considerations. There is clearly scope for the EU to act more ambitiously and more effectively, in cooperation with the Member States. Part II of this book is concerned precisely with this question, adopting a forward-looking perspective to examine the potential and limits of further action in the field of unhealthy lifestyles. Two central challenges emerge: the weight of the internal market and the difficulties posed by diversity, understood both in terms of the effectiveness of EU-level intervention and the desirability of such intervention.

[281] WHO, 'Tackling NCDs: Best buys and other recommended interventions for the prevention and control of noncommunicable diseases'.

PART II

Unhealthy Lifestyles and the EU's Internal Market Dilemmas

6 Building a Market for Unhealthy Products

Striking the Balance between Health and Free Movement

6.1 Introduction

The central contention of this book is that regulating unhealthy lifestyles through the prism of the internal market exposes EU law to a series of dilemmas. This chapter addresses the first of these dilemmas: the paradox of building a market for unhealthy products by removing barriers to their free circulation, while simultaneously seeking to reduce, or even eliminate, their consumption. It examines the balance struck between these two competing and, at times, contradictory objectives. The tension between market and non-market interests, health in this case, has long been a staple of EU scholarship. One of the most debated aspects of EU internal market law is its alleged 'liberal economic bias'[1] and the broader 'imbalance' between the market and 'the social' in the EU's constitutional framework.[2] At the risk of oversimplification, this diverse body of scholarship may be summarised as follows. A first line of critique focuses on negative integration and, in particular, the Court of Justice's interpretation of the TFEU free movement provisions. The central concerns here are the expansive understanding of the concept of 'restriction'[3] and the priority often accorded to free movement over competing social interests, such as health,[4] within the

[1] Martin Höpner and Susanne K Schmidt, 'Can We Make the European Fundamental Freedoms Less Constraining? A Literature Review' (2020) 22 Cambridge Yearbook of European Legal Studies 182, 184.

[2] Garben, 'The Constitutional (Im)Balance between "the Market" and "the Social" in the European Union'.

[3] See Catherine Barnard, 'Restricting Restrictions: Lessons for the EU from the US?' (2009) 68 The Cambridge Law Journal 575; Höpner and Schmidt, 'Can We Make the European Fundamental Freedoms Less Constraining?'.

[4] See in the context of food and alcohol: Baumberg and Anderson, 'Health, Alcohol and EU Law'; MacMaoláin, *Food Law* 67–116.

proportionality review of national measures.[5] A second strand centres on the imbalance between negative and positive integration,[6] most famously articulated in Fritz Scharpf's theory of the asymmetry of European integration. According to Scharpf, the liberalising and deregulatory effects of free movement provisions cannot be counterbalanced by re-regulation through EU legislation, given the difficulties of decision-making at the Union level, linked inter alia to its consensual character.[7] Most of these authors criticise not only the predominance of market interests in the EU's legal order, but equally the democratic cost of judge-made law, when compared to legislation adopted at the national or EU level.

This chapter seeks, modestly, to 'test' these theories and approaches in the field at hand. Can it be said that the free movement of unhealthy products has been prioritised over the health of Europeans? The answer, it is argued, is unequivocally no. The critical 'schools' capture part of the picture.[8] They provide a valuable account of certain historical developments in EU law and a useful framework for analysing specific judgments. Yet EU internal market law, as applied to unhealthy lifestyles, cannot be adequately characterised as systematically, or even predominantly, favouring free movement over health – importantly, this is meant as rebutting the existence of a pro-market bias embedded in the law, not as an appraisal of the policies adopted at the EU level. On the contrary, unhealthy lifestyles arguably constitute an area where the internal market has been instrumentalised, and at times even undermined, in the pursuit of health protection. This is especially apparent if one adopts a holistic perspective that considers both negative and positive integration, and the position of national as well as EU-level control measures within the internal market.

6.2 Reviewing National Measures: A Question of Evidence

The first step of our enquiry concerns the effects of the TFEU free movement provisions on national control measures, with particular

[5] See Garben, 'The Constitutional (Im)Balance between "the Market" and "the Social" in the European Union'; Garben, 'The "Fundamental Freedoms" and (Other) Fundamental Rights'.

[6] ibid.

[7] Fritz W Scharpf, 'The Asymmetry of European Integration, or Why the EU Cannot Be a "Social Market Economy"' (2010) 8 Socio-Economic Review 211.

[8] For recent re-evaluations of Fritz Scharpf's asymmetry theory, see Martijn van den Brink, Mark Dawson and Jan Zglinski, 'Revisiting the Asymmetry Thesis: Negative and Positive Integration in the EU' (2025) 32 Journal of European Public Policy 209; Schütze, '"Integration-through-Law"'.

attention to Article 34 TFEU, analysed through the standard formula of 'restriction – justification – proportionality'. The central question addressed in this section is whether the objective of eliminating restrictions to free movement has led, or could lead, to the disapplication of legitimate public health measures. The same issue arises where national measures are assessed against rules of secondary law, which essentially give effect to free movement provisions or codify their interpretation by the Court of Justice, such as the Services Directive.[9] Because of the Court's broad understanding of what constitutes a restriction to free movement, most national measures fall under its scrutiny. In principle, however, Article 36 TFEU ensures that any measure well-calibrated to achieve a public health objective should be exempt from the prohibition of Article 34 TFEU. The same applies to measures falling within the scope of Article 56 TFEU, benefitting from Article 62 TFEU. As we shall see, the Court generally recognises the harmfulness of unhealthy lifestyles and accepts Member States' defences in this regard, provided that the measures are proportionate and supported by adequate evidence. It is precisely at this evidentiary stage that difficulties may arise, leading to the invalidation of legitimate public health measures. This occurs in two main ways. First, the Court insists on the production of evidence, which may be difficult to obtain or is absent in the specific case. For unhealthy lifestyles in particular, the multifactorial nature of diseases and the interdisciplinary character of the evidence at stake renders the measurement of the effectiveness of different policy options inherently difficult.[10] Second, the Court may misjudge the available evidence and, as a result, incorrectly assess the justified and proportionate character of a measure.

Before proceeding, a brief note on Articles 37 and 110 TFEU is necessary. Unlike the 'traditional' free movement provisions of Articles 34, 56 or 49 TFEU, Articles 37 and 110 TFEU remain anchored in a discrimination model. As such, they capture fewer national measures but, conversely, do not provide for a formal system of justification. This inevitably affects the range of regulatory choices available to Member States. Since these provisions have largely lost their practical significance,[11] they will not be addressed in the subsequent analysis.

[9] See Case C-16/23, *FA.RO. di YK & C. Sas*, EU:C:2024:886.

[10] Alemanno and Garde, 'The Emergence of EU Lifestyle Risk Regulation' 155.

[11] For a complete assessment of both provisions in this context, see Vincent Delhomme, 'Regulating lifestyle risks in EU law: Promoting health in a diverse market' (2023)

6.2.1 *The Broad Scope of Restrictions*

There has been considerable judicial and doctrinal debate on what constitutes a 'restriction' to free movement.[12] This question matters not only conceptually, in revealing which economic or free-trade model underpins the internal market,[13] but also practically, as it determines whether a national measure may ultimately be struck down under the free movement provisions, depending on its justification and proportionality. Free movement provisions generally prohibit measures that, limit cross-border trade, in one way or another, irrespective of whether they discriminate on the basis of origin. In the field of establishment and services, for instance, all measures 'which *prohibit, impede or render less attractive* the exercise of the freedoms guaranteed by Articles 49 TFEU and 56 TFEU must be regarded as restrictions'.[14] This very broad scope encompasses most national interventions in the market. This so-called market access approach, focusing on the ability of foreign operators or products to penetrate a domestic market, has likewise been applied in the context of goods. Yet as regards Article 34 TFEU, the case law remains fragmented, with enduring uncertainty as to which test applies to national measures.

According to the classical formula developed in *Dassonville*, a measure having equivalent effect under Article 34 TFEU is 'any measure of the Member States that is capable of hindering, directly or indirectly, actually or potentially, intra-Union trade'.[15] As Schütze has noted, this definition is an 'abstract (jurisdictional)' one which 'must always be matched and mediated by – at least – one of the three substantive principles listed by the Court'.[16] These three principles were summarised in *Italian Trailers* and correspond to three categories of rules.[17] The first covers 'product

Doctoral thesis, https://dial.uclouvain.be/pr/boreal/object/boreal:275547 accessed 23 September 2025.

[12] For a recent account, see Rufat Babayev, *Private Autonomy in EU Internal Market Law* (Hart Publishing 2024) 86–116.

[13] Robert Schütze, *From International to Federal Market: The Changing Structure of European Law* (Oxford University Press 2017).

[14] *Stanley International Betting* para 45.

[15] *Austria v Germany* para 120. See *Dassonville* para 5.

[16] Robert Schütze, 'Of Types and Tests: Towards a Unitary Doctrinal Framework for Article 34 TFEU?' (2016) 41 European Law Review 826, 835. In some isolated judgments, however, the Court considers national measures to be measures having equivalent effect against the sole *Dassonville* formula, see Case C-573/12 *Ålands Vindkraft*, EU:C:2014:2037, paras 65–67; Case C-602/19 *Kohlpharma*, EU:C:2020:804, paras 38–39.

[17] Case C-110/05 *Commission v Italy (Trailers)*, EU:C:2009:66.

requirements', such as rules on composition, packaging and labelling, discussed in Section 4.2. The principle of mutual recognition applies to these requirements, meaning that, in the absence of harmonisation, 'applying, to goods coming from other Member States where they are lawfully manufactured and marketed, rules that lay down requirements to be met by such goods constitute measures of equivalent effect to quantitative restrictions even if those rules apply to all products alike'.[18] The second category covers national rules on 'selling arrangements', that is, 'provisions concerning inter alia the place and times of sale of certain products and advertising of those products as well as certain marketing methods to be provisions governing selling arrangements'.[19] Here, the *Keck* discrimination test applies: such measures fall outside Article 34 TFEU if they 'apply to all relevant traders operating within the national territory and that they affect in the same manner, in law and in fact, the marketing of domestic products and of those from other Member States'.[20] Advertising restrictions, for example, are typically classified as selling arrangements,[21] though they may also raise issues under the free movement of services.[22] The third category includes all other rules 'which hinder [...] access of products originating in other Member States to the market of a Member State'.[23] This residual 'market access' test has been used to capture a wide array of lifestyle-related measures, such as the Scottish minimum unit pricing of alcohol,[24] the Spanish system of retail licences for tobacco[25] and the Portuguese rules on the taxability of such products.[26]

As regards lifestyle-related measures, the treatment of price regulation has been particularly uncertain. Early case law suggested that price measures would not restrict trade if they applied equally to domestic and imported products, unless the level set placed imported goods at a disadvantage.[27] Where retail prices remained freely determined by the producer or importer, restrictive effects were considered unlikely. This approach essentially subjected price measures to a discrimination test,[28]

[18] ibid, para 35. See also *Cassis de Dijon* paras 6, 14 and 15.

[19] Case C-71/02 *Karner*, EU:C:2004:181, para 38.

[20] *Trailers* para 36, see also *Keck and Mithouard* para 16.

[21] Joined Cases C-34/95, C-35/95 and C-36/95 *De* Agostini, EU:C:1997:344; *Gourmet*.

[22] *Bacardi France*; *Commission v France* (C-262/02). [23] *Trailers* para 37. [24] *Scotch Whisky*.

[25] Case C-156/10, *ANETT*, EU:C:2012:241. [26] *Commission v Portugal* (C-126/15).

[27] See Section 4.2.

[28] See *Scotch Whisky*, Opinion of Advocate General Bot para 65. See also the analysis of the arguments put forward by the European Commission in this case in MacCulloch 202–203.

confirmed post-*Keck* through their classification as selling arrangements.[29] The Court, however, significantly departed from this approach in *Scotch Whisky*. The measure at issue was Scotland's MUP rule for alcoholic beverages, fixing a minimum price of 0.50 pounds per unit of alcohol. Unlike in earlier cases, the Court did not examine whether imported products were placed at a disadvantage compared to domestic ones. Instead, it applied a market access test, holding that because the measure 'prevents the lower cost price of imported products being reflected in the selling price to the consumer means, *by itself*, that that legislation is capable of hindering the access to the United Kingdom market of alcoholic drinks'.[30] This reasoning treated the MUP as a direct impairment of market access, away from the discrimination model. This raised questions as to the treatment of other retail price measures, such as those examined in *INNO v ATAB* and *Van de Haar*,[31] where retailers were prevented from selling at a price other than that set by the manufacturer, but the manufacturer remained free to set the price. The Court gave its answer in *Colruyt*, concerning a Belgian legislation that prohibited retailers from selling tobacco at a retail price lower than the price indicated by the manufacturer or importer on the revenue stamp. Here, the Court considered the measure to be a selling arrangement which applied to all traders alike and left importers free to set prices. As such, it was not of such a kind as to prevent or impede access to the Belgian market for tobacco products from another Member State any more than it did for domestic tobacco products and therefore escaped the prohibition of Article 34 TFEU.[32] The divergence between *Scotch Whisky*, where a market access test was applied, and *Colruyt*, where a discrimination test was applied, is unsatisfactory for at least two reasons. First, conceptually, all price measures could be considered selling arrangements. If they 'do not concern the characteristics of those goods, but solely the arrangements under

[29] In *LIBRO*, the price measures were found to put imported products at a disadvantage, see Case C-531/07 *LIBRO*, EU:C:2009:276, paras 21–22. For a price measure classified as non-discriminatory and therefore valid selling arrangement, see Case C-63/94 *Belgapom*, EU:C:1995:270.

[30] *Scotch Whisky* para 32, emphasis added.

[31] *INNO v ATAB*; *Van de Haar*.

[32] *Colruyt* paras 37–40. See also Case C-221/15 *Colruyt*, EU:C:2016:288, Opinion of Advocate General Wahl, para 56. For a critical reading of both the Court and the Advocate General's reasonings, see Oliver Bartlett, 'The CJEU Assesses Another Minimum Pricing Measure Without Properly Contextualising It' (2016) 7 European Journal of Risk Regulation 810.

which they may be sold, [and therefore] must be regarded as concerning selling arrangements',[33] this should hold for both MUP and retail price maintenance. Secondly, by classifying price measures differently depending on whether importers or manufacturers retain price-setting freedom, the Court imposes a rigid distinction that fails to capture the possible restrictive effects of retail price rules.[34] As recognised in *INNO v ATAB* and *Van de Haar*, such measures may, in certain circumstances, hinder access to the market. A degree of uncertainty therefore continues to surround the applicable legal test for price measures under Article 34 TFEU.

6.2.2 *The Recognition of the Harmfulness of Unhealthy Lifestyles*

The broad reach of the free movement provisions is counterbalanced by the Court's readiness to acknowledge the harmfulness of unhealthy lifestyles, thereby allowing Member States to defend measures adopted to address such harm. In principle, Member States must demonstrate that the product or substance at issue poses a threat to human health.[35] The existence of such a threat, the Court has repeatedly stressed, 'must be measured, not according to the yardstick of general conjecture, but on the basis of relevant scientific research'.[36]

The Court has long recognised alcohol and tobacco control as legitimate objectives justifying restrictions on free movement. The difference between the two lies merely in the number of judgments delivered: there are fewer decisions concerning tobacco under Articles 34 and 56 TFEU than there are concerning alcohol. The harmfulness of alcohol was acknowledged at an early stage,[37] and today the Court routinely affirms that:

> [L]egislation which has as its objective the control of the consumption of alcohol so as to prevent the harmful effects caused to health of humans and society by alcoholic substances, and which thus seeks to combat alcohol abuse, reflects health and public policy concerns recognised by Article 36 TFEU.[38]

[33] *Colruyt* para 37.
[34] Bartlett, 'The CJEU Assesses Another Minimum Pricing Measure Without Properly Contextualising It'.
[35] Case C-663/18, *B S and C A (CBD)*, EU:C:2020:938, para 87.
[36] Case C-148/15 *Deutsche Parkinson Vereinigung*, EU:C:2016:776, para 42.
[37] Case 152/78 *Commission v France*, EU:C:1980:187, para 17.
[38] *Visnapuu* para 115. See also *Aragonesa* para 15; *Franzen* para 76; *Ahokainen* para 28; *Rosengren* para 40.

The same approach applies under Article 52(1) TFEU.[39] In Heinonen, the Court also accepted Finland's reliance on a broad notion of public order, encompassing public policy, security and morality, such as the prevention of alcohol-induced violence or drunk driving.[40] As for tobacco, the Court has also recognised its 'proven harmfulness', its 'addictive effects' and 'the incidence of serious diseases caused by the compounds those products contain that are pharmacologically active, toxic, mutagenic and carcinogenic'.[41] In both areas, what is striking is the absence of discussion of evidence: once harm is sufficiently well-established, as with alcohol and tobacco, the Court no longer demands specific proof. After all, as noted by Advocate General Poiares Maduro, the harmfulness of alcohol 'has been *common knowledge* since at least as far back as the time of the Old Testament'.[42] A rare departure from this approach occurred in Franzen, where Advocate General Elmer examined the Swedish retail monopoly on alcohol. He suggested that drinking 'three to five glasses of wine a day was beneficial to health' and that 'normal' beer consumption was harmless.[43] His selective use of evidence led him to wrongly assess the justification of the Swedish system, provoking 'obvious consternation in official Swedish circles' and extended criticism, as Kurzer noted, for 'citing medical scientific data of which he knew nothing and could claim no expertise'.[44] This opinion, now three decades old, reflects different prevailing views on alcohol at the time, yet it still serves as a reminder that courts must tread carefully when dealing with scientific data beyond their expertise.

The judicial landscape is more complex regarding food and nutrition. While the Court has recognised that some nutrients can be harmful in excess, it has been more cautious in accepting measures aimed at improving the overall *quality* of diets. Much of the case law concerns additives such as vitamins. In *Sandoz*,[45] the Court upheld Dutch rules requiring prior authorisation for vitamin-fortified food, justified by the risk that 'the absorption of any vitamins in high doses or for a prolonged period may entail risks to health or at least undesirable side-effects such as *malnutrition*'.[46] Although

[39] *Commission v France*C-262/02 para 30; *Bacardi France* para 37.
[40] *Heinonen* paras 18, 30–35.
[41] *FA.RO.* para 102. See also Case 90/82 *Commission v France*, EU:C:1983:169, para 29; Case C-156/10 *ANETT*, EU:C:2012:241, para 51; *CDIL* para 40.
[42] Case C-434/04 *Ahokainen and Leppik*, EU:C:2006:462, Opinion of Advocate General Poiares Maduro, para 20.
[43] *Franzen*, Opinion of Advocate General Elmer para 113.
[44] Kurzer, *Markets and Moral Regulation* 85.
[45] *Sandoz*.
[46] ibid, para 10, emphasis added.

vitamins are 'not "in themselves" harmful substances', 'excessive consumption of them over a prolonged period may have harmful effects',[47] compounded by the fact that diets are 'unforeseeable and cannot be monitored'.[48] Later judgments confirmed that prohibitions on marketing fortified foods may be justified, provided they are based on a global assessment of the food's role in the general diet.[49]

The 'vitamins' cases reveal that the Court is prepared to accept defences based on both the immediate and long-term harmful effects of foodstuffs. Yet they also highlight a key difference with alcohol and tobacco: in the field of nutrition, the Court insists on the production of specific evidence. In these cases, the Court required that a 'detailed assessment of the risk alleged' be conducted.[50] The purpose of that risk assessment is 'to appraise *the degree of probability of harmful effects* on human health from the addition of certain nutrients to foodstuffs and *the seriousness* of those potential effects'.[51] Failure to adduce the necessary evidence results in the rejection of the measure.[52] This can be seen in the *Van der Veldt* case, where the rule prohibiting the sale of bread and bakery products with more than 2 per cent salt, thereby restricting imports from the Netherlands, was struck down. The Belgian authorities argued that the Dutch salt level was 'too high' and that consuming Dutch products would increase 'the daily intake [of salt] to 3.1 g, which represents, not counting those who eat bread in large quantities, a daily increase of 0.6 g of salt for the average person'.[53] The Court rejected this argument, holding that '*general conjecture of that nature* does not prove that increasing salt intake by such an amount poses a risk for public health', which must be measured 'on the basis of *relevant scientific research*'.[54] Unlike alcohol or tobacco, the harmfulness of salt was not considered self-evident. This raises the question of what constitutes, in the Court's view, 'appropriate'[55] evidence. This relates both to the standard of proof and the standard of review.[56] The Court usually refers to the

[47] ibid, para 11. [48] ibid, para 17.

[49] *Commission v Germany (Beer purity)* para 42; *Commission v DenmarkC-192/01*; *Commission v FranceC-24/00*; *Commission v Netherlands* C-41/02 para 30.

[50] *Commission v DenmarkC-192/01* para 47; *Commission v FranceC-24/00* para 54; *Commission v NetherlandsC-41/02* para 48.

[51] *Commission v DenmarkC-192/01* para 48; *Commission v FranceC-24/00* para 55; *Commission v NetherlandsC-41/02* para 49, emphasis added.

[52] See *Commission v Germany (Beer purity)* para 48–49. [53] *Van der Veldt* para 16.

[54] ibid, para 17, emphasis added. [55] *Scotch Whisky* para 54.

[56] According to Craig, it is important to distinguish between issues pertaining to the standard of proof 'to be required of the initial or primary decision-maker before it makes the decision' and that pertaining to the standard of review 'applied by the reviewing

'latest scientific data available'[57] at the date of the adoption of the measure and requires that 'the results of *international* scientific research' be considered.[58] The latter requirement can be seen as a way for the Court to prevent reliance on purely 'national' evidence, hence potentially tainted by non-scientific, protectionist interests. The Court does not generally go as far as requiring a certain quantum of studies or a specific type of study to be performed or produced.[59]

The 'vitamins' cases demonstrate the Court's willingness to uphold defences based on toxicity or the harmfulness of specific compounds. By contrast, it has been far more reluctant to accept arguments based on the overall quality of diets. In *Commission v France (Milk substitutes)*, concerning a prohibition on imports of milk powder substitutes, the Court ruled that:

> [A] Member State *may not invoke public health grounds* in order to prohibit the importation of a product by *arguing that its nutritional value is lower* or its fat content higher than another product already available on the market in question. It is plain that *the choice of foodstuffs available to consumers* in the Community is such that the mere fact that an imported product has a lower nutritional value does not pose *a real threat to human health.*[60]

The Court adopted a similar approach in *Commission v Germany (Meat products)*,[61] which concerned a prohibition on marketing meat products containing non-meat ingredients, and in *Commission v Denmark*, where it made the point even more explicit: 'general preoccupations relating to the desired composition of the nutritional regime of the population of those States cannot constitute a lawful justification for obstacles to trade

court in deciding whether the primary decision-maker has met the standard of proof required of it': Paul Craig, *EU Administrative Law* (Oxford University Press 2006) 469–470. Arguably, it is true that 'EU Courts have never drawn a clear line' between standard of proof and standard of review, which 'are not wo separate notions but two aspects of a single control system': Fernando Castillo de la Torre and Eric Gippini Fournier, *Evidence, Proof and Judicial Review in EU Competition Law* (Edward Elgar Publishing 2017) 16–17.

57 *Commission v Denmark* C-192/01 para 48; *Commission v (France*C-24/00) para 55; *Commission v Netherlands* (C-41/02) para 49; *CBD* para 88.

58 *Commission v Denmark* (C-192/01) para 46; *Commission v France* (C-24/00) para 53; *Commission v Netherlands* (C-41/02) para 47, emphasis added. See also *Commission v Germany (Beer purity)* para 44; *Commission v Greece* para 38; *CBD* para 87.

59 See, however, a rare case where the Court does require such a high threshold of evidence: Case C-73/08 *Bressol*, EU:C:2010:181, para 71.

60 *Commission v France (Milk substitutes)* para 15, emphasis added.

61 *Commission v Germany (Meat products)* para 10.

between them'.[62] This stance has been rightfully criticised, with some arguing that the Court 'simply refuses to accept that placing restrictions on the marketing of nutritionally inferior substitutes is ever justifiable on health protection grounds'.[63] MacMaoláin goes further, claiming that these rulings 'effectively prohibit [...] the adoption of measures at national level which are designed to promote good health' and deprive Member States of the capacity to take meaningful action to combat obesity.[64] Such a conclusion seems however exaggerated. First, these judgments date from 1989, a time when obesity and nutrition were not yet framed as major public health priorities and scientific knowledge was more limited. It is plausible that the Court would take a different stance today, in light of policy developments at the EU level. Second, judgments such as *Sandoz* demonstrate that Member States can still adopt meaningful policies on diet and obesity, provided they are supported by sufficient evidence. Fat and sugar, although not 'in themselves' harmful, may well produce 'harmful effects' when consumed 'over a prolonged period',[65] particularly in diets whose overall composition 'is unforeseeable and cannot be monitored'.[66] The Court is therefore not, in principle, hostile to national measures promoting healthier diets, but it requires them to be supported by adequate scientific evidence. It must itself resist the temptation to substitute judicial intuition for expertise in complex scientific matters.

6.2.3 *Proportionality*

Restrictive measures justified by a legitimate public interest must be proportionate to the objective pursued in order to be upheld. Proportionality review in EU law is traditionally structured as a three-pronged test comprising (i) suitability, (ii) necessity and (iii) proportionality *stricto sensu*,[67] also referred to as 'true' proportionality.[68] In the field

[62] *Commission v Denmark* (C-24/00) para 21. [63] MacMaoláin, *Food Law* 92.

[64] MacMaoláin, *Food Law* 90–91. [65] *Sandoz* para 11. [66] ibid, para 17.

[67] See Jan H Jans, 'Proportionality Revisited' (2000) 23 Legal Issues of Economic Integration 238, 240–241; Takis Tridimas, 'Proportionality in Community Law: Searching for the Appropriate Standard of Scrutiny' in Evelyn Ellis (ed), *The Principle of Proportionality in the Laws of Europe* (Hart Publishing 1999) 68. For judicial support see Case C-434/04, *Ahokainen*, Opinion of Advocate General Poiares Maduro paras 23–26; Case 159/90 *Grogan*, EU:C:1991:249, Opinion of Advocate General Van Gerven, para 35.

[68] Jukka Snell, 'True Proportionality and Free Movement of Goods and Services' (2000) 11 European Business Law Review 50.

of free movement under the TFEU, however, the Court's review generally extends only to the first two elements. Accordingly, a national measure will be considered proportionate if it is '*appropriate* for securing the achievement of the objective pursued and does not go beyond what is necessary in order to attain it'.[69] A measure must first 'be *suitable* actually to protect the interest that requires protection. There must, as it were, be a causal relationship between the measure and its object'.[70] Second, the measure must not go beyond what is necessary to meet the objective it purports to achieve. This means that there must be no other measure available which is equally capable of attaining that objective but is less restrictive of free movement. It is the criterion of the 'least restrictive alternative'.[71] In the context of lifestyle-related health risks, the Court's review of proportionality is concerned with risk management, 'the process of weighing policy alternatives in the light of the results of risk assessment and, if necessary, selecting and implementing appropriate control options, including regulatory measures'.[72] Unlike risk assessment, which concerns the technical and scientific evaluation of the existence and magnitude of a risk,[73] risk managers must integrate non-scientific concerns in their appraisal to determine the harm acceptable for society and the measures to be adopted in consideration. This has been recognised by the Court, which has repeatedly held that it was the Member States' responsibility 'to *determine the level of protection which they wish to afford to public health* and the way in which that level is to be achieved' and to adopt, with a '*measure of discretion*', appropriate measures in this regard.[74] In reality, however, that measure of discretion can prove elusive. A systematic analysis of lifestyle-related free movement cases reveals a more nuanced picture, in which Member States are not always entrusted with a margin of appreciation.[75] As for the question of justification, this is closely linked to evidence.

69 *Scotch Whisky* para 33. See also, Case C-137/09, *Josemans*, EU:C:2010:774, para 69; *ANETT* para 45.

70 Jans, 'Proportionality Revisited' 240. 71 ibid.

72 Alberto Alemanno, 'The Shaping of European Risk Regulation by Community Courts' (2009) Jean Monnet Working Paper 18/08, 33.

73 As regards food safety, see the definitions of 'risk assessment' and 'risk management' contained at art 3(11) and (12) GFLR.

74 *Visnapuu* para 118. See also *Heinonen* para 43; *Ahokainen* paras 32–33; *Rosengren* para 39; *Scotch Whisky* para 35; *CDIL* para 46; *FA.RO.* para 101.

75 Following Zglinski's terminology, we focus here on the 'margin of appreciation', which results in the Court deferring to the national legislatures in the way they design a measure – this therefore concerns the relationship between courts in general and other organs of government. This is to be distinguished with a 'decentralized judicial review,

Regarding suitability, the Court usually leaves a margin of discretion: Member States must show a reasonable degree of connection between the measure and the objective put forward, but do not have to establish a strict causality. Member States 'enjoy a margin of discretion in determining [. . .] the measures which are *likely to achieve concrete results*'.[76] This is evident in *Scotch Whisky*, where the Court held, regarding the appropriateness of the Scottish MUP, 'that [. . .] *it does not seem unreasonable* to consider that a measure that sets a minimum selling price of alcoholic drinks [. . .] is *capable* of reducing the consumption of alcohol',[77] without insisting further on tangible causation. Regarding necessity, the Court's assessment is essentially a comparative exercise: Member States must ensure that the objective cannot 'be achieved with *at least an equivalent level of effectiveness* by less restrictive methods'.[78] The question of necessity is thus intrinsically linked to the standard of protection chosen,[79] which is, according to the Court, in the hands of the Member States.[80] Such a deferent approach is apparent in *Commission v France (Loi Evin)*, where the Court, regarding the French rule prohibiting television advertising for alcoholic beverages, ruled that:

> [A]lthough there are less restrictive measures to ensure the protection of public health, [. . .] there is not currently any measure which is less restrictive which can exclude or conceal indirect television advertising for alcoholic beverages resulting from hoardings visible during the retransmission of sporting events.[81]

The Court acknowledged that measures less restrictive of free movement existed, but deferred to the choice made in France to eliminate all forms of television advertising for alcoholic beverages, direct and indirect.

where the Court of Justice lets the national judge conducting the review of a measure – in that latter case, this is not about the intensity of the review, but who performs it'. See Jan Zglinski, 'The Rise of Deference: The Margin of Appreciation and Decentralized Judicial Review in EU Free Movement Law' (2018) 55 Common Market Law Review 1341.

76 *Heinonen* para 43; *Ahokainen* para 32, emphasis added.

77 *Scotch Whisky* 36, emphasis added.

78 *Visnapuu* para 119, emphasis added.

79 Schütze, *From International to Federal Market* 219.

80 Miguel Poiares Maduro famously described the Court's approach to necessity as a form of 'majoritarian activism'. According to him, in its assessment, the Court compares the Member State's rule under scrutiny to those in place in other Member States, and discard that rule if it appears that a majority of other States made a different regulatory choice: Miguel Poiares Maduro, *We The Court: The European Court of Justice and The European Economic Constitution* (Hart Publishing 1998) 72–78. There is little to no trace of such an approach in the field of unhealthy lifestyles. For a broader refutation of Maduro's view, see Robert Schütze, 'Judicial Majoritarianism Revisited: "We, the Other Court"?' (2018) 43 European Law Review 269.

81 *Commission v France* (C-262/02) para 34. See *Bacardi France* paras 38–39.

These judicial examples of a more 'hands-off' approach must, however, be contrasted with cases where the Court applies a higher degree of scrutiny. *Rosengren* is a case in point. In that judgment, the Court reviewed the validity of the Swedish measure prohibiting the direct import of alcohol by private individuals and reserving this right to the State monopoly, *Systembolaget*. Sweden argued that this rule fulfilled two objectives: a general one of limiting the consumption of alcohol in the population and a specific one of preventing access to alcoholic beverages for underage persons. Regarding the first objective, the Court observed that the rule in place simply required individuals to place an order with *Systembolaget*, something which the Swedish monopoly had never refused to execute.[82] The Court accepted that the measure, in reducing the sources available to the consumer, '*may contribute, to a certain extent, because of the difficulty of supply*, to prevention of the harmful effects of [alcohol]'.[83] Yet, it considered that the rule had, at best, a marginal effect on alcohol consumption and was therefore unsuitable to achieving the first objective pursued by Sweden.[84] Clearly, the Court was not satisfied here with the loose degree of connection between a measure and its objective that it expected in other cases. There is much to criticise in this assessment, which seems to ignore that making access to the product more difficult is the very logic underlying many alcohol and tobacco control measures. This type of intervention, which adds excessive friction to people's choices, is recognised in the behavioural literature as an effective tool to impede decision-making.[85] Regarding the second objective, the protection of youth, the Court recognised that, by entrusting the right of import solely to the public monopoly, Sweden had set up a '*a centralised and coherent [system]* which must allow the monopoly's agents [. . .] to *satisfy themselves in a consistent manner that the goods are provided only to persons of more than 20 years of age*'.[86] Yet, the Court considered that the system failed to attain an '*irreproachable level of effectiveness*',[87] because age checks also happened to be carried out by third parties, for instance in bars and restaurants. Here again, the degree of scrutiny applied stands in stark contrast with the likeliness and reasonableness expected by the Court in other cases.[88] An explanation for the stricter approach taken in

[82] *Rosengren* paras 45–46. [83] ibid, para 45. [84] ibid, para 47.

[85] Sina Shahab and Leonhard K Lades, 'Sludge and Transaction Costs' (2024) 8 Behavioural Public Policy 327.

[86] ibid, para 52, emphasis added. [87] ibid, paras 53–54, emphasis added.

[88] See, in particular, in a comparable fact situation, the higher degree of deference showed by the Court in *Visnapuu* paras 121–122.

Rosengren may lie in the particularly restrictive effect of the Swedish measure on the free movement of goods, an import ban on individuals, which the Court categorised as a quantitative restriction to imports. Yet, the Court's evaluation of the measure led to lowering the degree of health protection sought by Sweden, contrary to the Court's continuous insistence on the opposite.

As it is the case at the risk assessment stage, the Court's ultimate conclusion regarding the proportionality of the measure often hinges on questions of evidence: how much is required, that is, the standard of evidence, and how is this evaluated, that is, the standard of review. As to the standard of evidence, little guidance, if any at all, is to be found in the case law on what kind of data is required to establish the proportionality of a given measure.[89] In a number of cases, such as *Aragonesa*, *Commission v France (Loi Evin)* or *Bacardi France*, the Court discusses and ultimately upholds the proportionality of the measures without any reference to specific evidence.[90] In *Aragonesa*, it was for the Court 'sufficient to observe' that 'advertising acts as an encouragement to consumption'[91] to establish the suitability of the advertising ban at stake, without the need for any kind of evidence to be adduced regarding the relationship between advertising and consumption and hence the likely effect of a restriction on advertising.

This may, however, be changing. In *Scotch Whisky*, the Court made a bigger inroad into the role played by evidence at the proportionality stage and provided more detailed guidance to national courts.[92] In particular, the Court held that:

> [I]t is for the national court called on to review the legality of the national legislation concerned to determine the relevance of the evidence adduced by the competent national authorities in order to determine whether that legislation is compatible with the principle of proportionality. On the basis of that evidence, that court must, in particular, examine objectively whether it may *reasonably* be concluded from the evidence submitted by the Member State concerned that the means chosen are appropriate for the attainment of the objectives pursued and whether it is possible to attain those objectives by measures that are less restrictive of the free movement of goods.[93]

[89] For an example of clear guidance given by the Court, see *Deutsche Parkinson* para 36.

[90] See Amandine Garde, 'Freedom of Commercial Expression and Public Health Protection: The Principle of Proportionality as a Tool to Strike the Balance' in Niamh Nic Shuibhne and Laurence W Gormley (eds), *From Single Market to Economic Union: Essays in Memory of John A Usher* (Oxford University Press 2012) 129.

[91] *Aragonesa* para 15.

[92] See *Scotch Whisky* paras 51–65.

[93] ibid, para 56, emphasis added.

Although the consequences of *Scotch Whisky* on the evidentiary requirement expected from national authorities as part of the proportionality assessment remain to be seen,[94] 'it could provide a precedent from which the CJEU could extend its shift towards greater engagement with evidence into more highly sensitive policy fields'.[95] Greater engagement with evidence should not necessarily result in fewer opportunities for Member States to act, but rather lead to a more transparent and open discussion of the regulatory options chosen by Member States and their evaluation.[96] This aligns with what Nic Shuibhne and Maci coined as 'a marked shift in recent case-law towards *positive* expression of and engagement with the standard of proof, which contrasts with the *negative* guidance more prevalent before'.[97]

Due in no small part to problems of evidence, the Court has, throughout its case law, repeatedly and mistakenly opposed two kinds of measures: minimum price measures for tobacco products and alcoholic beverages, and composition requirements for foodstuffs. In a series of cases involving the EU legal framework on excise duties for tobacco products, Member States had enacted rules imposing a minimum retail selling price for cigarettes (see Section 5.3.1). An increase in excise duty, they argued, was less effective than a minimum price to ensure a rise in the final price paid by consumers, since manufacturers and importers could decide, by reducing their profit margin, to absorb the increase so as not to pass it on to consumers.[98] The Court disagreed and discarded the minimum price measures, considering that the 'ability of manufacturers and importers not to pass on increases in excise duty on their products is in any event limited by the extent of their profit margin, with the result that *excise duty increases are sooner or later incorporated in retail selling prices*'.[99] It added that:

> [I]f the Member States wish to exclude once and for all any possibility for producers or importers to absorb, even temporarily, the impact of taxes on the retail

94 See Bartlett and Macculloch, 'Evidence and Proportionality in Free Movement Cases'.
95 ibid 116.
96 For an early application of such an approach, see Case C-320/03 *Commission v Austria*, EU:C:2005:684, paras 87–89.
97 Niamh Nic Shuibhne and Marsela Maci, 'Proving Public Interest: The Growing Impact of Evidence in Free Movement Case Law' (2013) 50 Common Market Law Review 965, 978.
98 *Commission v Greece*C-216/98 para 29; *Commission v Austria*C-198/08 para 37; *Commission v Ireland*C-221/08 para 49.
99 *Commission v Greece*C-216/98 para 32, emphasis added. See also *Commission v France*C-197/08 para 52; *Commission v Austria*C-198/08 para 42; *Commission v Ireland*C-221/08 para 54; *Commission v Italy*C-571/08 para 51.

selling price of manufactured tobacco products by selling them at a loss, it is inter alia open to them, while allowing those producers and importers to make effective use of the competitive advantage resulting from any lower cost prices, to prohibit the sale of manufactured tobacco products at a price below the sum of the cost price and all taxes.[100]

In *Scotch Whisky*, ironically, the Court followed a similar reasoning regarding the Scottish MUP for alcoholic beverages. Relying on the aforementioned cases on tobacco excise duties, the Court reiterated that 'the objective of ensuring that the prices of [alcoholic] drinks are set at high levels can adequately be pursued by their increased taxation, since increases in excise duties must sooner or later be reflected in increased retail selling prices, without impinging on the free formation of prices'.[101] An increase in taxation, the Court continued, 'is liable to be less restrictive of trade' than an MPU since the latter measure 'significantly restricts the freedom of economic operators to determine their retail selling prices' and therefore constitutes 'a serious obstacle' to market access and to the operation of fair competition.[102]

As appears from the *Scotch Whisky* judgment, the Court's reticence to accept the proportionality of national minimum price measures can be explained by the importance given to price competition in EU law, a central feature of a well-functioning market economy.[103] 'In contemporary European economies the direct regulation of prices is not normally seen as being the role of the State'.[104] Notwithstanding the restrictive nature of price measures for free movement, the Court's reasoning in these various cases appears misguided on multiple accounts. The idea that an increase in excise duties will sooner or later be passed on to consumers neglects the fact that tobacco companies can use a variety of techniques to continue supplying cheap products on the market, over-shifting, for instance, the increase on more expensive premium brands, for which demand is less elastic.[105] Similarly, an increase in excise duties for alcoholic beverages

[100] *Commission v France*C-197/08 para 53; *Commission v Austria*C-198/08 para 43; *Commission v Ireland*C-221/08 para 55; *Commission v Italy*C-571/08 para 52.

[101] *Scotch Whisky* para 44. [102] ibid, para 46.

[103] MacCulloch, 'State Intervention in Pricing'. [104] ibid 190.

[105] See Ian McLaughlin and others, 'Reducing Tobacco Use and Access Through Strengthened Minimum Price Laws' (2014) 104 American Journal of Public Health 1844; Ross Whitehead and others, 'Rapid Evidence Review: Strengths and Limitations of Tobacco Taxation and Pricing Strategies' (2018) NHS Health Scotland 28; Timea R Partos and others, 'Impact of Tobacco Tax Increases and Industry Pricing on Smoking Behaviours and Inequalities: A Mixed-Methods Study' (2020) 8 Public Health Research.

does not prevent supermarkets from continuing to offer discounts on cheaper products or the industry to absorb the increase and cross-subsidising products.[106] Only minimum price measures can ensure that the cheapest products, those which are most consumed, are swiftly driven out of the market. This is especially important for low-income consumers, the category of the population that is most price sensitive, and for hazardous drinkers who consume in particular cheaper products. The Court's reasoning in *Scotch Whisky* contains further problematic elements. In particular, the Court was told that the solution found in the tobacco excise duties cases would not necessarily hold true for alcoholic beverage, to which it replied that '[i]n the context of national measures which have as their objective the protection of human life and health, and *irrespective of the particular characteristics of each product*, an increase in the prices of alcoholic drinks can be achieved, as was the case with respect to tobacco products, by increased taxation'.[107] This is a regrettable mistake, as there are substantial differences between the markets in tobacco products and alcoholic beverages, which render the adoption of a minimum price measure even more pertinent for the latter.[108] The market for tobacco products is far more homogenous than that for alcoholic beverages. Cigarettes, the category most widely consumed, present very similar levels of harm and a fairly limited price range. Alcoholic beverages, by contrast, display significant variations in strength, price and organoleptic properties. This means that price measures targeting specific categories of cheap products may be even more warranted for alcoholic beverages than for tobacco products. Finally, the Court considers that an increase in taxation would not only be equally capable of attaining the objectives sought by the MUP – 'reducing, in a targeted way, [. . .] the consumption of alcohol by consumers whose consumption is hazardous or harmful' and reducing 'generally, the

[106] See Peter Rice and Colin Drummond, 'The Price of a Drink: The Potential of Alcohol Minimum Unit Pricing as a Public Health Measure in the UK' (2012) 201 The British Journal of Psychiatry 169; Ian Gilmore, 'A Minimum Unit Price: The "Holy Grail" of Alcohol Policy' (2015) 15 Clinical Medicine 5. See also Luca A Panzone, 'Alcohol Tax, Price–Quality Proxy and Discounting: A Reason Why Alcohol Taxes May Rebound' (2012) 63 Journal of Agricultural Economics 715.

[107] *Scotch Whisky* para 45, emphasis added.

[108] See Oliver Bartlett, 'Minimum Unit Pricing for Alcohol May Not Be a Proportionate Public Health Intervention' (2016) 7 European Journal of Risk Regulation 218, 220; Alberto Alemanno, 'Balancing Free Movement and Public Health: The Case of Minimum Unit Pricing of Alcohol in Scotch Whisky' (2016) 53 Common Market Law Review 1037, 1057; Bartlett and MacCulloch, 'Evidence and Proportionality in Free Movement Cases' 113–114.

population's consumption of alcohol' – [109]but would actually procure 'additional benefits as compared with the imposition of an [MUP]',[110] as it would equally impact both categories of the population.[111] This, however, was a clear misunderstanding of the objective of the Scottish authorities, which was to target drinkers whose consumption of alcohol is hazardous, moderate consumption being 'only secondarily' affected.[112]

A second type of measures which the Court has routinely opposed are those related to the composition of foodstuffs. The Court has repeatedly ruled that composition requirements were not necessary to protect consumers' legitimate expectations as to the content of products, and that appropriate labelling was sufficient to inform consumers in this regard.[113] For the Court, labelling 'enable[s] the consumer to make his choice in full knowledge of the facts'.[114] In most of these cases, Member States' measures sought to protect the use of certain product denominations, such as pasta, beer or vinegar, on grounds of consumer protection, but did not clearly involve any public health aspect, such as limiting the intake of certain nutrients or substances.[115] In some cases, however, the measures were prompted by nutrition-based considerations. This can be seen in *Van der Veldt*, where the Court ruled, regarding the Belgian rule limiting salt in bread and bakery products, that:

> [I]nstead of prohibiting and penalizing the marketing of bread and other bakery products whose salt content is higher than 2%, *the Belgian legislature could have*

[109] *Scotch Whisky* para 34. [110] ibid, para 48. [111] ibid, para 47.

[112] ibid, para 34. This point seems overlooked by a number of authors who have claimed that the outcome of the case could have been different had the Scottish authorities insisted on a single objective, that of targeting hazardous drinkers: see Alemanno, 'Balancing Free Movement and Public Health' 1052; Bartlett and Macculloch, 'Evidence and Proportionality in Free Movement Cases' 125–126. Yet, this would most likely not have changed the Court's appraisal since it anyway considers taxation to be as efficient as minimum pricing to raise the price of all alcoholic beverages.

[113] Case 193/80 *Commission v Italy (Vinegar)*, EU:C:1981:298, para 27; *Commission v Germany (Beer purity)* para 35; *Zoni* para 16. The same reasoning is applied in cases involving packaging requirements, see Case 261/81 *Rau v De Smedt* EU:C:1982:382, para 17; Case 16/83 *Criminal proceedings against Karl Prantl*, EU:C:1984:101, para 29; Case 179/85 *Commission v Germany (Sparkling wine)*, EU:C:1986:466, para 12.

[114] *Commission v Italy* (193/80) para 27; *Commission v Germany (Beer purity)* para 35.

[115] Some authors have argued that the Court's position had led to a lowering of the quality of the food available on the European market, see Brouwer, 'Free Movement of Foodstuffs and Quality Requirements'; Caoimhín MacMaoláin, 'Reforming European Community Food Law: Putting Quality Back on the Agenda' (2003) 58 Food and Drug Law Journal 549. Quality is used in that context to refer to the organoleptic properties of foods rather than its nutritional aspect.

prescribed suitable labelling to give consumers the desired information regarding the composition of the product. *The protection of public health would thus have been ensured* without such serious restrictions on the free movement of goods.[116]

Similarly, in *Commission v France (Milk substitutes)*, the Court applied the same reasoning regarding the French prohibition of milk substitutes, considering that 'appropriate labelling informing consumers about the nature, the ingredients and the characteristics of the milk substitutes on offer would enable persons liable to be adversely affected by vegetable fats or other constituents of the milk substitutes to decide for themselves as to whether to use them'.[117]

The Court's trust in the capacity of consumers to process the information given on products' labelling and packaging derives from a vision of 'an average consumer who is reasonably well-informed and reasonably observant and circumspect'[118] and who reads labels when their purchasing decisions depend on the composition of the products in question.[119] This has led to the development of an 'information paradigm' (see Section 5.5). The problem with this approach is twofold. First, as already exposed, the Court's vision of the average consumer is at odds with behavioural reality.[120] Most consumers, especially in a retail environment, lack the time and interest to properly check the information given on labels. Where they do so, they may not possess the appropriate knowledge to process that information and make a fully informed decision. Taking the *Van der Veldt* case as an example, it seems highly improbable that all consumers would carefully read the labels indicating the amount of salt in bread and, upon realising that the content exceeds

[116] *Van der Veldt* para 19.

[117] *Commission v France (Milk substitutes)* para 16. See also the similar line of argumentation held by the Commission in Case C-420/01 *Commission v Italy*, EU:C:2003:363, para 18: 'Finally, a mere obligation for the producer of the drinks in question to provide the consumer with accurate information as to their caffeine content is an effective way to protect persons at risk'.

[118] Case C-210/96 *Gut Springenheide*, EU:C:1998:369, para 31; Case C-220/98 *Estée Lauder*, EU:C:2000:8, para 27.

[119] Case C-51/94 *Commission v Germany*, EU:C:1995:352, para 34; Case C-465/98 *Darbo*, EU:C:2000:184, para 22.

[120] In the EU context, see e.g. Rossella Incardona and Cristina Poncibò, 'The Average Consumer, the Unfair Commercial Practices Directive, and the Cognitive Revolution' (2007) 30 Journal of Consumer Policy 21; Sibony and Helleringer, 'EU Consumer Protection and Behavioural Sciences' 214–215. See contra Stephen Weatherill, 'Who is the "Average Consumer"'in Stephen Weatherill and Ulf Bernitz (eds), *The Regulation of Unfair Commercial Practices under EC Directive 2005/29: New Rules and New Techniques* (Hart Publishing 2007) 123–133.

2 per cent, refrain from buying the product. Yet, this is precisely what labelling would need to achieve to be considered as effective as a mandatory salt limit. The Court's approach therefore results in a lowering of the degree of protection afforded to public health, a choice supposedly remaining firmly in the hands of the Member States. The second problem lies with the existence of the average consumer in itself as an 'autonomous European standard'[121] against which Member State measures are analysed. Regardless of the characteristics attributed to this average consumer, its existence denies Member States the possibility of setting their own level of protection. Some Member States may adopt a more protective interpretation of the average consumer, and measures calibrated accordingly risk appearing disproportionate when compared to the European benchmark.

6.2.4 *Interim Conclusion*

To conclude, nothing allows to say that the Court has overall favoured free movement over the protection of health in cases involving tobacco, alcohol and nutrition: 'EU law is not the threat for health that some [...] professionals appear to believe—yet neither it is inconsequential for health'.[122] The case law offers a nuanced picture, namely that of a broad scope of application of free movement provisions, compensated by a wide recognition of Member States' interests. Proportionality, as adequately described by De Witte, is a principle 'surprisingly amorphous and notoriously difficult to understand', whose 'application is not consistent' and whose 'intensity of review [...] seems to differ in light of the outcome that it can allow for'.[123] Overly strict cases, such as *Rosengren*, coexist with many others where the Court grants Member States a wide degree of discretion, such as *Aragonesa*, *Commission v France (Loi Evin)*, or *Bacardi France*. If it is difficult to discern a specific evolution in this field, the trend appears closer to the direction suggested by Zglinski, namely towards a greater margin of appreciation.[124] Where the Court mistakenly opposes national measures, this is most often due to a lack of engagement with, or misunderstanding of, evidence, as in *Scotch Whisky* and food labelling cases. The plea to be made is that of greater and more

[121] Schütze, *From International to Federal Market* 222.
[122] Baumberg and Anderson, 'Health, Alcohol and EU Law' 396.
[123] Floris De Witte, 'Sex, Drugs & EU Law: The Recognition of Moral and Ethical Diversity in EU Law' (2013) 50 Common Market Law Review 1545, 1567.
[124] Zglinski, 'The Rise of Deference' 55.

transparent use of evidence, without undue insistence on some sort of silver bullet, in a field characterised by complex scientific assessments. Whichever impact free movement provisions may have had should also be tempered by the fact that, at least in relation to goods, they no longer play a central role. There was never much case law on tobacco and HFSS foods. Most cases concerned alcohol, but there are less of these too since the landmark *Scotch Whisky* ruling. Harmonisation, as this book demonstrates, is the real driver and is arguably more to blame for constraining Member States' capacity to act, as Chapter 7 will show. A further methodological point is in order. To answer the question of the impact of TFEU free movement provisions in a meaningful way, it is not sufficient to look only at the outcome of preliminary reference cases. One should examine what becomes of these cases at the national level. A 'negative' judgment by the Court may ultimately lead to a 'positive' outcome at the national level, on the basis of the facts and the margin of appreciation left to the national judge. *Scotch Whisky* is a case in point. The UK Supreme Court, applying the law as in *Scotch Whisky* but with a different understanding of the measure's objectives and of the evidence, ultimately upheld the measure. Moreover, to obtain a reliable picture one must also consider cases fully decided by national courts, as well as the cases that never reached the courts, by examining the regulatory practices of Member States. In sum, offering a definitive answer is difficult, and there is much to be said for adopting a more measured approach when asserting that free movement provisions, as a whole, have produced deregulatory outcomes, beyond the specifics of each individual case.

6.3 Reviewing EU Measures: The Internal Market Instrumentalised

The second step of our inquiry into the balance between market and health concerns harmonisation. Here, unlike under the free movement provisions, market and non-market objectives are not placed in direct opposition. Rather, they operate in tandem. Harmonisation implies re-regulation, namely the adoption of standards that serve both the internal market, by eliminating regulatory divergences between Member States, and public health, by ensuring a common level of protection across the EU. Determining this level of protection is a political choice entrusted to the EU legislature, provided that the conditions for recourse to the TFEU internal market legal bases are fulfilled, Article 114 TFEU in particular. In this sense, the market functions as an auxiliary to public health. The

EU's ability to act is reinforced by the hands-off approach adopted by the Court of Justice when reviewing the proportionality of EU measures, which grants the EU legislature a considerable degree of latitude. Yet, the relationship between the internal market and health is far from entirely harmonious. Certain interventions lack a sufficient connection with market-making and therefore fail to satisfy the requirements of Article 114 TFEU. While the EU legislature has often pushed the market logic to its limits, and at times beyond, the Court has responded inconsistently. On some occasions, it has acknowledged the boundaries of the EU's competence under Article 114 TFEU, thereby restricting the possibilities for health protection. On others, it has favoured health in ways that sit uneasily with the concept of the internal market as a space for the free circulation of goods and services. This demonstrates that pursuing health objectives mostly through a market competence is not ideal, as it constrains regulatory possibilities in a manner ultimately detrimental to both the internal market and public health.

6.3.1 *Proportionality of EU Interventions*

Unlike in the case of the proportionality of Member State restrictions to free movement, the case law on the proportionality of EU lifestyle interventions is clear and consistent: the EU legislature is afforded a wide margin of discretion regarding the level of health protection it seeks to achieve and the measures appropriate to attain it. As with national measures, economic actors have repeatedly challenged EU lifestyle measures on grounds of restrictions to business opportunities or loss of revenue, to no avail. Proportionality, as applied by the Court of Justice, functions primarily as a procedural tool: the Court requires the EU legislature to explain its regulatory choices, without scrutinising in detail their objectives or effects. Proportionality is thus not an obstacle to the strengthening of EU lifestyle policies.

It is important to clarify that, unlike for national measures, the Court scrutinises the suitability, necessity but also the proportionality *stricto sensu* of EU measures, the third element of the test.[125] According to the Court, 'the EU legislature must be allowed *broad discretion*' in an area such as the regulation of lifestyle risks, 'which entails political, economic and social choices on its part, and in which it is called upon to undertake

[125] See e.g. *Philip Morris* para 165; *Pillbox 38* para 48; *Poland v Parliament and Council* para 78.

complex assessments'.[126] The legality of a measure adopted in that area can therefore only be affected if the measure is *manifestly* inappropriate or goes manifestly beyond what is necessary with regard to the objective sought, or leads to manifestly disproportionate consequences.[127] Hence, the judicial review of proportionality is attenuated with regard to these three constituent elements. Regarding suitability, the Court's review of EU measures resembles that applied to national measures. It is limited to establishing a reasonable degree of connection between the measure and its health objective. This is illustrated in *Pillbox 38*, where the Court considered that the TPD rules setting a maximum volume and a maximum nicotine concentration for e-cigarettes '*make it possible* to limit the risks linked to exposure to nicotine' and are therefore appropriate for ensuring a high level of protection of human health.[128] The Court similarly accepts that advertising restrictions are suitable to reduce the consumption of a given product, as it does for national measures.[129]

The difference in the standard of review between EU and national measures is most evident regarding necessity. Whereas the Court often engages in detailed discussion of alternative measures available to Member States, such analysis is largely absent from case law on EU measures. This is evident in the judgments on the ban on tobacco for oral use.[130] In *Swedish Match* and *Arnold André*, the Court observed that, as 'apparent from the preamble to the [2001 TPD]', 'the prohibition of the marketing of tobacco products for oral use was *the only measure that appeared appropriate* to cope with the real danger that those new products would be used by young people'.[131] The Court further noted that '*no other measures* aimed at imposing technical standards on manufacturers [. . .] or at regulating the labelling of packagings of the product and its conditions of sale, in particular to minors, *would have the same preventive effect* in terms of the protection of health, inasmuch as they would let a product which is in any event harmful gain a place in the market'.[132] For the Court, the harmful nature of the product is sufficient to justify the ban, a

126 *Poland v Parliament and Council* para 79; *Pillbox 38* para 49; *Philip Morris* para 166, emphasis added.

127 See *Poland v Parliament and Council* paras 79, 89, 96; *Pillbox 38* para 75; *Philip Morris* paras 166, 177, 184, 190.

128 *Pillbox 38* para 86, emphasis added.

129 ibid, para 113.

130 See also *Tobacco Advertising II* para 147.

131 *Arnold André* para 47; *Swedish Match* para 49, emphasis added.

132 *Arnold André* para 55; *Swedish Match* para 57, emphasis added. See also *Swedish Match II* para 50.

measure which is, by definition, more effective than any other alternative. This contrasts sharply with the approach taken regarding national measures, such as in *Van der Veldt*, concerning the salt limit for bakery products. Another point of comparison is the suitability of age limits. As discussed, in *Rosengren*, the Court considered that requiring consumers to simply declare in a document that they have reached the legal age for purchasing alcoholic beverages was a system as effective as requiring an identity check in stores.[133] In several judgments regarding EU measures, however, the Court refused to consider age limits as a suitable alternative to more stringent measures, such as prohibiting cross-border distance sales or banning flavoured tobacco, arguing that these could be 'easily circumvented'.[134]

An aspect of the Court's assessment that could have resulted into a greater scrutiny of the EU legislator's choices, compared to that of national legislatures, is the review of proportionality *stricto sensu*. Pure proportionality, however, is not systematically discussed in lifestyle-risk judgments, depending on whether an alleged breach thereof is raised by the claimant.[135] This conclusion holds true regarding the proportionality review of Union acts in general.[136] Further, where the Court does engage in a pure proportionality analysis, it does not take the form of a genuine balancing exercise, whereby the health benefits expected from EU measures would be openly confronted with the losses suffered by economic operators. This is illustrated in *Poland v Parliament and Council* and *Philip Morris*, concerning the alleged disproportionate effect of the ban on tobacco products with characterising flavours. In *Poland v Parliament and Council*, Poland argued in particular that the social and economic costs of the prohibition of menthol cigarettes were disproportionate to any advantages arising therefrom.[137] The Court upheld the validity of the ban, considering that the EU legislature had 'weighed up, on the one hand, the economic consequences of that prohibition and, on the other, the requirement to ensure [...] a high level of human health protection',[138] by ensuring that '*the negative economic and social consequences* of the prohibition on the placing on the market of tobacco products with a characterising flavour *were limited*'.[139] The decisive element in the eyes of

133 *Rosengren* para 56.
134 *Poland v Parliament and Council* para 93; *Pillbox 38* para 127; *Philip Morris* para 181.
135 Alemanno and Garde, 'The Emergence of EU Lifestyle Risk Regulation' 163.
136 See Craig, *EU Administrative Law* 644.
137 *Poland v Parliament and Council* para 73.
138 ibid, para 102; *Philip Morris* para 190.
139 *Poland v Parliament and Council* para 99; *Philip Morris* para 187, emphasis added.

the Court was the delayed application of the ban for tobacco products whose EU-wide sales volumes represented 3 per cent or more of total sales,[140] and the fact that the ban would only result 'in a decrease in cigarette consumption in the European Union of 0.5 to 0.8% over a five-year period'.[141] In these judgments, the Court did not genuinely balance health interests against economic considerations. It did not attempt to determine whether a certain number of saved lives justified the financial losses to the industry, but appeared satisfied that the negative economic consequences were limited or uncertain. This raises the question of whether the Court would reach a different conclusion if the consequences were not 'limited'. For instance, if the EU legislator introduced a ban on cigarettes, would the Court annul it on the grounds of disproportionate impact on tobacco companies? This seems unlikely, since the Court maintains that 'the objective of protection of health takes precedence over economic considerations, the importance of that objective being such as to justify even substantial negative economic consequences'.[142] As expressed by the Court's Advocate Generals, 'the protection of human health *has considerably greater importance in the value system under EU law than such essentially economic interests*'.[143]

This conclusion is further reinforced by the fact that reference to fundamental rights does not alter the nature of the Court's control of proportionality. Public health measures can restrict the business freedom of economic operators or their freedom to disseminate information – interests protected by Articles 11, 15, 16 and 17 of the Charter (CFR), relating respectively to the freedom of expression and information, the freedom to choose an occupation and engage in work, the freedom to conduct a business and the right to property. As a matter of principle, construing an EU measure as a restriction of fundamental rights would normally lead to greater scrutiny by the Court and a reduction of the legislature's margin of discretion.[144]

140 *Poland v Parliament and Council* para 100; *Philip Morris* para 188.

141 *Poland v Parliament and Council* para 101; *Philip Morris* para 189.

142 *Swedish Match II* para 54.

143 Case C-547/14 *Philip Morris Brands*, EU:C:2015:853, Opinion of Advocate General Kokott, para 179; Case C-358/14 *Poland v Parliament and Council*, EU:C:2015:848, Opinion of Advocate General Kokott, para 130, emphasis added; see also *Tobacco Advertising*, Opinion of Advocate General Fennelly para 165.

144 Craig, *EU Administrative Law* 656. See Joined Cases C-293/12 and C-594/12 *Digital Rights Ireland and Seitlinger and Others*, EU:C:2014:238, paras 47–48.

However, this has not been the case in the field of lifestyles.[145] The Court considers economic rights 'not absolute' but to be viewed in relation to their 'social function',[146] meaning that they may 'be subject to a *broad range* of interventions on the part of public authorities which may limit the exercise of economic activity in the public interest'.[147] Only 'a disproportionate and intolerable interference, impairing the very substance of the rights guaranteed' constitutes an unlawful limitation thereof.[148] The subordinate standing of economic rights is particularly evident where an alleged breach of Article 11 CFR or Article 10 of the European Convention on Human Rights (ECHR), on the freedom of expression and information, is claimed. In *Tobacco Advertising II*, the Court found that the prohibitions on tobacco advertising and sponsorship contained at Articles 3 and 4 of the TAD, 'even assuming' they indirectly weakened freedom of expression, did not impair journalistic freedom of expression and affect 'editorial contributions of journalists'.[149] The Court therefore concluded that the EU legislature had not exceeded the limits of its discretion in adopting such measures.[150] Thus doing, the Court drew a clear line between mere advertising and what constitutes a 'higher' version of the freedom of expression, such as the activity of journalists. None of the solutions adopted in these various judgments gives much cause for concern on substance. Considering the importance of the public interest at stake, with regard to tobacco consumption especially, such restrictions on the rights of economic operators appear largely justified and proportionate. What can be criticised, however, is that the standard of review applied in these judgments mirrors that used for non-rights-based proportionality claims, even when measures constitute far-reaching restrictions, such as a total advertising ban or a ban on an entire class of products.

Regarding, finally, the standard of proof and the judicial review of the evidence adduced, the EU legislature is also granted a broad margin of discretion. The Court's case law is largely devoid of the requirement

[145] *British American Tobacco* paras 149–153; *Planta Tabak* paras 91–100; *Swedish Match* para 72; *Pillbox 38* paras 156–165; *Deutsches Weintor* paras 56–57.

[146] *British American Tobacco* para 149; *Neptune Distribution* para 66; *Pillbox 38* para 157; *Swedish Match II* para 72.

[147] *Pillbox 38* para 158, emphasis added.

[148] *British American Tobacco* para 149; see also *Deutsches Weintor* para 54.

[149] *Tobacco Advertising II* para 156.

[150] ibid, para 157.

featuring in some free movement cases to produce a specific piece of evidence meeting certain standards. The Court considers that:

> As regards the assessments of *highly complex scientific and technical facts* [. . .], it must be recalled that the Courts of the European *Union cannot substitute their assessment* of that material for that of the legislature on which the FEU Treaty has placed that task. The EU legislature's *broad discretion*, which implies *limited judicial review* of its exercise, applies not only to the nature and scope of the measures to be taken but also, to some extent, to *the finding of the basic facts*.'[151]

The application of a limited *standard of judicial review* is not specific to lifestyle risks and can be seen in other areas of EU law involving the assessment of complex facts, such as food and feed safety[152] or competition law.[153] A striking feature of the Court's case law regarding the proportionality of EU measures is the absence of the general requirement applicable to national measures that 'the reasons which may be invoked [. . .] by way of justification [for their adoption] must be accompanied by *appropriate evidence* or by an analysis of the appropriateness and proportionality of the restrictive measure adopted by that State, and *specific evidence* substantiating its arguments'.[154] This is especially visible in the Court's early lifestyle case law, largely devoid of any discussion on proof and any reference to specific pieces of evidence.[155] While this has changed in more recent judgments,[156] the Court continues to avoid entanglement in scientific controversies and refrains from openly evaluating the quality of the evidence produced. This is especially visible where claimants rely on 'partisan expert evidence'[157] contradicting that put forward by the European Commission. In such cases, evidence coming from internationally recognised sources is favoured, as it provides the Court with a greater sense of certainty and objectivity

[151] *Swedish Match II* para 37, emphasis added; see also *Philip Morris*, Opinion of Advocate General Kokott paras 102–103.

[152] See Case T-13/99, *Pfizer Animal Health v Council*, EU:T:2002:209, para 393.

[153] See Joined Cases C-204/00 P, C-205/00 P, C-211/00 P, C-213/00 P, C-217/00 P and C-219/00 P *Aalborg Portland A/S*, EU:C:2004:6, para 279. On evidence and judicial review in competition law, see Castillo de la Torre and Gippini Fournier, *Evidence, Proof and Judicial Review in EU Competition Law* 275–288.

[154] *Scotch Whisky* para 54; see also *ANETT* para 50.

[155] See *British American Tobacco*; *Tobacco Advertising II*. Regarding *Tobacco Advertising II*, see Garde, 'Freedom of Commercial Expression and Public Health Protection' 121–122. See, however, a brief reference to evidence in *Swedish Match* paras 50–54.

[156] See *Philip Morris*; *Poland v Parliament and Council*; *Pillbox 38*; *Swedish Match II*.

[157] Barbier de la Eric Barbier de La Serre and Anne-Lise Sibony, 'Expert Evidence before the EC Courts' (2008) 45 Common Market Law Review 941, 964.

compared to studies presented by parties, which may have been selected purportedly to offer a partial account of the state of scientific knowledge. In *Pillbox 38*, confronted to the 'multiple scientific studies and reports' produced by the parties,[158] which contained contradicting evidence, the Court chose to rely on the WHO 'ENDS report' to determine its position regarding the health risks of e-cigarettes and the effectiveness of different regulatory options.[159]

Rather than evaluating the EU legislature's choices, the Court focuses on the quality of the decision-making process, ensuring that the interests of economic operators have been given due consideration, even if health takes ultimate precedence in a way that is particularly detrimental to them. This review can be defined as 'process-oriented', where rather than 'second-guessing the merits of the substantive choices made by the EU legislator, the ECJ prefer[s] to make sure that law-makers ha[ve] done their work properly'.[160] The limited nature of this review seems appropriate. In general, 'Courts should be wary of substituting their judgment for that of the primary decision-maker under the guise of proportionality',[161] particularly in an area such as lifestyle risks, where regulation entails the performance of complex assessments and the balancing of various political, economic and social interests. The rationale for this combines concerns relating to legitimacy and expertise.[162] Yet, the same considerations arguably apply to national legislatures and the Court's review of Member State measures derogating free movement, if not even more so, since the Court is less familiar with the workings of national legislators and the specific circumstances prompting the adoption of a given measure. That national measures are subject to more intense scrutiny than EU measures is observable across EU law and has been extensively discussed by scholars.[163] This difference in standard of review is usually justified, or at least explained, by the importance of internal market free movement provisions for European integration, and by the fact that proportionality serves different functions in these two contexts: balancing private and public interests for EU measures, and

[158] *Pillbox 38* para 50. [159] ibid, paras 51–53.

[160] Koen Lenaerts, 'The European Court of Justice and Process-Oriented Review' (2012) 31 Yearbook of European Law 3, 7. See in that regard Case C-310/04, *Spain v Council*, EU:C:2006:521, paras 122–123.

[161] Craig, *EU Administrative Law* 653. [162] ibid.

[163] See e.g. Maduro, *We The Court* 78; Tridimas, 'Proportionality in Community Law' 66; Craig, *EU Administrative Law* 682–683.

balancing EU and national interests for national measures.[164] However, while these observations may have descriptive value – indicating that the Court likely sees its role as an agent of EU (economic) integration and therefore shows less deference towards national legislators[165] – it is not clear that they should have prescriptive value. After all, if the protection of human health has considerably greater importance in the value system under EU law than purely economic interests, there is no reason to afford health less standing when reviewing the legality of national measures.

6.3.2 *The Limits to Indirect Internal Market Powers: Advertising and Smoke-Free Environments*

There is little doubt that a wide range of regulatory options are available to the EU legislature under Article 114 TFEU (see Section 3.4). This is particularly true of measures harmonising product requirements – rules concerning the designation, composition, packaging or labelling of products – which remove discrepancies in national legislation and facilitate the free movement of the products concerned.[166] Such measures form the bulk of the EU's lifestyle risk regulatory framework. Here, the 'weight' accorded to health may be freely determined while the measure remains relevant from a free movement perspective: a given labelling or composition rule may be more or less protective of health. Strengthening labelling obligations for alcoholic beverages, adopting mandatory food reformulation targets to reduce the salt, sugar or fat content of products or prohibiting harmful advertising directly targeting children and minors: all of these regulatory options are available to the EU legislature without raising competence issues. The same applies in the field of excise duties, where nothing prevents the EU from better integrating public health considerations into its legal framework, both regarding the rate and structure of taxes and the rules governing cross-border acquisitions by individuals.

The EU legislature's ability to strengthen its regulatory approach, however, is not without limits. The powers conferred by Article 114 TFEU are circumscribed by the requirement that the measure must genuinely serve to remove obstacles to free movement and/or restrictions

164 Tridimas, 'Proportionality in Community Law' 66.

165 According to Poiares Maduro, the Court is more concerned with '*State* intervention than with *public* intervention in the market': Maduro, *We The Court* 78.

166 *British American Tobacco* para 64.

on competition: '[i]n accordance with Article 114 TFEU, the legislature has competence to *eliminate* obstacles to free movement and to improve the functioning of the internal market. The latter essentially refers to *eliminating* distortions in competition'.[167] Merely identifying obstacles to free movement or distortions of competition arising from differences in national legislation is not sufficient to justify the harmonisation of those national provisions. What is required is their removal. In several instances, this condition has prevented the EU legislature from adopting public health measures. This is particularly evident with regard to two measures: the prohibition of 'static' forms of (tobacco) advertising and the design of smoke-free environments.

As explained in Section 5.4.1, most forms of tobacco advertising are currently prohibited under EU law. These prohibitions are lawful under Article 114 TFEU because they remove the obstacles resulting from national advertising bans, which constitute restrictions on free movement under Articles 34 and 56 TFEU.[168] The existing EU bans on tobacco advertising, covering television, radio and periodicals, facilitate the free circulation of these media by removing the differences in national legislation affecting them, thus creating a level playing field.[169] There are *constructive* bans. Conversely, as the Court ruled in *Tobacco Advertising*, the prohibition of static forms of advertising, such as the use of posters or advertising spots in cinemas, does not fall within the EU legislature's competence under Article 114 TFEU, because it does not remove obstacles to free movement.[170] Unlike press or audiovisual products, billboards and cinemas are not mobile once installed, which means that diverging national rules on advertising cannot affect their circulation. A prohibition of these static forms of advertising is therefore a *destructive* ban: it reduces opportunities for trade without opening a market for any other economic activity. Furthermore, as the Court underlined in the *Tobacco Advertising* judgment, differences in advertising regulation

[167] *Czech Republic v Parliament and Council*, Opinion of Advocate General Sharpston, para 44, emphasis added. See also *Tobacco Advertising* paras 84, 95; *Tobacco Advertising II* para 69. Although the case law has regrettably lost clarity on the matter, this condition still remains good law: see the direct and indirect references to previous cases made in *Philip Morris* paras 58 and 81; *Poland v Parliament and Council* para 32; Case C-482/17 *Czech Republic v Parliament and Council*, EU:C:2019:1035, para 34.

[168] See *Aragonesa*; *Gourmet*; *Commission v France*C-262/02; *Bacardi France*.

[169] *Tobacco Advertising* paras 96–98; *Tobacco Advertising II* para 71. See also TAD, recital 1.

[170] See *Tobacco Advertising* para 99. See also *Tobacco Advertising*, Opinion of Advocate General Fennelly para 113.

between Member States cannot be considered appreciable distortions of competition.[171] There are thus no possibilities for a binding prohibition of static forms of advertising at EU level,[172] which led the Court to annul the first version of the Tobacco Advertising Directive (Directive 98/43). The unlawful elements removed from the first TAD were subsequently included in the non-binding Council Recommendation of 2 December 2002.[173] This instrument covers types of advertising that cannot be prohibited by the EU, such as the use of promotional items (ashtrays, lighters, parasols), billboards, posters and other indoor or outdoor advertising techniques, or advertising in cinemas.[174]

Retail display bans represent another type of measure seeking to limit promotional opportunities for tobacco and other products. They prohibit stores from displaying a given product inside their premises, requiring that it be stored under the counter or inside a cupboard so as not to attract consumers' attention. The introduction of an EU-wide retail display ban was envisaged by the Commission as part of the revision of the 2001 TPD but was ultimately set aside on subsidiarity grounds.[175] It remains doubtful that the EU would have competence to adopt such a ban. It is far from obvious that a retail display ban constitutes an obstacle to free movement when enacted at the national level, or an appreciable distortion of competition. Such a measure would arguably qualify as a selling arrangement, and hence fall outside the prohibition in Article 34 TFEU if it satisfies the two conditions laid down in *Keck*. Considering that the display of tobacco products or alcoholic beverages could be assimilated to an advertising practice, the argument could nonetheless be made that a retail display ban has a greater adverse effect on imported products than on domestic ones, following the Court's reasoning in

[171] *Tobacco Advertising* paras 104–108.

[172] See TAD, recital 12: 'Other forms of advertising, such as indirect advertising, as well as the sponsorship of events or activities without cross-border effects, fall outside the scope of this Directive. Subject to the Treaty, Member States retain the competence to regulate these matters as they deem necessary to guarantee the protection of human health'.

[173] Council Recommendation of 2 December 2002 on the prevention of smoking and on initiatives to improve tobacco control, OJ L22/31.

[174] ibid, para 2.

[175] European Commission, 'Impact assessment accompanying the document: Proposal for a Directive of the European Parliament and of the Council on the approximation of the laws, regulations and administrative provisions of the Member states concerning the manufacture, presentation and sale of tobacco and Related products' (Staff Working Document) SWD (2012) 452 final, part 1, 50.

Gourmet.[176] The EFTA Court pointed in that direction in its judgment on the Norwegian retail display ban for tobacco products.[177] In any case, retail display bans prohibit a static form of promotion. Reasoning by analogy with advertising, an EU-wide retail display ban would not remove obstacles created by national bans but, by generalising such bans, would instead reduce opportunities for foreign products to penetrate national markets.[178]

The 2002 Recommendation also addresses other aspects of tobacco control. It recommends that Member States require vendors of tobacco products 'to establish that tobacco purchasers have reached the age for purchase of such products required in national law, where such an age limit exists', and to restrict the self-service of tobacco products in shops or limit the use of tobacco vending machines to places inaccessible to persons below the age limit.[179] As regards age limits for the purchase of tobacco or alcoholic beverages, even if these could be analysed as restrictions on use prohibited under Article 34 TFEU[180] – hence obstacles to free movement within the meaning of Article 114 TFEU – an EU measure generalising such rules would still not be capable of removing obstacles to trade or distortions of competition. The same is true of measures prohibiting or restricting vending machines. An EU regulation of this sales method was also considered during the revision process leading to the adoption of the TPD, but abandoned on subsidiarity grounds.[181] Here again, leaving aside doubts as to whether such national measures constitute obstacles to free movement or appreciable distortions of competition, any EU attempt to harmonise them would not remove but rather reinforce such obstacles or distortions.[182]

Finally, the limits arising from Article 114 TFEU have also prevented the EU from adopting binding measures on smoke-free environments. By prohibiting smoking in certain places (public buildings, parks, beaches, terraces) smoke-free environments protect people from second-hand smoke. In a 2005 Green Paper, the European Commission

176 *Gourmet* para 21.

177 Case E-16/10 *Philip Morris Norway AS v the Norwegian State*. See Alberto Alemanno, 'The Legality, Rationale and Science of Tobacco Display Bans After the Philip Morris Judgment' (2011) 2 European Journal of Risk Regulation 591.

178 For a diverging view, see Alemanno, 'Out of Sight, Out of Mind' 217.

179 Council Recommendation of 2 December 2002, para 1.

180 See *Trailers*; Case C-142/05, *Åklagaren v Percy Mickelsson and Joakim Roos*, EU:C:2009:336.

181 European Commission, TPD impact assessment part 1, 50.

182 See Alemanno and Garde, 'The Emergence of an EU Lifestyle Policy' 1767.

explored the possibility of binding legislation.[183] In 2009, however, only a Council Recommendation was adopted,[184] that invites Member States to 'provide effective protection from exposure to tobacco smoke in indoor workplaces, indoor public places, public transport and, as appropriate, other public places'.[185] The decision to act by way of recommendation reflects the absence of legislative competence, as acknowledged by the Commission.[186] Article 114 TFEU cannot serve as a basis here. First, because national rules prohibiting smoking in certain spaces are unlikely to constitute restrictions on the free movement of goods. These measures are rules on the use of products, which infringe Article 34 TFEU only if they have 'a considerable influence on the behaviour of consumers'.[187] That is the case only if 'consumers, knowing that the use permitted by such regulations is very limited, ha[ve] only a limited interest in buying that product'.[188] Extensive smoke-free environments may lead some consumers to reduce or quit smoking, but not to a 'considerable' extent. Smokers do not currently have 'only a limited interest' in buying cigarettes. Even assuming smoke-free rules did constitute restrictions under Article 34 TFEU, an EU measure prohibiting the use of tobacco in certain areas would merely generalise existing national obstacles or distortions rather than remove them. Hence, apart from the regulation of smoking in workplaces,[189] the EU lacks competence to impose smoke-free environments on Member States. It is therefore not the 'concerted activity [of] the tobacco industry [which] may explain why the EU has yet to take any further action in this area, despite evidence of widespread public support',[190] but the limits of its mandate.

[183] European Commission, 'Towards a Europe free from tobacco smoke: Policy options at EU level' (2007) Green Paper COM (2007) 27 final.

[184] Council Recommendation of 30 November 2009 on smoke-free environments, OJ C296/4.

[185] ibid, para 1.

[186] See Karen Banks, 'The Lisbon Treaty's Competence Arrangement Viewed from European Commission Practice' in Sacha Garben and Inge Govaere (eds), *The Division of Competences Between the EU and the Member States: Reflections on the Past, the Present and the Future* (Hart Publishing 2017) 196–197: 'Some years ago, the competent services of the Commission were convinced that there was a need for binding EU rules on smoking in public places. However, after examination of all possibilities, it was concluded that the most they could propose was a Council Recommendation. This resulted in Council Recommendation of 30 November 2009 on smoke-free environments'.

[187] *Mickelsson* para 26; *Trailers* para 56.

[188] *Mickelsson* para 27. See also *Trailers* para 57.

[189] The EU has the power to regulate smoking in workplaces under its social policy competence, laid down in Article 153 TFEU.

[190] Anna Gilmore and Martin McKee, 'Tobacco Control Policy: The European Dimension' (2002) 2 Clinical Medicine 335, 338.

6.3.3 *The Internal Market Diverted: Tobacco Bans*

In the examples just described, the EU's lack of competence has led to the adoption of non-binding incentive measures or, in some cases, to the absence of any action at all. In others, more problematic instances, this lack of competence has been disregarded by both the legislature and the Court of Justice. This is the case with the two EU-wide tobacco bans currently in place: those concerning tobacco for oral use and tobacco with a characterising flavour.

Member State rules prohibiting certain products from being placed on the market clearly constitute obstacles to the free movement of goods,[191] which the Union may harmonise away under Article 114 TFEU. Harmonisation, however, is conditional upon the removal of such obstacles, an element which is missing where the Union itself prohibits an entire class of products. As Advocate General Fennelly stated, 'a measure whose sole effect is to prohibit an economic activity cannot [...] be said to constitute the removal of barriers to trade affecting that activity'.[192] An EU-wide prohibition of a product cannot be considered as removing appreciable distortions of competition either, but rather as generalising a restriction of forms of competition, following the Court's reasoning in *Tobacco Advertising*.[193] Yet this has not prevented the EU from adopting the bans referred to above. A careful analysis of the various judgments rendered on the legality of these bans shows that no convincing argument has been put forward to explain how they contribute to the smooth functioning of the internal market.

The legality of the ban on tobacco for oral use was first contested in *Swedish Match* and *Arnold André*. In both cases, the Court upheld the ban, laying down the general principle that a measure under Article 114 TFEU 'may consist in [...] provisionally or definitively prohibiting the marketing of a product or products'.[194] The Court, however, fell short of explaining how such bans fulfil the necessary conditions for recourse to that provision. While the Court rightly observed that national prohibitions of tobacco for oral use constitute obstacles to the free movement of goods,[195] it completely disregarded the requirement that these obstacles be removed by the EU harmonisation measure. This approach was

[191] See *Arnold André* para 39; *Swedish Match* para 38.

[192] *Tobacco Advertising*, Opinion of Advocate General Fennelly para 113. See also Somek, *Individualism* 104.

[193] *Tobacco Advertising* para 113.

[194] *Arnold André* para 35; *Swedish Match* para 34.

[195] *Arnold André* paras 38–40; *Swedish Match* paras 37–39.

subsequently confirmed in *Swedish Match II*.[196] For a more detailed, though ultimately unconvincing, defence of the ban, one has to turn to Advocate General Geelhoed. He acknowledged that 'the prohibition on selling a product cannot itself improve the conditions for the marketing of that product' – the product in question is indeed excluded from the market.[197] He nonetheless argued that the ban on the marketing of tobacco for oral use improved trading conditions for 'related products', insofar as it reduced enforcement costs concerning these products.[198] According to him, 'if snus is not on the market of the European Union, the effort to control the marketing of other smokeless tobacco products can be reduced'.[199] Why this should be so is unclear. One might accept that monitoring compliance with prescribed standards consumes more resources than enforcing a ban. Yet Geelhoed does not explain how reduced enforcement costs benefit manufacturers or distributors of other products, or how such a reduction contributes to the removal of trade barriers.

The prohibition on tobacco with characterising flavours was upheld by the Court in *Poland v European Parliament and Council* and *Philip Morris*. Here too, as in *Swedish Match* and *Arnold André*, the Court offered little by way of justification, merely referring to the obstacles created by Member State bans on flavoured cigarettes. Once again, it failed to engage with the requirement that such obstacles be removed in order for Article 114 TFEU to be lawfully relied upon.[200] Advocate General Kokott's defence of the measure, although more persuasive than Geelhoed's, is equally problematic. She argued that the ban removed trade obstacles because it 'serves to create uniform trade conditions for all tobacco products throughout the European Union'.[201] Rather than prohibiting a class of products, she considered the measure a restriction of their composition: 'in other words, tobacco products may in principle still be placed on the market in the European Union, but only without characterising flavours'.[202] Kokott thus construed the prohibition of flavours as a product requirement. If that interpretation were accepted, the measure

[196] *Swedish Match II* paras 55–58.
[197] Cases C-434/02 *Arnold André* and C-210/03 *Swedish Match*, EU:C:2004:487, Joined Opinion of Advocate General Geelhoed, para 78.
[198] ibid, para 79. [199] ibid, emphasis added.
[200] *Poland v Parliament and Council* paras 57–64; *Philip Morris* paras 117–124.
[201] *Philip Morris*, Opinion of Advocate General Kokott para 83. This stands in contradiction with paragraph 82, where she mentions 'a class of other products', see also para 65.
[202] ibid, para 83.

would indeed fall within Article 114 TFEU.[203] But this presupposes that flavoured and unflavoured cigarettes are similar enough from the consumers' perspective, so that banning the former effectively opens a market segment for the latter. This assumption is contestable and, in any case, requires proof. Determining the 'common quality' of banned and authorised products is crucial for assessing the legality of a ban under Article 114 TFEU.[204] In this case, the use of a characterising flavour significantly alters the taste of a cigarette,[205] making it doubtful that flavoured and unflavoured cigarettes are similar products. Most importantly, if the two were indeed similar, there would be a sufficient degree of substitutability between them. It would follow that a consumer barred from smoking menthol cigarettes would simply switch to regular ones,[206] undermining the very rationale of a ban designed to reduce tobacco consumption.[207] Indeed, the ban can only achieve its public health objective if a significant number of people quit smoking altogether, or do not start in the first place. The prohibition of characterising flavours thus vividly illustrates the contradiction between market and health rationales. On the one hand, the ban aims to prevent people from starting or continuing to smoke. On the other hand, its internal market justification depends on the assumption that flavoured and unflavoured cigarettes are similar, which would make the ban ineffective in reducing consumption. This tension is evident in the TPD itself. Recital 16 states that 'products with characterising flavour with a higher sales volume should be phased out over an extended time period to allow consumers adequate time to switch to other products', thereby contradicting the public health rationale of the ban.[208]

203 See also Somek, *Individualism* 132: 'the prohibition of a certain product may be conducive to removing distortions of competition so that similar products (linked via cross-elasticity, of course) are made better off on the market'.

204 See Frederic Geber, 'Between a Rock and a Hard Place' in Alberto Alemanno and Amandine Garde (eds), *Regulating Lifestyle Risks: The EU, Alcohol, Tobacco and Unhealthy Diets* (Cambridge University Press, 2015) 168.

205 As recognised by Advocate General Kokott herself in *Philip Morris*, see para 103.

206 See, regarding dark-tobacco and light-tobacco cigarettes, the similar observation made by Advocate General Alber in Case C-302/00 *Commission v France*, EU:C:2001:449, para 69.

207 As accepted by the Court in *Philip Morris* para 108 and expressed by Advocate General Kokott in *Philip Morris* para 103. The same logic underlies the ban on tobacco for oral use: see *Arnold André* para 38; *Swedish Match* para 37.

208 See also *Planta Tabak* para 47.

In the case of tobacco for oral use and flavoured tobacco, the EU legislator has put in place *destructive* bans.[209] This situation must be distinguished from *constructive* bans, which operate within a class of products and can genuinely serve to create uniform trading conditions.[210] An example of a constructive ban is Directive 2002/46 on food supplements,[211] upheld in *Alliance for Natural Health*.[212] The Directive establishes a list of authorised vitamins and minerals that may be used in food supplements.[213] Thus, it excludes certain products from the market while simultaneously opening the market for other, similar food supplements.[214] Destructive bans expose the contradiction between the Court's interpretation of Article 114 TFEU's limits and its failure to enforce them. Nothing prevents the Court from changing its approach and its understanding of the legislature's role in building the internal market, clearly endorsing 'the principle that in a single market it is a central authority which decides which products or services may be placed on that market'.[215] The Court could embrace the idea that uniformity, rather than merely the removal of trade barriers, is a legitimate objective for the internal market. So far, however, it has refrained from acknowledging this openly. Arguably, doing so would come close to transforming Article 114 TFEU into a general legislative competence for the EU. This interpretation was explicitly rejected by the Court in *Tobacco Advertising*, yet it aptly describes current legislative practice, not only in health but also in other fields. It may therefore be time to bring principles and practice into alignment.

209 See the difference made by Scott Crosby between constructive and destructive bans in the case of the prohibition of ingredients: Scott Crosby, 'The New Tobacco Control Directive: An Illiberal and Illegal Disdain for the Law' (2002) 27 *European Law Review* 177, 186. See also Anatole Abasquene de Parfourus, '"Breaking through the Foul and Ugly Mists of Vapours" – Regulation of Alternative Tobacco and Related Products by the New TPD and Exercise of EU Competence' (2018) 18 German Law Journal 1291, 1302: the author considers the ban on characterising flavours to be a destructive ban.

210 Wyatt 117; Stephen Weatherill 'Protecting the Internal Market from the Charter', in Sybe de Vries, Ulf Bernitz and Stephen Weatherill (eds), *The EU Charter of Fundamental Rights as a Binding Instrument: Five Years Old and Growing* (Hart Publishing 2015) 229.

211 Directive 2002/46, arts 3, 4(1) and 15(b).

212 Case C-154/04, *Alliance for Natural Health and Others*, EU:C:2005:449.

213 Directive 2002/46, annex I and II.

214 Although neither the Court nor the Advocate General was able in this case to formulate such argument and failed to explain why the directive was indeed valid under Article 114 TFEU: see *Alliance for Natural Health* paras 34–39; *Alliance for Natural* Health, Opinion of Advocate General Geelhoed paras 31–36.

215 Wyatt, 'Community Competence to Regulate the Internal Market' 119–120.

6.3.4 *Interim Conclusion*

Measures that fall straightforwardly within EU competence are product requirements, such as information disclosures or warnings, or those that relate most closely to free movement, such as cross-border advertising.[216] These interventions are situated at the lower end of the regulatory spectrum: they 'provide information' and 'enable choice' rather than 'eliminate' or 'restrict choice'.[217] This is logical, as they are also less disruptive for economic operators. A market-making competence, even if it is limited to removing formal obstacles to trade rather than fostering actual increases in trade, cannot be stretched to justify the elimination of entire swathes of the market. The adoption of pure public health measures under the guise of internal market regulation raises problems not only for the vertical division of powers in the EU, but also for the legitimacy of EU policy. It impoverishes the law conceptually, since measures with no real connection to free movement must be defended as though they were about increasing trading opportunities.[218] From a health perspective, the current situation is unsatisfactory. Ideally, all regulatory options should be on the table. This does not mean that product bans or rules on the use of cigarettes in public spaces or retail environments should necessarily be enacted at the EU level. It does mean, however, that the decision whether or not to adopt such measures should rest on political judgment, not be foreclosed by the inadequacy of the current competence framework. Public health is not the only value compromised here. The internal market that emerges from tobacco legislation is one that makes little economic sense. It is a market which may be 'more perfect in a certain legal formal sense, but [is] in fact less active, and in which even cross-border trade [is] reduced'.[219] Although the internal market is primarily a legal rather than an economic concept, it cannot be dissociated from the economic gains expected from its establishment and its deepening.[220]

[216] The EU also has broad powers to enact measures in the field of indirect taxation under Article 113 TFEU, although the unanimity requirement contained in that provision and the wide differences in prices existing between Member States render the adoption of strengthened tax measures on unhealthy products unlikely.

[217] See the 'Nuffield ladder'.

[218] Davies, 'The Competence to Create an Internal Market' 85.

[219] ibid 80.

[220] See Panu Poutvaraa and others, 'Contribution to Growth: Free Movement of Goods. Delivering Economic Benefits for Citizens and Businesses' (2019) EPRS, <www.europarl.europa.eu/thinktank/en/document/IPOL_IDA(2019)631063> accessed 2 October 2025.

6.4 Conclusion

This chapter has sought to address the following paradox: building a market for unhealthy products by removing barriers to their free circulation, while at the same time seeking to reduce, or even eliminate, their consumption. It has examined the balance struck between these two competing and at times contradictory objectives. At the level of TFEU free movement provisions, EU law can accommodate trade-restricting measures on tobacco, alcohol and food, provided they are legitimate and supported by the relevant evidence. Where the case law can be improved is through greater consistency in the way evidence is assessed and greater recognition by the Court of its epistemic limits. Ultimately, a restrictive measure that is properly justified and proportionate will fragment the internal market. This is where harmonisation comes into play, in order to pursue both objectives at once, health and the market. Judicial practice leaves ample leeway to the EU legislature to regulate products as it sees fit and to give a certain shape to the market. Yet, this does not eliminate frictions entirely, since not all interventions can convincingly be said to contribute to the removal of obstacles to trade in lifestyle products. The market can provide the legal infrastructure for a health-oriented lifestyle policy only up to a certain point. These conclusions will be corroborated in the following chapters and ultimately call for reflection on the current EU competence framework and on the limits of its mandate in the field of health.

7 Managing Diversity I

Uncertainty and Experimentation in the Internal Market

7.1 Introduction

The second major dilemma explored in this book concerns the tension between the drive for uniformity at the heart of the internal market, where harmonisation seeks to smooth out regulatory differences and create a level playing field, and the need to preserve regulatory space at the national level. The latter can be justified on two main grounds, both linked to the diversity of lifestyle practices. One justification relates to the ethical and cultural dimensions of unhealthy lifestyles, and to the potential resistance against imposing uniform values and practices at the EU level: this issue is examined in Chapter 8. This chapter focuses on a second justification: the limits to the effectiveness of EU intervention in contexts of diversity and uncertainty. The plurality of lifestyles generates varying patterns of disease prevalence and might require tailored regulatory responses. Moreover, as in many other policy areas, scientific assessment remains uncertain regarding which regulatory tools are most effective. This uncertainty is reinforced by lifestyle diversity: what proves effective in one Member State may fail in another, pointing to the need for experimentation. Hervey and McHale capture the difficulty well:

> Can the intention to protect (national) population health justify different approaches to regulation of tobacco, food or alcohol, in the different Member States? After all, population health differs quite considerably across the EU, not only between Member States, but also within them. The logic of the internal market, and its mandating of free trade in goods throughout the EU, pulls against finely grained laws that seek to tackle specific public health problems,

which may be geographically or culturally limited to certain parts of the EU. Does EU health law support population health in those circumstances?[1]

This chapter examines the clash between market uniformity and diversity and experimentation in three stages. It begins with an analysis of how scientific uncertainty is treated in the proportionality review of lifestyle control measures, both at the national and EU levels. It then turns to two issues related to internal market legislation: the use of 'flexible' modes of harmonisation – referring to minimum and partial harmonisation – and the application of the subsidiarity principle. The chapter is based on concrete case studies in the fields of tobacco (plain packaging and harm-reduction products) and food (front-of-pack nutrition labelling). What emerges is a constitutional tension between the demands of the internal market and those of health protection. The conclusion mirrors that of Chapter 6: accommodation is possible, but that requires a reconceptualisation of the EU's internal market competence, and of its system of competences more broadly.

7.2 Uncertainty and Precaution in Proportionality Review

Unhealthy lifestyles give rise to health risks, most notably the risk of contracting disease. Uncertainty is inherent in the very notion of risk, since risk reflects the probability of an event that may or may not occur. This can be described as '*uncertainty in risk*': the severity and potential impact of the negative event are known, and the likelihood of its occurrence can be estimated.[2] It is a form of measurable uncertainty without which the concept of risk would lose its meaning. This must be distinguished from '*uncertainty on risk*', which concerns uncertainties about one or more components of risk, such as the inability to predict the severity of an outcome or to determine its probability with precision.[3] In the field of lifestyle-related health risks, regulators are rarely in a position of complete ignorance. The harmful effects of tobacco and alcohol, for example, are well-established in the scientific community, even if the probabilities of contracting a disease cannot be quantified with absolute accuracy. These are *certain risks*. Where uncertainty does remain, as with e-cigarettes or some dietary factors, there are grounds

[1] Hervey and McHale, *European Union Health Law* 390.

[2] Bernardo Delogu, *Risk Analysis and Governance in EU Policy Making and Regulation* (Springer International Publishing 2016) 26, emphasis added.

[3] ibid, emphasis added.

for allowing different regulatory approaches to coexist. Finally, a further layer of uncertainty arises not from the risks themselves, but from the effectiveness of policy responses. We cannot always know whether a given policy will achieve its intended effect, nor can we always compare the relative merits of competing regulatory strategies. This type of uncertainty is particularly relevant to unhealthy lifestyles, as we shall see. In such circumstances, experimentation is especially beneficial.

Situations of uncertainty regarding the existence or magnitude of risks raise the question of the appropriate regulatory response. Should authorities refrain from action until more certainty is achieved? Such an approach risks allowing unanticipated harm to materialise. This is precisely where the precautionary principle emerges, offering a framework for regulatory action in the face of scientific uncertainty. The precautionary principle is notoriously difficult to define and has generated intense debate in EU law, both as to its meaning and its scope.[4] As De Sadeleer puts it, this principle reflects 'a philosophy of anticipated action, not requiring that the entire corpus of scientific proof be collated in order for a public authority to be able to adopt a preventive measure'.[5] In its most simple form, it requires that 'where there is uncertainty as to the existence or extent of risks, protective measures may be taken without having to wait until the reality and seriousness of those risks become fully apparent'.[6] Maria Weimer distinguishes between two approaches to the principle. A *weak* version allows reliance on the precautionary principle only where there is a threat of serious or irreversible damage that is likely or probable, and where the measures adopted are cost-effective.[7] A *strong* version permits preventive action in the face of any threats to health or the environment, regardless of cost.[8] Over recent decades, the precautionary principle has gained prominence in EU risk regulation and is now recognised as a general principle of EU law. It plays a specific role within proportionality review, where it broadens legislative discretion and relaxes the standard of evidence required. This applies both to uncertainty about risk itself and to uncertainty about the effectiveness of regulatory policies.

[4] See Craig, *EU Administrative Law* 694–721; Nicolas de Sadeleer, 'The Precautionary Principle in EC Health and Environmental Law' (2006) 12 European Law Journal 139; Alessandra Donati, *Le Principe de Précaution en Droit de l'Union Européenne* (Bruylant 2021).

[5] De Sadeleer, 'The Precautionary Principle in EC Health and Environmental Law' 139.

[6] *Agenzia delle dogane* para 34.

[7] Weimer, *Risk Regulation in the Internal Market* 36.

[8] ibid.

As explained in Chapter 2, most lifestyle-related health risks are well established. The range of possible outcomes arising from exposure to lifestyle risk factors, as well as the nature of these outcomes, is generally well known. As a result, the precautionary principle, in its standard form, plays only a limited role, except in areas where significant uncertainty remains, for instance with respect to e-cigarettes. The Court of Justice has captured this point particularly clearly with regards to tobacco:

> As regards [. . .] the applicability of the precautionary principle in the present case, [. . .] it is sufficient to note, first, that none of the parties to the proceedings denies the risks linked to the consumption of tobacco products for smoking and, second, [. . .] that scientific evidence has unequivocally established that tobacco consumption and exposure to tobacco smoke cause death, disease and disability [. . .] Therefore, [. . .] *that principle does not apply* to the situation at issue in the main proceedings.[9]

Nonetheless, the Court has recognised the existence of uncertainty in certain cases concerning food risks and has readily applied the precautionary principle. These include cases on food additives, mainly vitamins, discussed in Section 6.2.2. In such instances, the Court's proportionality review takes a distinctly procedural turn. It requires that a 'detailed assessment of the risk alleged' be carried out.[10] With respect to food additives, the purpose of this assessment is 'to appraise *the degree of probability* of *harmful effects* on human health from the addition of certain nutrients to foodstuffs and *the seriousness* of those potential effects'.[11] What emerges here are the basic components of risk assessment: identifying and characterising the hazard linked to the addition of nutrients, and characterising the risk – considering not only the seriousness of potential adverse effects but also the likelihood of their occurrence.[12]

Where a risk assessment shows that 'scientific uncertainty persists as regards the *existence* or *extent* of real risks to human health',[13] the Court accepts reliance on the precautionary principle. This means that Member States may 'take protective measures without having to wait until the

[9] *Agenzia delle dogane* para 34, emphasis added.

[10] *Commission v Denmark* (C-192/01) para 47; *Commission v France* (C-24/00) para 54; *Commission v Netherlands* C-41/02 para 48.

[11] *Commission v Denmark* (C-192/01) para 48; *Commission v France* (C-24/00) para 55; *Commission v Netherlands* C-41/02 para 49, emphasis added.

[12] See Alemanno 'The Shaping of European Risk Regulation by Community Courts' 18–19.

[13] *Commission v Denmark* C-192/01 para 49; *Commission v France* (C-24/00) para 56, emphasis added. See also *Commission v Netherlands* (C-41/02) para 51; *CBD* para 90.

reality and seriousness of those risks are fully demonstrated'.[14] At the same time, the Court makes clear that a risk assessment cannot rest on 'purely hypothetical considerations'.[15] To prevent the precautionary principle from becoming a *carte blanche* for Member States, the Court reinforces its scrutiny of both the risk assessment procedure and the quality of the evidence, requiring 'a comprehensive assessment of the risk to health', 'based on the most reliable scientific data available and the most recent results of international research'.[16] Conversely, where 'it proves to be *impossible to determine with certainty* the existence or extent of the alleged risk because of [the lack of evidence] but *the likelihood of real harm to public health persists* should the risk materialise', the precautionary principle justifies the adoption of restrictive measures, provided they are non-discriminatory and objective.[17]

For the reasons already explained, the classic application of the precautionary principle, where uncertainty relates to the existence or extent of risks, is not the most pertinent dimension in the case of unhealthy lifestyles. Another dimension of precaution, developed more recently in the Court's case law, is more relevant: the use of precaution in relation to the *effects of policies*. A first clear instance appeared in *Scotch Whisky* (see Section 6.2.3). In reviewing proportionality, the Court stated that 'the referring court may take into consideration the possible existence of *scientific uncertainty as to the actual and specific effects on the consumption of alcohol of a measure such as the MPU* for the purposes of attaining the objective pursued'.[18] Without expressly naming it, the Court was in fact applying the precautionary principle.[19] This shift has significant implications. It relaxes evidentiary requirements, meaning that regulators are not required to prove with certainty that a measure will be effective to pass the proportionality hurdle. Although unconventional, this approach can be commended for acknowledging the inherent complexities – particularly in public health – of comparing the effectiveness of different policy options and assessing their respective contributions to a declared public interest objective.[20] This new approach was questioned shortly

[14] *Commission v Denmark* C-192/01 para 49; *Commission v France*(C-24/00) para 56. See also *Commission v Netherlands* (C-41/02) para 52; *CBD* para 90.

[15] ibid. [16] *CBD* paras 91–92. See also *Commission v Denmark* (C-192/01) paras 51–52.

[17] *CBD* para 92, emphasis added. See also *Commission v Denmark* (C-192/01) para 52.

[18] *Scotch Whisky* para 57, emphasis added.

[19] Alemanno, 'Balancing Free Movement and Public Health' 1061. [20] ibid.

after *Scotch Whisky* by Advocate General Szpunar in *Deutsche Parkinson*,[21] but more recently upheld by the Court in *Nordic Info*.[22]

This development connects to broader questions of regulatory experimentation. Where policy outcomes are uncertain, experimentation should be encouraged, but reflexivity becomes important so that lessons are properly drawn from such experiments. This dynamic is particularly visible in *Scotch Whisky*:

> As the Advocate General stated in point 85 of his Opinion, the fact that the national legislation provides that the setting of an MPU will *expire six years* after the entry into force of the MPU Order, unless the Scottish Parliament decides that it is to continue, *is a factor that the referring court may also take into consideration*.[23]

In its guidance to the national court, the Court took account of the sunset clause in the Scottish legislation – requiring the Scottish Parliament to review the measure after six years to decide whether to continue with it. Sunset clauses serve as a valuable proportionality tool: they allow Member States to experiment with new regulatory approaches, thereby relaxing evidentiary requirements, while ensuring that ineffective measures can be discontinued. The Court in *Scotch Whisky* further endorsed this dynamic approach. Asked whether scientific evidence not available at the time of adoption of a measure should be taken into account in the review of proportionality, the Court affirmed that 'the referring court must take into consideration *any relevant information*, evidence or other material of which it has knowledge under the conditions laid down by its national law', noting that such an assessment is 'all the more necessary in a situation [...] where there appears to be *scientific uncertainty* as to the actual effects of the measures'.[24] The importance of a dynamic assessment was also stressed by the Court in the context of gambling. In *Admiral Casinos*, where the national court referred a question similar to that in *Scotch Whisky*, the Court held that 'in a review of proportionality, the approach taken by the referring court must be *dynamic rather than static* in the sense that it must take account of the way in which circumstances have developed following the adoption of the legislation concerned',[25] meaning that 'a review of the proportionality of restrictive national legislation in the area of games of chance

[21] See Case C-148/15 *Deutsche Parkinson*, EU:C:2016:394, Opinion of Advocate General Szpunar, para 69.
[22] *Nordic Info* paras 82, 90 and 97.
[23] *Scotch Whisky* para 57, emphasis added.
[24] ibid, para 64, emphasis added.
[25] Case C-464/15 *Admiral Casinos & Entertainment*, EU:C:2016:500, para 36, emphasis added.

must be based not only on the objective of that legislation at the time of its adoption, but also *on the effects of the legislation, assessed after its adoption*'.[26]

Finding an equilibrium between effective judicial protection for those adversely affected by a given measure and respect for the legislator's complex choices is a difficult exercise. This challenge is also visible when the Court reviews the proportionality of EU legislation. Uncertainty and the precautionary principle played a central role in the *Swedish Match II* and *Pillbox 38* cases, concerning, respectively, the prohibition on oral tobacco products and the rules governing electronic cigarettes. Both areas of tobacco control share similar features: in each, uncertainty persists regarding the relationship between the consumption of these alternative products and that of cigarettes, whether as cessation aids or potential gateway products, and hence regarding the effect of regulatory measures on public health. As explained in Section 2.3, these cases illustrate a broader debate between two strands of tobacco control: the EU's endgame approach, seeking to eliminate the consumption of all tobacco products, and the alternative harm reduction approach, which aims to reduce the harmful effects of tobacco without necessarily eliminating it entirely.[27] In both *Swedish Match II* and *Pillbox 38*, the claimants, endorsing the harm reduction position, argued that restricting access to less harmful alternatives, as done by the EU, undermined public health protection.[28] In *Pillbox 38*, a 'heated debate' unfolded.[29] The claimant emphasised the limited risks associated with e-cigarettes and their potential as cessation aids, while EU institutions and intervening governments highlighted their addictiveness, possible gateway and normalisation effects, the existence of health risks such as poisoning and the lack of certainty regarding e-cigarettes' efficacy as cessation tools.[30] The Court did not assess the evidence submitted by the parties to endorse one position over the other.[31] Instead, relying on a WHO report,[32] it

[26] ibid, para 37, emphasis added.

[27] See Case C-151/17 *Swedish Match AB v Secretary of State for Health (Swedish Match II)*, EU:C:2018:241, Opinion of Advocate General Saugmandsgaard Øe, para 27.

[28] *Pillbox 38* para 47; *Swedish Match II* para 46.

[29] *Pillbox 38* para 50.

[30] ibid.

[31] Advocate General Kokott did not adopt the same degree of caution, holding that 'in assessing the lawfulness of Directive 2014/40, and in particular the proportionality of the provisions on e-cigarettes contained in Article 20 thereof, it is ultimately immaterial whether the health risks mentioned by the Union legislature – which seem very plausible to me personally – can be proven with sufficient accuracy in the current state of scientific research': *Pillbox 38*, Opinion of Advocate General Kokott para 64.

[32] *Pillbox 38* paras 51–54.

acknowledged the existence of uncertainty and ruled that 'in deciding to devote specific rules to the placing on the market of electronic cigarettes and refill containers, [...] the EU legislature did not manifestly infringe the limits of its discretion in the matter'.[33] Similarly, in *Swedish Match II*, the claimants challenged the ban on oral tobacco products, citing recent studies suggesting that snus consumption tends to replace, rather than supplement, cigarette use and does not act as a gateway to smoking.[34] Again, the Court did not evaluate the validity of the evidence but concluded that:

> Given that, if the prohibition on placing on the market tobacco products for oral use were to be lifted, *the positive effects would be uncertain* with respect to the health of consumers seeking to use those products as an aid to the cessation of smoking and, moreover, there would be risks to the health of other consumers, particularly young people, requiring the adoption, *in accordance with the precautionary principle*, of restrictive measures, Article 1(c) and Article 17 of Directive 2014/40 cannot be regarded as being manifestly inappropriate to the objective of ensuring a high level of public health.[35]

These cases illustrate several points. First, as in the free movement cases analysed earlier, the precautionary principle was applied to the effect of policies rather than to the existence of health risks. The issue was not the intrinsic harm of oral tobacco or e-cigarettes – though some uncertainty remains regarding the latter – but the appropriateness of EU measures in reducing overall exposure, considering the relationship between these products and cigarettes. Second, the cases exemplify the 'uncertainty paradox' described by Van Asselt and Vos: while acknowledging scientific uncertainty, the Court treats the evidence as providing sufficient certainty to justify regulatory action.[36] This was evident in *Pillbox 38*, where the WHO report was treated as determinative, obfuscating the political judgments underpinning the rules on oral tobacco and e-cigarettes. The Commission and the legislator's choice to pursue an endgame strategy is legitimate but would deserve to be articulated more clearly and openly acknowledged in Court, when science alone cannot fully justify the measures. The Court's approach encourages regulators

[33] ibid, para 61.
[34] *Swedish Match II* para 46; see also *Swedish Match II*, Opinion of Advocate General Saugmandsgaard Øe paras 43–57.
[35] *Swedish Match II* para 49, emphasis added.
[36] Marjolein B A van Asselt and Ellen Vos, 'The Precautionary Principle and the Uncertainty Paradox' (2006) 9 Journal of Risk Research 313.

to use science to rationalise political decisions rather than explicitly stating their normative choices.[37] Third, scientific uncertainty about policy effectiveness is amplified at the EU level, as will be discussed in relation to subsidiarity. The success of oral tobacco or e-cigarettes as cigarette substitutes depends on national preferences and habits, which vary widely across Member States, making it inherently difficult to achieve certainty at the EU level.

This evolution of the precautionary principle is, overall, a welcome one, both at the EU and national levels. It recognises the constraints under which regulators operate and avoids placing excessive hurdles *ex ante*, before legislation is adopted. At the same time, it cannot amount to a full *carte blanche*: rigorous review of the experimental measures adopted must be ensured *ex post*.

7.3 Minimum Harmonisation and the Building of Evidence

In the absence of EU harmonisation, free movement provisions can accommodate uncertainty and thus act as catalysers for regulatory experimentation. A lack of evidence does not mean, however, that the EU should refrain from legislating altogether. The choice is not between action and inaction. Rather, the EU can legislate in ways that do not fully pre-empt Member States' capacity to act – most notably through minimum harmonisation. In the context of unhealthy lifestyles, minimum harmonisation can serve several purposes. It allows Member States to progress at different speeds and to adopt varying levels of protection, reflecting both the severity of the public health problem in each country and the degree of public support for regulatory intervention. From a public health perspective, one might even argue that minimum harmonisation is always preferable, to avoid setting a ceiling on the level of protection across the EU. We have seen the problems that can arise from maximum harmonisation in the field of taxation and minimum pricing strategies (see Section 5.3). Minimum harmonisation also functions as a cautionary tool in contexts marked by scientific uncertainty, where the

[37] ibid 332; Ellen Vos, 'The European Court of Justice in the Face of Scientific Uncertainty and Complexity' in Mark Dawson, Bruno De Witte and Elise Muir (eds), *Judicial Activism at the European Court of Justice* (Edward Elgar Publishing 2013) 164. In that regard, the analysis of Advocate General Saugmandsgaard Øe in *Swedish Match II* appears more complete: see *Swedish Match II*, Opinion of Advocate General Saugmandsgaard Øe paras 61–63.

effects of regulatory instruments are not fully known and policy experimentation is therefore desirable. In such circumstances – and as the following two case studies will illustrate – EU legislation can act as a catalyst for evidence-building, informing the development of future EU-wide rules. The approach is dynamic rather than static. Nonetheless, the question remains whether experimentation can be reconciled with the internal market's demand for uniformity, in particular with the requirements attached to the use of Article 114 TFEU.

7.3.1 *Conceptual Clarification and Early Case Law*

Unlike other Treaty provisions – such as those in the fields of social policy,[38] public health,[39] consumer protection[40] or the environment[41] – where minimum harmonisation is expressly required, there is no 'con stitutionalisation' of minimum harmonisation in the internal market.[42] Under Article 114 TFEU, the legislator remains free regarding the method of harmonisation chosen. Although Article 114(4)–(10) TFEU provides mechanisms allowing Member States to maintain or introduce stricter requirements,[43] these derogation clauses are conceptually distinct from minimum harmonisation.[44] Minimum harmonisation is therefore not mandatory under Article 114 TFEU. What remains uncertain, however – and what the Court of Justice has so far failed to clarify – is the extent to which minimum harmonisation may be an available option under this provision. At first sight, a measure that seeks to eliminate obstacles to free movement and distortions of competition appears to undermine its own purpose if it simultaneously allows Member States to enact more stringent rules, thereby reintroducing

[38] Art 153(2)(b) TFEU. [39] Art 168(4)(a) TFEU. [40] Art 169(4) TFEU.

[41] Art 193 TFEU.

[42] Nina Boeger, 'Minimum Harmonisation, Free Movement and Proportionality' in Philip Syrpis (ed), *The Judiciary, the Legislature and the EU Internal Market* (Cambridge University Press 2012) 65–66.

[43] Article 114(4) to (10) TFEU.

[44] These provisions permit a derogation from the legislative act itself rather than constituting a derogation allowed under that act. The role of Article 114(4) to (10) TFEU is not explored further for two reasons. First, to the knowledge of the author, no decisions have been rendered by the Commission pursuant to these paragraphs in a matter related to lifestyles. Second, as extensive studies of these provisions have shown, their potential for allowing regulatory diversity remains limited: see Ellen Vos and Maria Weimer, 'Differentiated Integration or Uniform Regime? National Derogations from EU Internal Market Measures', in Bruno de Witte, Andrea Ott and Ellen Vos (eds), *Between Flexibility and Disintegration: The Trajectory of Differentiation in EU Law* (Edward Elgar Publishing 2017) 304–335; Weimer, *Risk Regulation in the Internal Market*, see especially 143–179.

the very obstacles and distortions it aimed to remove. More generally, as some have noted, 'the harmonised standard should not be set at a level so low that it becomes meaningless both from an internal market point of view and from a public health perspective'.[45] From a health policy standpoint, this is primarily a political choice concerning the Union's level of ambition. From the internal market perspective, however, it is first and foremost a legal issue of competence and compliance with Article 114 TFEU.

To address this question, a key conceptual and terminological distinction must be drawn between *minimum* harmonisation and *partial* harmonisation – two notions often conflated, even by the Court itself.[46] They concern different dimensions of an EU act: its intensity and its scope, respectively.[47] The scope of an EU measure, on the one hand, determines what the act covers and what it leaves unregulated. This is a matter of partial harmonisation: aspects of a product or policy area falling outside the act remain within Member States' residual powers.[48] Union law does not require full harmonisation of every product, service or policy area it touches. For instance, advertising rules for tobacco, alcohol and food are partially harmonised to varying degrees. The intensity of an EU act, on the other hand, concerns the possibility for Member States to go beyond the Union standard. Two main options exist here.[49] A measure may be of maximum harmonisation, precluding stricter national requirements, or of minimum harmonisation, permitting Member States to maintain or adopt higher standards. In what follows, the terms *minimum* and *maximum* harmonisation will be used to describe the intensity of an act, while *total* and *partial* harmonisation will refer to its scope.

Both methods – minimum and partial harmonisation – raise constitutional questions about their legality under Article 114 TFEU. Since Union measures adopted under that provision must genuinely remove barriers to free movement or distortions of competition, minimum

[45] Alemanno and Garde, 'The Emergence of an EU Lifestyle Policy' 1769.
[46] See Piet Jan Slot, 'Harmonisation' (1996) 21 European Law Review 378, 389.
[47] ibid, 388–389; Stephen Weatherill, 'Pre-Emption, Harmonisation and the Distribution of Competence to Regulate the Internal Market' in Catherine Barnard and Joanne Scott (eds), *The Law of the Single European Market: Unpacking the Premises* (Hart Publishing 2002) 52–63; Schütze, *From Dual to Cooperative Federalism* 194–196.
[48] For some elements on partial harmonisation and its different meanings: see Schütze, *From Dual to Cooperative Federalism* 195 and footnote 14. See also Case C-779/18 *Mikrokasa v XO*, EU:C:2019:1146, Opinion of Advocate General Hogan, paras 48–50.
[49] Leaving aside optional harmonisation: see Schütze, *From Dual to Cooperative Federalism* 197–198.

harmonisation appears prima facie problematic: if an EU act permits future divergences in national law, its contribution to free movement looks tenuous. As put by Boeger: 'since minimum harmonisation introduces more political diversity into the internal market, the key question remains to what extent such diversity continues to be accepted even if it impinges on the economic objective to harmonise regulatory standards in the internal market, so as to optimise conditions for undistorted competition and free trade'.[50] Much depends on whether stricter national rules apply equally to domestic and foreign operators. A 'thick' version of minimum harmonisation allows Member States to impose stricter rules on all actors – domestic and foreign alike. A 'thin' version restricts such rules to domestic operators only.[51] Given that Article 114 TFEU measures aim to facilitate free movement, the 'thin' model appears more consistent with its requirements, though it risks creating reverse discrimination against domestic actors.[52]

Despite the constitutional importance of this issue, the Court has not offered a clear and systematic answer. In early cases, the Court applied a 'thick' or 'thin' reading depending on whether the act contained a free movement clause preventing Member States from applying stricter rules to compliant foreign products or services.[53] Where no such clause was included, Member States could apply their higher standards to all actors, domestic and foreign alike.[54] The first major blow to minimum harmonisation came in *Tobacco Advertising*, where the Court partially annulled the directive for failing to guarantee the free movement of products lawfully placed on the market under its provisions.[55] The Court

[50] Boeger, 'Minimum Harmonisation, Free Movement and Proportionality' 62.

[51] Boeger, 'Minimum Harmonisation, Free Movement and Proportionality' 63. According to Weatherill, in cases where 'thin' minimum harmonisation is used, that latter term 'is a misnomer insofar as it is intended to refer to a standard which Member States must introduce but may surpass *even if to do so is to create obstacles to cross-border trade*': Stephen Weatherill, 'Supply of and Demand for Internal Market Regulations: Strategies, Preferences and Interpretation' in Niamh Nic Shuibhne (ed), *Regulating the Internal Market* (Edward Elgar Publishing 2006) 47, emphasis added.

[52] See regarding Directive 89/622 on the labelling of tobacco products: Case C-11/92 *Gallaher*, EU:C:1993:262, paras 20–22.

[53] Michael Dougan, 'Minimum Harmonization after *Tobacco Advertising* and *Laval Un Partneri*', in Mielle Bulterman and others (eds), *Views of European Law from the Mountain: Liber Amicorum for Piet Jan Slot* (Kluwer Law International 2009) 5. Such a clause was, for instance, present in Directive 89/622, art 8(1); see *Gallaher*.

[54] See e.g. Case 382/87, *Buet*, EU:C:1989:198.

[55] *Tobacco Advertising* paras 101–104. The Court based its decision on the fact that Article 5 of Directive 98/43/EC read as follows, '[t]his Directive shall not preclude Member States

suggested that allowing Member States to apply stricter rules to compliant foreign products undermined the directive's purpose of eliminating barriers to trade. This reasoning was confirmed in *Tobacco Advertising II*, where the directive was upheld in part because it contained a free movement clause.[56] Many commentators argued that *Tobacco Advertising* was context-specific and should not be read as a general rejection of 'thick' minimum harmonisation under Article 114 TFEU.[57] Yet in the *Philip Morris* case, concerning plain tobacco packaging and the Tobacco Products Directive, the Court not only reaffirmed the Tobacco Advertising line but appeared to go further – casting doubt on the very possibility of adopting internal market measures of a minimum harmonisation nature.

7.3.2 *Tobacco Plain Packaging: A Success Story?*

7.3.2.1 Plain Packaging under the Tobacco Products Directive

Article 24 TPD specifies the level of harmonisation reached under the Directive:

1. Member States may not, *for considerations relating to aspects regulated by this Directive*, and subject to paragraphs 2 and 3 of this Article, prohibit or restrict the placing on the market of tobacco or related products which comply with this Directive.
2. This Directive shall not affect the right of a Member State *to maintain or introduce further requirements*, applicable to all products placed on its market, in relation to the *standardisation of the packaging of tobacco products*, where it is justified on grounds of public health, taking into account the high level of protection of human health achieved through this Directive. [...]
3. A Member State may also *prohibit a certain category* of tobacco or related products, *on grounds relating to the specific* situation in that Member State and provided the provisions are justified by the need

from laying down, in accordance with the Treaty, such stricter requirements concerning the advertising or sponsorship of tobacco products as they deem necessary to guarantee the health protection of individuals', and that the directive contained no free movement clause.

[56] *Tobacco Advertising II* paras 73–74. Regarding Directive 2002/46 on food supplements, see *Alliance for Natural Health and Others*, Opinion of Advocate General Geelhoed para 37; regarding Directive 2001/37: *British American Tobacco* para 74.

[57] Dougan, 'Minimum Harmonization after *Tobacco Advertising* and *Laval Un Partneri*' 8–11. See also Boeger, 'Minimum Harmonisation, Free Movement and Proportionality' 73.

> to protect public health, taking into account the high level of protection of human health achieved through this Directive. [. . .][58]

Judging from Article 24(1), the Tobacco Products Directive (TPD) appears to be a measure of partial and maximum harmonisation. Member States are prevented from adopting further measures that would restrict or prohibit the marketing of products complying with the directive, but only with respect to those aspects regulated by it. This implies that certain aspects of tobacco products are left unregulated, and thus within Member States' residual competence. Articles 24(2) and (3) seem to introduce derogations from the principle laid down in paragraph 1. They allow: (i) under Article 24(2), Member States to maintain or introduce further requirements relating to the standardisation of packaging (i.e. plain packaging), and (ii) under Article 24(3), Member States to prohibit a category of products altogether, based on the specific situation prevailing within their territory.

Article 24(2) was inserted with a specific purpose: to enable Member States to adopt plain packaging rules ('standardisation of the packaging'). Plain or standardised packaging is the most stringent form of regulation affecting the presentation of tobacco products. It removes all visual elements – colours, logos or branding – that contribute to the attractiveness of products and shape consumer perceptions of harm, taste or strength.[59] The packaging area that is not covered by health warnings and other mandated elements must be in a standardised colour, typically brown or grey, with the brand name appearing only in a uniform font and size.

To date, eight Member States have introduced plain packaging.[60] An EU-wide obligation was contemplated during the revision of the 2001 TPD, but was excluded from the final proposal, partly due to opposition from the tobacco industry and partly because of the limited evidence available at the time regarding its effectiveness.[61] Allowing

58 Art 24 TPD, emphasis added.

59 Hammond and Parkinson, 'The Impact of Cigarette Package Design on Perceptions of Risk'; Lauren K Lempert and Stanton Glantz, 'Packaging Colour Research by Tobacco Companies: The Pack as a Product Characteristic' (2017) 26 Tobacco Control 307.

60 In August 2025, in the order of applicability of the measure: Finland, France, Ireland, Belgium Slovenia, the Netherlands, Denmark and Hungary.

61 European Commission, 'Impact assessment accompanying the document: Proposal for a Directive of the European Parliament and of the Council on the approximation of the laws, regulations and administrative provisions of the Member states concerning the manufacture, presentation and sale of tobacco and Related products' part 1, 95.

Member States to act created space for regulatory experimentation and the accumulation of evidence that could inform future EU legislation.[62] Indeed, the TPD impact assessment expressly observed that it was 'appropriate to wait for real life experience'.[63] Since then, empirical research has shown that plain packaging increases the salience of health warnings, reduces the appeal of both packaging and smoking itself and may also diminish misperceptions of harm.[64]

This provides a clear illustration of the benefits of minimum or partial harmonisation. The EU legislator was able to harmonise certain core aspects of labelling and packaging – such as the size and shape of packets and the inclusion of health warnings – while leaving scope for Member States to go further in pursuit of public health objectives. Article 24(2) thus not only allowed for some regulatory autonomy but also generated valuable evidence for potential future EU action. From a public health perspective, this is therefore a good provision. That said, this conclusion must be nuanced when viewed from the standpoint of the internal market. Article 24(2) implies that a manufacturer selling in a Member State products with traditional packaging must repackage its products in order to access the market of another Member State with plain packaging rules. The resulting fragmentation raises doubts about the compatibility of Article 24(2) with Article 114 TFEU, which requires the removal of barriers to trade and appreciable distortions of competition. Article 24(3), known as a 'safeguard clause',[65] similarly gives rise to tension by allowing Member States to prohibit products that would otherwise be permitted under the Directive. Here too, the obstacles to trade removed at the EU level appear only provisionally lifted if Member States may unilaterally reintroduce prohibitions.

7.3.2.2 The *Philip Morris* Judgment

In *Philip Morris*, the Court sought to reconcile Article 24(2) and (3) TPD with the requirements of Article 114 TFEU. Regarding Article 24(2) TPD – a provision 'not devoid of ambiguity'[66] – the Court held that two interpretations were possible. First, it could be read as permitting 'Member

[62] See European Commission, TPD impact assessment part 1, 118. See also, regarding reporting: TPD, art 28(2)(a).

[63] European Commission, TPD impact assessment part 1, 118.

[64] Crawford Moodie and others, 'Plain Tobacco Packaging: Progress, Challenges, Learning and Opportunities' (2022) 31 Tobacco Control 263.

[65] On the use of 'safeguard clauses' in EU legislation, see Slot, 'Harmonisation' 394–395.

[66] See *Philip Morris* para 69.

States to maintain or introduce further requirements *in relation to all aspects* of the packaging of tobacco products, including those which have been harmonised by the directive'.[67] This interpretation, however, 'would amount, in essence, to *undermining the harmonisation effected by the directive*' since 'the consequence of such an interpretation would be to permit Member States to *replace the requirements* relating to packaging which have been harmonised by the directive with other requirements, introduced at national level'.[68] 'Such an interpretation', the Court added, '*would render Article 24(2) of Directive 2014/40 incompatible with Article 114 TFEU*'.[69] In the Court's view, Member States wishing to derogate from the requirements of the TPD must instead follow the procedure laid down in Article 114(4)-(10) TFEU.[70] In a momentous statement, the Court thus openly rejected the use of minimum harmonisation under Article 114 TFEU – both, it seems, in its 'thick' and 'thin' versions.[71]

The second interpretation, favoured by the Court, was to read Article 24(2) TPD as a clause of partial harmonisation. In this view, 'Article 24 (2) of Directive 2014/40 may also be interpreted as meaning that it permits Member States to maintain or introduce further requirements *only in relation to aspects* of the standardisation of the packaging of tobacco products *which have not been harmonised by the directive*',[72] consistent with the directive's general scheme.[73] Even under this construction, however, Article 24(2) TPD does not guarantee the free circulation of products that comply with the directive.[74] The Court nonetheless considered that such 'partial harmonisation' is compatible with Article 114 TFEU, because 'whilst it does not eliminate all obstacles to trade, it does eliminate some'.[75] The result, according to the Court, is 'that manufacturers of tobacco products throughout the internal market are able to use cigarette packets which have a uniform basic design and are required to adapt that design to the specificities of their respective national laws, regulations and administrative

[67] ibid, para 71, emphasis added. [68] ibid, para 71, emphasis added.
[69] ibid, para 72, emphasis added.
[70] *Philip Morris* para 71. See Stephen Weatherill, 'The Fundamental Question of Minimum or Maximum Harmonisation' in Sacha Garben and Inge Govaere (eds), *The Internal Market 2.0* (Hart Publishing 2021) 274.
[71] According to Weatherill, only the thick version is rejected by the Court: ibid. Yet, the Court objects here to the substitution of national requirement for EU requirements generally, without making a reference to whom national requirements apply.
[72] *Philip Morris* para 73, emphasis added. [73] ibid, paras 74–77. [74] ibid, para 79.
[75] ibid, para 81.

provisions only in certain details (colours, for example), but no longer in every respect'.[76]

The Court's interpretation of Article 24(2) TPD appears formally correct from an internal market perspective, although one may doubt that this reflects the legislator's actual intention, given that it renders Article 24(2) largely redundant with Article 24(1).[77] By preventing divergence at least on some aspects, partial harmonisation, unlike minimum harmonisation, does bring clear benefits to free movement. In practice, however, such a 'piecemeal'[78] approach remains problematic. If harmonisation were so limited that manufacturers still needed separate production processes for different Member States, the removal of obstacles to trade or distortions of competition would be largely hypothetical. Economies of scale could not be guaranteed.[79]

In *Philip Morris*, the Court also examined the legality of Article 24(3) TPD under Article 114 TFEU. It acknowledged that 'it is true that by permitting the Member States to prohibit a certain category of tobacco or related products even though they comply with the requirements of Directive 2014/40, Article 24(3) of the directive is capable of impeding the free movement of those products'.[80] Following the logic applied to Article 24(2), this should have rendered Article 24(3) incompatible with Article 114 TFEU. Yet the Court again upheld its validity by construing it as a clause of partial harmonisation. According to the Court, the lawfulness of tobacco products is not regulated by the directive:[81]

> Article 24(3) of Directive 2014/40, read in conjunction with paragraph 1 of that article, thus seeks to *delineate the scope of the directive* by clarifying that tobacco and related products which comply with the requirements laid down by the directive *may move freely* on the internal market, *provided that those products belong to a category of tobacco products or related products which is, as such, lawful* in the Member State in which they are marketed.[82]

One may object that this stretches the logic of partial harmonisation to an extreme, particularly since the directive does regulate the lawfulness

[76] *Philip Morris*, Opinion of Advocate General Kokott para 119.

[77] Indeed, if Article 24(2) covers 'aspects of the standardisation of the packaging of tobacco products which have not been harmonised by the directive', then Article 24(1) alone is sufficient for allowing Member States to act.

[78] Davies, 'The Competence to Create an Internal Market' 79.

[79] Contrary to what was argued by the Court in *Philip Morris* para 103. See also *Philip Morris*, Opinion of Advocate General Kokott para 98.

[80] *Philip Morris* para 87. [81] ibid, para 90.

[82] ibid, para 91, emphasis added. See also *Swedish Match II* paras 73–74.

of some products, most notably tobacco for oral use. Advocate General Kokott proposed another interpretation:

> Article 24(3) of the Directive *may not be interpreted* so broadly that it effectively gives the Member States *carte blanche permanently to ban*, on public health grounds, the placing on the market of certain products covered by the Directive, *thereby unilaterally invalidating the free movement of those products*. The argument put forward by the Parliament and the Commission that, on the basis of Article 24(3) of the Directive, individual Member States are permitted for example to prohibit completely the placing on the market of cigarettes cannot therefore be accepted. Such *unilateral national prohibitions* are possible only in respect of products which have *not* been the subject of harmonisation in Directive 2014/40.[83]

Yet, according to Kokott, 'this does not mean, however, that Article 24(3) of the Directive would be unlawful and would thus have to be annulled'.[84] She considered the safeguards built into Article 24(3) – namely, that a Member State may act only on grounds relating to its specific situation, taking into account the level of protection achieved in the directive, and subject to Commission control – as sufficient to ensure compatibility with Article 114 TFEU.[85] Her argument, in essence, is that these strict conditions would make recourse to Article 24(3) rare, which has not exactly been the case.[86] Legally, however, nothing prevents Member States from relying on Article 24(3) TPD with respect to any tobacco product covered by the directive. Moreover, a similar reasoning could have been applied to Article 24(2) TPD – allowing its application to aspects already harmonised by the Directive, provided that the procedure set out therein prevented excessive derogations – yet the Court did not adopt this approach.

7.3.2.3 The Future of Minimum Harmonisation

Philip Morris is an important judgment. It provides a textbook example of the difficulty of reconciling provisions that have primarily a public health purpose, ensuring that Member States remain in command to adopt more stringent tobacco control measures, with their stated and

83 *Philip Morris*, Opinion of Advocate General Kokott para 125, emphasis added.

84 ibid, para 126. 85 ibid, paras 127–128.

86 In August 2025, five decisions had been adopted under this provision: <https://health.ec.europa.eu/tobacco/product-regulation/implementing-tobacco-products-directive-directive-201440eu/notifications-under-article-243-tobacco-products-directive_en> accessed 24 August 2025. In its decision, the Commission did not apply the condition that Member States only act on grounds related to their 'specific situation' particularly strictly.

required objective, which is to contribute to the smooth functioning of the internal market by removing obstacles to free movement or distortions of competition. In order to uphold provisions such as Article 24(2) and (3) TPD, without openly renouncing its case law regarding the validity of measures adopted under Article 114 TFEU, the Court is led to make interpretations that fail to convince. Legislating in the field of health with an internal market competence presents limits, a conclusion already drawn from the analysis found in Chapter 6.

This tension is also apparent in the Audiovisual Media Services Directive, whose Article 3(1) provides that 'Member States shall ensure freedom of reception and shall not restrict retransmissions on their territory of audiovisual media services from other Member States for reasons which fall within the fields coordinated by this Directive'. Under Article 4(1) AVMSD, 'Member States remain free to require media service providers *under their jurisdiction* to comply with more detailed or stricter rules *in the fields coordinated by this Directive*', and, provided a number of strict substantive and procedural conditions are met, may extend these rules to service providers established in other Member States.[87] Such 'thin' minimum harmonisation, although it sits awkwardly with the interpretation of Article 24(2) TPD adopted in *Philip Morris*,[88] does ensure the free movement of audiovisual media services coming from other Member States, at the expense, though, of public health. Under Articles 3(1) and 4(1) AVMSD, a Member State may prohibit alcohol advertising on television with regard only to operators established on its territory. In the case of two neighbouring countries sharing a language, where cross-border transmission tends to be a common phenomenon, France and Belgium for instance, or Germany and Austria, this can undermine the stricter advertising policy chosen by one of the two countries.[89] 'Isn't it paradoxical' then, as rightfully written by Amandine Garde, 'that

[87] See AVMSD, art 4(2)–(5), emphasis added. This possibility seems to have been used only once, by Sweden, whose request was ultimately rejected. See European Commission, 'Reporting on the application of Directive 2010/13/EU "Audiovisual Media Services Directive" for the period 2014-2019' 6.

[88] Article 4(1) AVMSD does allow Member States to 'replace requirements [. . .] which have been harmonised by the directive with other requirements, introduced at national level', a situation which, after *Philip Morris*, should lead to its incompatibility with Articles 53(1) and 62 TFEU, its legal bases: see *Philip Morris* paras 71–72. As ruled in *Tobacco Advertising*, the conditions for recourse to Articles 53(1) and 62 TFEU are similar to those for recourse to Article 114 TFEU: *Tobacco Advertising* para 87.

[89] Bartlett and Garde, 'Time to Seize the (Red) Bull by the Horns' 514.

Member States may be significantly better off in the absence of existing EU rules purporting to protect public health?'[90]

As the AVMSD example shows, from a public health perspective, minimum harmonisation does seem to be the best option: 'the aim of achieving a high level of protection within the Union would always be better served by allowing Member States to go beyond the federal compromise represented in European legislation'.[91] One could even make the argument that recourse to minimum harmonisation is required by the various health mainstreaming clauses contained in the TFEU and the Charter, which all refer to a 'high level of protection'.[92] Ideally, minimum harmonisation should be construed in a 'thick' manner, since having to accept foreign products or services offering a lesser degree of protection can act as a powerful deterrent for Member States to adopt a stricter regime.[93]

Such is not the logic of the internal market and of Article 114 TFEU, as shown in *Philip Morris*. The difference between that provision and other 'social' legal bases, where minimum harmonisation is constitutionally required, was also highlighted in the *Octapharma* case, dealing with the respective scopes of application of Directive 2001/83 on the Community code relating to medicinal products[94] and Directive 2002/98 on the quality and safety of human blood.[95] In its judgment, the Court reminded us that, in principle, Article 114 TFEU, unlike Article 168 TFEU, does not provide for the Member States to maintain or introduce more stringent protective measures.[96] A similar logic applies in consumer protection, where Article 169 TFEU only protects Member

[90] Garde, 'Harmful Commercial Marketing and Children's Rights' 845.

[91] Schütze, 'Classifying EU Competences' 48. The argument was made as regards environmental protection but equally applies to public health.

[92] See in the area of consumer protection: Stephen Weatherill, 'Maximum versus Minimum Harmonization: Choosing between Unity and Diversity in the Search for the Soul of the Internal Market' in Niamh Nic Shuibhne and Laurence W Gormley (eds), *From Single Market to Economic Union – Essays in Memory of John A Usher* (Oxford University Press 2012) 186–187 and 199.

[93] Michael Dougan, 'Minimum Harmonization and the Internal Market' (2000) 37 Common Market Law Review 867; Weatherill, 'Supply of and Demand for Internal Market Regulations' 47.

[94] Directive 2001/83/EC.

[95] Directive 2002/98/EC of the European Parliament and of the Council of 27 January 2003 setting standards of quality and safety for the collection, testing, processing, storage and distribution of human blood and blood components and amending Directive 2001/83/EC, OJ L33/30.

[96] Case C-512/12 *Octapharma v ANSM*, EU:C:2014:149, paras 43–44, emphasis added.

States' right to maintain or adopt stricter standards in cases where the EU adopts measures 'which support, supplement and monitor the policy pursued by the Member States'.[97] The Court made clear that this constitutional minimum harmonisation clause was not applicable to consumer protection legislation adopted under Article 114 TFEU.[98]

If one was to take seriously the Court's unambiguous rejection of minimum harmonisation, in its 'thick' version at least, this would have considerable repercussions on the EU acquis, in the field of lifestyles, consumer protection and beyond. As discussed, doubts exist as regards the validity of Article 4(1) AVMSD post-*Philip Morris*. A similar concern arises if looking at the provisions of the Food Information Regulation. Its Article 38 provides that '[a]s regards the matters specifically harmonised by this Regulation, Member States may not adopt nor maintain national measures unless authorised by Union law', adding that 'such measures shall not give rise to obstacles to free movement of goods, including discrimination as regards foods from other Member States'. This reads like a typical clause of partial and maximum harmonisation, similar to Article 24 TPD. At the same time, Articles 39 to 44 of the Regulation permit Member States, for a number of aspects harmonised under the directive, to adopt national measures applicable to all products, domestic and imported alike. Here as well, it seems that such provisions allow Member States to 'replace the requirements relating to [aspects] which have been harmonised by the directive with other requirements, introduced at national level',[99] 'an interpretation [that] would render [these provisions] incompatible with Article 114 TFEU'.[100] In the field of consumer law, where a number of legislative acts adopted under Article 114 TFEU are of a minimum harmonisation nature, a blanket application of *Philip Morris* would also have dramatic consequences.

Should *Philip Morris* be extended to other legislative acts than the TPD and to other fields of law where recourse to Article 114 TFEU is widespread? Nothing from the judgment indicates that the solution found was particularly contextual. Yet, as it has been rightfully observed, in recent years, 'there is no hint [. . .] that the Court finds anything constitutionally troubling' with minimum harmonisation.[101] The radical

[97] Article 169(2)(b) and (4) TFEU.

[98] Case C-52/00 *Commission v France*, EU:C:2002:252, para 15.

[99] *Philip Morris* para 71.

[100] *Philip Morris* para 72.

[101] Weatherill, 'The Fundamental Question of Minimum or Maximum Harmonisation'. See e.g. Case C-267/16 *Buhagiar v Minister for Justice*, EU:C:2018:26, para 49.

approach to minimum harmonisation and the internal market that *Philip Morris* invites us to take is not satisfactory if viewing the internal market in an embedded way, where non-market values and interests have to be integrated, and Member State autonomy somewhat accommodated. Full homogeneity is probably not an ideal perspective, if only a feasible one, for the Union internal market.[102] Yet, it belongs to the Court to clearly explain how a measure that does not ultimately ensure the free movement of goods or services can be validly adopted under Article 114 TFEU. Regulatory diversity should indeed be cherished and protected, but not at the expense of a proper understanding of the Union and Member States' respective powers, and of proper judicial review.

7.3.3 *Front-of-Pack Nutrition Labelling*

Despite lingering questions about the competence of the legislature under Article 114 TFEU, plain packaging can reasonably be regarded as a success story. By contrast, another regulatory experiment has been less successful: the introduction of front-of-pack (FoP) nutrition labelling. As discussed in Section 5.5.1.1, traditional textual and numerical back-of-pack (BoP) nutrition information shows clear limitations in terms of consumer understanding and behaviour change. To address these shortcomings, governments and food business operators have developed alternative labels. FoP labelling can be defined as the provision of nutrition information situated in the principal field of vision on food packaging.[103] Under the Food Information Regulation, the 'principal field of vision' is 'the field of vision [...] which is most likely to be seen at first glance by the consumer at the time of purchase and that enables the consumer to immediately identify a product in terms of its character or nature and, if applicable, its brand name'.[104] Beyond this common feature, FoP labels differ significantly in design (shape, colour, use of symbols, etc.) and purpose.[105] Their shared aim, however, is to simplify and support consumer choice. The label currently gaining traction in Europe is the Nutri-

[102] See Weatherill, 'Supply of and Demand for Internal Market Regulations' 47–49; Dougan, 'Minimum Harmonization after *Tobacco Advertising* and *Laval Un Partneri*' 17–18.

[103] Stefan Storcksdieck Gennant Bonsmann and others, 'Front-of-Pack Nutrition Labelling Schemes: A Comprehensive Review' (2020) Joint Research Centre, 18. See also Food Information Regulation, recital 41.

[104] Food Information Regulation, art 2(2)(l).

[105] For an overview, see Storcksdieck and others, 'Front-of-Pack Nutrition Labelling Schemes' 20–28.

Score, a scheme that attributes a 'grade' to food products, expressed as a coloured letter from A to E, based on their nutritional content.[106] It provides a summary evaluation of the overall nutritional quality of a product. All evaluative FoP labels rely on nutrient profiling to determine product healthiness, though methods differ: some use nutrient thresholds, such as those discussed in the context of the Claims Regulation (see Section 5.5.2.1), while others employ algorithms producing a summary score. Evidence shows that, in contrast to traditional BoP information required by the Food Information Regulation, simplified FoP labels offer better results in terms of consumer understanding and improved food choices.[107] By placing information in the principal field of vision, salience is increased: several studies have found that FoP labels are noticed earlier and attract more attention than BoP nutrition information.[108] Given the widespread difficulty consumers face in interpreting complex data, visual forms such as symbols are particularly effective and should be encouraged.[109]

The superiority of FoP nutrition information over BoP information is not new knowledge. Even before the adoption of the Food Information Regulation in 2011, a European Commission consultative document explored the possibility of introducing alternative forms of nutrition presentation, mentioning that 'simplified front of pack labelling ("sign-posting") may offer significant advantages in terms of increasing consumer use'.[110] The legislative proposal for the Food Information Regulation included the mandatory display of the energy value and the amount of key nutrients on the front of food packaging.[111] This provision, however, was later abandoned in the legislative process, partly due to strong opposition from the agri-food industry, backed by the

[106] For functioning and updates, see <www.santepubliquefrance.fr/en/nutri-score> accessed 2 October 2025.

[107] Sarah Campos, Juliana Doxey and David Hammond, 'Nutrition Labels on Pre-Packaged Foods: A Systematic Review' (2011) 14 Public Health Nutrition 1496; Storcksdieck and others, 'Front-of-Pack Nutrition Labelling Schemes'; Hanna Nohlen and others, 'Front-of-Pack Nutrition Labelling Schemes: An Update of the Evidence' (2022) Joint Research Centre. See also Vincent Delhomme, 'Front-of-Pack Nutrition Labelling in the European Union: A Behavioural, Legal and Political Analysis' (2021) 12 European Journal of Risk Regulation 825.

[108] Storcksdieck and others, 'Front-of-Pack Nutrition Labelling Schemes' 49.

[109] ibid 67; Bauer and Reisch, 'Behavioural Insights and (Un)Healthy Dietary Choices' 29.

[110] European Commission, 'Labelling: competitiveness, consumer information and better regulation for the EU' (2006) 8, <https://ec.europa.eu/food/system/files/2016-10/labelling-nutrition_better-reg_competitiveness-consumer-info_en.pdf > accessed 2 October 2025.

[111] European Commission, Food Information Regulation Proposal art 34.

European Parliament.[112] The decision not to introduce mandatory FoP information in the Food Information Regulation also reflected the uncertainty existing at that time regarding its use and its effectiveness. There was 'insufficient evidence across all the Union on how the average consumer understands and uses the alternative forms of expression or presentation of the information'.[113] The impact assessment observed in this regard that:

> At the moment there are different schemes for the presentation of information on the front of pack which are either endorsed by Governments, industry associations or are company specific schemes. However, *there is a need for mor research* on use and preference of consumers across the EU as the use of schemes is not universal across all the Member States. The provision of a framework for the inclusion of information on the front of pack would ensure that where such information is given then certain nutritional elements are included. It would be necessary to *provide some flexibility to allow for the evidence on the most useful presentation or interpretive elements to develop* and for voluntary mechanism to optimise a common approach.[114]

Unlike plain tobacco packaging, however, the legislature decided not to allow Member States to impose binding requirements on FoP labels. Such measures would have forced food businesses to comply with divergent national rules, thereby undermining the harmonising effect of the Regulation and the free movement of foodstuffs. Instead, in order to enable experimentation at the national level, a compromise system was established: FoP labels may be used voluntarily by food business operators under the official recommendation of Member States' public health authorities. '[I]n order to help consumers to easily see the essential nutrition information when purchasing foods',[115] the Food Information Regulation allows the repetition in the principal field of

[112] Kurzer and Cooper, 'Hold the Croissant! The European Union Declares War on Obesity' 64–65; Iris Goldner Lang, 'Public Health in European Union Food Law'in Tamara K Hervey, Calum Alasdair Young and Louise E Bishop (eds), *Research Handbook on EU Health Law and Policy* (Edward Elgar Publishing 2017) 410.

[113] Food Information Regulation, recital 43.

[114] European Commission, 'Impact assessment report on nutrition labelling issues accompanying the document: Proposal for a Regulation of the European Parliament and of the Council on the provision of food information to consumers' (Staff Working Document) SEC (2008) 63, emphasis added. See also European Commission, 'Report from the Commission to the European Parliament and the Council regarding the use of additional forms of expression and presentation of the nutrition declaration', COM (2020) 207 final 5.

[115] Food Information Regulation, recital 41.

vision of the most important elements of the mandatory declaration: the energy value alone or the energy value together with the amounts of fat, saturates, sugars and salt.[116] This supplementary and voluntary FoP nutrition information may be expressed using graphical forms or symbols, subject to further requirements.[117] Under Article 35(2) of the Regulation, Member States may recommend the use of FoP labels to food business operators, in which case they must notify the Commission.[118] The Commission is further invited to 'facilitate and organise the exchange of information between Member States, itself and stakeholders'[119] on FoP labelling practices, and to submit by December 2017 a report on the use of such additional forms of expression and presentation and on the advisability of further harmonisation.[120] The delayed report was submitted in May 2020,[121] paving the way for the adoption of a common and mandatory FoP nutrition label at the EU level.[122] The report confirms that both food business operators and Member States have made extensive use of the opportunity to voluntarily apply or recommend FoP schemes. From the perspective of evidence-gathering, the solution adopted in the Food Information Regulation can thus be regarded as a success. The diversity of labels used across different cultural contexts has enabled the Commission to produce a substantial study on FoP schemes and a comprehensive policy report,[123] both of which will play a central role in shaping the forthcoming revision of EU nutrition labelling rules.

Yet the 'hybrid' regulatory solution found in the Food Information Regulation is not without shortcomings, both from the standpoint of free movement and that of health and consumer protection. From a free movement perspective, even voluntary schemes can generate obstacles.

116 ibid, arts 30(3) and 34(3) and recital 41. 117 ibid, art 35(1). 118 ibid, art 35(2).

119 ibid, art 35(4). 120 ibid, art 35(5).

121 European Commission, 'Report from the Commission to the European Parliament and the Council regarding the use of additional forms of expression and presentation of the nutrition declaration'.

122 See European Commission, 'A Farm to Fork Strategy for a fair, healthy and environmentally-friendly food system'; European Commission, 'Europe's Beating Cancer Plan'. For further discussions of the legal and political implications of the development of an EU front-of-pack label, see Delhomme, 'Front-of-Pack Nutrition Labelling in the European Union'.

123 Storcksdieck and others, 'Front-of-Pack Nutrition Labelling Schemes'; European Commission, 'Report from the Commission to the European Parliament and the Council regarding the use of additional forms of expression and presentation of the nutrition declaration'.

Adapting to different national labels entails costs and uncertainty for operators, even where the schemes remain optional. Indeed, the fact that an FoP scheme is recommended by a Member State can create expectations for consumers that all products marketed in that country should be labelled with the official scheme, and could thus create a pressure on EU food business operators to label all products present on the national market with that official scheme.[124] This lack of uniformity also raises concerns from the perspective of health and consumer protection. The proliferation of different labels is a source of confusion and misunderstanding,[125] whereas a single label would allow consumers to better interpret information and make meaningful comparisons between products.[126] The mandatory nature of a label is crucial to ensure that consumers consistently have access to relevant and effective nutrition information. Moreover, voluntary schemes may bias consumers in favour of products that display a label, even where these are less nutritious than unlabelled products.[127]

Beyond these issues, which relate to the balance between unity and diversity in internal market legislation, further difficulties have emerged with FoP labelling, this time illustrating the broader limits of policy experimentation. As it stands, Article 35 of the Food Information Regulation does not actually cover summary indicators such as the Nutri-Score – that is, labels that combine information on several nutrients into one indicator – but only nutrient-specific schemes.[128] Ironically, the very provision designed to regulate FoP labelling fails to apply to the label now most widely used in the EU. Admittedly, the Nutri-Score was first conceptualised in 2014 and formally introduced in 2016, after the Food Information Regulation had been adopted, and its

124 European Commission, 'Report from the Commission to the European Parliament and the Council regarding the use of additional forms of expression and presentation of the nutrition declaration' 16. See also Gokani, 'Front-of-Pack Nutrition Labelling' 160.

125 Storcksdieck and others, 'Front-of-Pack Nutrition Labelling Schemes' 150–151. See also Gokani, 'Front-of-Pack Nutrition Labelling' 160.

126 Désirée Hagmann and Michael Siegrist, 'Nutri-Score, Multiple Traffic Light and Incomplete Nutrition Labelling on Food Packages: Effects on Consumers' Accuracy in Identifying Healthier Snack Options' (2020) 83 Food Quality and Preference 103894; Becher and others, 'Hungry for Change' 1348.

127 Storcksdieck and others, 'Front-of-Pack Nutrition Labelling Schemes' 148–149.

128 For further info on nutrient-specific schemes, see Storcksdieck and others, 'Front-of-Pack Nutrition Labelling Schemes'. Indeed, Article 35 refers to 'the energy value and the amount of nutrients referred to in Article 30(1) to (5)' of the Food Information Regulation.

development may not have been anticipated by the EU legislator. Nevertheless, the Commission and Member States have acted as if Nutri-Score fell under Article 35,[129] despite the fact that it is actually governed by Article 36 of the same Regulation, which concerns voluntary food information. That article does not provide for Member State recommendations or Commission notifications.[130]

Furthermore, schemes such as the Nutri-Score also fall within the scope of another EU instrument, the Claims Regulation, which was not conceived with policy experimentation in mind. On the contrary, its purpose was to address the proliferation of unverified food claims on the EU market. Its objective is to restrict the use of claims in order to prevent consumers from being misled. Evaluative FoP schemes that provide information on the overall quality of a product – as with the Nutri-Score, which uses the colour green and the letter A – constitute 'nutrition claims' within the meaning of the Claims Regulation: 'any claim which states, suggests or implies that a food has particular beneficial nutritional properties'.[131] The difficulty is that the Claims Regulation permits only a limited set of textual nutrition claims,[132] thereby excluding evaluative FoP schemes that positively assess products. Some commentators have further argued that these FoP schemes also amount to 'health claims', defined as 'any claim that states, suggests or implies that a relationship exists between a food category, a food or one of its constituents and health'.[133] Yet none of the evaluative FoP schemes currently in use in the EU comply with the substantive requirements for health claims under the Regulation.[134]

The result is that the creative compromise favoured by the EU legislator, designed to balance health protection with free movement, has produced a regulatory failure. Many FoP schemes now operate in legal limbo, while consumer health and interests remain insufficiently safeguarded. The adoption of a common and mandatory EU FoP nutrition label would resolve these shortcomings. Should the EU fail to take this

[129] See Gokani, 'Front-of-Pack Nutrition Labelling' 166–167.

[130] See in particular Food Information Regulation art 36(2).

[131] Claims Regulation, art 2(2) (4). This would not be the case for nutrient-specific evaluative claims, such as the MTL: Recital 46 of the Food Information Regulation. See also in that regard Van Nieuwenhuyze, 'Regulating nutrition and health claims' 71. See contra Gokani, 'Front-of-Pack Nutrition Labelling' 166.

[132] Claims Regulation, art 8 and annex.

[133] ibid, art 2(2) (5). See Gokani, 'Front-of-Pack Nutrition Labelling' 162.

[134] See in particular Claims Regulation, arts 5 and 10.

step, it ought at the very least to revise the food information framework to ensure that it does not stifle Member States' efforts to develop binding FoP labels. A robust solution would be the adoption of a single mandatory FoP scheme at the EU level. The Commission promised to present a proposal to this effect before the end of 2022,[135] a process unfortunately stalled for political reasons (see Section 8.3). Such a reform would address the legal uncertainties and practical problems described above. While the Commission has not expressed a preference for any specific scheme, the accumulated evidence and the support of a growing number of Member States make Nutri-Score the clear front runner. In its 2020 FoP report, the Commission itself concluded that evaluative schemes using colour-coding combined with a graded indicator appear the most promising to improve the nutritional quality of food choices.[136]

7.4 Subsidiarity and Tobacco Harm Reduction

In some instances, differences in patterns of disease and consumption, consumer behaviour or local preferences may justify that the EU refrains from action altogether, since local intervention would be better suited and more effective. In such circumstances, subsidiarity could emerge as a key principle for safeguarding national regulatory autonomy. Here again, market uniformity stands as an obstacle to the reflection of local diversity into the law.

7.4.1 Subsidiarity: What's in a Name?

Addressing this question requires first a clear definition of subsidiarity, arguably one of the most misunderstood principles of EU law. According to Article 5(3) TEU, in areas which do not fall within its exclusive competence, 'the Union shall act only if and in so far as the objectives of the proposed action *cannot be sufficiently achieved* by the Member States, [...] but can rather, by reason of the scale or effects of the proposed action, *be better achieved* at Union level'.[137] Subsidiarity may thus be understood as a principle of preference for local action, intimately linked

[135] European Commission, 'A Farm to Fork Strategy for a fair, healthy and environmentally-friendly food system' annex.

[136] European Commission, 'Report from the Commission to the European Parliament and the Council regarding the use of additional forms of expression and presentation of the nutrition declaration' 19.

[137] Art 5(3) TEU, emphasis added.

to federalism. Action at the higher level of government should take place only if there is a good reason for it. Legally speaking, subsidiarity is usually construed as entailing a two-stage test: a 'negative' test of national incapacity to achieve the set objectives of the given measure in a satisfactory manner – 'cannot be sufficiently achieved' – and a 'positive' test requiring that the EU be able to achieve these objectives in a better way – 'be better achieved'.[138] Only if these two conditions are met should the EU endeavour to act. The Protocol on the application of the principles of subsidiarity and proportionality, annexed to the TEU and TFEU, provides guidance for assessing compliance with those conditions and lays down procedures for both the judicial and political control of subsidiarity. The political control consists primarily in the so-called Early Warning Mechanism, whereby national parliaments may send reasoned opinions on draft legislative acts, which may in turn lead to a revision of the Commission's proposal.[139] The Court of Justice is tasked with the judicial control of subsidiarity, and must verify 'both compliance with the substantive conditions set out in Article 5 (3) TEU and compliance with the procedural safeguards provided for by [the] [P]rotocol'.[140]

Subsidiarity has generated considerable debate in the academic community and the political sphere.[141] 'The word that saves Maastricht',[142]

[138] *Poland v Parliament and Council*, Opinion of Advocate General Kokott para 142; *Philip Morris*, Opinion of Advocate General Kokott para 275; *Pillbox 38*, Opinion of Advocate General Kokott para 165.

[139] For further details and discussions on the 'Early Warning Mechanism', see Davor Jancic, 'The Game of Cards: National Parliaments in the EU and the Future of the Early Warning Mechanism and the Political Dialogue' (2015) 52 Common Market Law Review 939; Tomasz Jaroszyński, 'National Parliaments' Scrutiny of the Principle of Subsidiarity: Reasoned Opinions 2014–2019' (2020) 16 European Constitutional Law Review 91.

[140] *Philip Morris* para 217.

[141] In a vast literature, see Roger Van den Bergh, 'The Subsidiarity Principle in European Community Law: Some Insights from Law and Economics' (1994) 1 Maastricht Journal of European and Comparative Law 337; Gareth Davies, 'Subsidiarity: The Wrong Idea, in the Wrong Place, at the Wrong Time' (2006) 43 Common Market Law Review 63; Mattias Kumm, 'Constitutionalising Subsidiarity in Integrated Markets: The Case of Tobacco Regulation in the European Union' (2006) 12 European Law Journal 503; Groussot and Bogojević 'Subsidiarity as a Procedural Safeguard of Federalism' in Loïc Azoulai (ed), *The Question of Competence in the European Union* (Oxford University Press 2014) 234–252; Paul Craig, 'Subsidiarity: A Political and Legal Analysis' (2012) 50 Journal of Common Market Studies 72.

[142] Deborah Z Cass, 'The Word That Saves Maastricht? The Principle of Subsidiarity and the Division of Powers within the European Community' (1992) 29 Common Market Law Review 1107.

introduced at a time of existential fear over the seemingly unstoppable expansion of EU powers, seems to have failed to prevent the EU from expanding its reach in a growing number of fields. This explains why frequent political efforts are made to revive it. While general discussions on the meaning of subsidiarity and its role in the Union legal order go well beyond the scope of this work, it is still necessary to clarify certain terms of the debate in order to understand the role subsidiarity may play in the field of lifestyles. As it appears from Article 5(3) TEU, subsidiarity is essentially a 'technocratic' principle. It concerns how best to achieve a given policy objective, not whether that objective should be pursued in the first place. Crucially, in this sense, subsidiarity is not about deciding whether an objective should be pursued by the EU at the expense of Member States' interests.[143] Subsidiarity 'takes as its starting point that all levels are united in wishing to achieve certain goals and that none has any other interests or objectives in conflict with these'.[144] It is concerned with regulatory efficiency rather than respect for Member States' autonomy.[145] Where it is felt by one or several Member States that EU action would unduly interfere with a sensitive interest – the application of front-of-pack labelling to traditional food, for instance (see Section 8.3) – subsidiarity *stricto sensu*, as laid down in Article 5(3) TEU, cannot play a role.

Yet subsidiarity is often understood differently, as encapsulating the idea that the EU should not intrude excessively into Member States' internal affairs or citizens' daily lives, that it should not legislate on trivial matters in areas better left to national decision-making. One might say that this question is already addressed by the very existence of an EU act and by the fact that Member States have supported it so that it becomes law.[146] Subsidiarity is thus often used as an umbrella term to refer to all Union law principles or instruments that embody, in one way or another, the need to preserve sufficient regulatory space for Member States.[147] In this broader, more political sense it resonates with the principles of conferral and proportionality contained in Articles 5(2)

[143] Davies, 'Subsidiarity' 78. [144] ibid 78.
[145] Davies, 'The Competence to Create an Internal Market' 87.
[146] See Craig, 'Subsidiarity' 81, 83.
[147] Alemanno and Garde write for instance that '[a]nother manifestation of the principle of subsidiarity in EU policy, and EU lifestyle policy more specifically, is the use the EU has made of a broad range of harmonization techniques allowing for a degree of diversity between Member States to co-exist with harmonized EU standards': Alemanno and Garde, 'The Emergence of an EU Lifestyle Policy' 1767.

and 5(4) TEU, as well as with respect for national identities and fundamental structures of Member States enshrined in Article 4(2) TEU.[148] This wider understanding of subsidiarity is legitimate, but is far less amenable, if at all, to judicial review, and of limited pertinence for legal analysis. Unfortunately, public debate, policy and legislative practice, and even judicial review at times, have tended to blur the distinction between these two understandings of subsidiarity. As Davies aptly puts it, '[t]he public discourse around subsidiarity in the EU tends to use it as a shorthand for the general safeguarding of decentral choices, when this is not in fact its function, thereby adding a further potentially disillusioning layer of deception to speech about the EU'.[149] The Court itself, although well aware that its review is confined to subsidiarity *stricto sensu* as contained in Article 5(3) TEU, is not immune from this confusion. Advocate General Kokott, for instance, has defined subsidiarity as requiring that the EU's political institutions 'limit[ing] their action to regulating important matters in the common European interest'.[150]

7.4.2 *Tobacco for Oral Use and Harm Reduction*

The prohibition of tobacco for oral use raises important questions regarding competence and the balance between health, diversity and market uniformity. As explained in Section 6.3.3, if one adopts a rigorous approach to the use of the EU's internal market powers under Article 114 TFEU, the very existence of the ban is questionable. The push towards market uniformity raises a second problem, this time linked to compliance with the principle of subsidiarity in a harm-reduction context.

In *Swedish Match II*, the plaintiff argued for a breach of subsidiarity, claiming that 'the general and absolute prohibition on the placing on the market of tobacco products for oral use deprives Member States of any discretion in their legislation and imposes a uniform body of rules, with no consideration of the *individual circumstances* of the Member States'.[151]

[148] For a discussion on the links existing between subsidiarity and national identity, see Somek, *Individualism* 145; Barbara Guastaferro, 'Coupling National Identity with Subsidiarity Concerns in National Parliaments' Reasoned Opinions' (2014) 21 Maastricht Journal of European and Comparative Law 320. Under Article 4(2) TEU: 'The Union shall respect the equality of Member States before the Treaties as well as their national identities, inherent in their fundamental structures, political and constitutional, inclusive of regional and local self-government'.

[149] Davies, 'The Competence to Create an Internal Market' 87.

[150] *Pillbox 38* para 163.

[151] *Swedish Match II* para 64, emphasis added.

Although that plea was not further substantiated, one could have argued that the effect of the ban on snus on public health is dependent on local circumstances and that the decision would hence be better left to the national level. The report of the scientific committee that informed the adoption of the ban supports this view, stating that 'the association between patterns of smokeless tobacco use and smoking cessation differs between populations and is likely to be affected by cultural, societal and other factors', and concluding that 'it is not possible to extrapolate the trends in prevalence of smoking and use of oral tobacco if it were made available in an EU country where it is now unavailable'.[152] Recommending or discouraging the use of snus as a cessation aid should depend on how the harm caused by people taking up snus, either alone or in combination with cigarettes, compares to the harm reduction achieved when smokers substitute snus for cigarettes.[153] This assessment is likely to be influenced by social norms and local circumstances.[154] In countries neighbouring Sweden, such as Finland, where consumers are familiar with the product and already use it to some extent,[155] the effect of authorising and endorsing snus is likely to differ from that in countries where the product is virtually unknown. In sum, uncertainty could plead for regulatory diversity and should, at the very least, lead to a discussion of the legality of the ban under the principle of subsidiarity.

This discussion, unfortunately, did not take place in *Swedish Match II*. In its judgment, the Court did not address the question of subsidiarity from a health perspective but focused instead on the impossibility for

152 Scientific Committee on Emerging and Newly Identified Health Risks (SCENIHR), 'Health Effects of Smokeless Tobacco Products' (2008) 12, <https://ec.europa.eu/health/other-pages/health-sc-basic-page/scientific-committee-emerging-and-newly-identified-health-risks-0_en> accessed 2 October 2025.

153 Karl Erik Lund and Tord Finne Vedøy, 'A Conceptual Framework for Assessing the Public Health Effects from Snus and Novel Non-Combustible Nicotine Products' (2021) 38 Nordic Studies on Alcohol and Drugs 586.

154 See in that regard recital 20 of the TPD: 'the responsibility for regulating the ingredients of tobacco for oral use, which requires in-depth knowledge of the specific characteristics of this product and of its patterns of consumption, should, in accordance with the principle of subsidiarity, remain with Sweden'.

155 Marjut Salokannel and Eeva Ollila, 'Snus and Snus-like Nicotine Products Moving across Nordic Borders: Can Laws Protect Young People?' (2021) 38 Nordic Studies on Alcohol and Drugs 540; Kirsimarja Raitasalo and others, 'Single, Dual, and Triple Use of Cigarettes, e-Cigarettes, and Snus among Adolescents in the Nordic Countries' (2022) 19 International Journal of Environmental Research and Public Health 683.

Member States alone to contribute to the internal market objective, ruling that:

> *Even if the second of those objectives [health] might be better achieved at the level of Member States*, the fact remains that pursuing it at that level would be liable to entrench, if not create, situations in which some Member States permit the placing on the market of tobacco products for oral use, whilst others prohibit it, thus *running completely counter to the first objective* of Directive 2014/40, namely the improvement of the functioning of the internal market for tobacco and related products.
>
> The *interdependence of the two objectives* pursued by the directive means that the EU legislature could legitimately take the view that it had to establish a set of rules for the placing on the EU market of tobacco products for oral use and that, because of that interdependence, *those two objectives could best be achieved at EU level.*[156]

By analysing both objectives together, the Court severely restricts the possibility for Member States or other claimants to contest the validity of an EU measure based on the arguments outlined above. The EU will always be comparatively better placed than Member States to act for internal market purposes. Indeed, '[t]he removal of obstacles to cross-border trade in the European internal market, which is the focus of interest in Article 114 TFEU, is a prime example of action which cannot, *as a rule*, be sufficiently realised at national level'.[157] Member States alone cannot, by definition, take action to remove obstacles to trade or distortions of competition through harmonisation.[158] Hence, due to this interpretation, the internal market nature of legislative acts in the field of lifestyles prevents health-based subsidiarity claims from being made. Useful policy experimentation is therefore barred. The absence of any discussion on this point is even more ironic since, as already established, the prohibition of tobacco for oral use does not serve to remove obstacles to trade in the internal market. For the Court, adopting an alternative approach – requiring that the EU be better placed to achieve each objective considered separately – would mean weighing the relative importance of the two objectives. Yet this is precisely what the Court has refrained from doing since its ruling in *Tobacco Advertising*, in order to respect the legislator's intention to pursue both objectives

156 *Swedish Match II* paras 68–69.

157 *Poland v Parliament and Council*, Opinion of Advocate General Kokott para 154, emphasis added.

158 One could therefore conclude, with Davies, 'that subsidiarity has no relevance to those functional competences whose aim is to create the uniformity necessary for an internal market': 'Subsidiarity'.

simultaneously (see Section 3.4).[159] In *Poland v Council*, Advocate General Kokott suggested that '[a] stricter judicial review of subsidiarity may be necessary where an EU measure exceptionally affects matters of national identity of the Member States', within the meaning of Article 4(2) TEU.[160] She doubted however that 'problems relating to the manufacture, sale and consumption of menthol cigarettes [could] seriously to be regarded as a matter of national interest'.[161] Whether or not that latter point is correct, it seems problematic for the Court to take a stance on what constitutes a national interest, as this somewhat defeats the purpose.

The Court's reluctance to assess the achievement of the health objective as part of its subsidiarity review is regrettable. Understanding the extent to which EU-level action is necessary for health purposes would enhance both its legitimacy and acceptability, particularly in a field where health is clearly the main political objective. Even if it were shown that EU action was preferable only on internal market grounds, this would not necessarily lead to annulment of the legislation but could open a political debate about its pertinence. As Advocate General Kokott has observed, where 'national, regional or local features are central to [an] issue', 'this tends to suggest that intervention should be at the level of the Member States and that the matter should be addressed by the authorities which have greater proximity and expertise in respect of the action to be taken'.[162] Unhealthy lifestyles are precisely an area in which such infra-European features are likely to play a decisive role.

This problem may have repercussions in other areas of EU tobacco control, and for unhealthy lifestyles more broadly. E-cigarettes represent another category of 'tobacco' products with harm-reduction potential, since they emit vapour rather than combustion smoke. Evidence is mounting that, for some long-term smokers, e-cigarettes may be useful as a cessation aid.[163] In England, the use of e-cigarettes has been officially endorsed as such.[164] The controversy in this area mirrors that surrounding tobacco for oral use, with opponents of harm reduction pointing at the risk of gateway effect and dual use. While the EU does not ban e-

[159] See also *Poland v Parliament and Council*, Opinion of Advocate General Kokott para 157.
[160] ibid, para 148. [161] ibid, para 166; see also para 148. [162] ibid, para 152.
[163] Feeney, Rossetti andTerrien, 'E-Cigarettes – a Review of the Evidence – Harm versus Harm Reduction'.
[164] Virginia Berridge and others, 'E-Cigarettes: A Framework for Comparative History and Policy' (2024) 119 Addiction 1864.

cigarettes, it has subjected them to a drastic advertising and sponsorship ban, similar to that applicable to other tobacco products.[165] The EU legislator justified that decision on the ground that 'electronic cigarettes can develop into a gateway to nicotine addiction and ultimately traditional tobacco consumption, as they mimic and *normalise* the action of smoking'.[166] Proponents of harm reduction strategies are usually critical of total bans on e-cigarette advertising, arguing that a balance should be struck between shielding young people from exposure to such advertising, thereby preventing uptake of any tobacco-related product, and ensuring that current smokers develop an accurate perception of e-cigarettes, which remain less harmful than traditional tobacco.[167] Here too, that equilibrium is likely to be influenced by social norms,[168] and it is conceivable that some countries might benefit from more nuanced advertising regulation. Any subsidiarity claim made in this regard is, however, for the reasons outlined above, unlikely to succeed.

7.5 Conclusion

Regulating tobacco, food and alcohol is a challenging endeavour, given the difficulty of predicting how consumers will react to specific regulatory tools, a challenge further compounded by the diversity of lifestyle practices and health situations across the twenty-seven Member States. This necessitates to grant regulators a degree of leeway, to allow for experimentation. This chapter has shown that EU law can accommodate such an approach, and that EU legislation could even serve as a catalyst for regulatory experimentation, thereby improving evidence-based law-making. Yet the inherently fragmented approach that this presupposes sits uneasily with a fundamental feature of the internal market: regulatory uniformity, necessary for the removal of obstacles to the free movement of goods. The internal market nature of this field of law neutralises health-based subsidiarity claims and casts serious doubt on the feasibility of minimum harmonisation as a legislative technique. To address this tension, the EU legislature and the Court have responded in conflicting

[165] AVMSD, art 9(1)(d); TPD, art 20(5).
[166] TPD, recital 43, emphasis added.
[167] See Voigt, 'Smoking Norms and the Regulation of E-Cigarettes'.
[168] ibid; Máirtín S McDermott and others, 'Social Norms for E-Cigarettes and Smoking: Associations with Initiation of e-Cigarette Use, Intentions to Quit Smoking and Quit Attempts: Findings from the EUREST-PLUS ITC Europe Surveys' (2020) 30 European Journal of Public Health 46.

ways, placing health first, as in the case of tobacco plain packaging; prioritising (a certain vision of) the market, as with tobacco for oral use; or attempting to accommodate both, as in the case of front-of-pack nutrition labelling. *Philip Morris* is in some respects comparable to *Tobacco Advertising*: an isolated reminder that Article 114 TFEU should only be invoked to adopt measures genuinely contributing to the internal market, followed by a stream of cases which, without formally renouncing this principle, simply choose to disregard it. What emerges is a constitutional tension between the demands of the internal market and those of health, akin to the one described in Chapter 6. Accommodation is possible, but would require a reconceptualisation of the EU's internal market competence, and of its system of competences more broadly.

8 Managing Diversity II

Towards a Transnational Lifestyle?

8.1 Introduction

Lifestyles are not simply, or even primarily, health-focused. They are pleasurable activities that play an important role in the development and maintenance of social relationships. They also function as identity markers, signalling as belonging to particular social groups along (sub-) national or socio-economic lines. The norms governing the use of tobacco, alcohol and food, whether embedded in the social fabric or enshrined in law, express moral, ethical or cultural values. Sweden and Finland's strict alcohol policies – these two countries are the last in the EU to maintain retail monopolies – together with the Netherlands' notorious tolerance of cannabis consumption, form part of each nation's ethos, of what it means to be Nordic or Dutch, and shape the experience of living in or travelling to these countries.[1] In Finland and Sweden, alcohol has traditionally been consumed not for its organoleptic properties or to accompany meals, but for the purpose of intoxication. It 'symbolized moral degradation, poverty and social disorder, while temperance was considered a key to a better life, a sign of high social morality and general welfare'.[2] This is the root of the Nordic alcohol model. The Dutch tolerance policy on drugs also reflects a specific understanding of the State's role with regard to drug consumption, prioritising harm reduction over the prosecution of illegal behaviour.[3] These norms embody a particular relationship to risk and a collective

[1] See Kurzer, *Markets and Moral Regulation*; De Witte, 'Sex, Drugs & EU Law'.

[2] Trygve Ugland, 'Europeanisation of the Nordic Alcohol Monopoly Systems Collisions between Ideologies and Political Cultures' (1997) 14 Nordic Studies on Alcohol and Drugs 7, 9. See also Kurzer, *Markets and Moral Regulation* 27–72.

[3] Kurzer, *Markets and Moral Regulation* 97–120.

vision of what 'the good life' is.[4] Arguably, they do not 'lend themselves naturally to practices of *transnational rationalization*'.[5] Accordingly, in the EU context, the allocation of regulatory power over unhealthy lifestyles is not merely a matter of determining the most effective level of regulation – how health is best protected, the subject of Chapter 7 – but also of deciding whether, and to what extent, differences in cultural and ethical traditions may justify renouncing the EU's ambition to enhance citizens' welfare and legitimise its existence.[6] This is the final dilemma addressed in this book. This chapter examines how EU law engages with the cultural and moral dimensions of unhealthy lifestyles. It interrogates the emergence of a transnational lifestyle, as well as the resistance to it. To this end, it draws on the typology developed by Floris de Witte in his article 'Sex, Drugs & EU Law'.[7] According to De Witte, where national visions of 'the good life' clash, three main strategies exist for managing the conflict at the EU level: '(i) direct normative intervention and Europeanization of the contentious moral or ethical choice; (ii) the insulation of national autonomy; or (iii) balancing through either a substantive or procedural version of the principle of proportionality'. All three approaches have been employed in the field of unhealthy lifestyles, reflecting the distinct regulatory treatment of tobacco, alcohol and food. The overall conclusion of this chapter is twofold. First, in areas where a process of Europeanisation is underway, such as tobacco regulation, it is essential that EU law clearly sets out the reasons underlying the approach it chooses, quasi-prohibitive in this case, thereby enabling a discussion of its ethical implications. This is not the case at present. Second, in areas where Europeanisation is not (yet) possible or desirable, cultural and moral differences must be acknowledged, and EU law must allow sufficient flexibility so as not to prevent Member States from continuing to act. Once again, although less markedly than in the other phenomena examined in the preceding chapters, the internal market nature of the law is responsible for some of the malfunctions identified, because it obfuscates the cultural, moral and ethical disputes that arise in this field.

[4] Deborah Lupton and John Tulloch, '"Life Would Be Pretty Dull without Risk": Voluntary Risk-Taking and Its Pleasures' (2002) 4 Health, Risk & Society 113. See also Nick J Fox, 'Postmodern Reflections on "Risk", "Hazards" and Life Choices' in Deborah Lupton (ed), *Risk and Sociocultural Theory: New Directions and Perspectives* (Cambridge University Press 1999) 19.

[5] De Witte, 'Sex, Drugs & EU Law' 1545–1546, emphasis added.

[6] Somek, *Individualism* 94, 145.

[7] De Witte, 'Sex, Drugs & EU Law'.

8.2 Europeanisation and the Tobacco Endgame: The Missing Ethical Framework

A useful starting point is Floris de Witte's contention that the diversity of moral and ethical policies in Europe can be both explained and normatively justified by reference to self-determination, that is, the need to protect 'not only the expression of certain moral or ethical values, but also the autonomy of the political forum through which such values are articulated and renegotiated'.[8] For De Witte, the EU cannot reproduce 'the institutional and normative preconditions required for it to be a space of communal self-expression', because 'it lacks the sophisticated political framework, its law lacks the capacity for socialization, its system of governance is too rigid to allow for the continuous re-negotiation of first principles, and (therefore) the affective ties between its population are too weak to allow for a meaningful exercise in self-expression of the parameters of permissive behaviour'.[9] De Witte is therefore deeply sceptical of the emergence of a transnational morality. This is not, he stresses, 'about the protection of the nation State per se, but about the protection of the capacity of individuals to shape the fundamental norms that govern their society in conformity with their preferences and the horizontal commitments entered into with fellow citizens'.[10] While this view is contested,[11] it is safe to assume that it remains widespread among citizens and Member States in the EU. It helps explain why many of the most morally sensitive issues, such as reproductive rights, marriage or the wearing of religious symbols, are not regulated at the EU level.[12] This perspective also underpins the Union's commitment to respecting Europe's 'rich' cultural diversity and to safeguarding and enhancing its cultural heritage.[13]

Yet, this has not prevented the EU from acting in certain sensitive areas, directly intervening and 'Europeanising' contentious moral, ethical or cultural choices. This first strategy of Europeanisation is most visible in the case of tobacco. The EU has developed some of the most

[8] ibid, 1547. [9] ibid, 1550. [10] ibid, 1551.

[11] See the alternative view put forward by Martijn van den Brink, defending an input oriented vision of the EU's legitimacy: Martijn van den Brink, *Legislative Authority and Interpretation in the European Union* (Oxford University Press 2024), 30, 37–44.

[12] This does not mean that EU law does not affect these issues, for instance through free movement and non-discrimination provisions: see e.g. Case C-673/16, *Coman*, EU:C:2018:385; Case C-148/22, *Commune d'Ans*, EU:C:2023:924; Case C-4/23, *Mirin*, EU:C:2024:845.

[13] Art 3 TEU.

stringent tobacco control policies worldwide, wholeheartedly endorsing the endgame strategy, that is, the end of smoking, seemingly with little resistance or contestation. In this area, EU law is less and less a medium allowing individuals to move to another country in order to pursue a different life, that would be the role of the free movement provisions, but a vehicle for equalising conditions throughout the EU. In addition, EU tobacco law is vigorously paternalistic.[14] This paternalistic approach is rarely acknowledged or debated. The language of tobacco regulation is framed in terms of the market, its legal anchor, and health, its political objective. This vision is evident in the discussion of a possible general ban on all tobacco products, included in the TPD impact assessment.[15] That option was rejected as unfeasible, owing to 'unreasonable compliance costs' and the likely emergence of an illegal market that would undermine the very objective of eliminating tobacco use in the EU. At no point, however, did the Commission discuss the ethical implications of banning a product as widely consumed and available as tobacco. While the adoption of an EU-wide tobacco ban remains a distant prospect, the idea is gaining traction among experts and civil society. On 24 August 2022 the Commission officially registered a European Citizens' Initiative titled 'Call to achieve a tobacco-free environment and the first European tobacco-free generation by 2030', whose first objective is to 'promote the first tobacco-free European generation by 2028, ending the sale of tobacco and nicotine products to citizens born since 2010'.[16] This raises the question whether tobacco regulation is in fact (still) a morally controversial issue at all, or whether it simply reflects, as has been observed in relation to EU consumer law and policy, that 'paternalism is not a hot issue' in the EU.[17] It seems indeed to go back such a long way in the

[14] Paternalism may be defined as the interference with an individual's decision-making, against that person's will, without their consent or contrary to their preferences, with the declared purpose of furthering that person's own good: see Danny Scoccia, 'The Concept of Paternalism', in Kalle Grill and Jason Hanna (eds), *The Routledge Handbook of the Philosophy of Paternalism* (Routledge, Taylor & Francis Group 2018) 11.

[15] European Commission, TPD impact assessment part 1, 49–50.

[16] Commission Implementing Decision (EU) 2022/1430 of 24 August 2022 on the request for registration of the European citizens' initiative titled 'Call to achieve a tobacco-free environment and the first European tobacco-free generation by 2030', pursuant to Regulation (EU) 2019/788 of the European Parliament and of the Council, OJ L221/103, recital 2.

[17] Sibony and Helleringer, 'EU Consumer Protection and Behavioural Sciences' 211.

national traditions of some of the Member States that it is hardly questioned.[18] The issue with paternalistic State interventions in lifestyles is not only their coercive nature, but also their potential to affect the social position of those targeted.[19]

> The drunk, the smoker, the fatty, the problem gambler, and the drug fiend have long been objects of derision. Those deemed to be out of control have been viewed as needing to be brought back into line. If they, themselves, did not have the willpower to conform, then society would have to take charge and do the job for them.[20]

Public health interventions may, consciously or not, lead to the stigmatisation of the person engaging in the targeted behaviour.[21] The risk is particularly acute for overweight and obese individuals, whose bodies are frequently subject to social reprobation, who may be seen as lazy or incapable, and who face discrimination in a plurality of professional and social settings.[22] But it also exists for smokers, especially since tobacco regulation has embraced the strategy of 'denormalisation': making smoking less visible and less acceptable on the assumption that changing the social norms surrounding smoking will help changing smoking behaviours.[23] This strategy is visible in the design of smoke-free environments, which aim not only to protect bystanders from exposure to tobacco smoke but also to render smokers less visible. It is also at stake in the regulation of e-cigarettes, criticised for perpetuating the gesture of smoking as something socially acceptable. Stigmatisation can be

[18] ibid. See also Alberto Alemanno and Anne-Lise Sibony, 'Epilogue: The Legitimacy and Practicability of EU Behavioural Policy-Making' in Alberto Alemanno and Anne-Lise Sibony (eds), *Nudge and the Law: A European Perspective* (Hart Publishing 2015) 335.

[19] Deborah Lupton, 'Risk as Moral Danger: The Social and Political Functions of Risk Discourse in Public Health' (1993) 23 International Journal of Health Services 425; Ayo, 'Understanding Health Promotion in a Neoliberal Climate and the Making of Health Conscious Citizens'.

[20] W A Bogart, *Permit But Discourage* (Oxford University Press 2010) xviii.

[21] Erving Goffman, *Stigma: Notes on the Management of Spoiled Identity* (Simon & Schuster 1963) 3; cited by Mette Hartlev, 'Stigmatisation as a Public Health Tool against Obesity - A Health and Human Rights Perspective' (2014) 21 European Journal of Health Law 365, 370.

[22] Lee F Monaghan, Rachel Colls and Bethan Evans, 'Obesity Discourse and Fat Politics: Research, Critique and Interventions' (2013) 23 Critical Public Health 249; Schorb, 'Fat Politics in Europe'; Michael Gard, Darren Powell and José Tenorio (eds), *Routledge Handbook of Critical Obesity Studies* (Routledge 2022); Nuttall, 'Body Mass Index' 117.

[23] Voigt, 'Smoking Norms and the Regulation of E-Cigarettes'.

internalised and negatively affect the motivation to cease a certain behaviour, it may also worsen outcomes for already vulnerable groups, including racial or ethnic minorities and individuals of lower socio-economic status.[24] The use of law as a social stigma is, for instance, visible in the opinion of Advocate General Kokott in *Philip Morris*. Referring to the impossibility under Article 13(1) TPD to use the term 'organic' for tobacco products, she notes that:

> An 'organic cigarette' is still a product that is extremely harmful to health. Information on the product packaging should not suggest *even to consumers who are aware of the health risks of smoking* – even merely subconsciously – that it is desirable for them or beneficial to the environment to smoke 'organic cigarettes'. In addition, *any poor conscience* on the part of smokers on account of the health risks associated with the consumption of tobacco products *should not be appeased* by the fact they are doing something good for themselves or for the planet by turning to 'organic cigarettes' rather than conventional cigarettes.[25]

Advocate General Kokott expresses her opposition to smoking and seems to suggest that smokers are condemned to be perpetually reminded of the harmful aspect of their habit.

There are complex legal and ethical trade-offs involved in using the law to bring smoking prevalence close to zero.[26] These are largely absent from the regulatory discussion. Because this body of law is framed almost entirely as internal market regulation, the debate tends to present economic operators as the primary stakeholders affected by tobacco control, overshadowing the impact on individual choice. This is clear from the case law on proportionality examined in Section 6.3.1, where the adverse impact on personal autonomy is never addressed. Fundamental rights challenges are framed exclusively in terms of the economic rights of business operators, while EU measures are construed as being beneficial to consumers. That vision is too reductive. That interventions adopted in the name of public health may also negatively affect individual rights should not be controversial. Many such measures impose restrictions on individuals to achieve broader population-wide

[24] Shaon Lahiri and others, 'Social Norms Change and Tobacco Use: A Protocol for a Systematic Review and Meta-Analysis of Interventions' (2021) 18 International Journal of Environmental Research and Public Health 12186.

[25] *Philip Morris*, Opinion of Advocate General Kokott para 222.

[26] Bryan P Thomas and Lawrence O Gostin, 'Tobacco Endgame Strategies: Challenges in Ethics and Law' (2013) 22 Tobacco Control i55.

objectives,[27] requiring to draw a careful balance between the collective good and personal freedom.[28] The absence of any discussion on autonomy and individual rights is apparent in the TPD Proposal:

> The proposal affects several fundamental rights as laid down in the Charter of Fundamental Rights of the European Union, notably the protection of personal data (Article 8), the freedom of expression and information (Article 11), freedom of economic operators to conduct business (Article 16), and the right to property (Article 17). The obligations imposed on manufacturers, importers and distributors of tobacco products are necessary to improve the functioning of the internal market while ensuring a high level of health and consumer protection as set out in Articles 35 and 38 of the Charter of Fundamental Rights of the European Union.[29]

No reference is made to rights that may be affected by a loss of freedom or autonomy. It is important to note that no general right to freedom or autonomy exists under the Charter or the ECHR, perhaps because these concepts are too vague and broad in character. The 'right to liberty' in Article 6 CFR concerns the physical liberty of the person and possible restrictions thereof by the State, not a general right to be free from State interference.[30] Respect for private autonomy may nonetheless be reflected in other provisions of the Charter, such as Articles 1, 3 and 7, which protect, respectively, human dignity, the integrity of the person and private and family life.[31] Article 7 CFR appears in this regard the most promising, as it may be construed as requiring public authorities to abstain from any unjustified interference in people's private sphere of autonomy[32]

[27] de Ruijter, *EU Health Law & Policy* 46–50. See also Hartlev, 'Stigmatisation as a Public Health Tool against Obesity' 368.

[28] de Ruijter, *EU Health Law & Policy* 48.

[29] European Commission, 'Proposal for a Directive of the European Parliament and of the Council on the approximation of the laws, regulations and administrative provisions of the Member States concerning the manufacture, presentation and sale of tobacco and related products' COM (2012) 788 final, Explanatory Memorandum 11.

[30] See Tobias Lock, 'Article 6 CFR – Right to Liberty and Security' in Manuel Kellerbauer, Marcus Klamert and Jonathan Tomkin (eds), *The EU Treaties and the Charter of Fundamental Rights: A Commentary* (Oxford University Press 2019) 2111–2114.

[31] On the right to privacy and nudging, see Alberto Alemanno and Alessandro Spina, 'Nudging Legally: On the Checks and Balances of Behavioral Regulation' (2014) 12 International Journal of Constitutional Law 429, 447. On Article 1 and paternalism, see Anne Van Aaken, 'Judge the Nudge: In Search of the Legal Limits of Paternalistic Nudging in the EU' in Alberto Alemanno and Anne-Lise Sibony (eds), *Nudge and the Law: A European Perspective* (Hart Publishing 2015) 103.

[32] In the original text: 's'abstenir de toute ingérence injustifiée dans la sphère d'intimité et d'autonomie des personnes': Nicolas Cariat, 'Article 7. Respect de la vie privée et

or as safeguarding a 'right to be left alone'.[33] Article 8 ECHR, to which Article 7 CFR corresponds almost word for word, encapsulates 'the ability to conduct one's life in a manner of one's own choosing', which 'may also include the opportunity to pursue activities perceived to be of a physically or morally harmful or dangerous nature for the individual concerned'.[34] Article 8 ECHR and Article 7 CFR, may thus reasonably be interpreted as covering the enactment of paternalistic lifestyle interventions by public authorities.[35]

Alliance for Natural Health is the only instance in which a potential breach of the right to private and family life was discussed in relation to one of the EU's lifestyle interventions. The claimants argued that the provisions of Directive 2002/46 on food supplements, which restricts the use of certain supplements in food, breached Article 8 ECHR and constituted 'an infringement of consumer's rights, because the Directive restricts their choice'.[36] The Court swiftly rejected the claim, holding that:

> The fact that Articles 3, 4(1) and 15(b) of Directive 2002/46 may deprive people of the right to consume food supplements which do not comply with the directive cannot be regarded as amounting to a breach of respect for private and family life.[37]

Although one may agree with the conclusion reached, the brevity of the Court's reasoning is regrettable, particularly given how rarely the rights of private individuals are raised in challenges to EU lifestyle measures. It remains unclear whether the absence of a breach was due to the relatively minor nature of the restriction in this case, or to the fact that restrictions on access to certain food products simply do not fall within

familiale', in Fabrice Picod, Cecilia Rizcallah and Sébastien Van Drooghenbroeck (eds), *Charte des Droits Fondamentaux de l'Union Européenne: Commentaire Article par Article* (Bruylant 2019). See also Lock, 'Article 7 CFR' 2115–2117.

33 Maris Burbergs, 'How the Right to Respect for Private and Family Life, Home and Correspondence Became the Nursery in Which New Rights Are Born: Article 8 ECHR' in Eva Brems and Janneke Gerards (eds), *Shaping Rights in the ECHR: The Role of the European Court of Human Rights in Determining the Scope of Human Rights* (Cambridge University Press 2014) 324.

34 *Pretty v The United Kingdom* App no 2346/02 (ECtHR, 29 April 2002), para 62.

35 Anne Van Aaken, 'Constitutional Limits to Regulation-by-Nudging' in Holger Straßheim and Silke Beck (eds), *Handbook of Behavioural Change and Public Policy* (Edward Elgar Publishing 2019) 310; Van Aaken, 'Judge the Nudge' 102–103.

36 *Alliance for Natural Health and Others*, Opinion of Advocate General Geelhoed para 101.

37 *Alliance for Natural Health and Others* para 124.

the scope of the right to private and family life. Would a general ban on all tobacco products, such as that briefly envisaged in the TPD impact assessment, amount to a breach of Article 7 CFR, the legality of which would then need to be assessed by weighing the limitation on individual autonomy against its protective effect on public health?[38]

A closely related issue to that of autonomy is information, since adequate information is a prerequisite for deliberation and choice. As discussed in Section 6.3.1, various EU measures restricting the freedom of expression and information have been challenged in this regard, though invariably from the perspective of companies marketing the products in question. From the consumers' perspective, however, the right to receive information, covered by Article 11 CFR[39] and, arguably, by Article 38 CFR on consumer protection,[40] is absent from the analysis, even though such measures undeniably limit consumers' access to information about products they wish to purchase. This is particularly evident when restrictions concern the provision of inherently truthful information, such as claims on HFFS foods that currently comply with the Claims Regulation, or TNCO information for tobacco products. The Court has yet failed to recognise this restrictive dimension. In *Philip Morris*, it held that the elements and features prohibited on tobacco packaging under Article 13(1) TPD could not be construed as

> [G]iving consumers *clear and precise information*, inasmuch as they are intended more to *exploit the vulnerability of consumers* of tobacco products who, because of their nicotine dependence, are particularly receptive to any element suggesting there may be some kind of benefit linked to tobacco consumption, in order to vindicate or reduce the risks associated with their habits.[41]

Regarding the same provision, Advocate General Saugmandsgaard Øe argued the following in *Planta Tabak*:

> Nor, in my view, is there any doubt as to whether Article 13(1)(c) of Directive 2014/40 is proportionate in terms of a purported requirement to *keep consumers*

[38] For Van Aaken, such a ban would be a disproportionate interference with the autonomy of the individual: Van Aaken, 'Judge the Nudge'.

[39] Under Article 11 CFR, the right to freedom of expression includes 'freedom to hold opinions and to *receive* and impart information and ideas', emphasis added. Regarding Article 10 ECHR, see Garde, 'Freedom of Commercial Expression and Public Health Protection' 119.

[40] According to the Explanations relating to the Charter of Fundamental Rights (2007) OJ C303/17, the principles set out in Article 39 is based on Article 169 TFEU, the latter provision making an explicit reference to consumers' right to information.

[41] *Philip Morris* para 160, emphasis added.

properly informed. In certain fields, including that of *food, consumers must indeed be given information about the ingredients in the products they consume*, so that they can identify and make appropriate use of a food and make choices that suit their individual needs.

However, *tobacco products are not ordinary commodities*. The aim is not to enable consumers to choose more easily between different products. Here, *giving consumers appropriate information amounts essentially to highlighting the particularly harmful effects of tobacco on their health.*[42]

What is striking and objectionable here is not that the proportionality of the provision is upheld – it was within the legislator's prerogative to consider that the harmful nature of tobacco products justifies restrictions on elements that could reinforce their appeal – but rather that the interest some consumers may have in knowing the content and characteristics of tobacco products, in order to 'make choices that suit their individual needs', is entirely ignored.

Advocate General Saugmandsgaard Øe's approach mirrors that adopted by the Court in *Deutsches Weintor*, concerning the prohibition of health claims for alcoholic beverages. Relying on Article 35 CFR, the Court upheld the measure on the ground of the 'ambiguous or even misleading' character of such claims, which is 'likely to encourage [...] consumption and, ultimately, to increase the risks for consumers' health inherent in the immoderate consumption of any alcoholic beverage'.[43] The national court's reference invited a discussion of the prohibition of 'inherently correct' information.[44] The Court could, as it did for Article 35 CFR, have referred to Article 11 or Article 38 CFR of its own motion, and integrated the right to information into its reasoning. This would have acknowledged that consumers may have a legitimate interest in accessing health information about alcoholic beverages, even when that information is not related to the risks of consumption. Moreover, accessing relevant information is not only a matter of the right to information, but also of the right to health. By restricting the provision of information on the grounds of its potentially misleading character, EU measures prevent some consumers from making health-based choices and from favouring products which, notwithstanding their overall harmfulness, are still less harmful than others (harm reduction). In *Deutsches Weintor*, the health claim at issue was a statement that a wine was 'easily

[42] *Planta Tabak*, Opinion of Advocate General Saugmansgaard Øe paras 76–77, emphasis added.

[43] *Deutsches Weintor* para 42.

[44] ibid, paras 26, 42.

digestible', yet the Court failed to consider that such a prohibition effectively prevents health-based choices.[45] As noted, '[w]ithout the possibility to present even scientifically tested health claims in a balanced manner, obtaining easily digestible information for example about the acidity or antioxidant or polyphenol levels in red wines, and their relation to health, is difficult'.[46] It is not inconceivable that the absence of such information, for consumers with low levels of alcohol consumption but other health concerns, may have, 'on balance', negative consequences for human health.[47] Similarly, the prohibition may also act as a disincentive for manufacturers to develop healthier versions of their alcoholic drinks if they are unable to communicate such qualities to consumers.[48]

The argument that EU lifestyle risk regulation may restrict the right to health was made explicitly in *Swedish Match II*. One of the claimants argued that the ban on tobacco for oral use constituted a 'breach of Articles 1, 7 and 35 of the Charter, since [its effect] is that individuals who want to stop smoking cannot use products that would improve their health'.[49] This claim highlights that even if, on balance, the prohibition can be justified for its overall positive effects on the population as a whole, smokers and non-smokers alike, it nonetheless represents for smokers a loss of opportunity to switch to a healthier alternative. The Court could have responded in a manner similar to its reasoning on proportionality: noting that uncertainty did not permit a precise evaluation of the combined effects of the gateway and cessation phenomena, yet that the ban was still defensible under the precautionary principle. Regrettably, the Court chose not to engage in this way, simply observing that even if the prohibition did limit fundamental rights,[50] it was intended 'not to restrict the right to health but, on the contrary, to give expression to that right and, consequently, to ensure a high level of protection of health with respect to all consumers, by not entirely depriving people who want to stop smoking of a choice of products which would help them to achieve that goal'.[51] While the outcome itself may be satisfactory, it represents a missed opportunity for the Court to acknowledge the contradictory impacts that certain EU measures may have on health.

[45] Tuomas Mylly, 'CJEU Approves Ban on Health Claims Related to Alcoholic Beverages' (2013) 4 European Journal of Risk Regulation 271, 274.
[46] ibid. [47] ibid. [48] ibid. [49] *Swedish Match II* para 86. [50] ibid, para 88.
[51] ibid, para 89.

There may be different explanations for this one-sided vision of what the rights and interests of consumers entail. With respect to fundamental rights, the Court's reluctance to scrutinise EU measures from the perspective of consumer autonomy likely results from the nature of the legal challenges brought against them, which originate primarily from companies. Naturally, these actors argue on the basis of breaches of their own rights. Since companies are those directly and most tangibly affected by EU regulation – whether through the impossibility of marketing a product, restrictions on advertising or obligations to change packaging and product composition – restrictions appear more concrete from their perspective. Limitations on freedom and autonomy, by contrast, are more diffuse and difficult to grasp. Yet, the extent to which an individual may freely decide to engage in harmful behaviour and to access information about hazardous products raises fundamental ethical questions concerning public intervention. The near absence of these questions in the regulatory debate is therefore all the more remarkable, and regrettable. The current picture does not do justice to the complexity of lifestyle choices. For many, to fully engage with these thorny ethical issues is seen as pandering to the industry, whose interest is to frame unhealthy behaviours as a matter of individual freedom.[52] That the industry has relied on such argumentation to oppose stronger control measures is undeniable, and it is equally clear that manufacturers of unhealthy products are more concerned with their profits than with the preservation of individual freedom. This, however, does not mean that the reality of restrictions on individual freedom should be ignored. Recognising that lifestyle interventions limit the freedom of individuals, sometimes drastically so, does not mean that such measures are illegitimate or should not be adopted. The argument is rather that, to 'Europeanise' an area, and thus contribute to building a European morality, it is necessary to develop a convincing ethical framework, and indeed a broader narrative, to explain why and how such intervention is pursued.

8.3 Insulation, Food and Alcohol: The (Mis)use of Heritage Politics

In certain areas, the logic of self-determination described by De Witte is fully at play, insofar as particular national cultural or moral choices and norms are insulated from the dynamics of integration. Such divergences

[52] See e.g. Robert N Proctor, 'Why Ban the Sale of Cigarettes? The Case for Abolition' (2013) 22 Tobacco Control i27–i28. Elizabeth A Smith and Ruth E Malone, 'An Argument for Phasing out Sales of Cigarettes' (2020) 29 Tobacco Control 703–704.

may be addressed at the political level. This logic is most evident in the case of opt-outs, such as that secured by Sweden to escape prohibition on the marketing of smokeless tobacco products. The opt-out was obtained upon its accession to the European Union in 1995.[53] Conversely, other forms of smokeless tobacco, such as chewing or nasal tobacco, may still be placed on the market precisely on the grounds of their traditional use in other Member States.[54]

The clearest case of insulation in the field of lifestyles is alcohol. As noted, EU regulation of alcohol is minimal: there are limited rules on advertising, no health warnings are prescribed and exemptions exist even with regards to the disclosure of nutrition information or ingredients. The prohibition of food claims is one of the few measures that can be said to reflect the harmfulness of alcohol, as examined in *Deutsches Weintor*. The reasons for this regulatory restraint are manifold, and economic considerations loom large: the European Union is the world's largest producer of wine and has a strong spirits sector, with alcohol representing 16 per cent of EU agri-food exports.[55] EU wine policy, one of the central pillars of the CAP, almost entirely ignores health concerns.[56] On the contrary, the EU actively promotes wine and spirits, both within the internal market and in third countries, financing information campaigns and promotional material for these products.[57]

The EU relies heavily on the cultural importance of alcohol to justify the absence of action. In its 2006 Alcohol Strategy, the Commission stated that:

> *There is no intention to substitute Community action to national policies*, which have already been put in place in most of the Member States and relate to national competences in accordance with the *principle of subsidiarity* and Article 152 of the

[53] The Act concerning the conditions of accession of the Kingdom of Norway, the Republic of Austria, the Republic of Finland and the Kingdom of Sweden and the adjustments to the Treaties on which the European Union is founded, OJ C241/9, art 151. See also Article 17 TPD.

[54] Council Directive 92/41, recitals. See also Tobacco Products Directive, recital 32.

[55] European Commission, 'Monitoring EU agri-food trade: developments in January 2025' (2025) <https://agriculture.ec.europa.eu/document/download/61ebe68b-1fe5–4a30-af56-bbd7151c83fb_en?filename=monitoring-agri-food-trade_apr2025_en.pdf> accessed 4 September 2025.

[56] For an overview of EU wine policy, see Eugenio Pomarici and Roberta Sardone, 'EU Wine Policy in the Framework of the CAP: Post-2020 Challenges' (2020) 8 Agricultural and Food Economics 17.

[57] Regulation (EU) No 1144/2014 of the European Parliament and of the Council of 22 October 2014 on information provision and promotion measures concerning agricultural products implemented in the internal market and in third countries and repealing Council Regulation (EC) No 3/2008, OJ L 317/56.

EC Treaty. In particular, the Commission *does not intend as a consequence of this Communication to propose the development of harmonised legislation* in the field of the prevention of alcohol-related harm.[58]

The 'different cultural habits' existing between Member States are mentioned several times in the text, the Commission emphasising the variations in 'drinking patterns and cultures [existing] across the EU',[59] as well as the particular context in which 'measures adopted by Member States to reduce alcohol-related harm with a view to protecting public health are based'.[60] It is undeniable that types and patterns of alcohol consumption differ widely between Member States, which could justify a supporting role for the EU. The same could, however, be said of dietary habits and, to a lesser extent, tobacco consumption. Yet, no references to cultural diversity or subsidiarity appear in the EU Nutrition Strategy or in any tobacco-related document. Even where the Union refrains from acting on subsidiarity grounds, it does not clearly articulate the reasons justifying its choice (see Section 6.3.2). The EU Alcohol Strategy, which invokes subsidiarity on several occasions, refers in this regard to 'different cultural habits related to alcohol consumption' without clarifying why such differences undermine the appropriateness of EU action: for example, how these habits would diminish the effectiveness of EU health warnings on alcoholic beverages or binding restrictions on advertising directed at minors. The Commission has failed to set out a convincing argument as to why the market for alcoholic beverages should be treated differently from the markets for tobacco products or other foodstuffs.[61] In this respect, subsidiarity and cultural diversity appear to have been instrumentalised rather than genuinely applied.[62]

This lack of action, while insulating national choices and allowing Member States to pursue their own policies,[63] also reflects the shared vision of alcohol in society, generally perceived as less risky than it in fact is,[64] and subject to lighter regulation than comparable risk factors

[58] European Commission, EU Alcohol Strategy. [59] ibid 4. [60] ibid 13.

[61] Alemanno and Garde, 'The Emergence of an EU Lifestyle Policy' 1770.

[62] Bartlett and Garde, 'EU Public Health Law and Policy – on the Rocks?' 394.

[63] Nino Berdzuli and others, 'Alcohol Control Policy in Europe: Overview and Exemplary Countries' (2020) 17 International Journal of Environmental Research and Public Health 8162.

[64] On the various dimensions of risk perception and the characterisation of hazards by lay people, see Glynis M Breakwell, *The Psychology of Risk* (2nd edition, Cambridge University Press 2014) 37–43.

such as illicit drugs or tobacco.[65] There is, in truth, no clear scientific justification for prohibiting cannabis while permitting the sale of alcohol.[66] This discrepancy reflects the particular place alcohol occupies in many societies, which varies across countries and historical periods. This is visible in the reactions to the Commission's intention, under the Beating Cancer Plan, to extend the listing of ingredients and nutrition declarations provided for in the Food Information Regulation to alcoholic beverages, and to introduce health warnings on their packaging.[67] The very idea that wine, a flagship European product, could be labelled as unhealthy has generated strong resistance. This prompted Margaritis Schinas, former EU Commissioner in charge of the 'European way of life',[68] to clarify that wine was 'part of who we are and of our way of life', adding that '[c]ertainly the European Union will not ban wine, and we will not label wine as being something that is toxic'.[69] Wine is toxic, however, and such rejection of science is troubling, to say the least.

Food is another area in which cultural diversity has been invoked. In 1987, the Commission observed, in relation to the European Cancer Code, that '[a]t European level, however, it would be unrealistic to go into too much detail, especially as regards food. Indeed, *eating habits are an integral part of the culture of a community and vary considerably between countries, regions or even towns*'.[70] Likewise, in its 2000 Resolution on health and nutrition, the Council acknowledged that '*the diversity of food cultures throughout the European Union constitutes a valuable asset that ought to be respected*, and that it is necessary to take this into account when drawing up and implementing nutritional health policies, which must therefore be defined first of all at national level'.[71] Interestingly, when compared to alcohol, the EU's position is here also grounded in the

[65] Rehm, Lachenmeier and Room, 'Why Does Society Accept a Higher Risk for Alcohol than for Other Voluntary or Involuntary Risks?'. See also Robin Room, 'Global Intergovernmental Initiatives to Minimise Alcohol Problems: Some Good Intentions, but Little Action' (2021) 12 European Journal of Risk Regulation 419.

[66] Upton and Thirlaway, *Promoting Healthy Behaviour* 356.

[67] European Commission, 'Europe's Beating Cancer Plan' 10.

[68] On the 'European way of life' narrative, see Francois Foret and Noemi Trino, 'The "European Way of Life", a New Narrative for the EU? Institutions' vs Citizens' View' (2023) 24 European Politics and Society 336.

[69] Euractiv, 'EU goes easy on alcohol in cancer plan' (2021), <www.euractiv.com/section/agriculture-food/news/eu-goes-easy-on-alcohol-in-cancer-plan/> accessed 3 October 2025.

[70] European Commission, 'Europe against cancer' programme: Proposal for a plan of action 1987 to 1989 32, emphasis added.

[71] Council Resolution of 14 December 2000 on health and nutrition, recital 11, emphasis added.

respect for consumers' responsibility and autonomy. As discussed in Section 4.3.3, central to the Commission's vision of nutrition is the notion that the individual is ultimately responsible for her lifestyle.[72] Most recently, in its 2025 communication on 'A Vision for Agriculture and Food', the Commission also relied on a vocabulary related to sensitivity, subsidiarity and respect for individual choice:

> Food is a crucial part of any discussion on the future of agriculture and food production in Europe. *But it is also sensitive, as experience shows, where social and cultural traditions come into play.* This chapter identifies areas where Union action can bring added value, *without encroaching on the national and regional competences in health policy and the freedom to choose.*[73]

Food resonates strongly with both individual and collective identities. It affects and responds to political agendas, and within the EU serves as a medium of cultural politics, marking boundaries and reinforcing identities.[74] Numerous past and current examples illustrate how real or perceived threats to culinary traditions can trigger political mobilisation. In 2017, Belgians reacted with outrage to reports of a possible EU ban on the double cooking of fries, a method regarded as essential to the local *frietcultuur*.[75] More recently, fears in France that the new Packaging and Packaging Waste Directive would prohibit the sale of Camembert in its traditional wooden boxes prompted a last-minute amendment exempting such packaging from the new rules.[76] Questions of paternalism also loom in the background. Citizens tend to react

[72] European Commission, EU Nutrition Strategy 3.

[73] European Commission, Communication from the Commission to the Council, the European Parliament, the European Economic and Social Committee and the Committee of the Regions, 'A Vision for Agriculture and Food: Shaping together an attractive farming and agri-food sector for future generations' COM(2025) 75 final 22, emphasis added.

[74] Michaela DeSoucey, 'Gastronationalism: Food Traditions and Authenticity Politics in the European Union' (2010) 75 American Sociological Review 432.

[75] The Belgian method of cooking fries generates acrylamide, a molecule associated with cancer risk. On the controversy, see Het Nieuwsblad, 'Ben Weyts versus de experts: wat is er belangrijker: onze frietcultuur of onze gezondheid?', 19 June 2017, <www.nieuwsblad.be/cnt/dmf20170618_02930135>, accessed 3 October 2025.

[76] Proposal for a regulation of the European Parliament and of the Council on packaging and packaging waste, amending Regulation (EU) 2019/1020 and Directive (EU) 2019/904, and repealing Directive 94/62/EC, COM/2022/677 final. See Euronews, '"We have saved our Camemberts": Wooden boxes saved from recycling rules in last-minute amendment', 16 November 2023, <www.euronews.com/green/2023/11/16/could-new-eu-recycling-laws-mean-the-end-of-camemberts-traditional-wooden-boxes>, accessed 3 October 2025.

negatively to public injunctions about what they should eat. Conflicts between laypersons and experts in the management of food risks can readily be reframed as opposition to EU intervention,[77] as shown by the Nutri-Score controversy explored below.

If the Union has not refrained from acting in the field of food overall, one category of products presents distinctive challenges for regulation. This concerns 'heritage' products, as understood by De Witte:

> Heritage, conceptually, is best understood as a claim made in space and in time. Tasting Parmigiano Reggiano is a physical manifestation of "how things are done" in a specific place (even when we eat it in Amsterdam we "are" in Parma) and a claim rooted in time (someone tasting it in 1254, 1712 or 2003 will have had a similar taste perception). This reference to space and time are what renders the narrative of heritage authentic and, thereby, legitimate.[78]

In the EU, such products are generally protected through specific quality schemes. These schemes safeguard the names of certain foodstuffs and agricultural products in order to promote their unique characteristics, usually linked to their geographical origin and traditional methods of production. There are three main types of such schemes: the protected designation of origin (PDO) and the protected geographical indication (PGI), which concern food and wine, and the geographical indication (GI), for spirit drinks and aromatised wines.[79] While these traditional products carry significant cultural value, they also tend to be high in fat, salt, or sugar, energy-dense or to contain alcohol. As a result, policies aimed at encouraging healthier lifestyles are unlikely to favour them, at least where their nutritional composition is not advantageous. Moreover,

[77] Damian Chalmers, '"Food for Thought": Reconciling European Risks and Traditional Ways of Life' (2003) 66 Modern Law Review 532.

[78] De Witte, 'You Are What You Ate' 647.

[79] The traditional speciality guaranteed (TSG) is another EU quality scheme, applicable to food and agricultural products, which highlight the traditional aspects of these products without being linked to a specific geographical area. The main rules on EU quality schemes are contained in Regulation (EU) No 1151/2012 of the European Parliament and of the Council of 21 November 2012 on quality schemes for agricultural products and foodstuffs, OJ L343/1; CMO Regulation; Regulation (EU) No 251/2014 of the European Parliament and of the Council of 26 February 2014 on the definition, description, presentation, labelling and the protection of geographical indications of aromatised wine products, OJ L84/14; Regulation (EU) 2019/787 of the European Parliament and of the Council of 17 April 2019 on the definition, description, presentation and labelling of spirit drinks, the use of the names of spirit drinks in the presentation and labelling of other foodstuffs, the protection of geographical indications for spirit drinks, the use of ethyl alcohol and distillates of agricultural origin in alcoholic beverages, OJ L130/1.

products protected under EU quality schemes must comply with strict requirements concerning their composition, method and place of production, and the origin of raw materials. Once such protection is granted, the characteristics of these products are fixed and cannot be modified at will. This differs from industrial products, whose composition may be reformulated and which are therefore less likely to be penalised by policies based on the nutritional composition of products. A telling example is that of the nutrient profiles provided for in the Claims Regulation, which have still not been adopted (see Section 5.5.2.1). Several Member States opposed the Commission's 2009 proposal on nutrient profiles for fear that it would divide the market between traditional products, protected by quality schemes, and processed foods. Their concern was that applying the proposed profiles would result in a market split between 'traditional products, for which reformulation would be challenging, if not impossible, due to their legal composition specifications [...] and [which] therefore would be perceived as non-healthy foods' and 'processed foods which could be more easily reformulated and [...] would be perceived as healthy foods'.[80]

Similar considerations have arisen in the debate on front-of-pack (FoP) nutrition labelling (see Section 7.3.3). As early as 2016, the Council delegations of seven Member States signalled their opposition to a specific label developed in the United Kingdom (the MTL label),[81] pointing to the detrimental effect it could have on EU quality products. They deplored that some of these products 'would get a "red label" in reason of their composition' and thus risk being shunned by consumers, in contradiction with European quality policy.[82] In its 2020 report on FoP labelling, the Commission likewise noted that '[e]xperts from a few EU national competent authorities favoured reductive FoP schemes providing nutrient-specific information, based on portion sizes, without evaluating foods and are concerned that under evaluative FOP schemes some

[80] European Commission, 'Evaluation of the Regulation (EC) No 1924/2006 on nutrition and health claims made on foods with regard to nutrient profiles and health claims made on plants and their preparations and of the general regulatory framework for their use in foods' 17. See also Pierre Médevielle, 'Allégations nutritionnelles et de santé : pour une application effective de la réglementation' (2021) Rapport d'information fait au nom de la commission des affaires européennes 346, 35, <www.senat.fr/notice-rapport/2020/r20-346-notice.html> accessed 3 October 2025.

[81] Council of the European Union, '"Hybrid" Nutrition Labelling System Recommended in Some Member States: Information from the Delegations of Italy, Cyprus, Greece, Portugal, Romania, Slovenia and Spain' (2016) 6585/16.

[82] ibid 2.

traditional products and regional specialities (e.g. cheeses, edible oils, meat products) might display labels that deter consumer purchase'.[83] Some Member States have therefore called for an exemption for PDO, PGI products and single-ingredient products such as olive oil, arguing that such measures are necessary to protect the European cultural heritage.[84] Member States' sensitivity with regard to these products has been particularly evident in the controversy over Nutri-Score, the FoP label most widely used within the EU and a strong candidate for a pan-European roll-out. Italy has emerged as the most vocal opponent of the colour-coded label, seeing it as a major threat to its traditional products and food heritage.[85] This opposition is shared across the Italian political and social spectrum: food industry groups, government, political parties, newspapers, etc.[86] While some criticisms target the scientific soundness of the label and its underlying algorithm, resistance is primarily rooted in the defence of the 'Mediterranean diet' and the excellence of Italian cheeses, cured meats and olive oil against what is perceived as a stigmatising tool,[87] and even as a deliberate 'French' plot to undermine Italian cuisine and traditions.[88] Evidence suggests that Italy's activism has at least in part succeeded in persuading the Commission to adjourn its legislative proposal *sine die*.[89]

The Nutri-Score debate exemplifies the excesses of gastronationalism, defined as 'a defense mechanism [. . .] deployed mainly by the state when

[83] European Commission, 'Report from the Commission to the European Parliament and the Council regarding the use of additional forms of expression and presentation of the nutrition declaration' 17.

[84] Council of the European Union, 'Non Paper on the "Front of Pack Nutrition Labelling – FOPNL" by Cyprus, Czech Republic, Greece, Hungary, Italy, Latvia and Romania' (2020) 10846/20, 4.

[85] Fialon, Nabec and Julia, 'Legitimacy of Front-of-Pack Nutrition Labels'.

[86] ibid.

[87] ibid. As pointed out by the authors, though, the products usually singled out as being penalised by the Nutri-Score are actually those whose consumption should be limited as part of the Mediterranean diet: cheese, cured meat, etc.

[88] Politico, 'Italy claims it's winning the war against French food labels' (2022), <www.politico.eu/article/italys-war-against-french-food-label-starts-to-pay-dividends/>, accessed 3 October 2025; Euractiv, 'France might drop support for Nutri-score, say Italians' (2021), <www.euractiv.com/section/agriculture-food/news/france-might-drop-support-for-nutri-score-say-italians/>, accessed 3 October 2025.

[89] Mediapart, 'Le « gastro-nationalisme » italien met un coup d'arrêt au Nutri-Score en Europe' (2023), <www.mediapart.fr/journal/international/301223/le-gastro-nationalisme-italien-met-un-coup-d-arret-au-nutri-score-en-europe>, accessed 3 October 2025. See also BEUC, 'Food Label Ambush: How intense industry lobbying halted EU plans' (2023), <www.beuc.eu/blog/food-label-ambush-how-intense-industry-lobbying-halted-eu-plans/>, accessed 3 October 2025.

symbolic boundaries represented by food are perceived to be violated or under threat'.[90] As De Witte aptly argues, gastronationalism today pervades the management of EU quality schemes, which are often captured by Member States and international conglomerates to serve their own economic and political purposes, frequently to the detriment of small producers and local communities.[91] The cultural relevance of such products cannot obscure the fact that wine is toxic and that Parma ham and Parmigiano Reggiano contain significant amounts of salt and fat. Their traditional character and cultural importance should not be invoked as an obstacle to providing consumers with appropriate information about the health risks linked to their consumption. The resistance goes beyond the preservation of cultural practices or market shares but has to do with risk perception. Products such as wine, traditional cheeses or cured meats are perceived positively, and the idea that a public authority, let alone a European one, could label them as unhealthy is anathema to many consumers and manufacturers. These positions may be regrettable, but they cannot simply be dismissed. Not only can they lead to political deadlock, as demonstrated with nutrient profiles and FoP labelling, but they can also undermine the EU's efforts to promote healthier lifestyles. Indeed, the effectiveness of labelling depends on consumer acceptance, trust and perceived legitimacy. Introducing Nutri-Score in Italy would be plainly ineffective, and perhaps even counterproductive, if the vast majority of consumers chose to ignore it or deliberately act against it.

These cases reveal a further intertwining of health and cultural considerations. Differences in national food cultures pose a challenge to the development and adoption of an EU nutrition policy, generally speaking. The European Food Safety Authority (EFSA)[92] acknowledged that setting nutrient profiles at the EU level was a difficult task due to the absence of uniform data on food composition and consumption across the Union, as well as divergent nutrient intake recommendations and food-based

[90] Atsuko Ichijo, 'Food and Nationalism: Gastronationalism Revisited' (2020) 48 Nationalities Papers 215. See also DeSoucey.

[91] De Witte, 'You Are What You Ate'.

[92] The European Food Safety Authority was established by the General Food Law Regulation, see art 22(1). Its task is to 'provide scientific advice and scientific and technical support for the [EU]'s legislation and policies in all fields which have a direct or indirect impact on food and feed safety': GFL Regulation, art 22(2). Alongside its core food safety activity, EFSA also has responsibilities in the field of nutrition, see art 22(5)(a).

dietary guidelines in the Member States.[93] Food-based dietary guidelines vary across Member States and are strongly shaped by cultural factors and local consumption patterns. EFSA therefore concluded that 'it was not feasible to establish detailed and effective food based dietary guidelines which could be used at the EU level'.[94] It pointed to several factors: diverging public health priorities between countries; diverging approaches to selecting principal nutrients, 'depending on the country-specific nutrient intake levels and on the impact of the related diseases on morbidity and mortality rates'; and 'wide disparities in dietary/cultural habits and the availability of food products between European Member States'.[95] EFSA concluded that food-based dietary guidelines would fail if found culturally unacceptable by the public.[96] Recommending the consumption of a food virtually unknown in a given country, or consumed only by a minority of the population, is unlikely to influence behaviour or yield meaningful health outcomes. Whatever their purpose, nutrient profiles must therefore categorise foods in a manner consistent with national dietary habits and guidelines.

8.4 Balancing: A Narrow Approach to Proportionality

The third approach identified by De Witte lies in the middle, between Europeanisation and insulation. Internal market freedoms allow for self-determination while limiting parochial biases in national norms and enabling citizens to move freely between Member States with diverse moral and ethical standards. The legal method used to strike a balance between both interests is proportionality, which ensures that limits on individual rights imposed by national policy remain reasonable.[97]

[93] EFSA Panel on Dietetic Products, Nutrition and Allergies, 'The Setting of Nutrient Profiles for Foods Bearing Nutrition and Health Claims Pursuant to Article 4 of the Regulation (EC) No 1924/2006' 4. See also Friant-Perrot and Garde, 'From BSE to Obesity' 142. Food-based dietary guidelines are 'policy recommendations in the form of guidelines for healthy eating [. . .] primarily intended for consumer information and education': EFSA Panel on Dietetic Products, Nutrition, and Allergies, 'Scientific Opinion on Establishing Food-Based Dietary Guidelines' (2010) 8 The EFSA Journal 1460–1461.

[94] EFSA Panel on Dietetic Products, Nutrition, and Allergies, 'Scientific Opinion on Establishing Food-Based Dietary Guidelines' 1484; See also Angela Bechthold and others, 'Perspective: Food-Based Dietary Guidelines in Europe – Scientific Concepts, Current Status, and Perspectives' (2018) 9 Advances in Nutrition 544.

[95] EFSA Panel on Dietetic Products, Nutrition, and Allergies, 'Scientific Opinion on Establishing Food-Based Dietary Guidelines' 1484–1485.

[96] ibid. [97] De Witte, 'Sex, Drugs & EU Law' 1565.

Proportionality arbitrates between the argument for containment (i.e. restrictions on free movement) and the argument for self-determination, which serves as a prima facie justification for such restrictions.[98] The field of alcohol policy offers numerous examples. Cases like *Franzen* or *Rosengren* involve Swedish nationals invoking free movement law against stricter local rules, while Sweden relies on self-determination to defend its regulatory model.[99] Similar dynamics arise in cases concerning Finland[100] or the French *Loi Evin*, which severely restricts alcohol advertising in audiovisual media.[101]

In its standard form, proportionality ensures that Member States may pursue legitimate policy objectives without unduly restricting free movement. The proportionality of a measure is assessed in relation to its stated goal and the interests it seeks to protect. In lifestyle cases, Member States have expectedly mainly invoked public health objectives, and, less frequently, objectives linked to the preservation of public order, a concept encompassing public policy, public security and sometimes moral considerations.[102] Focusing on public health as a justification is useful both for Member States and the Court. A measure grounded in health and scientific evidence is easier to defend and evaluate than one based on moral or cultural grounds, values which are harder to assess objectively. For the Court, health provides a supranational lens to review restrictions on free movement, avoiding entanglement in debates about morals or culture. Yet, as discussed at length in this book, lifestyle regulation is never solely about health. Measures may exist not only because behaviours are harmful, but also because society deems them morally wrong. Conversely, an activity may be lightly regulated despite its harmful nature if it plays a significant cultural or social role. A measure may appear disproportionate when viewed only through the prism of health but may be justified on other grounds. The Nordic alcohol monopolies do not only limit access to alcohol, their very organisation has become part of the Nordic lifestyle: visiting the same shops, at specific hours, with access to a standardised range of beverages. Neither the Court nor the Member States addressed this cultural dimension in *Franzen* or *Rosengren*.

This absence of concern for the broader cultural and moral considerations underpinning national measure echoes Gareth Davies' work on

[98] ibid, 1566. [99] *Franzen* and *Rosengren*. [100] *Heinonen, Visnapuu*.
[101] *Bacardi France*; *Commission v France* (C-262/02). [102] See *Heinonen* paras 18, 30–35.

the Court's treatment of 'quality of life' arguments.[103] Davies examines the 'changes wrought by free movement [. . .] on the texture of national life, on the wider social relations between individuals, and between individuals and their state,' which are 'not captured merely by looking at the parties to transactions, but by understanding how market regulation affects society more broadly, for example by creating shared experiences, a sense of equality, and social bonds'.[104] He defines this 'quality of life' as comprising 'traditions, practices, habits' and other matters, 'such as the sense of a shared identity and belonging which arise when a community lives and consumes in a common way'.[105] These interests are not adequately protected under free movement law, largely due to proportionality, as they cannot be rationalised within the available grounds of justification. What matters is not the purpose of the rules, which is central to proportionality, but the fact that the rules exist and shape life in a particular country.[106] These rules concern lifestyles broadly, if not lifestyle health risks specifically. Davies' most telling examples involve food composition requirements: beer,[107] pasta,[108] foie gras.[109] Allowing products manufactured differently to enter the German, Italian or French market does not so much endanger consumers' ability to access their traditional products, but it does undermine the shared cultural practices solidified by market uniformity. The pasta cases are particularly illustrative: because no 'quality of life' argument could prosper, Italy sought to defend its rules with a public health argument, claiming that chemical additives and colourants are often used to give pasta made from common wheat the organoleptic characteristics of durum wheat pasta, and that consuming large quantities of the former could harm human health. Yet the Italian Government admitted it had no evidence that pasta made from common wheat contained these additives or colorants.[110]

[103] Gareth Davies, 'Internal Market Adjudication and the Quality of Life in Europe' (2015) 21 Columbia Journal of European Law 289; Gareth Davies, 'Free Movement, the Quality of Life and the Myth that the Court Balances Interests' in Panos Koutrakos, Niamh Nic Shuibhne and Phil Syrpis (eds), *Exceptions from EU Free Movement Law: Derogation, Justification and Proportionality* (Hart Publishing 2016) 218–239.

[104] Davies, 'Internal Market Adjudication and the Quality of Life in Europe' 290.

[105] Davies, 'Free Movement, the Quality of Life and the Myth that the Court Balances Interests' 220.

[106] Davies, 'Internal Market Adjudication and the Quality of Life in Europe' 313–317.

[107] *Commission v Germany (Beer purity).*

[108] *Zoni; 3 Glocken.*

[109] *Commission v France (Foie gras).*

[110] *Zoni* paras 12–13; *3 Glocken* paras 12–13.

To the author's knowledge, none of the food, alcohol or tobacco cases examined in this study has seen the Court directly address proportionality arguments based on 'quality of life'. An exception is *Visnapuu*, where Finland's retail licensing scheme allowed producers of certain fermented alcoholic beverages to sell their products on-site, but only if established in Finland. The Court noted that this could protect national production,[111] to which the Finnish government responded that:

> [T]he licencing scheme in question pursued – *in addition to the health and public policy grounds* mentioned above – *the objective of promoting tourism*, since the measure is intended to allow a limited number of alcoholic beverage manufacturers established in Finland, *using traditional and artisanal methods*, to sell their products at the site of production.[112]

Thus, Finland relied on a cultural argument to defend a measure which, although part of a broader licensing scheme with clear health-related aspects, did not itself pursue health or public policy objectives. The Court did not address that argument specifically, leaving it to the referring court to assess whether the measure was justified based on health and public policy.[113] This suggests that the Court is not, in principle, hostile to such arguments. In *Commission v France*, the Court acknowledged the possibility of favouring the traditional and customary production of natural sweet wines from economically disadvantaged regions through tax.[114]

Thus, as it is the case for EU legislation, the cultural, moral and ethical aspects of unhealthy lifestyles are largely absent from the case law on alcohol, food and tobacco. This should be contrasted with the Court's approach in the field of gambling, which, as explained in Chapter 2, can also be conceptualised as a 'lifestyle risk'. Unlike the case for other lifestyles, national rules on gambling are subject to a light standard of scrutiny. In particular, the proportionality test is applied in a way that affords Member States a wide margin of discretion in organising gambling activities on their territory.[115] Despite the many judgments handed down by the Court of Justice in this field, national rules have only rarely been declared unlawful under Articles 49 or 56 TFEU.[116] Access to

[111] *Visnapuu* para 126. [112] ibid, para 127, emphasis added. [113] ibid, para 128.

[114] Case 196/85, *Commission v France*, EU:C:1987:18, para 9.

[115] See Van den Bogaert and Cuyvers, '"Money for Nothing"'.

[116] For such occasions, see Joined Cases C-338/04, C-359/04 and C-360/04, *Placanica*, EU:C:2007:133; Case C-153/08 *Commission v Spain*, EU:C:2009:618; Case C-142/02 *Lindman*, EU:C:2003:613; Case C-64/08 *Engelmann*, EU:C:2010:506; C-410/07 *Stoß*, EU:C:2010:504.

national gambling markets remains difficult for foreign service providers, raising questions about the existence of an internal market for cross-border gambling.[117] This specific treatment, unique in the application of internal market provisions, is grounded in what the Court considers the special nature of gambling: an activity giving rise to significant risks for individuals and society, and one to which particular moral and cultural considerations apply. This was clearly articulated by Advocate General Bot in *Liga Portuguesa*:

> First, in all the Member States, *moral, religious or cultural considerations* tend to restrict, or even prohibit, such games to prevent them from being a source of private profit. Secondly, games of chance and gambling involve *a high risk of crime or fraud*, given the size of the potential winnings. In addition, they are an encouragement to spend which may have *damaging individual and social consequences*. Finally, [. . .] it is not without relevance that lotteries may make a significant contribution to the financing of benevolent or public interest activities such as social works, charitable works, sport or culture.[118]

The Court not only recognises the diversity of Member States' 'scale of values'[119] regarding gambling but has also adopted its own stance towards it, denying it the status of a fully legitimate economic activity. It considers the morality of lotteries to be 'at least questionable'[120] and gambling in general to have 'morally [. . .] harmful consequences'.[121] The Court has particularly recognised 'the idea of the moral superiority of allocating gambling proceeds to good causes compared to mere private profit'.[122] This is most evident in *Sjöberg* and *Gerdin*, where the Court accepted that 'it might be considered unacceptable to allow private profit to be drawn from the exploitation of a social evil or the weakness of players and their misfortune'.[123] This language is striking when compared to the Court's approach in *Grogan*,[124] where, regarding the claim that abortion was 'grossly immoral and involves the destruction of the

[117] See Dimitrios Doukas, 'In a Bet There Is a Fool and a State Monopoly: Are the Odds Stacked Against Cross-Border Gambling?' (2011) 36 European Law Review 243, 262.

[118] Case C-42/07, *Liga Portuguesa*, EU:C:2008:560, Opinion of Advocate General Bot, para 62, emphasis added.

[119] *Placanica*, para 48; Joined Cases C-447/08 and C-448/08, *Sjöberg and Gerdin*, EU:C:2010:415, para 43.

[120] Case C-275/92, *Schindler*, EU:C:1994:119, para 32.

[121] Case C-243/01, *Gambelli and* Others, EU:C:2003:597, para 63.

[122] Planzer, *Empirical Views on European Gambling Law and Addiction* 69. See e.g. *Schindler* para 57; Case C-67/98 *Zenatti*, EU:C:1999:514, para 30.

[123] *Sjöberg and Gerdin* para 43.

[124] Case C-159/90, *Grogan*, EU:C:1991:378.

life of a human being, namely the unborn child',[125] the Court simply responded that 'whatever the merits of those arguments on the moral plane, they cannot influence the answer to the national court'.[126] For the Court, all these factors 'justify national authorities having a sufficient degree of latitude to determine what is required to protect [gambling] players and, more generally, in the light of the specific social and cultural features of each Member State, to maintain order in society'.[127] Member States thus enjoy a 'margin of appreciation'[128] or even a 'wide discretion'[129] when defining the level of protection sought in relation to gambling and adopting the necessary measures. In practice, the Court only pays lip service to the principle of proportionality.[130] This position stands in stark contrast with the absence of similar concerns regarding other types of trade in harmful commodities, such as tobacco and alcohol, for which allowing private profit from consumers' misfortune might appear equally unacceptable, or at least objectionable.[131] If the sensitive moral aspect of an activity warrants a different approach from the Court and a lighter application of the proportionality principle, this should be done for all such activities, including for instance alcohol. In such sensitive fields, De Witte defends the application of procedural version of proportionality focusing on 'policy coherence, consistency and transparency', rather than on the substance of the rule.[132] This also begs the following question: is the Court's hands-off approach really about moral or cultural diversity or is it rather about the preservation of the 'golden eggs' of gambling,[133] or, as Planzer says, about 'the cutting of the copious cake'?[134]

8.5 Conclusion

Should unhealthy lifestyles form part of the 'European way of life'? As far as Union law and policy are concerned, the answer is nuanced.

[125] ibid, para 19 [126] ibid, para 20 [127] *Schindler* para 61.
[128] *Gambelli* para 63; *Zenatti* para 33.
[129] Case C-347/09 *Dickinger and Ömer*, EU:C:2011:582, para 99.
[130] See in that regard Van den Bogaert and Cuyvers, '"Money for Nothing"' 1995–1996.
[131] See in that regard the statement of reasons of the Swedish law on alcohol: 'The fundamental aim of Swedish alcohol policy throughout the twentieth century has been to limit the effect of market forces, namely competition and private profits. The reason for this was the conviction that competition and private profits encourage active marketing and active selling, which lead to increased consumption'. *Franzen*, Opinion of Advocate General Elmer para 6.
[132] De Witte, 'Sex, Drugs & EU Law' 1571.
[133] Van den Bogaert and Cuyvers, '"Money for Nothing"' 1211.
[134] Planzer, *Empirical Views on European Gambling Law and Addiction* 74.

The declared objective of EU tobacco regulation is to eliminate these products from the market as far as possible, a stance that stands in stark contrast with the treatment of alcoholic beverages and 'heritage' products more generally. Regardless of the approach adopted, the EU faces sensitive normative questions that it is not fully equipped to answer: what role should risk, harm and pleasure play in everyday activities, and is the plurality of lifestyle practices, including unhealthy ones, something worth preserving? Overall, the regulation of unhealthy lifestyles remains marked by a dialectical relationship between market and health, in which cultural, moral and ethical considerations are not systematically acknowledged. This becomes apparent at the level of proportionality. For EU measures, a narrow vision of consumers' rights and interests emerges, based on the collective need for a healthier population. For national measures, proportionality fails to capture the reality of national regulations that are genuinely rooted in cultural considerations. The omission is all the more striking when compared to other policy fields, such as gambling, where the Court has explicitly recognised the cultural and moral dimensions of such activity and the need for Member States to retain broader discretion.

This neglect is particularly problematic in areas where Europeanisation is at play, as in the case of tobacco. The difficulty lies not in the fact of Europeanisation itself, but in the lack of discussion of the ethical implications of the strategy chosen: that of eliminating a habit which forms part of the daily life of 20 per cent of Europeans. In the field of food, by contrast, controversies surrounding heritage products tend to result in political deadlock, as illustrated by the disputes over nutrient profiles and Nutri-Score. Combined with the rigidities created by maximum harmonisation, discussed in Chapter 7, such deadlock can also have negative repercussions for health. The law must therefore become more creative. One possibility would be to allow more opt-outs for those few Member States genuinely unwilling to proceed in a given direction. These do not necessarily need to be Treaty-based. Another would be to rely more systematically on minimum harmonisation, or even to reconsider the derogation clause in Article 114(5) TFEU, which is currently drafted and interpreted in an unduly narrow manner.

9 Conclusion

At the conclusion of this book, it is fitting to return to the three questions at the heart of the enquiry: (i) What are the powers of the EU to regulate unhealthy lifestyles and how have these powers been used to date? (ii) How does EU law balance the objective of building a market for unhealthy products with that of reducing and eliminating their consumption? (iii) How does EU law balance market uniformity with the diversity and scientific uncertainty associated with lifestyle practices?

As to the first question, the book has shown that the EU possesses broad powers to address the harmful consequences of tobacco, alcohol and unhealthy diets, despite its limited direct competence in the field of health. Because unhealthy lifestyles are embedded in an economic activity, that of buying and selling the goods in question, the EU can rely on its internal market competence to regulate the matter. This occurs in a 'negative' way, through the application of the TFEU free movement provisions to national measures, and in a 'positive' way, through the adoption of harmonisation measures. Only the latter amounts to a policy in the strict sense, allowing the EU to set objectives and harmonised market standards. Legally speaking, EU law on unhealthy lifestyles remains essentially a form of economic and market regulation, with Article 114 TFEU playing a central role.

The way in which these powers have been exercised reveals both continuity and divergence across the products concerned. Since the early 2000s, a genuine 'lifestyle policy' has emerged, identifying tobacco, alcohol use and unhealthy diets as major health risk factors whose prevalence must be reduced within the European population. Overall, the EU follows a 'permit but discourage' approach, as there is for the moment no question, leaving minor exceptions aside, of prohibiting the placing on the market of unhealthy products. In order to discourage unhealthy behaviours, the EU has relied on four main types of tools: (i) measures restricting choice, such as bans or composition requirements, (ii) tax measures in the form of excise duties, (iii) rules limiting or prohibiting commercial communications and finally, (iv) rules on information disclosure, usually targeting the packaging and labelling of products. Overall, the EU has made only limited use of the first two categories of measures. Product bans remain the exception, and the lack of EU engagement on composition rules is particularly regrettable, given that the food supply is a major driver of unhealthy diets and obesity. The EU has favoured the adoption of packaging and labelling rules and, as regards tobacco, of rules prohibiting commercial communications. The protection of minors emerges as a central concern, reflecting both the vulnerability of this group and the importance of acting early to prevent the formation of unhealthy habits.

Yet, the regulatory mix also reveals significant divergences across risk factors. Regarding tobacco, the objective is to communicate clearly and vividly the hazards of the product and to deprive manufacturers of most available promotional tools. This is not the approach chosen in the regulation of food or alcohol, where consumers are trusted to evaluate the merits of products and to limit their exposure to risk. While the EU actively pursues a 'smoke-free future', it does not call into question the presence of alcohol or unhealthy foods in our lives. These differences reflect divergent risk perceptions and different evaluations of the cultural and economic importance of the products in question. The weakest dimension of EU lifestyle risk policy is undoubtedly alcohol. To date, only some limited EU measures exist, on taxation, labelling or commercial communication, and it is unlikely that the current body of rules contributes in any meaningful way to reducing alcohol consumption in Europe. More troublingly, EU policy continues to rest on questionable assumptions, notably the persistent belief that alcohol is risk-free under a certain threshold, and that 'moderate' and 'responsible' consumption is harmless. The issue is not merely that EU alcohol policy is limited, but that it is not evidence-based, which contradicts the EU's stated regulatory commitments.

Although this book did not aim to evaluate the effectiveness of EU policy – this is an empirical question that lies beyond the scope of this study and exceeds the author's competence – the analysis deployed allows nevertheless for a critical assessment of the adequacy of the EU's response to the so-called NCDs epidemic. It is clear that classic disclosure-based information tools, while they may be justified on other grounds, do not significantly influence consumer behaviour. It is equally clear that reliance on self-regulatory schemes in the area of commercial communications is misguided, if the protection of children and minors is taken seriously. Some of these shortcomings stem from political choices, often influenced by commercial interests, as in the case of labelling and advertising. There, the EU could undoubtedly do more. Whether the Beating Cancer Plan, and the European Health Union will provide a new impetus remains to be seen.[1] Other shortcomings are linked to the limits of EU competences, as exemplified by the absence of binding EU rules on smoke-free environments. Here, the tension between market and health becomes visible. If progress is to be made in certain areas, certain constitutional limitations must be acknowledged and addressed.

This leads directly to the second and third questions, which concern the structural dilemma at the heart of EU lifestyle regulation. The regulation of unhealthy lifestyles has been approached here as a 'privileged forum for thinking about Union law',[2] a way of reflecting on some perennial questions: the raison d'être of EU action, the boundaries of its competences, the management of diversity and the place of free movement in relation to competing non-market objectives.

The field at hand invites us to view the internal market not as an area of undeterred free movement but as a space where the health and safety of consumers can be safeguarded, provided there is political will. Judging from policy developments at both national and Union levels, EU law has so far provided fertile ground for the adoption of lifestyle risk control measures. Free movement provisions can accommodate national rules that restrict trading opportunities for manufacturers and importers of harmful products. In the field of alcohol, for instance, overly strict cases such as *Rosengren* should be considered alongside those more respectful of Member State prerogatives, such as *Aragonesa* or *Bacardi France*. In any event, the deregulatory effect of free movement provisions, if it is to be convincingly assessed, must be approached from an empirical perspective. The ultimate outcome of a case is dependent on the way national courts receive it and on the use subsequently made of it by economic

[1] On the European Health Union, see Vincent Delhomme and Carina van Os, 'Building the European Health Union (2019–2024): Successes, Limits and Future Perspectives' (2025) European Journal of Risk Regulation 942.

[2] Alexandre Saydé, *Abuse of EU Law and Regulation of the Internal Market* (Hart Publishing 2014) 370.

operators.[3] At the same time, EU law also provides the legislator with a range of regulatory options to reduce the consumption of tobacco, alcohol and unhealthy foods. This legislative practice reflects what Azoulai describes as an evolution in both the scope and the quality of EU internal market harmonisation.[4] As regards the scope, unhealthy lifestyles are a clear example of a law that extends well beyond the removal of obstacles to trade, shaping instead the institutional, social and moral infrastructure of the market, 'protecting the non-market interests that are deemed to be essential to the pursuit of European integration'.[5] As regards quality, which Azoulai defines as the integration of fundamental rights and values into internal market law, this book also shows that harmonisation 'does not simply influence the lifestyle of European populations through the regulation of environmental and public health risks' but 'directly affects the basic ethical and social conditions of human life'.[6] Lifestyle regulation thus contributes to an understanding of the market that is more embedded in social life, providing greater substance and texture to internal market law. Once one takes a broader view of the internal market, combining negative and positive integration, a more complex and nuanced picture emerges. The EU is not as constitutionally hard-wired in favour of free movement as is often claimed.

That being said, pursuing a health policy through internal market instruments has inherent limits. Through free movement, consumers are exposed to new products and services, which may encourage new unhealthy behaviours. The Court of Justice sees the internal market as a dynamic space where consumer habits evolve over time and should not be 'crystallised' for the benefit of domestic operators.[7] Yet opening markets to a broader range of products not only endangers traditional ways of life, such as the consumption of Italian pasta or German beer, but also poses risks to public health. A greater supply of alcoholic drinks or ultra-processed food products increases the likelihood that harmful habits will spread. Increased choice, lower prices and greater market concentration rarely foster healthier consumption patterns. At the end

[3] Gareth Davies, 'Activism Relocated. The Self-Restraint of the European Court of Justice in Its National Context' (2012) 19 Journal of European Public Policy 76.

[4] Loïc Azoulai, 'The Complex Weave of Harmonization' in Damian Chalmers and Anthony Arnull (eds), *The Oxford Handbook of European Union Law* (Oxford University Press 2015) 589–611.

[5] ibid 593. [6] ibid 594.

[7] *Commission v United Kingdom (beer and wine I)* para 14; See also *Commission v Germany (Beer purity)* para 32.

of this enquiry, the tension thus evolves into more radical questions. Is an internal market for products hazardous to human health desirable? Is the free movement of tobacco products a legitimate objective for the EU? Do we really want to preserve, as the excise duties regime does, 'the imperative needs of competition' in the tobacco sector, with the implication of 'a system of freely formed prices'?[8] Unhealthy lifestyles ultimately question the very 'soul of the internal market',[9] and by extension, that of the EU itself.

This connects with the second dilemma, and the third core question addressed here, namely the equilibrium between uniformity and diversity, linked to the scientific uncertainty over risks and policies to address them, as well as to the cultural, moral and ethical dimensions of lifestyles. Regulating tobacco, food and alcohol is a challenging endeavour, given the difficulty of predicting how consumers will react to a specific regulatory tool, a challenge further compounded by the diversity of lifestyle practices and health situations across the twenty-seven Member States. This necessitates to grant regulators with a degree of leeway to enable experimentation. This book has shown that EU law can accommodate such an approach, and that EU legislation could even serve as a catalyst for fostering regulatory experimentation and thereby improving evidence-based law-making. Yet the inherently fragmented approach that this presupposes sits uneasily with a fundamental feature of the internal market, regulatory uniformity, necessary for the removal of obstacles to free movement. The internal market nature of this field of law neutralises health-based subsidiarity claims and casts serious doubt on the feasibility of minimum harmonisation as a legislative technique. To address this tension, the EU legislature and the Court have responded in conflicting ways, sometimes placing health first, as in the case of tobacco plain packaging, sometimes prioritising market uniformity, as with tobacco for oral use, or sometimes attempting to accommodate both, as in the case of front-of-pack nutrition labelling. What is again visible is a constitutional tension between the demands of the internal market and those of health protection. Accommodation is possible, but it requires a reconceptualisation of the EU's internal market competence and of its system of competences more broadly.

To alleviate the concrete legal problems identified in Chapters 6 and 7, resulting from the conceptual mismatch between the internal market

[8] Tobacco Excise Duties Directive, recital 10.
[9] Weatherill, 'Maximum versus Minimum Harmonization'.

and health promotion, one could defend a change of approach as regards the scope of the Union's internal market competence. Leaving *Tobacco Advertising* behind, Article 114 TFEU could be construed as empowering the EU with a general competence to regulate the internal market, disconnected from the facilitation of cross-border trade. This would have the advantage of avoiding the judicial circumvolutions contained in cases such as *Swedish Match*, *Philip Morris* or *Poland v Parliament and Council*. How this would be in line with Article 26 TFEU, which defines the internal market as 'an area without internal frontiers in which the free movement of goods, persons, services and capital is ensured', remains however an open question. Moreover, broadening the Union's internal market competence would only lead to further contradictions between a carefully defined catalogue of competences and sweeping general harmonisation powers. The best way forward, even if not the most feasible, would be a Treaty change, to address the various legal malfunctions outlined above and provide a solid foundation for any further expansion of EU action in the field of lifestyles, and of health more broadly.[10]

Finally, by regulating unhealthy lifestyles, the EU is inevitably confronted with their cultural, moral and ethical dimensions, as well as with the diversity of relationships to the products and the risks involved. This diversity is addressed in different ways across policy areas. Tobacco is a field where Europeanisation is clearly at play. Concretely, this means that tobacco is no longer regarded as a desirable part of the 'European way of life', with the explicit objective that only a small minority of people will continue to smoke. This process does not appear to generate significant resistance among Member States or citizens, perhaps because smoking and cigarettes are not considered habits or goods of cultural value worth protecting. What is striking, however, is that the ethical dimensions of the endgame strategy remain unaddressed. This is true more broadly: the impact of lifestyle regulations on consumer autonomy is a question that has largely gone unaddressed.

It is in the regulation of food and alcohol that cultural aspects are most clearly invoked as obstacles to EU-level action. While the genuine cultural significance of these products cannot be denied, references to 'culture' and 'heritage' are often instrumentalised to justify inaction.

[10] See Vincent Delhomme, 'Emancipating Health from the Internal Market: For a Stronger EU (Legislative) Competence in Public Health' (2020) 11 European Journal of Risk Regulation 747.

This is particularly visible in the absence of a coherent EU alcohol policy and in the protection of certain food products under quality schemes, dynamics that can easily result in regulatory deadlock, as the controversies surrounding Nutri-Score illustrate. Combined with the rigidities created by maximum harmonisation, such deadlock also has negative repercussions for health. To overcome these obstacles, more creative solutions must be explored. One possibility would be to allow opt-outs for those few Member States that are genuinely unwilling to follow the common approach, akin to Sweden's derogation concerning tobacco for oral use. Another would be to rely more systematically on flexible modes of harmonisation, as identified in Chapter 7, or to re-draft or re-interpret the derogation clause contained at Article 114(5). And if the impossibility to act persists, the EU must ultimately accept to cede regulatory power back to the Member States, so that those willing to go further are able to do so.

EU legislation in this field continues to be framed primarily in economic terms, conceived as necessary to remove obstacles to trade, and the regulatory debate remains largely confined to a dialectic between the internal market and scientific or health-related concerns. Whatever the future may bring, further intervention at the EU level would ideally be accompanied by reforms to the constitutional framework of competence and by greater engagement with the political, moral and cultural dimensions of unhealthy lifestyles. Only under these conditions can a body of law emerge that is more coherent, more persuasive and ultimately more legitimate.

Bibliography

Abel T and McQueen DV, 'Current and Future Theoretical Foundations for NCDs and Health Promotion' in David V McQueen (ed), *Global Handbook on Noncommunicable Diseases and Health Promotion* (Springer 2013) 21–35

Afshin A and others, 'Health Effects of Dietary Risks in 195 Countries, 1990–2017: A Systematic Analysis for the Global Burden of Disease Study 2017' (2019) 393 The Lancet 1958

Albors-Llorens A, Barnard C and Leucht B (eds), *Cassis de Dijon: 40 Years On* (Hart Publishing 2021)

Alemanno A, 'The Shaping of European Risk Regulation by Community Courts' (2009) Jean Monnet Working Paper 18/08

Alemanno A, 'Nudging Smokers: The Behavioural Turn of Tobacco Risk Regulation' (2012) 3 European Journal of Risk Regulation 32

Alemanno A, 'Out of Sight Out of Mind: Towards a New EU Tobacco Products Directive' (2012) 18 Columbia Journal of European Law 197

Alemanno A, 'Balancing Free Movement and Public Health: The Case of Minimum Unit Pricing of Alcohol in Scotch Whisky' (2016) 53 Common Market Law Review 1037

Alemanno A and Garde A, 'The Emergence of an EU Lifestyle Policy: The Case of Alcohol, Tobacco and Unhealthy Diets' (2013) 50 Common Market Law Review 1745

Alemanno A and Garde A, *Regulating Lifestyle Risks: The EU, Alcohol, Tobacco and Unhealthy Diets* (Cambridge University Press 2015)

Alemanno A and Garde A, 'The Emergence of EU Lifestyle Risk Regulation: New Trends in Evidence, Proportionality and Judicial Review' in Hans-W Micklitz and Takis Tridimas (eds), *Risk and EU Law* (Edward Elgar Publishing 2015) 134–168

Alemanno A and Garde A, 'Risk and Regulation' in Adam Burgess, Alberto Alemanno and Jens O Zinn (eds), *Routledge Handbook of Risk Studies* (Routledge 2016) 289–301

Alemanno A and Spina A, 'Nudging Legally: On the Checks and Balances of Behavioral Regulation' (2014) 12 International Journal of Constitutional Law 429

Al-Hamdani M and Manly E, 'Harm Reduction in Tobacco Control: Where Do We Draw the Line?' (2022) 43 Journal of Public Health Policy 149

Ayo N, 'Understanding Health Promotion in a Neoliberal Climate and the Making of Health Conscious Citizens' (2012) 22 Critical Public Health 99

Azoulai L, 'The Complex Weave of Harmonization' in Damian Chalmers and Anthony Arnull (eds), *The Oxford Handbook of European Union Law* (Oxford University Press 2015) 589–611

Azzopardi-Muscat N and others, 'EU Country Specific Recommendations for Health Systems in the European Semester Process: Trends, Discourse and Predictors' (2015) 119 Health Policy 375

Babayev R, *Private Autonomy in EU Internal Market Law* (Hart Publishing 2024).

Baggio M and others, 'The Evolution of Behaviourally Informed Policy-Making in the EU' (2021) 28 Journal of European Public Policy 658

Baldwin R, Cave M and Lodge M, 'Introduction: Regulation – the Field and the Developing Agenda' in Robert Baldwin, Martin Cave and Martin Lodge (eds), *The Oxford Handbook of Regulation* (Oxford University Press 2010) 2–16

Banterle A, Ricci EC and Cavaliere A, 'Environmental Sustainability and the Food System' in Harry Bremmers and Kai Purnhagen (eds), *Regulating and Managing Food Safety in the EU: A Legal-Economic Perspective* (Springer International Publishing 2018) 57–88

Barents R, 'The Internal Market Unlimited: Some Observations on the Legal Basis of Community Legislation' (1993) 30 Common Market Law Review 85

Barnard C, 'Restriction Restrictions: Lessons for the EU from the US?' (2009) 68 The Cambridge Law Journal 575

Bartlett O, 'The EU's Competence Gap in Public Health and Non-Communicable Disease Policy' (2016) 5 Cambridge International Law Journal 50

Bartlett O, 'Minimum Unit Pricing for Alcohol May Not Be a Proportionate Public Health Intervention' (2016) 7 European Journal of Risk Regulation 218

Bartlett O, 'The CJEU Assesses Another Minimum Pricing Measure without Properly Contextualising It' (2016) 7 European Journal of Risk Regulation 810

Bartlett O, 'Power, Policy Ideas and Paternalism in Non-communicable Disease Prevention' (2018) 24 European Law Journal 474

Bartlett O and Garde A, 'Time to Seize the (Red) Bull by the Horns: The EU's Failure to Protect Children from Alcohol and Unhealthy Food Marketing' (2013) 38 European Law Review 498

Bartlett O and Garde A, 'EU Public Health Law and Policy – on the Rocks? A Few Sobering Thoughts on the Growing EU Alcohol Problem' in Tamara K Hervey, Calum Alasdair Young and Louise E Bishop (eds), *Research Handbook on EU Health Law and Policy* (Edward Elgar Publishing 2017) 369–397

Bartlett O and Garde A, 'The EU's Failure to Support Member States in Their Implementation of the WHO Recommendations: How to Ignore the Elephant in the Room?' (2017) 8 European Journal of Risk Regulation 251

Bartlett O and Macculloch A, 'Evidence and Proportionality in Free Movement Cases: The Impact of the Scotch Whisky Case' (2020) 11 European Journal of Risk Regulation 109

Bartlett O and Naumann A, 'Reinterpreting the Health in All Policies Obligation in Article 168 TFEU: The First Step towards Making Enforcement a Realistic Prospect' (2021) 16 Health Economics, Policy and Law 8

Bates C and others, 'European Union Policy on Smokeless Tobacco: A Statement in Favour of Evidence Based Regulation for Public Health' (2003) 12 Tobacco Control 360

Bauer JM and Reisch LA, 'Behavioural Insights and (Un)Healthy Dietary Choices: A Review of Current Evidence' (2019) 42 Journal of Consumer Policy 3

Baumberg B and Anderson P, 'The European Strategy on Alcohol: A Landmark and a Lesson' (2007) 42 Alcohol and Alcoholism 1

Baumberg B and Anderson P, 'Health, Alcohol and EU Law: Understanding the Impact of European Single Market Law on Alcohol Policies' (2008) 18 The European Journal of Public Health 392

Beard E, Brown J and Shahab L, 'Association of Quarterly Prevalence of E-Cigarette Use with Ever Regular Smoking among Young Adults in England: A Time–Series Analysis between 2007 and 2018' (2022) 117 Addiction 2283

Becher SI and others, 'Hungry for Change: The Law and Policy of Food Health Labeling' (2019) 54 Wake Forest Law Review 1305

Bechthold A and others, 'Perspective: Food-Based Dietary Guidelines in Europe—Scientific Concepts, Current Status, and Perspectives' (2018) 9 Advances in Nutrition 544

Berdzuli N and others, 'Alcohol Control Policy in Europe: Overview and Exemplary Countries' (2020) 17 International Journal of Environmental Research and Public Health 8162

Berridge V and others, 'E-Cigarettes: A Framework for Comparative History and Policy' (2024) 119 Addiction 1864

Berteletti F and others, 'Campaign for a Revised Tobacco Products Directive in the European Union: Lessons Learnt' (2017) 26 Tobacco Control 464

Birt C, 'A CAP on Health?' (Faculty of Public Health 2010)

Bjartveit K and Tverdal A, 'Health Consequences of Smoking 1–4 Cigarettes per Day' (2005) 14 Tobacco Control 315

Black J, 'Critical Reflections on Regulation' (2002) 27 Austrian Journal of Legal Philosophy 1

Blackwell AKM and others, 'Should Cigarette Pack Sizes Be Capped?' (2020) 115 Addiction 802

Blum A, 'Tobacco in Sport: An Endless Addiction?' (2005) 14 Tobacco Control 1

Boada LD, Henríquez-Hernández LA and Luzardo OP, 'The Impact of Red and Processed Meat Consumption on Cancer and Other Health Outcomes: Epidemiological Evidences' (2016) 92 Food and Chemical Toxicology 236

Boeger N, 'Minimum Harmonisation, Free Movement and Proportionality' in Philip Syrpis (ed), *The Judiciary, the Legislature and the EU Internal Market* (Cambridge University Press 2012) 62–91

Bogart WA, *Permit But Discourage: Regulating Excessive Consumption* (Oxford University Press 2010)

Boyland E and others, 'Systematic Review of the Effect of Policies to Restrict the Marketing of Foods and Non-Alcoholic Beverages to Which Children Are Exposed' (2023) 8 Obesity Reviews e13447

Boyland E and Tatlow-Golden M, 'Exposure, Power and Impact of Food Marketing on Children: Evidence Supports Strong Restrictions' (2017) 8 European Journal of Risk Regulation 224

Breakwell GM, *The Psychology of Risk* (2nd edition, Cambridge University Press 2014)

Brouwer O, 'Free Movement of Foodstuffs and Quality Requirements: Has the Commission Got It Wrong?' (1988) 25 Common Market Law Review 26

Burbergs M, 'How the Right to Respect for Private and Family Life, Home and Correspondence Became the Nursery in Which New Rights Are Born: Article 8 ECHR' in Eva Brems and Janneke Gerards (eds), *Shaping Rights in the ECHR: The Role of the European Court of Human Rights in Determining the Scope of Human Rights* (Cambridge University Press 2014) 315–329

Burci GL, 'A Global Legal Instrument for Alcohol Control: Options, Prospects and Challenges' (2021) 12 European Journal of Risk Regulation 499

Butler G, 'State Monopolies and the Free Movement of Goods in EU Law: Getting Beyond Obscure Clarity' 48 Legal Issues of Economic Integration 285

Campos S, Doxey J and Hammond D, 'Nutrition Labels on Pre-Packaged Foods: A Systematic Review' (2011) 14 Public Health Nutrition 1496

Cass DZ, 'The Word That Saves Maastricht?: The Principle of Subsidiarity and the Division of Powers within the European Community' (1992) 29 Common Market Law Review 1107

Casswell S, 'Will Alcohol Harm Get the Global Response It Deserves?' (2019) 394 The Lancet 1396

Castillo de la Torre F and Gippini Fournier E, *Evidence, Proof and Judicial Review in EU Competition Law* (Edward Elgar Publishing 2017)

Chalmers D, '"Food for Thought": Reconciling European Risks and Traditional Ways of Life' (2003) 66 Modern Law Review 532

Chalmers D, 'The Unconfined Power of European Union Law' (2016) 1 European Papers 405

Chambers T and Sassi F, 'Unhealthy Sponsorship of Sport' (2019) 367 BMJ l6718

Chandon P, 'How Package Design and Packaged-Based Marketing Claims Lead to Overeating' (2013) 35 Applied Economic Perspectives and Policy 7

Chapman S, Bareham D and Maziak W, 'The Gateway Effect of E-Cigarettes: Reflections on Main Criticisms' (2018) 21 Nicotine & Tobacco Research 695

Chikritzhs T and others, 'Has the Leaning Tower of Presumed Health Benefits from "moderate" Alcohol Use Finally Collapsed?' (2015) 110 Addiction 726

Clarke E and others, 'Snus: A Compelling Harm Reduction Alternative to Cigarettes' (2019) 16 Harm Reduction Journal 62

Cockerham WC, 'Health Lifestyle Theory and the Convergence of Agency and Structure' (2005) 46 Journal of Health and Social Behavior 51

Cockerham WC, Rütten A and Abel T, 'Conceptualizing Contemporary Health Lifestyles: Moving beyond Weber' (1997) 38 The Sociological Quarterly 321
Constant J, 'Alcohol, Ischemic Heart Disease, and the French Paradox' (1997) 20 Clinical Cardiology 420
Coppens P, 'Regulation (EU) No. 432/2012 Establishing a List of Permitted Health Claims' (2012) 2012 European Food and Feed Law Review 162
Cowburn G and Stockley L, 'Consumer Understanding and Use of Nutrition Labelling: A Systematic Review' (2005) 8 Public Health Nutrition 21
Cox S and Dawkins L, 'Global and Local Perspectives on Tobacco Harm Reduction: What Are the Issues and Where Do We Go from Here?' (2018) 15 Harm Reduction Journal 32
Craig P, *EU Administrative Law* (Oxford University Press 2006)
Craig P, 'Subsidiarity: A Political and Legal Analysis' (2012) 50 Journal of Common Market Studies 72
Crompton JL, 'Sponsorship of Sport By Tobacco and Alcohol Companies: A Review of the Issues' (1993) 17 Journal of Sport and Social Issues 148
Crosby S, 'The New Tobacco Control Directive : An Illiberal and Illegal Disdain for the Law' (2002) 27 European Law Review 177
Cummings KM, 'What's in a Number?' (2020) 115 Addiction 814
Davesne A and Guigner S, 'La Communauté Européenne de la Santé (1952-1954): Une Redécouverte Intergouvernementaliste du Projet Fonctionnaliste de 'Pool Blanc'' (2013) 41 Politique Européenne 40
Davies G, 'Can Selling Arrangements be Harmonized?' (2005) 30 European Law Review 370
Davies G, 'Subsidiarity: The Wrong Idea, in the Wrong Place, at the Wrong Time' (2006) 43 Common Market Law Review 63
Davies G, 'Activism Relocated. The Self-Restraint of the European Court of Justice in Its National Context' (2012) 19 Journal of European Public Policy 76
Davies G, 'Democracy and Legitimacy in the Shadow of Purposive Competence' (2015) 21 European Law Journal 2
Davies G, 'Internal Market Adjudication and the Quality of Life in Europe' (2015) 21 Columbia Journal of European Law 289
Davies G, 'Free Movement, the Quality of Life and the Myth that the Court Balances Interests' in Panos Koutrakos, Niamh Nic Shuibhne and Phil Syrpis (eds), *Exceptions from EU Free Movement Law: Derogation, Justification and Proportionality* (Hart Publishing 2016) 218–239
Dawson M and Witte F de, *EU Law and Governance* (Cambridge University Press 2022)
de Coninck P and Gilmore I, 'Long Overdue: A Fresh Start for EU Policy on Alcohol and Health' (2020) 395 The Lancet 10
de Ridder D, Adriaanse M and Fujita K (eds), *The Routledge International Handbook of Self-Control in Health and Well-Being: Concepts, Theories, and Central Issues* (Routledge 2018)
De Witte F, 'Sex, Drugs & EU Law: The Recognition of Moral and Ethical Diversity in EU Law' (2013) 50 Common Market Law Review 1545

De Witte F, 'You Are What You Ate: Food Heritage and the EU's Internal Market' (2022) 47 European Law Review 647

Delhomme VN, 'Emancipating Health from the Internal Market: For a Stronger EU (Legislative) Competence in Public Health' (2020) 11 European Journal of Risk Regulation 747

Delhomme VN, 'Front-of-Pack Nutrition Labelling in the European Union: A Behavioural, Legal and Political Analysis' (2021) 12 European Journal of Risk Regulation 825

Delhomme VN, 'The Legality of Covid-19 Travel Restrictions in an "Area without Internal Frontiers": Court of Justice (Grand Chamber) 5 December 2023, Case C-128/22, Nordic Info' (2024) 20 European Constitutional Law Review 307

Delhomme VN and Hervey T, 'The European Union's Response to the Covid-19 Crisis and (the Legitimacy of) the Union's Legal Order' (2022) 41 Yearbook of European Law 48

Delhomme VN and van Os C, 'Building the European Health Union (2019–2024): Successes, Limits and Future Perspectives' (2025) 16 European Journal of Risk Regulation 942

Delnevo CD and others, 'The Influence of Menthol, e-Cigarettes and Other Tobacco Products on Young Adults' Self-Reported Changes in Past Year Smoking' (2016) 25 Tobacco Control 571

Delogu B, *Risk Analysis and Governance in EU Policy Making and Regulation* (Springer International Publishing 2016)

DeSoucey M, 'Gastronationalism: Food Traditions and Authenticity Politics in the European Union' (2010) 75 American Sociological Review 432

Diallo A and others, 'Red and Processed Meat Intake and Cancer Risk: Results from the Prospective NutriNet-Santé Cohort Study' (2018) 142 International Journal of Cancer 230

Dixon H, Lee A and Scully M, 'Sports Sponsorship as a Cause of Obesity' (2019) 8 Current Obesity Reports 480

Donati A, *Le principe de précaution en droit de l'Union européenne* (Bruylant 2021)

Dougan M and Currie S (eds), *50 Years of the European Treaties: Looking Back and Thinking Forward* (Hart Publishing 2009)

Driezen P and others, 'Cross-Border Purchasing of Cigarettes among Smokers in Six Countries of the EUREST-PLUS ITC Europe Surveys' (2019) 16 Tobacco Induced Diseases 13

Edinger WH, 'Food, Safety and the Behavioural Factor of Risk' (2014) 5 European Journal of Risk Regulation 491

Edinger WH, 'Food Health Law: A Legal Perspective on EU Competence to Regulate the "Healthiness" of Food' (2014) 9 European Food and Feed Law Review 11

EFSA Panel on Dietetic Products, Nutrition, and Allergies, 'Scientific Opinion on Establishing Food-Based Dietary Guidelines' (2010) 8 The EFSA Journal 1460

Eijk Y van der, 'Development of an Integrated Tobacco Endgame Strategy' (2015) 24 Tobacco Control 336

Elshiewy O, Jahn S and Boztug Y, 'Seduced by the Label: How the Recommended Serving Size on Nutrition Labels Affects Food Sales' (2016) 1 Journal of the Association for Consumer Research 104

Everson M, 'Three Intimate Tales of Law and Science: Hope, Despair and Transcendence' in Ellen Vos and Michelle Everson (eds), *Uncertain Risks Regulated* (Routledge-Cavendish 2009) 347–358

Fagerström K and Schildt E-B, 'Should the European Union Lift the Ban on Snus? Evidence from the Swedish Experience' (2003) 98 Addiction 1191

Faid M and Gleicher D, 'Dancing the Tango: The Experience and Roles of the European Union in Relation to the Framework Convention on Tobacco Control' (2011) Global Health Europe

Fairchild AL, Bayer R and Colgrove J, 'The Renormalization of Smoking? E-Cigarettes and the Tobacco "Endgame"' (2014) 370 The New England Journal of Medicine 293

Farsalinos K, 'Snus: Swedish Snus Is Different' (2019) 226 British Dental Journal 85

Farvid MS and others, 'Consumption of Red Meat and Processed Meat and Cancer Incidence: A Systematic Review and Meta-Analysis of Prospective Studies' (2021) 36 European Journal of Epidemiology 937

Faure M, 'The Economics of Harmonization of Food Law in the EU' in Harry Bremmers and Kai Purnhagen (eds), *Regulating and Managing Food Safety in the EU* (Springer International Publishing 2018) 263–290

Feeney S, Rossetti V and Terrien J, 'E-Cigarettes—a Review of the Evidence—Harm versus Harm Reduction' (2022) 15 Tobacco Use Insights 1179173X2210875

Fialon M, Nabec L and Julia C, 'Legitimacy of Front-of-Pack Nutrition Labels: Controversy Over the Deployment of the Nutri-Score in Italy' (2022) 11 International Journal of Health Policy and Management 2574

Filippidis FT and others, 'Changes in Smoking Cessation Assistance in the European Union between 2012 and 2017: Pharmacotherapy versus Counselling versus e-Cigarettes' (2019) 28 Tobacco Control 95

Flegal KM and others, 'Association of All-Cause Mortality With Overweight and Obesity Using Standard Body Mass Index Categories: A Systematic Review and Meta-Analysis' (2013) 309 Journal of the American Medical Association 71

Friant-Perrot M and Garde A, 'From BSE to Obesity: EFSA's Growing Role in the EU's Nutrition Policy' in Alberto Alemanno and Simone Gabbi (eds), *Foundations of EU Food Law and Policy: Ten Years of the European Food Safety Authority* (Ashgate 2013) 135–153

Garben S, 'The Constitutional (Im)Balance between "the Market" and "the Social" in the European Union' (2017) 13 European Constitutional Law Review 23

Gard M, Powell D and Tenorio J (eds), *Routledge Handbook of Critical Obesity Studies* (Routledge 2022)

Garde A, *EU Law and Obesity Prevention* (Kluwer Law International 2010)

Garde A, 'Freedom of Commercial Expression and Public Health Protection: The Principle of Proportionality as a Tool to Strike the Balance' in Niamh Nic

Shuibhne and Laurence W Gormley (eds), *From Single Market to Economic Union: Essays in Memory of John A Usher* (Oxford University Press 2012) 117–134

Garde A, 'Harmful Commercial Marketing and Children's Rights: For a Better Use of EU Powers' (2020) 11 European Journal of Risk Regulation 841

Garde A, 'For a Children's Rights Approach to Obesity Prevention: The Key Role of an Effective Implementation of the WHO Recommendations' (2017) 8 European Journal of Risk Regulation 327

Garde A, 'Lobbying, Transparency and Trust: Power Imbalances and the Failure to Implement Europe's Beating Cancer Plan' (2025) 51 The Lancet Regional Health – Europe 101238

Garde A, Jeffery B and Rigby N, 'Implementing the WHO Recommendations Whilst Avoiding Real, Perceived or Potential Conflicts of Interest' (2017) 8 European Journal of Risk Regulation 237

Garde A and Xuereb G, 'The WHO Recommendations on the Marketing of Food and Non-Alcoholic Beverages to Children' (2017) 8 European Journal of Risk Regulation 211

Gilmore A and McKee M, 'Tobacco Control Policy: The European Dimension' (2002) 2 Clinical Medicine 335

Gilmore I, 'A Minimum Unit Price: The "Holy Grail" of Alcohol Policy' (2015) 15 Clinical Medicine 5

Gispen ME and Toebes B (eds), *Human Rights and Tobacco Control* (Edward Elgar Publishing 2020)

Gokani N, 'Regulation for Health Inequalities and Non-Communicable Diseases: In Want of (Effective) Behavioural Insights' (2018) 24 European Law Journal 490

Gokani N, 'Front-of-Pack Nutrition Labelling: A Tussle between EU Food Law and National Measures' (2022) 47 European Law Review 153

Goldner Lang I, 'Public Health in European Union Food Law', Tamara K Hervey, Calum Alasdair Young and Louise E Bishop (eds), *Research Handbook on EU Health Law and Policy* (Edward Elgar Publishing 2017) 398–425

Gornall J, 'Europe under the Influence' (2014) 348 British Medical Journal g1166

Gravely S and others, 'European Adult Smokers' Perceptions of the Harmfulness of e-Cigarettes Relative to Combustible Cigarettes: Cohort Findings from the 2016 and 2018 EUREST-PLUS ITC Europe Surveys' (2020) 30 European Journal of Public Health iii38

Gray N and Boyle P, 'Publishing Tobacco Tar Measurements on Packets' (2004) 329 BMJ: British Medical Journal 813

Greer SL, 'The Three Faces of European Union Health Policy: Policy, Markets, and Austerity' (2014) 33 Policy and Society 13

Greer SL, 'Health, Federalism and the European Union: Lessons from Comparative Federalism about the European Union' (2021) 16 Health Economics, Policy and Law 90

Greer SL and Kurzer P (eds), *European Union Public Health Policy: Regional and Global Trends* (Routledge 2016)

Griffiths PE and West C, 'A Balanced Intervention Ladder: Promoting Autonomy through Public Health Action' (2015) 129 Public Health 1092

Grill K and Dawson A, 'Ethical Frameworks in Public Health Decision-Making: Defending a Value-Based and Pluralist Approach' (2017) 25 Health Care Analysis 291

Grill K and Hanna J (eds), *The Routledge Handbook of the Philosophy of Paternalism* (Routledge, Taylor & Francis Group 2018)

Griswold MG and others, 'Alcohol Use and Burden for 195 Countries and Territories, 1990–2016: A Systematic Analysis for the Global Burden of Disease Study 2016' (2018) 392 The Lancet 1015

Groussot X and Bogojević S, 'Subsidiarity as a Procedural Safeguard of Federalism' in Loïc Azoulai (ed), *The Question of Competence in the European Union* (Oxford University Press 2014) 234–252

Guastaferro B, 'Coupling National Identity with Subsidiarity Concerns in National Parliaments' Reasoned Opinions' (2014) 21 Maastricht Journal of European and Comparative Law 320

Guigner S, 'La Dynamique d'Intégration par Sédimentation: Retour sur l'Inscription de la Santé dans les Compétences de l'Union' in Estelle Brosset (ed), *Droit Européen et Protection de la Santé – Bilan et Perspectives* (Bruylant 2015) 38–43

Guigner S, 'De « La Santé dans Toutes les Politiques » à « Toutes les Politiques dans la Santé » : le Régime de Visibilité de la Prise en Compte de la Santé dans les Politiques de l'Union Européenne' (2016) 34 Sciences Sociales et santé 71

Guthman J, 'Fatuous Measures: The Artifactual Construction of the Obesity Epidemic' (2013) 23 Critical Public Health 263

Hajek P and others, 'A Randomized Trial of E-Cigarettes versus Nicotine-Replacement Therapy' (2019) 380 New England Journal of Medicine 629

Halberstam D, 'Federalism: Theory, Policy, Law' in Michel Rosenfeld and Andras Sajo (eds), *The Oxford Handbook of Comparative Constitutional Law* (Oxford University Press 2012) 576–608

Hammond D and Parkinson C, 'The Impact of Cigarette Package Design on Perceptions of Risk' (2009) 31 Journal of Public Health 345

Hartlev M, 'Stigmatisation as a Public Health Tool against Obesity - A Health and Human Rights Perspective' (2014) 21 European Journal of Health Law 365

Hawkins B and Holden C, 'European Union Implementation of Article 5.3 of the Framework Convention on Tobacco Control' (2018) 14 Globalization and Health 79

Helberger N and others, 'Choice Architectures in the Digital Economy: Towards a New Understanding of Digital Vulnerability' (2022) 45 Journal of Consumer Policy 175

Helleringer G and Sibony A-L, 'European Consumer Protection Through The Behavioral Lens' (2017) 23 Columbia Journal of European Law 607

Herforth A and others, 'A Global Review of Food-Based Dietary Guidelines' (2019) 10 Advances in Nutrition 590

Hersey JC and others, 'Are Menthol Cigarettes a Starter Product for Youth?' (2006) 8 Nicotine & Tobacco Research 403

Hervey TK and De Ruijter A, 'The Dynamic Potential of European Union Health Law' (2020) 11 European Journal of Risk Regulation 726

Hervey TK and McHale JV, *European Union Health Law: Themes and Implications* (Cambridge University Press 2015)

Hervey TK, Young CA and Bishop LE, *Research Handbook on EU Health Law and Policy* (Edward Elgar Publishing 2017)

Hood C, Rothstein H and Baldwin R, *The Government of Risk: Understanding Risk Regulation Regimes* (Oxford University Press 2001)

Höpner M and Schmidt SK, 'Can We Make the European Fundamental Freedoms Less Constraining? A Literature Review' (2020) 22 Cambridge Yearbook of European Legal Studies 182

Husten CG, 'How Should We Define Light or Intermittent Smoking? Does It Matter?' (2009) 11 Nicotine & Tobacco Research 111

Ichijo A, 'Food and Nationalism: Gastronationalism Revisited' (2020) 48 Nationalities Papers 215

Incardona R and Poncibò C, 'The Average Consumer, the Unfair Commercial Practices Directive, and the Cognitive Revolution' (2007) 30 Journal of Consumer Policy 21

Ireland R and others, 'Commercial Determinants of Health: Advertising of Alcohol and Unhealthy Foods during Sporting Events' (2019) 97 Bulletin of the World Health Organization 290

Jancic D, 'The Game of Cards: National Parliaments in the EU and the Future of the Early Warning Mechanism and the Political Dialogue' (2015) 52 Common Market Law Review 939

Jans JH, 'Proportionality Revisited' (2000) 23 Legal Issues of Economic Integration 238

Jaroszyński T, 'National Parliaments' Scrutiny of the Principle of Subsidiarity: Reasoned Opinions 2014–2019' (2020) 16 European Constitutional Law Review 91

Jernigan D and others, 'Alcohol Marketing and Youth Alcohol Consumption: A Systematic Review of Longitudinal Studies Published since 2008: Alcohol Marketing and Youth Drinking' (2017) 112 Addiction 7

Jha P, 'Avoidable Deaths from Smoking: A Global Perspective' (2011) 33 Public Health Reviews 569

Julia C and others, 'Are Foods "healthy" or "Healthier"? Front-of-Pack Labelling and the Concept of Healthiness Applied to Foods' (2022) 127 The British Journal of Nutrition 948

Julia C, 'Ten Years of Nutri-Score Front-of-Pack Nutrition Labelling in Europe' (2025) 6 Nature Food 239

Kalkhoran S and Glantz SA, 'E-Cigarettes and Smoking Cessation in Real-World and Clinical Settings: A Systematic Review and Meta-Analysis' (2016) 4 The Lancet. Respiratory Medicine 116

Kaur A, Scarborough P and Rayner M, 'A Systematic Review, and Meta-Analyses, of the Impact of Health-Related Claims on Dietary Choices' (2017) 14 International Journal of Behavioral Nutrition and Physical Activity 93

Kellerbauer M, Klamert M and Tomkin J (eds), *The EU Treaties and the Charter of Fundamental Rights: A Commentary* (Oxford University Press 2019)
Klausner K, 'Menthol Cigarettes and Smoking Initiation: A Tobacco Industry Perspective' (2011) 20 Tobacco Control ii12
Kliemann N and others, 'Serving Size and Nutrition Labelling: Implications for Nutrition Information and Nutrition Claims on Packaged Foods' (2018) 10 Nutrients 891
Koop C and Lodge M, 'What Is Regulation? An Interdisciplinary Concept Analysis' (2017) 11 Regulation & Governance 95
Kortleve AJ and others, 'Over 80% of the European Union's Common Agricultural Policy Supports Emissions-Intensive Animal Products' (2024) 5 Nature Food 288
Koski A and others, 'Alcohol Tax Cuts and Increase in Alcohol-Positive Sudden Deaths-a Time-Series Intervention Analysis' (2007) 102 Addiction 362
Kozlowski LT, O'Connor RJ and Quinio Edwards B, 'Some Practical Points on Harm Reduction: What to Tell Your Lawmaker and What to Tell Your Brother about Swedish Snus' (2003) 12 Tobacco Control 372
Kumm M, 'Constitutionalising Subsidiarity in Integrated Markets: The Case of Tobacco Regulation in the European Union' (2006) 12 European Law Journal 503
Kurzer P, *Markets and Moral Regulation: Cultural Change in the European Union* (Cambridge University Press 2001)
Kurzer P and Cooper A, 'Hold the Croissant! The European Union Declares War on Obesity' (2011) 21 Journal of European Social Policy 107
Lacoste-Badie S and others, 'How Do Smokers Respond to Pictorial and Threatening Tobacco Warnings? The Role of Threat Level, Repeated Exposure, Type of Packs and Warning Size' (2019) 36 Journal of Consumer Marketing 461
Lahiri S and others, 'Social Norms Change and Tobacco Use: A Protocol for a Systematic Review and Meta-Analysis of Interventions' (2021) 18 International Journal of Environmental Research and Public Health 12186
Lahiri S, 'Understanding the Mechanisms of Change in Social Norms around Tobacco Use: A Systematic Review and Meta-Analysis of Interventions' (2025) 120 Addiction 215
Lai JC and Becher SI, 'Front-of-Pack Labelling and International Trade Law: Revisiting the Health Star Rating System' (2020) 21 Melbourne Journal of International Law 144
Lancet T, 'A Framework Convention on Alcohol Control' (2007) 370 The Lancet 1102
Lang T and Rayner G, 'Obesity: A Growing Issue for European Policy?' (2005) 15 Journal of European Social Policy 301
Langlet D and Mahmoudi S, *EU Environmental Law and Policy* (Oxford University Press 2016)
Larsen SR and Larsen SR, *The Constitutional Theory of the Federation and the European Union* (Oxford University Press 2021)

Le Houezec J, Mcneill A and Britton J, 'Tobacco, Nicotine and Harm Reduction' (2011) 30 Drug and Alcohol Review 119

Lee PN, Coombs KJ and Afolalu EF, 'Considerations Related to Vaping as a Possible Gateway into Cigarette Smoking: An Analytical Review' (2019) 7 F1000Research 1915

Leeuwen B van, 'Repositioning Free Movement of Services: A Substantive Perspective on the Structure and Dynamics of the Internal Market' (2025) 62 Common Market Law Review 705

Lempert LK and Glantz S, 'Packaging Colour Research by Tobacco Companies: The Pack as a Product Characteristic' (2017) 26 Tobacco Control 307

Lenaerts K, 'The European Court of Justice and Process-Oriented Review' (2012) 31 Yearbook of European Law 3

Lund KE and Vedøy TF, 'A Conceptual Framework for Assessing the Public Health Effects from Snus and Novel Non-Combustible Nicotine Products' (2021) 38 Nordic Studies on Alcohol and Drugs 586.

Lupton D, 'Risk as Moral Danger: The Social and Political Functions of Risk Discourse in Public Health' (1993) 23 International Journal of Health Services 425

Lupton D (ed), *Risk and Sociocultural Theory: New Directions and Perspectives* (Cambridge University Press 1999)

Lupton D and Tulloch J, '"Life Would Be Pretty Dull without Risk": Voluntary Risk-Taking and Its Pleasures' (2002) 4 Health, Risk & Society 113

MacCulloch A, 'State Intervention in Pricing: An Intersection of EU Free Movement and Competition Law' (2017) 42 European Law Review 190

MacMaoláin C, 'Reforming European Community Food Law: Putting Quality Back on the Agenda' (2003) 58 Food and Drug Law Journal 549

MacMaoláin C, *EU Food Law: Protecting Consumers and Health in a Common Market* (Hart Publishing 2007)

MacMaoláin C, *Food Law: European, Domestic and International Frameworks* (Hart Publishing 2015)

Malone RE, 'The Race to a Tobacco Endgame' (2016) 25 Tobacco Control 607

Mamudu HM and Studlar DT, 'Multilevel Governance and Shared Sovereignty: European Union, Member States, and the FCTC' (2009) 22 Governance: An International Journal of Policy, Administration, and Institutions 73

Martinelli T and others, 'Exploring the Gateway Hypothesis of E-Cigarettes and Tobacco: A Prospective Replication Study among Adolescents in the Netherlands and Flanders' (2023) 32 Tobacco Control 270

McDaniel PA, Smith EA and Malone RE, 'The Tobacco Endgame: A Qualitative Review and Synthesis' (2016) 25 Tobacco Control 594

McKeown RE, 'The Epidemiologic Transition: Changing Patterns of Mortality and Population Dynamics' (2009) 3 American Journal of Lifestyle Medicine 19S

McLaughlin I and others, 'Reducing Tobacco Use and Access Through Strengthened Minimum Price Laws' (2014) 104 American Journal of Public Health 1844

McNeill A and others, 'Evidence review of e-cigarettes and heated tobacco products 2018: A report commissioned by Public Health England' (2018) Public Health England

Meier E and others, 'A Randomized Clinical Trial of Snus Examining the Effect of Complete Versus Partial Cigarette Substitution on Smoking-Related Behaviors, and Biomarkers of Exposure' (2020) 22 Nicotine & Tobacco Research 473

Mitsilegas V, *EU Criminal Law* (Hart Publishing 2022)

Mohr GS, Lichtenstein DR and Janiszewski C, 'The Effect of Marketer-Suggested Serving Size on Consumer Responses: The Unintended Consequences of Consumer Attention to Calorie Information' (2012) 76 Journal of Marketing 59

Monaghan LF, Colls R and Evans B, 'Obesity Discourse and Fat Politics: Research, Critique and Interventions' (2013) 23 Critical Public Health 249

Moodie C and others, 'Plain Tobacco Packaging: Progress, Challenges, Learning and Opportunities' (2022) 31 Tobacco Control 263

Mossialos E and others (eds), *Health Systems Governance in Europe: The Role of European Union Law and Policy* (Cambridge University Press 2010)

Murray CJL and others, 'Global Burden of 87 Risk Factors in 204 Countries and Territories, 1990–2019: A Systematic Analysis for the Global Burden of Disease Study 2019' (2020) 396 The Lancet 1223

Mylly T, 'CJEU Approves Ban on Health Claims Related to Alcoholic Beverages' (2013) 4 European Journal of Risk Regulation 271

Ní Chaoimh E, *The Legislative Priority Rule and the EU Internal Market for Goods: A Constitutional Approach* (Oxford University Press 2022)

Nic Shuibhne N and Maci M, 'Proving Public Interest: The Growing Impact of Evidence in Free Movement Case Law' (2013) 50 Common Market Law Review 965

Nonnemaker J and others, 'Initiation with Menthol Cigarettes and Youth Smoking Uptake' (2013) 108 Addiction 171

Notley C and others, 'The Unique Contribution of E-Cigarettes for Tobacco Harm Reduction in Supporting Smoking Relapse Prevention' (2018) 15 Harm Reduction Journal 31

Novotny TE and Slaughter E, 'Tobacco Product Waste: An Environmental Approach to Reduce Tobacco Consumption' (2014) 1 Current Environmental Health Reports 208

Nutt DJ and others, 'Estimating the Harms of Nicotine-Containing Products Using the MCDA Approach' (2014) 20 European Addiction Research 218

Nuttall FQ, 'Body Mass Index' (2015) 50 Nutrition Today 117

O'brien P, 'Public Health and the Global Governance of Alcohol' (2021) 12 European Journal of Risk Regulation 415

O'Leary R and Polosa R, 'Tobacco Harm Reduction in the 21st Century' (2020) 20 Drugs and Alcohol Today 219

Oliver A, 'Nudging, Shoving, and Budging: Behavioural Economic-Informed Policy' (2015) 93 Public Administration 700

Ollila H and others, 'Tobacco Endgame Goals and Measures in Europe: Current Status and Future Directions' (2024) 34 Tobacco Control 114

Omran AR, 'The Epidemiologic Transition: A Theory of the Epidemiology of Population Change' (2005) 83 The Milbank Quarterly 731
Örnberg JC, 'The Europeanization of Swedish Alcohol Policy: The Case of ECAS' (2008) 18 Journal of European Social Policy 380
Örnberg JC, 'Escaping Deadlock – Alcohol Policy-Making in the EU' (2009) 16 Journal of European Public Policy 755
Örnberg JC, 'Sweden, the EU and the Alcohol Traveller's Allowances' (2010) 37 Contemporary Drug Problems 3
Örnberg JC, 'Alcohol Policy in the European Union' in Scott Greer and Paulette Kurzer (eds), *European Union Public Health Policy* (1st edition, Routledge 2012)
Panel on Dietetic Products, Nutrition and Allergies, 'The Setting of Nutrient Profiles for Foods Bearing Nutrition and Health Claims Pursuant to Article 4 of the Regulation (EC) ° No 1924/2006' (2008) 6 The EFSA Journal 1
Pang B and others, 'The Effectiveness of Graphic Health Warnings on Tobacco Products: A Systematic Review on Perceived Harm and Quit Intentions' (2021) 21 BMC Public Health 884
Panzone LA, 'Alcohol Tax, Price–Quality Proxy and Discounting: A Reason Why Alcohol Taxes May Rebound' (2012) 63 Journal of Agricultural Economics 715
Papadakis S and others, 'Quitting Behaviours and Cessation Methods Used in Eight European Countries in 2018: Findings from the EUREST-PLUS ITC Europe Surveys' (2020) 30 European Journal of Public Health iii26
Partos TR and others, 'Impact of Tobacco Tax Increases and Industry Pricing on Smoking Behaviours and Inequalities: A Mixed-Methods Study' (2020) 8 Public Health Research
Peeters S and others, 'The Revision of the 2014 European Tobacco Products Directive: An Analysis of the Tobacco Industry's Attempts to "Break the Health Silo"' (2016) 25 Tobacco Control 108
Petersen A and Lupton D, *The New Public Health: Health and Self in the Age of Risk* (SAGE 2000)
Picod F, Rizcallah C and Van Drooghenbroeck S (eds), *Charte des droits fondamentaux de l'Union européenne: Commentaire article par article* (2nd edition, Larcier 2020)
Pisinger C and others, 'ERS and Tobacco Harm Reduction' (2019) 54 European Respiratory Journal
Planzer S, *Empirical Views on European Gambling Law and Addiction* (Springer 2014)
Planzer S and Alemanno A, 'Lifestyle Risks: Conceptualising an Emerging Category of Research' (2010) 1 European Journal of Risk Regulation 335
Poiares Maduro M, *We The Court: The European Court of Justice and The European Economic Constitution* (Hart Publishing 1998)
Pomarici E and Sardone R, 'EU Wine Policy in the Framework of the CAP: Post-2020 Challenges' (2020) 8 Agricultural and Food Economics 17
Proctor RN, 'Why Ban the Sale of Cigarettes? The Case for Abolition' (2013) 22 Tobacco Control i27
Purnhagen K, van Herpen E and van Kleef E, 'The Potential Use of Visual Packaging Elements as Nudges' in Klaus Mathis and Avishalom Tor (eds),

Nudging - Possibilities, Limitations and Applications in European Law and Economics (Springer International Publishing 2016) 197–216
Pushkarev N, 'A CAP for Healthy Living Mainstreaming Health into the EU Common Agricultural Policy' (2015) 2 AIMS Public Health 844
Raitasalo K and others, 'Single, Dual, and Triple Use of Cigarettes, e-Cigarettes, and Snus among Adolescents in the Nordic Countries' (2022) 19 International Journal of Environmental Research and Public Health 683
Ramström L, Borland R and Wikmans T, 'Patterns of Smoking and Snus Use in Sweden: Implications for Public Health' (2016) 13 International Journal of Environmental Research and Public Health 1110
Ramström L and Wikmans T, 'Mortality Attributable to Tobacco among Men in Sweden and Other European Countries: An Analysis of Data in a WHO Report' (2014) 12 Tobacco Induced Diseases 14
Ramström LM, 'Much Safer with Snus' (2019) 226 British Dental Journal 85
Ramström LM, 'If There Had Been No Snus in Sweden: The Impact of Snus on Mortality Attributable to Smoking' (2024) 21 Harm Reduction Journal 176
Rayner M and others (eds), *An Introduction to Population-Level Prevention of Non-Communicable Diseases* (Oxford University Press 2017)
Recanati F and others, 'Assessing the Role of CAP for More Sustainable and Healthier Food Systems in Europe: A Literature Review' (2019) 653 Science of The Total Environment 908
Rehm J, Lachenmeier DW and Room R, 'Why Does Society Accept a Higher Risk for Alcohol than for Other Voluntary or Involuntary Risks?' (2014) 12 BMC Medicine 189
Renaud S and Gueguen R, 'The French Paradox and Wine Drinking' (1998) 216 Novartis Foundation Symposium 208
Rice P and Drummond C, 'The Price of a Drink: The Potential of Alcohol Minimum Unit Pricing as a Public Health Measure in the UK' (2012) 201 The British Journal of Psychiatry 169
Room R, 'Global Intergovernmental Initiatives to Minimise Alcohol Problems: Some Good Intentions, but Little Action' (2021) 12 European Journal of Risk Regulation 419
Room R and Örnberg JC, 'A Framework Convention on Alcohol Control: Getting Concrete about Its Contents' (2021) 12 European Journal of Risk Regulation 433
Rosen H, 'Is Obesity A Disease or A Behavior Abnormality? Did the AMA Get It Right?' (2014) 111 Missouri Medicine 104
Ruijter A de, *EU Health Law & Policy: The Expansion of EU Power in Public Health and Health Care* (Oxford University Press 2019)
Ruiz Cairo E, *The Promotion of Public Health in EU External Relations* (Schulthess LGDJ 2021)
Sadeleer N de, 'The Precautionary Principle in EC Health and Environmental Law' (2006) 12 European Law Journal 139
Sadeleer N de, *EU Environmental Law and the Internal Market* (Oxford University Press 2014)

Salokannel M and Ollila E, 'Snus and Snus-like Nicotine Products Moving across Nordic Borders: Can Laws Protect Young People?' (2021) 38 Nordic Studies on Alcohol and Drugs 540

Saydé A, *Abuse of EU Law and Regulation of the Internal Market* (Hart Publishing 2014)

Schane RE, Ling PM and Glantz SA, 'Health Effects of Light and Intermittent Smoking: A Review' (2010) 121 Circulation 1518

Scharpf FW, 'The Asymmetry of European Integration, or Why the EU Cannot Be a "Social Market Economy"' (2010) 8 Socio-Economic Review 211

Schebesta H, 'How to Save the Farm to Fork Strategy: A Two-Phased Approach' (2023) 18 European Food and Feed Law Review 231

Schebesta H and Purnhagen K, *EU Food Law* (Oxford University Press 2024)

Schorb F, 'Fat Politics in Europe: Theorizing on the Premises and Outcomes of European Anti-"Obesity-Epidemic" Policies' (2013) 2 Fat Studies 3

Schütze R, *From Dual to Cooperative Federalism: The Changing Structure of European Law* (Oxford University Press 2009)

Schütze R, 'Of Types and Tests: Towards a Unitary Doctrinal Framework for Article 34 TFEU?' (2016) 41 European Law Review 826

Schütze R, *From International to Federal Market: The Changing Structure of European Law* (Oxford University Press 2017)

Schütze R, 'Judicial Majoritarianism Revisited: "We, the Other Court"?' (2018) 43 European Law Review 269

Schütze R, '"Integration-through-Law": Grand Theory, Revisionist History' (2025) 2 European Law Open 162

Schüz J and others, 'European Code against Cancer 4th Edition: 12 Ways to Reduce Your Cancer Risk' (2015) 39 Cancer Epidemiology 1

Selvan ST, Yeo XX and Eijk Y van der, 'Which Countries Are Ready for a Tobacco Endgame? A Scoping Review and Cluster Analysis' (2024) 12 The Lancet Global Health e1049

Serre EB de L and Sibony A-L, 'Expert Evidence before the EC Courts' (2008) 45 Common Market Law Review 941

Sherk A and others, 'Calorie Intake from Alcohol in Canada: Why New Labelling Requirements Are Necessary' (2019) 80 Canadian Journal of Dietetic Practice and Research 111

Sibony A-L and Helleringer G, 'EU Consumer Protection and Behavioural Sciences: Revolution or Reform?' in Alberto Alemanno and Anne-Lise Sibony (eds), *Nudge and the Law: A European Perspective* (Hart Publishing 2015) 209–234

Slot PJ, 'Harmonisation' (1996) 21 European Law Review 378

Smed S and others, 'The Effects of the Danish Saturated Fat Tax on Food and Nutrient Intake and Modelled Health Outcomes: An Econometric and Comparative Risk Assessment Evaluation' (2016) 70 European Journal of Clinical Nutrition 681

Smith EA and Malone RE, 'An Argument for Phasing out Sales of Cigarettes' (2020) 29 Tobacco Control 703

Snell J, 'True Proportionality and Free Movement of Goods and Services' (2000) 11 European Business Law Review 50

Somek A, *Individualism: An Essay on the Authority of the European Union* (Oxford University Press 2008)

Studlar DT, 'Tobacco Control: The End of Europe's Love Affair with Smoking?' in Scott L Greer and Paulette Kurzer (eds), *European Union Public Health Policy: Regional and Global Trends* (Routledge 2012) 181–193

Sundar A and others, 'Is Unnatural Unhealthy? Think about It: Overcoming Negative Halo Effects from Food Labels' (2021) 38 Psychology & Marketing 1280

Sunstein CR, 'Social Norms and Social Roles' (1996) 96 Columbia Law Review 903

Swinburn BA and others, 'The Global Syndemic of Obesity, Undernutrition, and Climate Change: The Lancet Commission Report' (2019) 393 The Lancet 791

Talati Z and others, 'Consumers' Responses to Health Claims in the Context of Other on-Pack Nutrition Information: A Systematic Review' (2017) 75 Nutrition Reviews 260

Thirlaway K and Upton D, *The Psychology of Lifestyle: Promoting Healthy Behaviour* (Routledge, Taylor & Francis Group 2009)

Thomas BP and Gostin LO, 'Tobacco Endgame Strategies: Challenges in Ethics and Law' (2013) 22 Tobacco Control i55

Tridimas T, 'Proportionality in Community Law: Searching for the Appropriate Standard of Scrutiny' in Evelyn Ellis (ed), *The Principle of Proportionality in the Laws of Europe* (Hart Publishing 1999) 65–84

Trubek L, Nance M and Hervey T, 'The Construction of Healthier Europe: Lessons from the Fight against Cancer' (2008) 26 Wisconsin International Law Journal 804

Ugland T, 'Europeanisation of the Nordic Alcohol Monopoly Systems Collisions between Ideologies and Political Cultures 1' (1997) 14 Nordic Studies on Alcohol and Drugs 7

Ugland T, 'Promoting Policy Consistency and Continuity in the EU through the Trio: Alcohol-Related Harm on the Council Presidency Agenda' (2019) 29 Journal of European Social Policy 515

Upton D and Thirlaway K, *Promoting Healthy Behaviour: A Practical Guide* (2nd edition, Routledge, Taylor & Francis Group 2014)

Vallgårda S, Holm L and Jensen JD, 'The Danish Tax on Saturated Fat: Why It Did Not Survive' (2015) 69 European Journal of Clinical Nutrition 223

van Aaken A, 'Constitutional Limits to Regulation-by-Nudging' in Holger Straßheim and Silke Beck (eds), *Handbook of Behavioural Change and Public Policy* (Edward Elgar Publishing 2019) 304–318

van Amsterdam J and van den Brink W, 'The High Harm Score of Alcohol. Time for Drug Policy to Be Revisited?' (2013) 27 Journal of Psychopharmacology 248

van Asselt MBA and Vos E, 'The Precautionary Principle and the Uncertainty Paradox' (2006) 9 Journal of Risk Research 313

Van den Bergh R, 'The Subsidiarity Principle in European Community Law: Some Insights from Law and Economics' (1994) 1 Maastricht Journal of European and Comparative Law 337

Van den Bergh R, 'Farewell Utopia?: Why the European Union Should Take the Economics of Federalism Seriously' (2016) 23 Maastricht Journal of European and Comparative Law 937
Van den Bogaert S and Cuyvers A, '"Money for Nothing": The Case Law of the EU Court of Justice on the Regulation of Gambling' (2011) 48 Common Market Law Review 1175
van den Brink M, *Legislative Authority and Interpretation in the European Union* (Oxford University Press 2024)
van den Brink M, Dawson M and Zglinski J, 'Revisiting the Asymmetry Thesis: Negative and Positive Integration in the EU' (2025) 32 Journal of European Public Policy 209
Vandenberghe D and Albrecht J, 'The Financial Burden of Non-Communicable Diseases in the European Union: A Systematic Review' (2020) 30 European Journal of Public Health 833
Viet Cuong P and others, 'Cross-country Comparison of Proportion of Alcohol Consumed in Harmful Drinking Occasions Using the International Alcohol Control Study' (2018) 37 Drug and Alcohol Review S45
Vos E, 'The European Court of Justice in the Face of Scientific Uncertainty and Complexity' in Mark Dawson, Bruno De Witte and Elise Muir (eds), *Judicial Activism at the European Court of Justice* (Edward Elgar Publishing 2013) 142–166
Weatherill S, 'Pre-Emption, Harmonisation and the Distribution of Competence to Regulate the Internal Market' in Catherine Barnard and Joanne Scott (eds), *The Law of the Single European Market: Unpacking the Premises* (Hart Publishing 2002) 41–74
Weatherill S, 'The Limits of Legislative Harmonization Ten Years after Tobacco Advertising: How the Court's Case-law has become a "Drafting Guide"' (2011) 12 German Law Journal 827
Weatherill S, *The Internal Market as a Legal Concept* (Oxford University Press 2017)
Weatherill S, 'The Fundamental Question of Minimum or Maximum Harmonisation' in Sacha Garben and Inge Govaere (eds), *The Internal Market 2.0* (Hart Publishing 2021) 261–284
Weatherill S and Bernitz U (eds), *The Regulation of Unfair Commercial Practices under EC Directive 2005/29: New Rules and New Techniques* (Hart Publishing 2007)
Weimer M, *Risk Regulation in the Internal Market: Lessons from Agricultural Biotechnology* (Oxford University Press 2019)
Wettlaufer A, 'Can a Label Help Me Drink in Moderation? A Review of the Evidence on Standard Drink Labelling' (2018) 53 Substance Use & Misuse 585
Whitehead R and others, 'Rapid Evidence Review: Strengths and Limitations of Tobacco Taxation and Pricing Strategies' (2018) NHS Health Scotland
WHO, 'Global Noncommunicable Diseases (NCD) Compact 2020–2030', <https://cdn.who.int/media/docs/default-source/ncds/final_ncd-compact-(1).pdf?sfvrsn=d8895106_1> accessed 8 September 2025
Wilding JPH, Mooney V and Pile R, 'Should Obesity Be Recognised as a Disease?' (2019) 366 BMJ l4258

Wiley LF, Berman ML and Blanke D, 'Who's Your Nanny? Choice, Paternalism and Public Health in the Age of Personal Responsibility' (2013) 41 The Journal of Law, Medicine & Ethics 88

Willett W and others, 'Food in the Anthropocene: The EAT–Lancet Commission on Healthy Diets from Sustainable Food Systems' (2019) 393 The Lancet 447

Woelbert E and d'Hombres B, 'Pictorial Health Warnings and Wear-out Effects: Evidence from a Web Experiment in 10 European Countries' (2019) 28 Tobacco Control e71

Wood AM and others, 'Risk Thresholds for Alcohol Consumption: Combined Analysis of Individual-Participant Data for 599 912 Current Drinkers in 83 Prospective Studies' (2018) 391 The Lancet 1513

Wyatt D, 'Community Competence to Regulate the Internal Market' in Michael Dougan and Samantha Currie (eds), *50 Years of the European Treaties: Looking Back and Thinking Forward* (Hart Publishing 2009) 93–136

Zamir E and Teichman D, *Behavioral Law and Economics* (Oxford University Press 2018)

Zglinski J, 'The End of Negative Market Integration: 60 Years of Free Movement of Goods Litigation in the EU (1961–2020)' (2024) 31 Journal of European Public Policy 633

Zhou S, 'What Difference Would a Binding International Legal Instrument on Alcohol Control Make? Lessons from the World Health Organization Framework Convention on Tobacco Control's Impact on Domestic Litigation' (2021) 12 European Journal of Risk Regulation 514

Zhou S and Liberman J, 'The Global Tobacco Epidemic and the WHO Framework Convention on Tobacco Control – the Contributions of the WHO's First Convention to Global Health Law and Governance' in Gian Luca Burci and Brigit CA Toebes (eds), *Research Handbook on Global Health Law* (Edward Elgar Publishing 2018) 340–388

Znyk M, Jurewicz J and Kaleta D, 'Exposure to Heated Tobacco Products and Adverse Health Effects, a Systematic Review' (2021) 18 International Journal of Environmental Research and Public Health 6651

Index

For EU product safety concerns, contact us at Calle de José Abascal, 56–1°, 28003 Madrid, Spain or eugpsr@cambridge.org.

www.ingramcontent.com/pod-product-compliance
Ingram Content Group UK Ltd.
Pitfield, Milton Keynes, MK11 3LW, UK
UKHW021630270926
476026UK00011B/289
* 9 7 8 1 0 0 9 7 4 6 9 5 3 *